HISTORIANS AT WORK

Other Books by Peter Gay

Style in History (1974)

The Bridge of Criticism: Dialogues on the Enlightenment (1970)

The Enlightenment: An Interpretation
Volume II, The Science of Freedom (1969)

Weimar Culture: The Outsider as Insider (1968)

A Loss of Mastery: Puritan Historians in Colonial America (1966)

The Enlightenment: An Interpretation
Volume I, The Rise of Modern Paganism (1966)

The Party of Humanity: Essays in the French Enlightenment (1964)

Voltaire's Politics: The Poet as Realist (1959)

The Dilemma of Democratic Socialism: Eduard Bernstein's Challenge to
Marx (1952)

Translations with Introductions:

Voltaire: Candide (1963)

Voltaire: Philosophical Dictionary, 2 vols. (1962)

Ernst Cassirer: The Question of Jean Jacques Rousseau (1954)

Anthologies and Collective Works

The Enlightenment: A Comprehensive Anthology (1973)

Eighteenth Century Studies Presented to Arthur M. Wilson (1972)

The Columbia History of the World (with John A. Garraty) (1972)

Deism: An Anthology (1968)

John Locke on Education (1964)

NEW YORK, EVANSTON, SAN FRANCISCO, LONDON

Historians
at Work

VOLUME IV

Edited by Peter Gay

and Gerald J. Cavanaugh

Harper & Row, Publishers

1817

FIRST EDITION

Designed by Sidney Feinberg

Library of Congress Cataloging in Publication Data (Revised)

Gay, Peter, 1923–   comp.
  Historians at work.
  Vol.   edited by P. Gay and V. G. Wexler.
  Includes bibliographical references.
  1. History—Addresses, essays, lectures.
I. Cavanaugh, Gerald J., joint comp. II. Wexler,
Victor G., joint comp. III. Title.
D6.G35   908   75-123930
ISBN 0–06–011473–8 (v. 1)
ISBN 0–06–011472–X (v. 2)
ISBN 0–06–011474–6 (v. 3)
ISBN 0–06–011476–2 (v. 4)

---

75 76 77 78 79 10 9 8 7 6 5 4 3 2 1

Contents

Preface to Volume IV   IX

1. Wilhelm Dilthey (1833–1911)   1
   THE EIGHTEENTH CENTURY AND THE HISTORICAL WORLD

2. Friedrich Meinecke (1862–1954)   34
   COSMOPOLITANISM AND THE NATIONAL STATE

3. Eckart Kehr (1902–1933)   64
   THE SOCIAL AND FINANCIAL BASES OF TIRPITZ' NAVAL PROPAGANDA

4. Henri Pirenne (1862–1935)   82
   HISTORY OF BELGIUM

5. Lucien Febvre (1878–1956)   104
   THE PROBLEM OF UNBELIEF IN THE SIXTEENTH CENTURY

6. Marc Bloch (1886–1944)   131
   FEUDAL SOCIETY

7. Georges Lefebvre (1874–1959)   161
   STUDIES ON THE FRENCH REVOLUTION

8. Élie Halévy (1870–1937)   186
   ENGLAND IN 1815

9. Jaime Vicens Vives (1910–1960)   215
   AN ECONOMIC HISTORY OF SPAIN

10. Federico Chabod (1901–1960)   244
    HISTORY OF ITALIAN FOREIGN POLICY FROM 1870 TO 1896

11. Lewis B. Namier (1888–1960)   272
    PERSONALITIES AND POWERS

12. Erwin Panofsky (1892–1968)   296
    RENAISSANCE AND RENASCENCES IN WESTERN ART

13. Charles Beard (1874–1948)   324
    AN ECONOMIC INTERPRETATION OF THE CONSTITUTION OF THE
    UNITED STATES

14. Perry Miller (1905–1963)   353
    THE NEW ENGLAND MIND: THE SEVENTEENTH CENTURY

15. Richard Hofstadter (1916–1970)   384
    THE AGE OF REFORM

Preface to Volume IV

It is still too early to characterize the historical craft of the twentieth century; we are too much of it and in it to see it steadily, let alone whole. The temper of our time seems to be one of experimentation, of restlessness with results, and of innovation in techniques; and we may speculate that this contemporary assessment is likely to remain valid as future historians look back on twentieth-century history writing with some serenity and detachment. At the same time, it is equally likely that the continuities of our century with its great predecessor will emerge into focus more sharply as time passes. We are too embattled now to recognize how much we owe our fathers.

The nineteenth century, as the third volume of this collection should have amply shown, was a century of classics, of comprehensive works spanning great periods and embracing great nations. These classics were as substantial, as crowded with incident, and as intricately plotted as the bulky novels and expansive symphonies of their day. They seem in many ways old-fashioned now, with their vigorous narrative, their sumptuous detail, and their striking self-assurance. But these classics turn out on inspection to be more than museum pieces to be admired and ignored. Their authors were thoroughly professional in temper and sophisticated in technique; however timebound they were in their failure to detect, and hence minimize, their prejudgments, they have secured permanent validity in their lusting after dependable documentation, their demand for precision, and their commitment to veracity. And in method as in substance, they adumbrated concerns that have come to dominate the history writing of our own era: Burckhardt, by exploring the possibilities of cultural history; Ranke, by compelling attention to the weight of power; Mommsen, by demonstrating the connection of class with politics. Even Marx, though little recognized in his time as a historian, was both in way of thinking and lifespan a complete nineteenth-century man. His teachers were Hegel and the classical economists, and he died, after all, in 1883. In short, the history of the historical profession since the French Revolution documents not merely the pressure for change but also, and impressively, the strands of continuity.

Yet, though it is important to insist on this continuity—for without such a reminder it is easily overlooked—change and thirst for more change are doubtless the dominant realities in the historical scholarship of our day. Both are highly visible alike in subject matter and in method. The historical profession has steadily democratized, even radicalized, the first and complicated the second. And these two shifts go together: to write the history of illiterate peasants or inarticulate proletarians poses technical problems of unprecedented difficulty and compels historians to resort to new, and highly specialized, auxiliary sciences like demography and econometrics. Until fairly recently, history was by and large an account of the lives and fates of political, social, artistic, and religious elites. The "people" emerged into the light of such history mainly as docile recipients of religious revelation or political decisions, as hapless victims of pestilence and pillage, as spectators to great events, and, on very rare occasions, as actors: as demonstrators, as looters, as collective executioners. But in recent decades, historians have raised the poor of country and city from their passivity and ignominious anonymity. In his widely popular, passionate *The Making of the English Working Class,* published in 1963, the English historian E. P. Thompson has given voice to this new orientation: "I am seeking," he writes in the preface, "to rescue the poor stockinger, the Luddite cropper, the 'obsolete' hand-loom weaver, the 'utopian' artisan, and even the deluded follower of Joanna Southcott, from the enormous condescension of posterity." Thanks in part to historians like Thompson, enormous condescension has given way to what may seem, to many, excessive concentration. In any event, mobs have been promoted to crowds, while the cultural life of the poor and the political activities of the disenfranchised have moved to the center of the historian's stage. Birth control, popular sports, seasonal migrations, mass religiosity, working class newspapers have become the staple of the social historian of our day. Until fairly recently, intellectual history meant the history of great ideas, normally studied in splendid isolation, in the rarefied atmosphere of the library. It was not that all earlier historians of ideas were snobbishly indifferent to the social roots and cultural diffusion of ideas. Arthur O. Lovejoy, the father of what is called "the history of ideas" in this country, explicitly included "the collective thought of large groups of persons" within the purview of the kind of history he was advocating; it was not enough, he insisted, to remain with "the doctrines or opinions of a small number of profound thinkers or eminent writers." Yet, in general, historians neglected this part of Lovejoy's program and concentrated on the first-rate, or at least the second-rate, products of the human mind. All this has changed now; Friedrich Meinecke's proud, if innocent, boast that he liked to walk along the summits seems discredited today, and historians instead have taken to the streets.

Some of the animus behind what I have called the democratization and radicalization of historical interest has, of course, been political; appropriately, several historians represented in this volume were deeply indebted to Marxism. But by no means all the social historians of our century have been Marxists—witness Marc Bloch, Lucien Febvre, and some of their followers. And by no means all innovating historians of our century have chosen social history on which to practice their skills; the political anatomies of a Lewis Namier and the intellectual morphologies of a Perry Miller prove otherwise. They prove that the possibilities of historical writing have not been confined by new views, but have, on the contrary, been enlarged. We may hope for some sort of synthesis, for a cultural history that will give some of the old and some of the new choices their due and draw a map of the past that will provide space for statesmen and publics, priests and believers, great novels and mass publications, for sports, art, and religion. Meanwhile, much to our benefit, the debate continues.

HISTORIANS AT WORK

Wilhelm Dilthey 1833—1911

1

Wilhelm Dilthey died in 1911 at the age of seventy-eight. He was thus very much a man, a historian-philosopher, of the nineteenth century. His influence on historiography, however, was not felt until the twentieth century. As H. Stuart Hughes puts it: "Like his contemporary Henry Adams, Wilhelm Dilthey was so old-fashioned that by the end of his life he had become a modern . . . ; as an old man he found himself rather surprisingly cast in the role of a pathfinder to the thought of the new century that was opening." That thought concerned itself particularly with the nature and definition of history. Dilthey became convinced that neither the positivistic belief in "objective" history—in history as "simply a science, no less and no more," as J. B. Bury put it—nor the original historicist interpretation of history which heavily relied on feeling, inference, or intuition, any longer sufficed as a definition or methodology of history. Dilthey devoted most of his intellectual life to the task of integrating the scientific and subjective elements that were the inevitable and apparently contradictory components of modern historiography.

By background and training Dilthey was well prepared to attempt such a reconciliation. Born in 1833 in Rhineland Nassau, the son of a Calvinist minister, he grew up in a liberal and stimulating atmosphere congenial to the study and appreciation of music, literature, and philosophy. Dilthey originally intended to enter the ministry, and his first studies concerned the theology of Schleiermacher. But perhaps because his minister-father himself regarded philosophy as more important than theology, Dilthey soon found his interests engaged by philosophy and history, subjects to whose study he devoted his life. By 1864, he was a lecturer in philosophy at the University of Berlin; there followed professorships at Basel (1867), Kiel and Breslau (1871–1882), and, again, at Berlin (1882–1902). Only during the last decade of his tenure at Berlin, however, did his lectures attract a wide audience.

Dilthey's academic progress was marked by the publication of historical-philosophical works that have attained the status of classics, for example, *The*

1

Life of Schleiermacher (1867, 1870), and the *Introduction to the Cultural Sciences* (1883); his *Collected Writings* fill twelve volumes. Outstanding among the influences Dilthey acknowledged as stimulating his thought were the works of Kant, Hegel, Schleiermacher, Ranke, Droysen, and Mommsen. Dilthey was also inevitably touched by the prevailing "realism" of his formative years, an outlook which led him to accept the positivist view that the historical world was "lawful" in the same sense as the physical world. Theological and metaphysical abstractions could never satisfy his intellectual needs, because, as he wrote, "Thought is fruitful only when it is based upon the special investigation of some aspect of the real." However, Dilthey's definition of "reality" transcended the positivistic notion of the physical, measurable world.

Reality to Dilthey was "life" itself, it was "history," a continuum in time, which meant that individuals, societies, forms of understanding, consciousness, and expression can only be understood historically. Dilthey thus rejected the claim that positivism alone sufficed as an approach to and an explanation of the world. In Dilthey's view, positivism, besides being metaphysical in its own way, did not encompass all of reality; in fact, as he put it, "it mutilates historical reality." But if neither positivistic science nor abstract metaphysical systems adequately cover the manifold aspects of reality, how could man understand himself and his world? Dilthey spent his mature life seeking the answer to this question.

Without denigrating the natural science of positivists and empiricists, Dilthey sought to demonstrate that the method appropriate for the study of nature was inadequate and misleading when applied to the human or cultural sciences *(Geisteswissenschaften)*. Thus, just as Kant had asked how scientific knowledge was possible, Dilthey inquired into the question of the independent validity of the "human sciences." His "epistemological standpoint" was that "all knowledge is knowledge of experience; but the original unity of all experience and its resulting validity are conditioned by the factors which mold the consciousness within which it arises, i.e., by the whole of our nature." We cannot get beyond or behind these conditioning factors, Dilthey concludes, and consequently, "from this standpoint our view of the whole natural world turns out to be a mere shadow cast by a reality hidden from us, while it is only in the facts of consciousness given in inner experience that we possess reality as it is. The analysis of these facts lies at the center of the human studies and so, in accord with the standpoint of the historical school, in knowing the principles which govern the world of mind we remain within that world, and the human studies form an independent system by themselves."

Dilthey defined "consciousness" to include feelings, sensations, volition, as well as rational thought; "consciousness" entails an "awareness" *(In-*

newerden), a "lived experience" *(Erleben)* of the totality of human capabilities. "Only from his actions, his fixed utterances, his effects upon others can man learn about himself . . . to know himself only by the roundabout way of understanding. . . . The human studies [*Geisteswissenschaften*] are thus founded on this relation of lived experience, expression, and understanding." From this relation, man forms his world picture *(Weltbild)* and his view of what it ought to be *(Weltanschauung).* Thus, what man is cannot be learned through introspection but only through history informed by critical philosophy. Dilthey further believed that far from "extinguishing himself" (in Ranke's words), the historian must invoke intuition and empathy in order to capture that genuine historical knowledge which is an inward experience *(Erlebnis).*

In his effort to establish the "human sciences" on a firm foundation, Dilthey wrestled with profound and intractable problems in epistemology, psychology, history, and philosophy. That Dilthey failed in his task (as he himself knew) does not detract from the luster of his real contributions to historical understanding. He was (in Hajo Holborn's words) "the greatest historian of ideas" and "more than any other scholar he was the father of the history of ideas." He redefined the nature of human consciousness and expanded the concept of mind. He broke with the traditional *Geistesgeschichte* which tended to see all of history reflected in ideas, unrelated to other aspects of reality. Dilthey never ignored the economic, social, and political components of history; and his theory of history influenced both Alfred Weber's "sociology of culture" and Karl Mannheim's "sociology of knowledge." He also posed and sought to answer the essential philosophical problem in the history of thought: "Life is given to us not immediately, but elucidated through the objectification of thought. If the objective conception of life is not to become dubious by the fact that it passes through the operations of thought, the objective validity of thinking will have to be demonstrated."

If Dilthey did not succeed in demonstrating this validity, he did succeed, however, in winning wide acceptance for his distinction between the natural and the human or cultural sciences. This was liberating in part; thanks to his efforts, historians and social scientists were freed from the need to justify their disciplines on the basis of a strict comparison with, say, physics and chemistry. But for many unrepentant positivists among historians, Dilthey's principled distinction between natural and historical science was a kind of treason or, even worse, a failure of nerve—it illegitimately stressed the art of history at the expense of its science. The debate continues.

The "crisis of historicism," coupled with his sense of the sterility of positivist history, impelled Dilthey to a redefinition of history and historiography. At the end of his life, he knew he had not provided a solution to the problem of historical knowledge. If nothing else (in Dilthey's words), "historical consciousness demonstrates ever more clearly the relativity of every metaphysical or religious doctrine which has appeared in the course of time"; we see in history "a vast field of ruins of religious traditions, metaphysical positions, demonstrated systems, possibilities of all sorts." And yet, in the face of this "anarchy of convictions," Dilthey did not despair; "modern historical consciousness breaks the last chains which philosophy and natural science could not tear apart. Now man stands completely free."

Dilthey's speculations on the role of theory and philosophy in history were profound. "The sociological theories and the philosophies of history, which see in the description of the singular a mere raw material for their abstractions," he wrote, "are false. This superstition, which subjects the works of the historians to a mysterious process in order by a kind of alchemy to turn the material of particular facts which is found there into the pure gold of abstraction and compel history to yield its last secret, is quite as fanciful as was ever the dream of an alchemistic nature philosopher who thought to entice nature into giving up her word of power. There is no such last simple word of history, uttering its true sense, any more than there is such a thing to be extracted from nature. And quite as erroneous as this superstition is the procedure which commonly goes with it. This procedure seeks to unify the views already formulated by the historians. But the thinker who has the historical world for his object must become master of history and all its methods by direct contact with the immediate raw material. He must subject himself to the same law of hard work on the raw material to which the historian is subject. To take the material which through the eye and the labor of the historian has already been combined into an artistic whole, and bring it into a system by means of psychological or metaphysical principles, is an operation which will always be stricken with sterility. If we are to speak of a philosophy of history, it can only mean historical research with a philosophical aim and with philosophical aids."

Yet, Dilthey was not merely a thoughtful philosopher but also a superb practitioner of history. Among his many historical essays, his study of the historical consciousness of the eighteenth century is among the best. Dilthey was one of the first historians to recognize the contribution of the Enlightenment to modern historiography. That essay, which we excerpt below, manifests among other things Dilthey's conviction of the historical conditioning of all thought.

Selected Bibliography

Perhaps the best introduction to Dilthey's work in English is Hajo Holborn's sensitive and probing essay "Wilhelm Dilthey and the Critique of Historical Reason," *Journal of the History of Ideas*, XI: 1 (January, 1950), 93–118. Holborn includes extensive bibliographic references and a helpful discussion of the German term *Geisteswissenschaften* and its English equivalents (pp. 98–99, and note 25).

Also valuable is Holborn's presidential address, "The History of Ideas," *American Historical Review,* LXXIII: 3 (February, 1968), 683–695. We have drawn heavily on Holborn's interpretation of Dilthey's work.

H. A. Hodges performed a valuable service for students of Dilthey in his *Wilhelm Dilthey: An Introduction* (1944) and *The Philosophy of Wilhelm Dilthey* (1952). (Except for a short passage taken from Hajo Holborn's essay, all quotations from Dilthey's works in the above headnote are from Hodges' *Introduction.*) H. P. Rickman has translated and edited a short compilation, *Wilhelm Dilthey: Pattern and Meaning in History, Thoughts on History and Society* (1962); his introduction is perceptive and enlightening. Carlo Antoni, *From History to Sociology: The Transition in German Historical Thinking* (1959), has an excellent chapter on Dilthey. Antoni stresses (perhaps too much) Dilthey's failure to reconcile the antinomies he faced, e.g., between history and psychology, and in contrast to Holborn he places Dilthey squarely in the tradition of *Geistesgeschichte.*

H. Stuart Hughes has a short but incisive and intelligent passage on "Dilthey and the Definition of the 'Cultural Sciences' " in *Consciousness and Society: The Reorientation of European Social Thought, 1890–1930* (1958). Particularly helpful is Hughes's clear formulation of the basis of Dilthey's importance: "One may state Dilthey's significance in most general fashion by characterizing his work as the first thoroughgoing and sophisticated confrontation of history with positivism and natural science" (p. 194). It should be noted that Ranke also believed that recognition of the intellectual and spiritual forces in history "depends rather on a kind of feeling or belief than on exact knowledge," but this position was obscured by Ranke's more dramatic "scientific-objective" pronouncements. On this point see Friedrich Engels-Janosi, *The Growth of German Historicism* (Baltimore, 1944).

Georg Iggers, *The German Conception of History: The National Tradition of Historical Thought from Herder to the Present* (1968), and Gordon Leff, *History and Social Theory* (1971), include helpful sections on Dilthey and his influence. Students who read German will find appropriate bibliographic references in Holborn's article, cited above. An excellent analysis in French is Jean F. Suter, *Philosophie et histoire chez Wilhelm Dilthey* (1960).

An interesting assessment of the state of the problem Dilthey addressed is Edgar Wind's essay "Some Points of Contact Between History and Natural Science," in *Philosophy and History: The Ernst Cassirer Festschrift,* edited by Raymond Klibansky and H. J. Paton (1936; 1963), 255–264.

THE EIGHTEENTH CENTURY
AND THE HISTORICAL WORLD

The Enlightenment of the eighteenth century, which is condemned as being unhistorical, produced a new approach to history, an approach which, in brilliant works of historical art, Frederick the Great, Hume, Robertson and Gibbon put into practice. In these works the idea of the solidarity and the progress of the human race cast its light over all peoples and all times. Now, for the first time, universal history acquired a unifying principle drawn from empirical observation itself. It was rational in that it related all events one to another in terms of cause and effect. And it was critically superior in that it rejected any preconceived notions which would distort given reality. Its bases were a completely unprejudiced application of historical criticism, one which did not spare even the most sacred relics of the past, and a method of comparison which took in all the stages of human existence.

This new conception of pattern in the life of humanity, founded as it was upon empirical observation, made it possible for the first time to tie natural science to history. Through the idea of evolution, hypotheses regarding the origin of the universe, the formation of the earth and man's emergence from among the animals could now be related to the course of history.

But at the same time, the very vitality of this century set a limit to its historical vision. As they strode joyously and confidently forward, these men of the Enlightenment saw in the past only a set of steps leading upward to their own heights. They were filled with a godlike insolence toward the methodical learning of past centuries and with an exceedingly immodest view of their own merit—with the full, happy sovereignty of the new spirit which the name Voltaire represents.

I

Ever since the Greeks, with their clear artists' eyes, looked into the affairs of the world, there have been great historians. But as the historical world

From *Gesammelte Schriften* (Stuttgart: B. G. Teubner), III, pp. 209–238, 265–268. Translated by James W. Moore. Translated by permission of the publisher.

develops over time, so our scientific understanding of man's historical nature matures. This is the inner law of historiography. For no amount of introspective brooding will teach man to know himself; therein lies only an overwrought subjectivity, the great Nietzschean disorder. Only by understanding the historical reality which he creates can man gain a consciousness of his capacity, both for good and for evil.

It is the Greeks who created the great historical art. Herodotus and Thucydides are their imperishably active models. This historiography reached perfection in an age of unparalleled brilliance in all the arts. The artistic capacity of the age, the most highly developed which the world has ever seen, was creatively active in it. But in this great time of the free city-states, the horizon of the Greeks was still limited in time and in space. From the time of Herodotus, they could with the utmost clarity grasp that which outwardly characterized those nations with which they were in contact, through commerce, through war or through journeys. But their ignorance of foreign languages kept them from penetrating the earlier history, the political structures or the literature of other countries. Thus, they expressed beautifully the characterizing distinction which they found between themselves and the others, but they did not develop a scientifically based concept of the historical development of civilization or of their own place in this development.

So, too, their political thought was limited, during the age of their independent political development, to the analysis of their own states and of those of the peoples with which they were in closest contact: the Macedonians, the Persians and the Carthaginians. They studied the conditions which governed the existence and the form of their city-states. They investigated the economic bases of these political bodies, their structure and the law which governed changes in their constitutions. They discovered the great golden mean of political achievement and of political rights which must be held to if internal order is to be maintained. From it they deduced the proper causes of revolutions. And from the time of Plato, they were concerned with the problem of giving permanence, perhaps immortality, to the state—an accomplishment which, under the political conditions of the day, would have been equivalent to that of squaring the circle. They further analyzed the forms of their own poetry and rhetoric. And in Dicaearchus' work on the *Life of Hellas* they achieved a conception of Greek culture as a whole and made the attempt to study it systematically. For, building on the basis of natural conditions, the great student of Aristotle differentiated the facets of this culture and portrayed the life of Greece in terms of its political structures, its manners and morals, its religious cults and its festivals.

Thus, the analytical talents of this gifted nation were turned for the

most part inward, to its own rapidly ebbing culture. For the noble, radi-
ant Greek experience had also its dark side: the plantlike cycle of birth,
fruition and decay, the quick decline of its great art, the vain effort to
make its little city-states endure. And if, among this beautifully endowed
[schönheitsseligen] people, a pessimistic sense of the vanity of human
existence comes repeatedly to light, then this is the necessary consequence of these conditions.

If the majority of their thinkers made periods of origin, development
and decline in the universe succeed one another with a dull hopelessness,
then this attitude was certainly conditioned by the very basis of their
view of the world. But at the same time, this cyclical view became for
them the loftiest symbol of the transience of our kind. They were conscious that they had left barbarism and unfreedom behind them. However, they had no concept of continuing progress, no consciousness of any
work achieved for the future of mankind which might have led them to
look forward toward a a greater future.

From the time of Alexander the Great, the geographical and historical
horizon of the Greeks constantly expanded. They developed a concept of
human knowledge as a totality, a totality which extended from astronomy through geology to chronology and to the cataloguing of the
collected stock of Greek cultural achievements. In the age in which the
Roman state, in its origin a city-state like those of the Greeks, was rising
to mastery of the world, Polybius then composed his great historical
work. He wrote the history of the period from the beginning of the first
Punic War to the destruction of Carthage and of Corinth. The advance
of history itself, the close interrelatedness of events upon a broad stage
during this struggle for mastery of the Mediterranean, set a new task for
the writing of history and for political thought. Now, one could achieve
a universal-historical standpoint, for the broadening of historical outlook necessary to take in the interaction of states and the relationship
between the two greatest civilizations of the Mediterranean required
such a standpoint.

The historian who was to accomplish this had to be schooled in the
political thinking of the Greeks, and at the same time he needed a position at the center of contemporary world politics, a position from which
he could survey the relationships between the nations and could learn to
understand their leading personalities. History itself seems to have
formed Polybius for this task.

When Polybius joined the circle of the Scipios in Rome, he was already
well versed in all the achievements of Greek thought and schooled in the
turbulent politics and in the wars of his native land. Here, he adopted
that universal standpoint which saw the future of the cultivated world
to lie in a fusion of Roman mastery and Greek civilization.

Aemilius Paulus, the great-minded victor of Pydna, took him into his home, as a companion and to see to the scholarly training of his sons. The historian himself tells us—a bit boastfully—how he won the heart of one of them, the younger of the two great Scipios. The timid yearning with which this masterful young man turned to the wisdom of the Greeks reminds us how in a later era our Germanic ancestors yielded themselves, modestly and yet demandingly, to Greco-Roman culture. The friendship which now grew up between the two was to contemporaries a symbol of the newly developing alliance between the Roman will to rule and the intellectual powers of Greece.

The aristocracy of this, the age of the Scipios, is one of the high points in man's existence. Here, Roman force of will was wedded to the aesthetic and contemplative spirit of Greece. The finest monument to this alliance is *Scipio's Dream,* by Cicero. The great hero of this family appeared before the younger Scipio; he explained to him the metaphysical connection by which the order of the immeasurable universe, as the Greeks knew it, is bound up with the duty to live for the state. The necessities of empire were already leading the great Roman personalities to gather in themselves the totality of all that human thought had achieved. They wished to free Greek thought from the crust of oversubtle theorizing which adhered to it. They brought it into harmony with the genius of their own people. At this time Panaetius was introducing the Stoic philosophy into the Scipios' circle, and it was destined to penetrate the Roman spirit. But who can say whether it influenced the Roman spirit more, or was more influenced by it?

Polybius was conscious of this junction of the two greatest forces which the world had yet produced. Out of his relationship with the Scipio circle arose his universal-historical understanding for the process in which the lifework of the two greatest nations of antiquity was fused into a single culture: a culture which would dominate intellectual life until the entry of Christianity and of the Germanic peoples into history. And the confidence with which he and other talented Greeks like Panaetius could move among their conquerers was also based on this understanding. Certainly, Polybius had his fair share of the vanities of the Greeks, and of the subservience which they displayed toward the new rulers of the world. But for his practiced political intellect, it was a matter of course that in Rome, and especially in the aristocratic circles in which he lived, he should have recognized the historical realities and have submitted himself to them. That he did so does not reflect unfavorably upon his character. The pose of the unteachable, irreconcilable statesman, filled with resentment against destiny, was not for him. His was a clear and a sober intellect. Surrounded though he was by the grandiose historical fictions of the Greeks, he devoted himself to reality in truth and with a good critical intelligence.

The detailed portion of his account began with Hannibal's crossing the

Alps into Italy and with the alliance of Philip III of Macedon with the Carthaginians. Thus he was faced with the task of evaluating the strengths which had enabled Rome to overcome this crisis and to press on to mastery of the world. After the manner of Aristotle's *Politics,* he sought the true and lasting causes of Roman greatness. These causes he found in Roman morals, Roman law and Roman institutions. If he repeatedly returns to the manly virtue of the Romans as being the most basic explanation, then surely this is what one would expect of the pupil of Attic philosophers and the contemporary of Greek rhetoricians. But at the same time it also illustrates the objective historical impression which the customs and characteristics of this great democratic epoch of Rome had made, and that precisely upon a contemporary Greek. And if he sees the basic cause for the tenacity of the Roman state in its mixed constitution, then there is also a kernel of truth in this, couched though it is in doctrinaire Aristotelian terms. The main thing was that he undertook to apply all the results of political analysis to history. In so doing, he meant to raise it to the level of a science, a science which would make it possible to predict the future and which could become the school of statesmen. Faced with such a task, the art form of Herodotus and Thucydides melted away.

But his main original contribution to universal history lay in this, that in his writing he took in the interplay between the states which constitute history at a given time, and that he then sought to explain individual political events on the basis of this interplay. Proudly he called this his great achievement in advancing the understanding of history. He insisted on the fact that it was the object of his study itself which had led him to adopt this approach. For he saw that the events of his time in Italy, in Asia, in Greece and in Africa were most intimately related one to another, and that together they had brought about Rome's domination of the world. And he recognized that his theme required a new kind of historical method, a method which rises above the history of single nations and which considers the universal process in which the events of three continents are bound together.

And yet the cyclical view, which for the Greeks embraced all earthly things, held even Polybius in its spell. This intensely vital Roman nation, which even now has subdued the Semitic race, will itself decline. Amid all the exuberance of the Roman will to power, the Greek observer maintains a rational coolness refreshing, but at the same time chilling, to the reader. Precisely because of Rome's unchallenged mastery, because of the growth of wealth and of luxury, her aristocratic constitution must decay. Democracy and mob rule will break in. Thus also Scipio, standing in the full flush of victory before ruined Carthage, spoke of his presentiment that Rome would decline. Polybius was with him then, and the victor turned to him with the prophetic words: "So, too, some day some other man, standing on the ruins of Rome, will recall the words of Homer." It was only in the time of Pompey and Cicero that the eternal permanence of Rome became an article of faith which appreciably influenced historical thought.

II

History moves forward. The peoples of three continents are united under Roman administration. Now the revealed religions of the East find their way into the composite which has developed out of Greek and Roman culture. The Christian Church expands. Within it the question arises, what the essential relationship is between the Roman Empire, the knowledge of the Greeks, and the Christian religion. Such great historical changes have produced a new concept of the unifying principle in human history. Mankind is now seen as a unit, a unit which realizes a preordained goal through the succession of peoples. Within this teleological ordering of history, the individual nations fulfill functions given them for the sake of the whole, through the development of knowledge, the building of political power and the process of revelation. Polybius' vision had, in a manner of speaking, extended over the breadth of history. Now the concept of universal history was enlarged and perfected by an idea of coherence over time. But this coherence is conceived not scientifically but in religious and metaphysical terms. It is seen as a divinely ordained teleology. And the tie which binds its beginning to its end is the story of salvation.

This new concept was first developed in Augustine's work *On the City of God.* As Augustine wrote, the Greek-speaking peoples in the Eastern Roman Empire were breaking free from the Western world and sinking into torpor; the philosophical schools of the Greeks were in decline; and the Germanic tribes were pushing into the Roman Empire. Only the Church remained upright and continued to stride victoriously forward. For Augustine, this "City of God" had grown progressively upward since the beginnings of the human race, and the future history of humanity depended upon its development. The work is permeated by a sense of the senility of ancient culture, of the approaching ruin of political order, of the worthlessness of all earthly existence.

This new universal-historical outlook had its basis in the idea of the Kingdom of God. The brutal egoism of the oligarchy, the exploitation of conquered provinces and the bloodshed of the civil wars had dispelled all the fine illusions of Scipio's time. The happiness which a relieved world enjoyed under the rule of Augustus was a happiness based upon peace, civilization and a wise administration. In the sensibilities of this aging world there was no longer a place for the independent worth of nations, for the progress of mankind.

And now by the quiet shores of Galilee Jesus found, in nature and in the simple life around him, the image of the divine order described in his holy scriptures. Thus he conceived the idea of the Kingdom of God, not only of the Kingdom which is to come, but of that which has always been. Then, with the development of the Christian communities, this idea of God's Kingdom was fused with the Stoic concept of world community and with the universal Roman concept of the Church. In this way there grew up for the first time a consciousness of the solidarity of all peoples and of their progress in realizing the Kingdom of God. And as the expectation of a Second Coming faded, this realization retreated ever further into the distance of history.

To this idea Augustine subordinates all the concepts of Church philosophy: the education of the human race, as Clement teaches; its passage through the ages of life, as Tertullian has it; or through the six days of creation, according to Cyprian; the succession of the Four Monarchies, which Jerome draws from the Book of Daniel. Above all these, Augustine sets the dichotomy between the Kingdom of God and the City of Man, that dualism which has torn history asunder.

The later development of his standpoint has consisted primarily in the increasingly high value which has been given to the external ordering of life. Augustine derived property and authority from the Fall. The temporal state was for him the creature of egotism. He confronts Rome with the tally of her crimes, and, if even he recognizes in the manly virtue of Rome the source of her power, then virtue in the pursuit of fame and power is to the ascetic bishop only a glorified vice. Worthless in itself, the temporal state acquires its religious significance only as an instrument in the hands of the Church. For Albertus and for St. Thomas Aquinas, the internal order of the state is grounded in the moral nature of man. But this realizes only the preconditions necessary for the fulfillment of the religious purpose of humanity. Dante was the first to recognize the independent value of the state: in the state, temporal happiness is realized; it is for the Church to prepare man for eternal life.

This was the earliest conception of the solidarity and of the progressive development of mankind. It was a satisfactory conception only so long as the conditions remained out of which it had arisen. It was a teleological interpretation of world history. One looked for a meaning in history, just as one looks for meaning in a poetical epic; one found it only because one had in Revelation a ready key to the great riddle. Beginning, middle and end of the life of mankind were all laid down by holy scripture. On this basis, history was construed in terms of the real conditions prevailing from the time of Augustine until the end of the medieval order.

Christ's ideal had found its first form in theocracy, but the course of events itself proved this form to be transitory. Christendom was confronted by Islam, and it strove in vain to overcome this historical barrier to its Divine Kingdom. Even earlier, the Greek-speaking peoples had withdrawn themselves from the Papacy. Now it was confronted by the Protestant churches, and the unity of the Christian theocracy was completely lost. So, too, the active idea of a cosmopolitan and progressive task, which Christianity had been given in realizing the Kingdom of God on Earth, now vanished from the life of the Christian churches. It had been the Church's great intention to lead, with a wise moderation, the progressive powers of the nations. In the Catholicism of Trent this intention was lost. And the living consciousness of the united progressive strength of Protestantism, the consciousness in which Luther in his great early years, Calvin, Coligny and the Oranges had lived, withered and shrank in the Protestant churches of the seventeenth century. And slowly the deepest contradiction emerged, which is immanent in the Christian City of God. Every religion is from the time of its origin limited by the historical nature of that religious condition of mind which gave birth to its dogmas and its ecclesiastical structure. And so long as it remains bound to this origin, its claim to mastery over mankind will be in conflict with man's universal spirit.

III

Once more history surges forward, and there is an advance in the historical disciplines, an advance which established the conditions under which in the eighteenth century the first attempt could be made to give universal history a scientifically based cohesiveness and under which, in the nineteenth, our own historical *Weltanschauung* could arise.

In the fifteenth and sixteenth centuries the modern mind advanced to the point where it could conceive historical life, and the forces which govern it, in natural terms. As the medieval Church and its metaphysical system broke apart, it called forth intellectual and economic progress and a restructuring of social and political relationships. With these changes there arose a consciousness of the independent value of worldly life and labor, a consciousness which everywhere victoriously broke through the transcendental world view of previous centuries. Individual, state and nation took cognizance of their own sovereignty. They began to suit their mode of action to their natural interests, and they never hesitated openly to admit their motives. And just as the revival of ancient culture was based upon the inner affinity which existed between the life of modern peoples and that of the Greco-Roman world, so, too, everything which antiquity had achieved in the systematic treatment of morals, law,

history and the state was now revived. And the inadequacy of all metaphysical cosmologies was even more deeply felt, the need of a natural
foundation for the temporal order grew even more compelling as the
powerful religious movement of the sixteenth century produced, not a
new cultural unity among Christian peoples, but the bloody rivalry of
sects and denominations. Out of these elements arose the beginnings of
a new theory of man and of society. This theory abandoned all supernatu-
rally derived concepts and explanations. It sought to explain this world
of human will and action in terms of its own laws, laws accessible to
observation and description and therefore also practically applicable.
The natural system of social and humane sciences was then brought to
completion under the influence of the new physical science of the seventeenth century, and its power to influence life and scholarship was infinitely increased.

It was in Italy that this new manner of conceiving the kingdom of man
was first made usable for the historian. This occurred in the most intimate connection with modern politics, which was here for the first time
being developed into a practical and theoretical system. Machiavelli, the
first modern political thinker, is also the father of modern historiography. And like the great Florentine, so, too, his younger contemporary
Guicciardini was a busy diplomat and deeply involved in the varied
workings of Italian party politics.

This historiography is exceedingly narrow in scope. Its content is
purely political. It considers man only in his relationship to the state; all
other aspects of his life—economics, art and science, morals and religion
—are of interest only insofar as they can be made useful for the purposes
of the state. And its purpose is also political. It wishes to show how
political power is gained and held. At its very highest standpoint, it asks
how the patriotic statesman is to hold this variety of competing interests
in balance and to secure the good and the permanence of the whole. But
it is precisely this one-sidedness which gives it its importance, and which
explains its influence until the time of Frederick the Great and on down
to Ranke and his school. For its viewpoint was derived from reality itself,
and it was and remains the most important from which history can be
written. And the manner in which Machiavelli and Guicciardini used it
made them the creators of dynamic historiography.

The writing of valid history must begin with a criticism of sources,
which, from the remains of the event itself and from reports of the event,
establish the facts of the case. And proper historiography only begins
with an interpretation of the sources, which can comprehend these facts
as an expression of the inner life of man.

In this respect the great philology of the sixteenth and seventeenth
centuries rendered a valuable service to historiography. It undertook to

reconstruct a lost world out of the decayed remnants of its literature, and in the process, criticism and interpretation developed into an art and a conscious method. The religious struggles and confrontations which filled these two centuries brought further assistance. Biblical exegesis became extremely important to the two great Protestant faiths. For when they rejected the authority of Catholic tradition, they were forced, in order to defend themselves against the unbridled individualism of the sects, to seek in the letter of the scriptures a firm basis for their dogmas and institutions. Flacius was led by his struggle with Tridentine Catholicism to consider the principles of exegesis, and in his *Key to the Scriptures* he created the first new system of biblical interpretation since the days when the theologians of Alexandria had quarreled with those of Antioch. Spinoza, Richard Simon, the English freethinkers, the Dutch Arminians and Bayle submitted the scriptures to criticism. From the Lutheran standpoint, the authors of the *Magdeburg Centuries* began the critical study of ecclesiastical history. Basagne continued it from the Calvinist point of view. With Arnold, the young Pietist faith entered the field; Tillemont, the Jansenist of Port-Royal, surpassed them all.

Specifically historical criticism developed along lines set down by this critical activity in the fields of philology and theology. In the introductions to works of narrative history and to documentary collections, and in special works on methodology, there was an ever-increasing emphasis on the need to investigate the value of sources: to consider the personality of the author, the entire situation in which he wrote and the degree to which one source is dependent upon another. Such an investigation was increasingly regarded as the first prerequisite of all historical work, and, in the honest effort to live up to these demands, the technique of textual criticism slowly developed a firm set of principles.

To an equal degree, there was increasing recognition for the great importance of written documents. And the whole basis for the special field of paleography was already laid down in the seventeenth century. This new discipline grew up out of the very practical interest which this age of tangled legal relationships had in determining the validity and the conclusiveness of century-old parchments. The remarkable war of documents which the city of Lindau had to wage in order to establish its status as a free Imperial City gave rise to Conring's excellent studies. And a hundred years later, in France, the attack which the Jesuit Papebroch launched against the oldest Benedictine charters of St. Denis called forth the classical work of Mabillon.

And now, too, the age of the Humanists and polyhistorians heaped up, with an unrivaled diligence, the material on which the eighteenth century would base its own historical narratives.

Through the labor of philologists of all countries, the entire treasury

of ancient literature was slowly brought to light—insofar as it had survived the poverty, the enmity and the indifference of previous centuries
at all. The texts were made ever purer and more reliable. These writings
were studied and interpreted, and commentaries were written, from every standpoint, and it is in this context that the individual branches of
classical scholarship had their origin. When the methods of the new
philology were brought to bear upon the needs of justice and administration, the imposing structure of Roman law was restored, after centuries
of distortion and mutilation, to its original purity and completeness.

Because of religious conflicts, more material became available for the
study of Church history. Seeking to refute history with history, Cardinal
Baronius opposed his own *Annales* to the *Magdeburg Centuries.* To this
end, he and a supporting staff of scholars spent forty years working
through the Vatican archives and the libraries of the most important
European churches. Now for the first time a part of the treasure which
they held was published and made available for general study. The *Lives
of the Saints* of the Bollandists was a product of the same tendencies in
restored Catholicism. Again, the eternally fruitful combination of political and scholarly interests operated in the case of Paolo Sarpi. He wrote
a well-documented history of the Council of Trent, and his work was so
thorough, so honest, that it had to be published abroad and under a
pseudonym.

The work of collecting and ordering undertaken in preparation for the
historiography of individual states and nations was perhaps even richer
and more massive. The source collections of Duchesne and Baluze are
still as valuable today to the historian of France as is the *Glossary* of their
countryman Du Cange to anyone who must venture into the jungle of
medieval latinity. Muratori collected the authors and antiquities of Italy.
And in Germany, this kind of historical work grew to an enormous extent. Here the existence of numerous political entities, each of which had
its own history and wished to pass it on to posterity, came to aid the
scholar's zeal. A further incentive came from the practical necessity of
having the legal monuments of the Empire and of the individual territories brought together in usable editions. By far the majority of the annals
and chronicles, on which today our knowledge of medieval Germany is
based, were already discovered and printed in those days. At the same
time, there was a constant and growing stream of documented territorial
histories. The old forms—dry annals or gossipy chronicles—yielded
everywhere to new demands for a maximum of completeness and reliability. Formless and verbose as they were, more source collection than
history, these folios were the secure basis on which the German historian
of the future would build, and to which he often refers even today. And
the age of Leibniz already planned to unite its powers and to work this

enormous material into a great German history, a history to be based in every detail upon original sources. To this end, Hiob Ludolf worked for the foundation of an Imperial Institute of History, and Leibniz gave him his full support.

The eighteenth century knew the sixteenth and seventeenth centuries themselves from the great contemporary histories of that era. The list of classical Italian historians runs from Machiavelli and Guicciardini to Strada and Davila, men who took in what they experienced, at home or abroad in France or Holland, with the keen vision of statesmen, and who portrayed it in the artistic form of the great ancients. Beside them stands Thuanus, who could never equal them in classical expression, in clear ordering of events or in psychological explanation, but who far surpassed them in his historical vision—just as the new monarchy of Henry IV excelled the petty circumstances of the Italian state system. The heroic age of Dutch Calvinism produced the historical works of Grotius and Hooft.

Germany could produce nothing comparable. There was no national historiography in the grand style, which might have reflected the fateful developments which took place here. Contemporaries could only take up individual events and tendencies, or they considered matters from the petty standpoint of this or that government. But here, too, within these limitations there were accomplishments of unique value.

Greatest of all was Pufendorf's immortal work. At the end of their lives, Samuel Pufendorf and Frederick William, Elector of Brandenburg, met. These two men belonged together, in their work and in their very essence. For the one was the hardest realist among German publicists, the other among German princes. Just as Frederick William, at the dramatic moments of his career when German interests conflicted with those of Brandenburg, unscrupulously abandoned the common cause to follow the promptings of his own natural egoism, so, too, Pufendorf saw in the great temporal principalities the only element in the German state system to hold promise for the future. Both were filled with a sense for the reality of power, as against all the obsolete structures of the past.

Pufendorf was called to Berlin in the summer of 1686. He arrived in February 1688, a few months before Frederick William died. And Pufendorf himself had only time to sign the manuscript of his work before he followed his great master to the grave. His *Nineteen Books on the Deeds of Frederick William, Great Elector of Brandenburg* was only published a year after his death. The book is one-sided in the extreme. Everything is seen only from the standpoint of the policy of Brandenburg; attention is directed solely to the action outside. But for precisely this reason, the work expressed perfectly the nature, both of the young state of Brandenburg and of its first great historian. And as one trait of this common nature was a most ruthless frankness, the Elector had permitted his historian an unrestricted use of the archives, and Pufendorf made such candid use of this permission that immediately upon publication his work was reproached with damaging the reputation of Brandenburg. In all this, Pufendorf was the beginning and the model of all specifically Prussian historiography: Frederick the Great, Droysen and Treitschke were all conscious of their inner affinity with him.

I V

The art of writing history requires a reasoned concept of the unifying principle which joins the individual occurrences and which gives them life and an inner emotional force. The sixteenth and seventeenth centuries had produced the scholarly tools for handling the enormous material of history. But it was the eighteenth century which first produced the great leading ideas which could master this material. Here again, these ideas grew out of historical life itself, from a combination of the greatest universal-historical events. For the play of forces, both on the broad stage of contemporary history and in the distant past which was then being uncovered, could be grasped only from a standpoint of an entirely universal-historical kind.

The concept of the solidarity and the progress of mankind was derived from that of a universally valid natural science, of a coherent universe governed by laws. What religion had conceived symbolically was now the object of scientific knowledge. Thus a central idea, one susceptible, within limits, of proof, was found for the study of history—however much later generations would restrict and limit it. Like all the earlier ideas, it was derived from the observation of what happened in life itself. In the course of the seventeenth century and through the cooperation of philosophers and scientists in every civilized country, a mathematically based science arose, was given its philosophical basis and was applied to every phase of life. In this cooperation among men of learning and in the steady progress of their work lay the great new fact which effected a revolution of ideas.

Voltaire says of the early eighteenth century: "At no time has there been a more general union of philosophical minds; Leibniz animated it. Despite the wars and religious confrontations, a republic of learning gradually emerged in Europe. This republic was made up of the Academies. Modern scholars in every branch of knowledge joined together in a great society of minds which is everywhere present, everywhere independent. This union endures, and it is one consolation against the evil which ambition and policy have spread over the earth." Thus together arose the principal ideas of the new epoch: the autonomy of reason, the mastery of the human mind over the earth through knowledge, the solidarity of peoples despite all their struggles, and the firm trust in constant progress, founded on the universal validity of scientific truth which enables us to found one truth upon another.

These ideas have given mankind a new vitality. In all human history I can think of no greater occasion than the rise of this new complex of ideas, a complex extending from the recognition of the laws of nature to the mastery of reality through the power of thought, and from there to the highest ideas which govern all our lives. It is because of this that any one of us is, in his vital sensibilities, superior even to the greatest thinkers and heroes, the loftiest religious minds of the old world. For now for the first time humanity stands upon firm ground, a goal before it which is set in reality and a clear path by which to reach it.

This certainty of the progress of civilization was increased by the development of the great European monarchies. Those robust political bodies grew up which have become the bearers of modern history. First France was consolidated. Then, with the accession of William of Orange, England achieved the internal stability which was the basis of her remarkable rise to power. In the same era, the Austro-Hungarian monarchy arose out of the dual struggle against France and the might of the Ottomans; something of an anomaly among these national states, it was still able to maintain itself through the force of circumstances. Then, in the first generation of the eighteenth century, Russia became a European state and since that time has pressed irresistibly westward. Finally there arose the Prussia of Frederick the Great, the boldest and most modern form of state, and it, too, held firm.

These "great powers" shared the mastery of the Continent. But as they held one another in check, wars gradually diminished, and in the last half of the eighteenth century, Europe saw a more lasting peace than at any other time since the bloom of the Roman Empire. Literature was filled with the ideal of an eternal peace and with plans for its realization. These states secured and assisted their subjects in producing the economic blessings of life. They created that continuity of material civilization which is everywhere essential to the advancement of culture. They placed themselves directly at the service of science and civilization, as the sure and capable bearers of their progress. They needed these intellectual forces to maintain and to strengthen their political power. In affording protection to the Muses, the great princes sought to heighten the glory of their government and to assure the immortality of their names. All this strengthened, in the political and historical thinkers of the eighteenth century, a cheerful confidence in the continuing progress of civilization. Everywhere an optimism which made spirits rejoice and which urged them onward—until the catastrophe of the French Revolu tion broke in over this entire order of things.

And in these modern states, scholarly work received a new, firm organization, and this, too, strengthened the faith in the constant, irresistible progress of knowledge and of its effect upon life. The Academies were created. Now, for the first time, the capitals of Europe sustained centers of learning. And now, because it was organized into permanent corporations supported by the state, this learning received a clear direction. The Academies promoted the division of labor, the restriction of the individual within a definite area and the positive, exact and methodical spirit of research. Laplace once remarked that their essential advantage lay in the philosophical spirit which developed within them. Because they wished to convince one another, their members agreed to favor investigations of a certain and unmetaphysical kind. They were the permanent bearers of the extremely complex and extensive enterprise of modern empirical science, an enterprise which requires continuity in disciplined work. They spread to all the capital cities. Twenty-five years after the Berlin Academy came the Academy in Petersburg. Then came the one in Stockholm, whose first president was the great Linné, then the one in Copenhagen, and even the smaller German states founded such institutions.

Then the modern scientific spirit took hold in the universities, and here, too, the division of scholarly labor moved steadily forward. Here those studies were continued which the Academies neglected but which these modern states required: administrative studies, jurisprudence and medicine. Science was utilized for the training of the governing class, and especially of future officials. The first model of the new university was Halle, where administration was taught from the standpoint of contemporary philosophy. Then Göttingen was established as the center of historical studies, which were under the influence of England. Consider the constant expansion of scientific enterprise, organized by the state, and the acceleration of intellectual work which it produced; consider the intellectual authority of the persons involved and their influence on high officials of state who had been their students, and how all this strenghtened the power of science and its influence upon life. How just this organization of intellectual effort increased confidence in the progress of civilization through the influence of reason. How this central idea of the Enlightenment spread from the scholars to officials, jurists and writers.

Thus arose the idea of the *great culture,* a culture having its firm foundation in the power of lawfully ordered monarchy, in the development of industry, of commerce and of wealth, a culture which builds upon these foundations a firmly grounded, progressive, universally valid system of knowledge, of enlightenment and of power for man over nature, a civilization which blossoms forth in an art ennobled by thought, in a purified, disciplined taste and in a high culture uniting the upper classes of all nations. This concept the Enlightenment created in its own image. It became the measure for judging earlier times. It was convincing because the progress of physical science had, in the great states, given civilization a new sense of security. Even artists and poets were considered in terms of this rule of thought over life. The measure of their worth lay in their capacity to express the humane ideal of this culture and that joy in existence which springs from the sovereignty of the intellect. This is an idea of the function of art to which no one-sidedly aesthetic standpoint can do justice.

It was England, under the rule of the great William and of Queen Anne, which first developed a unified civilization of this kind. Shaftesbury best exemplifies this era. He was conscious of the relationship which existed between the power and independence of his country and the growth of the human personality to inner harmony. All conditions were fulfilled: that great culture, which in Roman times had been inhibited by continual war, is now to be realized in England. It demands that imagination be subordinated to a thought which accords with reality. Then it will produce a higher form of personality, a purer art, a more noble culture.

Voltaire, when he came to England, was filled with this ideal of a powerful and yet a free ordering of society. And yet he was a Frenchman to the bone, and he held firm to the unique value of the culture of his own vivacious nation. Voltaire was the first to apply the new idea of culture to history. In his *Age of Louis XIV* he undertook to organize all aspects of French life under this king's reign within a coherent framework. For him Louis XIV personified the will to power of the French monarchy. His cult of Louis rested on the idea that only the greatness and solidity of his state had made possible the improvement of man's whole existence: the bloom of science, of the nobility and of the greatness of artistic form and the courtly refinement of manners.

Where this will to power has done violence, he condemns it: in the devastation of Germany, in the insatiability of its warlike ambition, in the expulsion of the Protestants and in the persecution of the Jansenists. And yet his heart is with every action of the king's which had as its goal the unified power and the expansion of France. "The great soul," the urge, "to great things of every kind," in this man's will to power impress Voltaire. He seeks to grasp him in his warlike and political actions. In a collection of anecdotes which illuminate the most intimate details of his private life, he tries to make him comprehensible. But ultimately it is not this king who matters to Voltaire. What he wants is to understand the structure of this French century, which the power of Louis' monarchy had made possible.

From the development, in war and in policy, of France's political power, he passes to the progress of commerce and industry, of legislation, of military organization and of finance, and finally to what was done for knowledge in this era. He notes that "sound philosophy" did not make the same advances under Louis as did poetry or rhetoric, and, as the comparison with England is ever present in his mind, he freely admits that their intellectual achievements were greater. The reasons for this fact, reasons which cast so dark a shadow over Louis' reign, he passes over in silence.

As he now turns to literature and the arts, the special standpoint of the work becomes perfectly clear. For him, the immeasurable importance of this literature lies, not in the excellence of single poets, but in the perfection of language. For now this language is equal to any task; in the expansion of art into every variety of poetry and prose and to every object of reality, and in the power with which it everywhere permeated polite society, with which it mixed princes, statesmen and generals with writers and contributed to developing a higher form of human and social existence. Here Voltaire truly grasps the progress which leads from the poetry of imagination to the era of Racine, Diderot, Lessing, Goethe and Schiller. These new men are more than poets. Because from their intellectual heights they dominated the age, they became the teachers of humanity in a more comprehensive, if not in a higher, sense than were the earlier poets—even Shakespeare.

And now Voltaire's history rises to the highest point of observation. He attempts to gain a comprehensive overview of the entire intellectual culture of the era, which began shortly before the reign of this king and which Voltaire could now examine in its completed form. In his opinion it is philosophy, the queen of sciences, which gives this century an immeasurable superiority over all preceding centuries. If one compares Locke to Plato, one recognizes what progress culture has made in this, the greatest age of human history. From Milton to Pope, Addison and Swift, the English were masters of the poetry of ideas, and in Locke and Newton they are man's teachers in true philosophy. And maliciously as he might ridicule Leibniz elsewhere for his optimism, here he does him justice as the most universal thinker of Europe. For him, the greatness of this time lay in the universal coherence of all sciences in the different civilized nations, borne by the Academies.

And since for him enlightenment, tolerance and humanity are ultimately the most important product of the great culture, his story ends with a description of religious and ecclesiastical conditions. He plunges into the thicket of religious conflict. He recognizes the errors of Louis' Church policy, although he fails to see through its political motivation. And since to him the intolerance of the king, the fanatical obstinacy of the Huguenots, the theological squabbles of the Jansenists and of their opponents are alike contemptible, indeed incomprehensible, his work ends with a kind of desperation at the power of narrowness and superstition over mankind. He did not understand the emotional forces which move history.

Voltaire does not fulfill the need for a full understanding of this culture. He describes, he judges, but he does not explain. But he had a special understanding for the kind of greatness which lived in this French monarchy. He knew three great nations well. He understood great men of action through a kind of inner affinity, for he himself was led by the interests of his own literary power, a power which extended throughout Europe.

And most of all, at Sans Souci he had known the greatest representative of contemporary kingship. We know enough about Voltaire's influence on Frederick; the king made no secret of the matter. How great Frederick's influence was upon Voltaire is difficult to say. Voltaire knew everything that the king had written, and everything that he was considering and had not yet written. When one reads Frederick's essay "On Morals, Usages, Customs, Industry and the Progress of the Human Spirit in the Arts and Sciences," which was published a few years before Voltaire's work, it becomes clear that the two men agreed in their approach to cultural history. It was one of the great king's main ideas that the Prussian state, more backward than the other great powers, had first to establish its power and to develop its economy. Only then would follow the blossoming of science and the arts.

Thus there came a change in the writing of history, a change which distinguishes the work of this century, more strikingly than any other, from all that had come before. History began to deal with the pattern of culture. This has nothing to do with the false ideal of a cultural history which isolates great men from the conditions around them, or the regular progress of civilization from the struggles of nations. It is precisely the connection among all these which the great histories of Hume, Gibbon and Robertson portray. For the Enlightenment was conscious of the importance of the great monarchies and interested in the shifting balance of power among them. Even its ideals of freedom were integrated within this context. Nor was it any philosophy of history—as a new branch of study—which brought about these great advances in conceiving the historical world. Taken in isolation, no philosophy of history would be worth anything. But the philosophical spirit was active in everyone's mind, and it increased the capacity to understand the historical world. It sought out those causal relationships which bind the laws of nature to the life of the spirit and the earth's development to man's life upon it.

And it was its greatest achievement that it brought its universal-historical standpoint, that of the progress of human culture, into the foreground. The struggles of states, war and politics kept their place in history. Even Voltaire devotes the greater part of his two works to them. To be sure, war is to him like an unfathomable act of God which disturbs the even march of civilization. He stands before religious enthusiasm—or before Louis' unlimited lust for conquest—as if before a natural force interrupting the gentle rule of reason. This, then, was to be the task for the future development of true historiography: to investigate the reasons for these power struggles and to explain the diminution of these struggles, in number and in intensity, which followed especially from the development of the great monarchies and of a condition of equilibrium among them. It is here that the political and historical ideas of Frederick the Great fit in.

To deal with culture itself, the best historians of the century developed a technique of dividing it according to its different facets. At the same time, *cross sections* were taken through the progress of civilization at especially important points in its development. Hume, after 1763, was the first to apply this method with sufficient exactitude. Montesquieu's principal works had already appeared, and Voltaire had just published his *Age of Louis XIV*, as in Edinburgh Hume steeped himself in the sources of his native history. And as he was half finished, Voltaire's work on morals was published. Beside his political history Hume places a thorough, comprehensive account of constitution, laws and customs under the Anglo-Saxon Heptarchy, then another for Norman feudalism, and he concludes with the famous description of morals and the scientific spirit as they had developed, after the long struggles between King and Commons, under William of Orange. Then in 1769 Robertson, in the fine introduction to his *History of Charles V,* brought an inner sequence to the conditions of European society. And Gibbon, the greatest historian of the century, begins his work with a description of the entire culture of Rome under the Antonines—that long and happy time in which Rome, under the wise rule of noble emperors, enjoyed a condition of greatest peace and domestic well-being, until the decline began with the death of Marcus Aurelius. This description is the greatest achievement of its kind which the eighteenth century produced. He dedicates a similar passage to conditions among the Germans at the time of their invasion of the Empire under Decius. So, too, he analyzes at other points the spirit of nations when they come into contact with the Empire. And, in his brilliant analysis, he was the first to set forth the character of early Christianity and to develop the reasons for its growth. It was indeed the great age of English analysis. They were the first methodically to dissect economic life, moral facts, artistic creation and the methodical working of the human mind. After this, Adam Ferguson and Henry Home began their analysis of society as a whole and of progress in history.

But now, from the concepts which had been established, the concepts of the unity of the human race, of the common pattern of aspects of its culture in every epoch, of development toward the great culture of the present, another task also arose. It was the task of describing the *line* of progress which had led upward from primitive barbarism to the creation of the great monarchies, to the development of a universally valid science, of enlightenment and of civilized manners. For this historiography of the eighteenth century, this was the real problem. All Enlightenment historians are related in the basics. For all of them, the goal of history lies in the independence of scholarly investigation, in tolerance, in religious enlightenment, in well-crafted art and in the new freedom of the individual to develop his personality, which the security offered by the great states now permitted him. By this time natural science, the accounts of travelers and the combination of these with the oldest human artifacts have established the origin of history in the primitive stages of mankind. The age of myths concerning the origins of man is over. How the human race climbed upward, step by step through madness, illusion and impassioned chaos to civilization: this is the standpoint from which historians now treat every part of the past. And the mood of the historian varies from sympathy to amusement at the great delusions of the past, between an honest hatred of the despots and charlatans of all times and that optimistic confidence with which this age of reason looks proudly forward to a boundless progress of man under the guidance of knowledge. Voltaire has settled accounts with the theological historiography of Bossuet. And in his "Essai sur les moeurs" he was also the first to undertake the writing of a new universal history of human culture.

This task attended him throughout his life. In about 1740, he wrote for the Marquise de Chatelet a philosophy of history and an essay on the history of the human spirit from Charlemagne to his own time. He then combined the two for publication in 1756. Twenty years later he took up the project anew. His performance was not equal to the magnitude of his intent. And yet there was an extraordinary force in the application of the new ideas to the data of history. It was strengthened in two ways. In submitting all tradition to the measure of sound common sense, Voltaire strengthened the critical spirit. He is desultory and often wrong, in what he rejects as in what he accepts. He is far beneath the profound synthetic criticism of Vico and the methodically schooled criticism of Perizonius. However, he is more effective than all of his predecessors, through the principle of universal doubt.

But what is most important is the power of Voltaire's prose style, which is more perfect here than in almost any other work. It is entirely different from everything that had previously been written about history. Here, after the long and painful work of scholars, a sovereign human being appears, firmly convinced that he possesses, in his modern consciousness and in the culture of his century, the measure of all history. Priests of all religions he covers with ridicule, down to those who, under Louis XIV, had filled the land with their quarreling. He hates every kind of intolerance or slavery, down to the great nobility, which in the court of Louis XIV still lived off the state. And yet at the same time, he is aware of the distance between his own intellectual emancipation and the vulgar mass, lurking in the depths, below history, composed of the cheaters and the cheated. Every advance of knowledge, every work of good taste, he pursues with the enthusiasm of a young man. History elicits from him a thousand outcries at the power of stupidity and superstition and at the iron rule of chance. History comes alive when this liveliest of men brings each event into relationship to himself. The power of subjectivity now makes its entry into the realm of Tillemont and of Muratori. And in its train the art of historiography, which is always grounded in inner vitality. For the time being, it remains an exceedingly subjective and irregular form. But the true art works will come, when emancipated subjectivity yields itself, quieter, steadier, more scientific, to the great reality of the historical world.

It was necessary to proceed to a methodical system of explanation. And the compulsion to broaden Voltaire's approach lay in the historical facts themselves. At the same stage in the development of society there are many forms of life. The political thinker of this era confronted the religious despotism of the Turkish Empire, the lawful monarchies of France and of Prussia, and the free political systems of England and the Venetian Republic, of Switzerland and then of North America. He found these distinctions combined with differences of national character, of civil law and of intellectual life. Thus arose the task of deriving these differences from the traits common to human nature and of setting them in relation to the great stages of human development. The comparative approach of the ancients and its results, present in the works of Plato, Aristotle, Polybius and Cicero and in the comprehensive insights of the medical schools, with regard to differences of climate and to their effects, had now to be utilized. Vico, Grotius and Bodin must be carried further. Montesquieu was the first to undertake this task.

V

Montesquieu's *Spirit of the Laws* is the most important political work of the eighteenth century. The author belonged to the nobility of the robe, which held as its hereditary property the judicial offices of Old France. But in him, the scientific spirit of the age was now joined to Bodin's humanistic and juridical training. He had, as a member of the Academy in Bordeaux, published essays on natural science. And when he now visited England, he understood the free constitution in mechanical terms, as a mutual balancing of political forces—a metaphor drawn from the world of physical science. His life work was published in 1748—the *Spirit of the Laws.*

Three main ideas make up the central theme of his work. These ideas are concealed in the text. For much of the artistry which made the book's enormous popularity possible lies in its division into individual reflections.

"That which is common to the legal and moral orders of all nations stems from the natural laws of unanimous human reason." With this thesis he adopts the standpoint of natural law. But his problem is now to explain the differences which exist among these orders and to establish their unique value. He starts from the political thinkers of antiquity. He deepens their comparative method by tracing the connections which lead back from the orders of society to the natural conditions on which they rest. Climate and the nature of the soil create differences in economic life and in the distribution of wealth. From these arise the differentiation of customs, of legislation and of political structure. He masters this connection with a thorough study. At the same time, he appreciates that the collective spirit of nations is conditioned by history, and in the end perhaps by an innate predisposition. Every people maintains a definite character throughout its history. Its legislation must be adapted to this national character, and it determines its legal and political structure.

With these chapters of Montesquieu's begins a new epoch in political and historical thought. They are filled with the profoundest insights: how climate influences the functioning of the human body, and thus sets a definite stamp upon the spirit of individual regions; how the geography of the broad plains, where no physical barriers restrict the spread of the power of the strongest, produces the great states; how the migrations and conquests of peoples proceed from the poorer to the better soils; how in mountainous countries or on islands smaller states find protection and freedom can develop; how man in history gradually emancipates himself from his bondage to the soil. Here the first bases of a historical geography are adumbrated.

With Montesquieu, political thought makes a second great advance. He inquires as to the psychic and moral forces necessary to maintain a given form of government. He perceives that these are different in despotic, aristocratic, democratic and monarchical states. The principal forms of constitution arise and maintain themselves through the force of appropriate types of communal spirit. Here Vico had preceded him; and politi-

cal writers in his own time and thereafter, Frederick the Great and
Hertzberg, took a lively interest in the problem which he raised. They
saw through the weaknesses of his solution. And yet they did not fully
grasp his profound central idea, that monarchy under law is less dependent upon the religious convictions or the moral characteristics of its
citizens than is any earlier constitution. Precisely from this, Montesquieu
derives his hope in its greater permanence. For to him, too, the task is to
prove the superiority of this great lawful monarchy. "It is this form
which enables policy to accomplish great things with the least possible
expenditure of virtue, just as, in the most perfect machines, technology
utilizes the least possible number of movements, forces and wheels."

And so, too, for him the development of monarchy under law to the
political freedom which England enjoyed becomes a mechanical problem. The solution lies in the mutual balancing of political powers. Only
then will the executive power be held within its limits when the legislative and judicial powers are founded in themselves, independently of the
executive, and have a power adequate to maintain themselves.

This theory is a valuable step forward for science. If one conceives it
as an interpretation of the English constitution, then it deserves all the
reproaches which have been leveled against it. But considered as a theory which has at once the dynamics and the statics of political power as
its object, it does justice for the first time to this aspect of political life.
England has realized political freedom before all other states, and in it
Montesquieu studied the conditions to which this freedom is bound: so
long as one takes into account only the relationship of powers within a
political unit. Thus arose his theory of the separation of powers as the
precondition of English freedom. From this he derives the necessity of
the distribution of these powers among different subjects, the veto of the
monarch, the responsibility of the ministers. Everything is a system of
weights and counterweights, of restraining mechanisms, of guarantees
against the self-aggrandizement of any one of the powers. So perceived,
political freedom seemed to be transferrable from one country to another
through the will of the legislator. He did not consider the deep ties which
bound England's political freedom to the character of the nation and to
its tradition of administrative decentralization [Selbstverwaltung].

Montesquieu only solved the problem which he set for himself very
imperfectly. Profoundly thoughtful and entirely free from prejudice, he
dealt with an enormous volume of material; he took the time to allow his
work to mature. But his explanations refer only to causal relationships
between factors which he sees as firm and immutable facts. Individual
statutory or constitutional provisions he explains in terms of individual
causes. His method of comparison never takes in the entire structure of
a social order, nor its development, nor the relationship in which it

stands as a whole to the religion and the customs of a people. He does not think historically. He has no eye for the special qualities of a social body which have their roots in the vitality of human nature. He did not investigate the steps which law and constitution pass through in the course of their development.

Turgot proceeded from just this concept of a set of regular steps in the progress of society. Turgot's reading of the *Spirit of the Laws* gave him a powerful impulse more completely to solve Montesquieu's problem.

On 11 December, 1750, Robert Jacques Turgot read in the Sorbonne his discourse "On the Successive Advances of the Human Mind." He was then twenty-three years old, a precocious genius pursuing studies of vast extent with plans for the foundation of new sciences. One is struck by the similarity to Herder, as at the same age his mind was stirred by ideas, boundless in their extent, concerning the entire historical world. But while Herder could devote his life to the development of these ideas, the great French statesman was able to take up the plans of his youth only after he left political affairs. And nothing was published, either from this speech and his early papers or from his last years. His view of progress in history was first made effective by his friend and pupil Condorcet. His papers were only published in 1809. Either directly or through Condorcet, they became the bases for the development of Comte's philosophy of history.

Turgot was at the center of the movement of the French spirit from which the Encyclopedia emerged. He, too, was directed by mathematically based science and the positivist spirit of his friend d'Alembert, who left every kind of metaphysics behind him. And just as the physiocratic school, to which he belonged, had proceeded from natural science to political economy and sought natural laws of economic life, he saw the connection between the geographical structure of the earth's surface and the forms of economic life upon it, and he saw these as determining the historical and political life of nations.

At the same time, this idea can be seen as the broadest conceivable statement of Montesquieu's doctrine regarding the influence of climate and the soil upon historical life. The science which has these relationships as its object he called political geography and designated as a cross section through history. He wishes to discover the influence of the configuration of the earth's surface on the production and distribution of goods in the various regions. Then the effect of the distribution of land, sea and rivers on intercourse, on the relations among peoples, on conquests and on trade. Finally the relationship of these outward causes to the moral forces which create the different characters of nations, their genius and their constitutions. His brilliant surmises touch upon a great portion of the problems which Kant and Herder dealt with, and whose solution has occupied historical geography since Karl Ritter. The manner in which they are treated expresses his training in natural science, which opens to him the understanding of form and structure, of quantitative distinctions and of the relationship of forces.

There is in this political geography a thought which carries over into universal history, which in its turn anticipates the central thesis of Comte. In the present situation of the earth's surface, with its multiplicity of more or less cultivated peoples, the entire line of progression of human development is still present today. A look at the earth enables us to take in the whole history of mankind in *one* picture. If one compares the wild peoples of the American West with the Moslem or with the denizen of a Spanish monastery, and, again, the scholastics of the Sorbonne with the *philosophes,* then one finds side by side the same steps in the development of our race which we encounter in history. "Ah! our ancestors, and the Pelasgians who preceded the Greeks—they were like the American Indians!" Thus the general idea of the progress of mankind in history acquires a more definite form. The observation of cultures of different levels, scattered simultaneously over the earth, leads to the same conclusion as that of the course of history.

Man stands thus amid the dry uniformity of the course of nature, an atom in the immeasurable universe—and yet, if one can grasp him philosophically, as a part of the whole of humanity, victoriously unfolding himself in the constant working succession of generations: *one* great unity, throughout the rise and fall of historical change like the water of the sea in storms, striding constantly forward to greater perfection. This insight covers the whole breadth of culture. Everywhere the progress of mankind is derived from the facts: "Manners grow gentler, the mind is enlightened, the isolated nations come together, commerce and politics finally unite all the parts of the globe, and the totality of mankind moves through alternating violence and repose, through good and evil, slowly but surely forward to greater perfection."

To be sure, these great intentions do not fully correspond to what is accomplished. For it remains an outline. Progress in moral and political civilization is postulated rather than proven. The nations progress from despotism to free and just systems of government; from a moral world in which little tribes are the outer limit of benevolence and obligation toward others to ever milder and more humane customs which finally take in all humanity. Then for a moment appears the idea of development in art which Schiller and his generation evolved. There is a naïve stage of art, one that in poetry is favored by the metaphorical character of language. It is directed by instinct and imagination. After the decline of the first great art, humanity must achieve through reflection what it once produced naïvely and effortlessly. Thus arises a new and different kind of perfection. Thought directs imagination, and this is reason's highest achievement.

In *one* area of history Turgot made a contribution of enduring value. He was the first to draw up the law of the three stages in the intellectual development of mankind. The human intellect passes through a theological stage, a metaphysical stage and a stage of empirical science. This conception arose from the scientific mood of the time, and it could only have been stated in France, for here, in d'Alembert's circle, positive science was breaking free of the metaphysics of the scholastics, of Descartes and of Leibniz. All around him, Turgot saw the best minds make this transition to positive experimentation. At the same time, he was still surrounded by the rule of every kind of religious superstition in the Catholic Church.

Thus, he posits the existence of a period of metaphysical illusion. In this stage the human mind ascribes reality to metaphysical entities. Positive thought dissolves this illusion when it sees through the subjectivity of sense impressions and learns to see concepts as abstractions from factual data. And throughout a long, long period of time before this metaphysical stage extends a primitive level of our intelligence, the stage of mythical consciousness. This perceives will and personality in everything. Today, in primitive peoples and in the child, we still find the unrestricted rule of this imaginative stage. For the first time, this law of three stages uncovered an intrinsic regularity of progress in history. Surely Turgot, like Comte, is mistaken, in that he fails sufficiently to differentiate the myth—seen as a primitive way of perceiving reality— from religion as an eternal life-impulse of peoples. And if they would have the metaphysical stage to yield completely to the positive stage, then here again a question remains which demands another kind of answer. But a more exact restatement of the law, one suited more closely to the facts, can remove these shortcomings. Its kernel stands.

[Translator's note. These final paragraphs follow a discussion of ecclesiastical history as it was pursued by Spitteler and others at Göttingen, in the spirit of the Enlightenment.]

The limits of the pragmatic historiography of the eighteenth century become visible with a special clarity when it deals with this material. Let us call to mind once more the nature of this method. Characteristically, it is directed toward the knowledge of causes. It holds individuals to be the only true causes, i.e., the only causes susceptible of empirical proof, and it considers these individuals, not in terms of unconscious powers active within them, but in terms of intent, of plan, in short, of a rational activity which is governed primarily by their own interest. Thus, characteristically it has no concept of inner ties between individuals in society —no concept of the people or the state as an original historical quantity.

Related to this is another main feature of this pragmatic historiography. It is meant to be useful; it seeks to instruct the reader regarding the motives of men of action, of parties, of religious schools, or of the masses which they influence. It seeks to make its readers "not only learned, but also wise," by showing how the human spirit "has made its way through the mightiest efforts and the most incredible perplexities." It wishes to make the present comprehensible. Spitteler defines history as the study of the origins of the present.

This manner of considering man in history arose when the eighteenth century took man, as the society of this century shaped him, to be the norm of human existence. It is customary to regard Bolingbroke as the founder of this historiography. This politician without a conscience; this little man who wavered between the ambition and the disappointments of courtly politics and the studied pose of a philosophical abstention from affairs; so ignorant that he could equate Guicciardini with Thucydides; so shallow that he disdained the study of historical beginnings and of antiquity, and had no feeling for Herodotus; this dilettante who in his book said nothing true which had not been said before, whose knowledge would not have fitted him for any solid historical work of a petty and subordinate nature, let alone to sit as judge upon history. The only merit of this Bolingbroke was that he played with truths which serious thinkers, like Polybius, Machiavelli, Guicciardini and Hobbes, had discovered; and that he said boldly what the statesmen and men of the world of his time thought about history.

The first work in which pragmatic historiography was practiced with thoroughness and on a major subject is Montesquieu's *Observations on the Causes of the Greatness and Decline of the Romans* (1734). Here a new light is cast upon the great theme of Polybius and Machiavelli, through the methodical application of psychological concepts to a political whole and to the manner in which it functions. "Since men have at all times had the same passions, so, although the occasions for great changes differ, their causes are always the same." He begins with the Romans who fought the wars of the monarchical period. They are firm in their religion, true to their oaths, inspired to the utmost of bravery by the distribution of loot which followed successful wars. He recalls how this population was surrounded by walls, continually ready for war, forever fighting with other tribes and everywhere seeking its own advantage. He considers the psychological effects of such a situation, the habits which arise from it—in short, he seeks to explain that condition of mind which the old writers called the "manly virtue of the Romans" and estimated to be the primary cause of their success, on the basis of the conditions in which they lived. By the same token, the causes which decided in the struggle between Rome and Carthage lie for him primarily in psychological strengths, determined by the conditions of life in both states. So, too, the decline of Roman freedom is derived from the relaxation of moral forces which had tended to keep the whole together and whose strength had to be maintained, and which now succumb to the influence of changed conditions brought about by the expansion of the Empire.

And when pragmatic historiography is elevated to the universal-historical standpoint of the eighteenth century, it becomes itself a historical power of the greatest importance. For its consciousness of its goal, the solidarity and the progress of our kind and of culture, becomes a universally effective force which permeates the whole educated world. What it has drawn from the changed sensibilities of man it gives back to the time, heightened and confirmed by the fullness of historical reality. To accomplish this, it becomes popular. It becomes a work of art, because it is borne by the inner power of a new life-consciousness.

Now the work of writing history itself produces insights which restrict the basic ideas of the Enlightenment. The question arises of the collective force which gives a state its power and which maintains constitutions. And from the beginning, the German mind had a way of looking at history which carried the most outstanding historical minds of our people over the limits of the Enlightenment's understanding of the historical world. Möser and Winckelmann stand alone in the midst of the Enlightenment, the founders of a new epoch. The crisis came with Herder. His intellectual basis lay in knowledge of the evolution of the physical universe, the formation of the earth, the influence of geographical conditions upon the life of nations; in this he is the son of the eighteenth century and the student of Buffon and Kant. But his conception of the unique value of every stage in history and of every form of existence on every patch of ground, of the realization of happiness and of perfection under the most varied conditions, of the unconsciously developing powers of human nature, carry him past the limitations of this eighteenth century. With him begins the development which, united, cohesive, progressing unceasingly, carries through Romanticism to Humboldt, Niebuhr, Schleiermacher and Hegel, and thus on into the nineteenth century.

Friedrich Meinecke 1862—1954

2

Friedrich Meinecke was doubtless the most distinguished German practitioner of the history of ideas in the first half of the twentieth century. He was also quite possibly the most influential. Through his long tenure as editor of the prestigious *Historische Zeitschrift,* from 1896 to 1935 (in which he saw himself as resisting the spread of positivistic history), and through his numerous essays on political and historical theory (e.g., those in the collection *Schaffender Spiegel),* his views on history and the role of ideas reached a wide professional audience. His three great works—*Cosmopolitanism and the National State* (1907), *Machiavellism* (1924), and *Historism* (1936)—are regarded as classics of modern historiography, and not least because they tell us as much about the historian and his time as they do of the subjects themselves. The three works have all been translated into English since 1957, a testimony to Meinecke's enduring importance. His influence extended to America in a particularly effective manner: Hajo Holborn, Hans Rothfels, Hans Baron, Fritz Gilbert, Dietrich Gerhard, Hans Rosenberg, and Gerhard Masur, all distinguished historians and every one a Meinecke student, migrated to America in the 1930's.

Meinecke was born in 1862 in the small Prussian town of Salzwedel. Like so many other German professors in the nineteenth century, he came from a family of Prussian civil servants (his father was a postal official) and Protestant ministers (there were several Lutheran pastors in his background). Meinecke grew up in an atmosphere of deep piety tempered somewhat by a love of the idyllic natural environment which surrounded his isolated country town. As a young student he was drawn to the poets and writers of the *Sturm und Drang* school. He later referred to their literature as his "spiritual home." Meinecke was particularly attracted by Goethe's emphasis on the uniqueness and importance of individual human beings, an emphasis which was to reappear in his historical works. He entered the University of Berlin in 1882. Johann Gustav Droysen, in his last seminar, introduced him to the importance of ideas in history, that is, of man's contemplation of his experiences over time. From Droysen, too, Meinecke learned to consider the individual in history, to become aware of the unpredictable and incalculable human factor in historical developments, a view for which Goethe had already prepared him.

Yet Droysen's influence on Meinecke was surpassed by that of Ranke, whose "Historicist" school dominated the German universities at that time. Meinecke had already experienced and rejected Treitschke's vehement and one-sided Prussian nationalist historiography; he looked to Ranke as his "guiding star." From Ranke he learned to apply the sense of the "unique" to the writing of history. Every historical phenomenon was to be viewed sympathetically on its own terms and working out its own inner logic. Hegel's view had reduced men and epochs to shadows merely imbued with the Idea, having no meaning in themselves. Ranke rejected this, as Meinecke approvingly noted: "I claim that every epoch is in direct contact with God, and its value is not based on what emerges from it but is found in its own existence, in its own being." Implicit in this individualizing view of history is an antipositivist stand which rejects generalizing mechanistic theories of causality appropriate only to the physical sciences. It was also a view which allowed for the play of irrational, intuitive forces. "The essence of Historicism," Meinecke writes, "is the substitution of a process of individualizing observations for a generalizing view of human forces in history." (It should be noted that Meinecke began to appreciate Dilthey's work only after he had attained scholarly maturity; his appreciation then was deep.)

From Goethe, Hegel, and Ranke, among many others, Meinecke also assimilated the philosophy of "identity," so called because it posited the basic identity, despite seeming disparities, of nature and spirit, is and ought, world and God, in a great Unity. For Ranke, as for Meinecke during most of his life, the violent excesses that the student of history encounters were quite understandable when viewed from the proper perspective. If one steps far enough away from the immediate scene, one sees that even the most tragic actions have their proper and acceptable place in the universal drama. In Ranke's words: "Over everything there lies the divine ordination of things which we cannot indeed directly prove, but which we can sense. . . . Belief in Providence is the sum and substance of all belief; in it I cannot be shaken." Ranke was indeed a "scientific," empirical researcher, but he was, even more, a "spiritual" and metaphysical historian.

Ranke also transferred the philosophical idea of individuality to history, and one of the individualities he found to be suffused with the divine essence was the state. The state clothed in power and marching, at times storming, through history held a special fascination for Ranke which Meinecke shared. Meinecke, referring to Ranke's essay on "The Great Powers," asks, "Who does not know those mighty figures [the modern states] which Ranke's sketch makes pass . . . before our eyes, how they now gather strength and now clash with each other, and, by their violent struggle, grow in marrow and muscle?" As Meinecke put it in 1914: "The state is mightier than civilization." Like Ranke, he believed that the community of nations was stronger than their individual diversities and that in the end a genuine international concord would be attained. But in working out their individual paths to that end, no restrictions could or should be placed on their sovereignty or autonomy. Conflict between states is, then, unavoidable. However, their conflict is not evil, is even in some sense good, since the individualities, while proceeding toward the same end, strengthen their inner beings and heighten their vital powers. The optimism which inhered in their world view allowed Ranke and Meinecke to suspend their judgment over the obvious evils of war.

As Philip J. Wolfson writes, they "saw in the stream of history a fundamental moral or ethical purpose, and endeavored to evoke its essence in their writings." It seemed one way, at least, to counter the "anarchy of values or convictions" that Dilthey had analyzed as characteristic of modern life. In the sunny days of Wilhelmine Germany, such a congenial philosophy was both satisfying and understandably held; the horrors of World War I and of the later totalitarian regimes were to force a reassessment of Historicism.

Meinecke received his doctorate in 1886 and began his professional career in the Prussian State Archives. In 1902, after the publication of his masterful biography of the Prussian military reformer Hermann von Boyen, he became Professor of Modern History at the University of Strasbourg. He moved to the University of Freiburg in 1906 before joining, in 1914, the faculty of the University of Berlin, where he remained until his retirement. He retained his editorship of the *Historische Zeitschrift* until forced out by the Nazi regime in 1935, and he survived the "thousand-year Reich" to return to a new University of Berlin in 1945.

The publication of *Cosmopolitanism and the National State (Weltbürgertum und Nationalstaat)* in 1907 at once established Meinecke's high reputation and initiated a new and fruitful form of *Geistesgeschichte*. The work deals with the process of German unification during the course of the nineteenth century; it focuses on the long and painful transformation of the *idea* of German national unity from its origins in eighteenth-century cosmopolitan humanitarianism and German particularism, particularly stressing the tension between Prussian and German "nationalism." Instead of studying archival sources and documents, Meinecke analyzed the thought of philosophers and poets like Humboldt, Novalis, Schlegel, Fichte, and Hegel, of scholars like Haller and Ranke, and of men of affairs like Stein, Gneisenau, and Bismarck. As Meinecke explains in his introduction: "The lofty insight that the state is an ideal supraindividual personality . . . could only come to life when the political feelings and energies of individual citizens permeated the state and transformed it into a national state." These creative individuals are found only at the heights of German political and cultural life, among an elite: "We must grasp the ideas at their high source and not on the broad plain of so-called public opinion, in the insignificant political dailies."

In Fritz Gilbert's words, "This is a book on the influence of ideas on the course of politics and also of the influence of politics on the development of ideas." Meinecke was not interested in, nor did he ever discuss, the relationships of ideas to social and economic conditions. By relating the world of political action to the world of ideas, by stressing individuals as the mediums by which ideas were translated into social forces, by analyzing the actions and reactions of ideas upon events and events upon ideas, by integrating thought and action over time, Meinecke both expanded the concept of political history and initiated a new approach to the history of ideas.

But, underlying Meinecke's methodological and historiographical breakthrough is his uncritical, wholehearted acceptance of the manner by which Germany was united. The glorification of nationalism, the admiration for Bismarck and his methods of *Realpolitik,* the vindication of the autonomous state unaccountable to any external moral law, inform his account of a process which in his eyes possessed "necessity, greatness, and ethical dignity." World War I shattered Meinecke's world and his world view. He attempted to redefine the meaning of German history after the war in his work on Machiavellism *(Die Idee der Staatsräson in der neueren Geschichte,* 1924). Events forced him to look at the state with new eyes and to recognize "the danger that the evils of war and power politics are threatening to choke the blessings they are capable of producing." Meinecke had to grapple seriously with the problem of reconciling ethics and political power. He reluctantly conceded that Hegel's (and Ranke's) acceptance and justification of *Machtpolitik* "was almost like the legitimization of a bastard." He concluded that not even the state was absolute and autonomous.

Meinecke's despair deepened after Hitler's triumph, and he sought hope and solace in the realm of the spirit, in his study of Historicism, "the highest stage so far reached in the understanding of human affairs." *Historism (Die Entstehung des Historismus,* 1936) ignores the problems of ethics and power; by culminating, or conveniently halting, with Goethe, it evades the vexing questions of relativism and irrationalism that inhere in Historicism. This was to withdraw from the social realities, to abdicate any role in shaping events, to flee inward to a contemplative world. Despite its vast erudition, *Historism* is a flawed work. Because Meinecke wrote it out of passionate political commitment—"to exalt the superiority of a specifically *German* mode of thought," in Robert A. Pois's words—not much could be said about Historicism's contribution to a philosophy of ethical nihilism which helped prepare the way for, or at least did not obstruct, the rise of Hitler. A younger Meinecke might have written the history of the interaction of those ideas and that monstrous regime.

In his old age, Meinecke returned to Berlin as Rector of the Free University (1945), and in his last years he advocated a program of studies which he saw as necessary but that he himself could not undertake. Forsaking a lifelong scholarly position and admitting his own fundamental failure, he called for a total re-examination of the Rankean tradition of German historiography. In what was his last scholarly effort before his death in 1954, he called for a new synthesis based upon the disparate views of Ranke and Burckhardt, particularly vis-à-vis the state.

Selected Bibliography

The literature on Meinecke is enormous. Beyond the works by Antoni, Hughes, and Iggers cited in the headnote to the Dilthey selection, students may profitably consult Robert A. Pois's admirable and incisive analysis, *Friedrich Meinecke and German Politics in the Twentieth Century* (1972), and Richard W. Sterling's balanced essay, *Ethics in a World of Power* (1958). The English translations of *Die Idee der Staatsräson in der neueren Geschichte* (*Machiavellism*; translated by Douglas Scott, 1957) and *Weltbürgertum und Nationalstaat* (*Cosmopolitanism and the National State*; translated by Robert B. Kimber, 1970) include informative introductions by, respectively, W. Stark, and Felix Gilbert (a typically magisterial essay). J. E. Anderson's translation of *Die Entstehung des Historismus* (*Historism: The Rise of a New Historical Outlook,* 1972) is excellent.

Philip J. Wolfson's perceptive article "Friedrich Meinecke," *Journal of the History of Ideas,* XVII (1956), 511–525, is drawn from his sound University of Chicago dissertation, "Friedrich Meinecke: A Study in German Historiography" (1951). Eugene Anderson has written an essential article, "Meinecke's *Ideengeschichte* and the Crisis in Historical Thought," in *Medieval and Historiographical Essays in Honor of James Westfall Thompson* (edited by James L. Cate and Eugene Anderson, 1938). J. L. Herkless, "Meinecke and the Ranke-Burckhardt Problem," *History and Theory,* IX (1970), 290–321, is a critical examination of Meinecke's approach to his two great predecessors.

The various definitions of "Historicism" are discussed in Dwight E. Lee and Robert N. Beck, "The Meaning of Historicism," *American Historical Review,* LIX (1953–1954), 568–577, and in Georg C. Iggers, *The German Conception of History,* 287–290. See also the exchange between Helen Liebel and Georg Iggers on "The Rise of German Historicism," *Eighteenth Century Studies,* IV:4 (Summer, 1971), 587–603. Karl Kupisch has an interesting essay on Meinecke in his collection *Die Hieroglyphe Gottes: Grosse Historiker der bürgerlichen Epoche von Ranke bis Meinecke* (1967). In German, the following are important: Ludwig Dehio, *Friedrich Meinecke: Der Historiker in der Krise* (1952); Hans Rothfels, *Friedrich Meinecke: Ein Rückblick auf sein wissenschaftliches Lebenswerk* (1954); Ernst Schulin, "Friedrich Meinecke" in *Deutsche Historiker* (edited by Hans-Ulrich Wehler, 1972) I, 39–57. All of these have bibliographic references for further study.

COSMOPOLITANISM AND THE
NATIONAL STATE

Hegel

... A major idea from the period when both cosmopolitan and national ideas came together is still alive in Hegel and takes on a new and unusual form in his philosophy of history. This is the idea of the representative nation of humanity. He did not think, as Fichte, Schiller, and, to a certain extent, Humboldt and the early Romantics had, that the German nation as such was the representative and universal nation of all mankind. His view was that there is in every epoch of world history a "nation of world historical consequence" that acts as the bearer of the universal spirit in its current stage of development. This nation, he thought, should therefore receive absolute privileges, against which the spirits of other nations had no claim. The nation of world historical consequence would also be the dominant nation of the world. He was not thinking here of the actual rights of nations or of the practical matter of ruling the world. He saw the different nations gathered before the forum of the absolute world spirit; and, from this point of view, he distributed grants of ideal rights and dominance. But to the historical sensibility, such a classification and evaluation of nations will seem rigid and unacceptable. For even though all nations are not of equal value in the eyes of the historian, he still recognizes in every highly developed nation something of unique and irreplaceable historical value, because every substantial historical individuality is irreplaceable. Hegel's view led inevitably to depriving all historical individualities of their proper rights and making them mere unconscious instruments and functionaries of the world spirit.

It was this aspect of Hegel that repelled Ranke. According to this view, Ranke once said, all men were mere shadows or phantoms imbued with idea; and the successive epochs and generations of mankind were mediatized by this, as it were, and had no meaning in themselves. "But I claim

From *Cosmopolitanism and the National State*, translated from the original German title, *Weltbürgertum und Nationalstaat*, by Robert M. Kimber (Princeton, N.J.: Princeton University Press, 1970), pp. 201–230. Reprinted by permission of the publisher.

39

that every epoch is in direct contact with God, and its value is not based on what emerges from it but is found in its own existence, in its own being."

This applied to the "being" of the state and of the nation, too. Hegel, with the remarkable duplicity that permeates his entire philosophy, had both recognized and denied this being, giving it all possible freedom in the sphere of conscious reality only to limit it again in the most rigorous way in the higher sphere of the absolute. The state and the historical world as a whole led a double existence of apparent freedom in the realm of reality and of actual servitude in the realm of the spirit. It was a great advance over Fichte that Hegel did not tear the historical world in two as Fichte had done, and that he removed existence in the rational order to the transcendent sphere rather than wanting, as Fichte had, to realize it on earth. This relieved some of the pressure that reality had had to bear from ideas; and because of this, reality could enjoy greater freedom. But this freedom was a precarious affair in Hegel, only a concession that the philosopher condescendingly made to the world of experience. He much preferred to linger in the world of the transcendent, and he tried to force his contemporaries to judge actual historical life from this point of view, to see it with his eyes. We feel a cutting irony when he describes how states, nations, and individuals live aimlessly, deeply absorbed by their interests, but are in reality only instruments of that "inmost activity in which these figures pass away but in which spirit as such prepares and achieves the transition to its next higher level." Whoever surrendered completely to the spirit of Hegel's theory always stood in danger of trans-forming actual life in this world into a phantasmagoria—stood in danger, too, in terms of our basic theme here, of forcefully and prematurely imposing the universal element onto the life of the state and nation. For it was universalism in its most extreme form that motivated Hegel and let the world spirit advance by means of its unconsciously functioning instruments. Thus, this aspect of his theory is still closely connected with the tendencies we have been tracing.

It was not necessary to completely dispense with the universalistic principles that had previously limited historical life in order to reestab-lish its full autonomy. All that was needed was to draw new and more accurate borders between the two spheres and to span the curve of uni-versal ideas high and wide enough so that history could lead its full and undisturbed life beneath them. Hegel's attempt to do this was imposing and profound, but it was still not completely successful. As the example of Ranke will show, it was possible to go still further in recognizing the proper claims of historical individualities; it was possible to embrace them more warmly, yet at the same time to direct the spiritual vision upwards to the eternal constellations.

Ranke and Bismarck

The "nation" belongs to the basic concepts that Ranke's overall view of history employs, concepts that are so remarkably fruitful because he never demands too much of them, never misuses them for an overly simple classification of historical material, and because he knows that they have no absolutely clear limits of application. When he uses them, he always hints at their origins, which keep blending continually into the infinite. Only a talent as unusual as his, only a mode of thinking simultaneously empirical, philosophical, and artistic could dispense with sharp, clear limits and firm categories without becoming blurred and unclear. A study undertaken with ordinary scholarly means cannot do without them and must make use of such concepts as "cultural nation," "political nation," "liberal idea of the national state," "conservative idea of the national state," and so forth—concepts that Ranke would probably never have used, although his historical writings lead to them often enough and are rich in observations that can easily be fitted into such categories.

It would be to go beyond the scope of this study to examine the national idea in his entire historical work. We shall instead single out one phase in his development when, as a historian and political thinker, he influenced the evolution of the idea of the nation and of the national state in Germany in a significant and, I believe, an epoch-making way. He accomplished this with his essays in the *Historischpolitische Zeitschrift*. The most important of these essays are "Frankreich und Deutschland" (1832), "Über die Trennung und die Einheit von Deutschland" (1832), "Die Grossen Mächte" (1833), and "Politisches Gespräch" (1836).

What he says here about the relationship of nationality to the state and about his own inner relationship to these two forces radiates a genuine originality and a profound sensibility; and even if we were to discount these qualities, his use of language alone would still create an inimitable aura. Yet if we listen carefully, we hear echoes of almost all the voices we have heard earlier. Sometimes we think we hear Humboldt speaking, sometimes Fichte or even Schiller, sometimes the Romantics, from Novalis to Adam Müller and Savigny; and there is even some affinity with the ideas of the *Berliner Politische Wochenblatt,* the extreme feudal counterweight to the historico-political disinterestedness of Ranke's magazine. These influences cannot be traced by the usual literary means and by comparison with sources; and even if they are so traced, the results are still problematic. Passages in Ranke that are reminiscent of his predecessors are not necessarily drawn directly from them. They represent only the finest quintessence of the entire development of thought over the previous four decades transformed into a highly personal view. These intellectual developments were more important for Ranke than the great national experiences in the period of the Wars of Liberation, for these events did not affect his thinking in a direct and powerful way. But filtered through the medium of contemplation, they too could communicate their inner meaning to him.

The earliest elements of his own national sensibility do not stem from these events but from the period preceding them, when the German nation suddenly felt itself to be a great cultural nation once more because of its new literature. German literature, Ranke says with the authority of personal experience, "became one of the most important factors of our unity. Through it we first became aware of this unity again. German literature forms the atmosphere in which our childhood arises, our youth draws breath. It animates all the veins of our existence with a characteristic breath of life. Not one German, we must admit, would be what he is without it." Ranke's German national feeling was first and foremost of an intellectual, not political, nature. It was a feeling of inspiration, a feeling of being totally permeated and carried along, a feeling—as Ludwig von Gerlach would have skeptically called it—of a pantheistic relationship between his spirit and the spirit of the nation. "Our fatherland is with us, in us," his "Politisches Gespräch" claims. "Germany lives in us. We enact it, whether we choose to do so or not, in every country we enter, in every zone. We stand upon it from the very beginning and cannot escape it. This mysterious something that informs the lowest among us as well as the highest—this spiritual air that we breathe—precedes any form of government and animates and permeates all its forms." The subjective element seems to be completely extinguished here, the element of the conscious will that usually has an important role elsewhere in the rise of modern national consciousness. The principle is not: Whoever wants to be a nation is a nation. It is just the opposite: A nation simply *is,* whether the individuals of which it is composed want to belong to that nation or not. A nation is not based on self-determination but on predetermination.

Here we see mirrored once again in a brilliant mind that earlier stage in the development of a nation when unconscious, instinctive, rationally inexplicable processes dominate it, creating and maintaining its unity and character. If we take away the refinements that Ranke's language and thought added to this conception, we have the same view of the character of nationality as that which formed the basis of the conservative idea of the national state for some members of the *Wochenblatt* group. Nationality is a dark, impenetrable womb, a mysterious something, a force arising from hidden sources that is incorporeal itself but that creates and permeates the corporeal. The richness of personal and individual being arises from it; but, for our eyes at least, it remains in the sphere of the impersonal. Ranke thought that every attempt to define the limits of nationality was a restriction and trivialization of the infinite. "Who can name it and who can profess it?" he said, almost in those words, to whoever tried "to raise the flag of an intellectually conceived Germanness." "Who would ever want to capture in concepts or words what 'German' means? Who would want to call it by name—that genius of our past and future epochs? Such a name could only be another phantom that would lead us in false directions." One who rejected such trivial worship of the Germanic in this way would also have to reject the attempt of the *Wochenblatt* politicians to present the feudal-patrimonial state as the flowering of the German spirit and as the Christian-Germanic state as such. The entire tendency of his journal was against these men. Unlike them, he had not conceived of the nation in a purely intellectual and bodiless form for purposes of idealizing the crude material existence of agrarian-feudal institutions. He had not ascribed such an infinite—we might even say such a universal—character to the spirit of the nation only to draw such a narrow conclusion. A slight but clear trace of the spiritual universalism that filled Humboldt, Fichte, Schiller, and the early Romantics still hovers over Ranke's concept of the nation. What else is the nation here but a modification of human existence as such, conceived of as both hidden and revealed? "In the different nations, God gave expression to the idea of human nature." Does Ranke not intentionally define the essence of the nation with words that could also be applied to God in the form of the world spirit? But the name here is not the important thing. For a man imbued with this idea of nationality, nationality was not a burden that confined him to the soil of a limited national existence. It was a pinion that bore him to heights from which he could look down upon his own national soil with grateful affection yet also look up with awe at the incomprehensible, infinite forces of the universe. There is a special evocative quality in this concept of the nation. As we noted before, not only the epoch of the early vegetative development of nations is echoed here, but, as we have just seen, the universalistic epoch of the German national idea is also present. Thus, Ranke himself showed an unusual instinctive awareness of historical developments by responding to his times as he did; for, as we remarked earlier, the rise of this very universalistic epoch and its national literary movement showed again the role of the unconscious, vegetative element in the development of nations. Ranke was also keenly aware of how different national development in Germany was from that in France where conscious will and rational intention dominated. Our countries, he says, are fundamentally different. They have completely different needs and represent completely different points of view. "The complete reorientation of property and law, the creation of a new nation and a new existence, the total renunciation of the past—all these things that have taken place in France have not taken place with us." The contrast between German and French national development is drawn too sharply here, because the "new nation" of the French after 1789 was much more closely attached to the old nation of the *ancien régime* than these words give us to believe. This kind of judgment is rare in Ranke's historical thinking; in this instance he let his German feelings carry him too far. But his German feelings here were also personal feelings. The way in which the German spirit had developed was extremely sympathetic and congenial to him. It had grown from quiet social and political circumstances; rising simultaneously to a state of national consciousness and to the heights of human ideals.

We know how close Ranke's ties with Germany's literary epoch of Classicism and Romanticism were, and we know that the great universalistic aspect of his historical writing derived from it. We often hear the quite correct assertion that he united an awareness of the national element in history with the universalistic historical legacy of the eighteenth century; but if we remember that this awareness of the national had already come alive in the universalistic epoch itself with Herder, Humboldt, and the early Romantics, and that a clear separation of the two tendencies was impossible, then we shall be able to say of Ranke in similar fashion that his own German national feelings and his awareness of the universal existed side by side. But unlike Humboldt, Fichte, Schiller, and Novalis, he did not elevate the German nation as such to a universal, spiritual nation representative of all mankind. His consciousness and the consciousness of his time were too realistic and concrete for that. Too much had happened to shatter faith in this idealistic—but, in the long run, too ethereal—mission for the German nation. Novalis' definition of the German character as cosmopolitanism mixed with the strongest individualism could not have satisfied Ranke; but both in his scholarly considerations and in expressing his own national sensibility, Ranke used Novalis' other statement that everything national, local, and individual could be universalized and that the common must be given a higher meaning, the known the dignity of the unknown, and the finite the appearance of the infinite. Novalis called this procedure "romanticizing" and, in the course of applying it, allowed the infinite and the universal to eclipse and obscure the finite and the national. It is characteristic of the great change in the intellectual climate that Ranke did not "romanticize" but gave reality its due. He did justice, however, not only to the reality that served particular political interests, as the *Wochenblatt* group had done, but to everything that was animated by the breath of German nationality. Pantheistic as his view of the German national spirit may seem, his pantheism is by no means mystic and purely emotional but is instead a realistic, worldly pantheism that moves directly from the realm of feeling to that of facts. Speaking of the German genius, he wrote very accurately that "we can easily see that the emotions alone accomplish nothing. As with other fermenting agents, they are there to spiritualize matter, to act on its ingredients and bring them to life. If the emotions are isolated and left to themselves they have no value, and are more a deadening and harmful influence than a vitalizing one."

Because he always saw the actual and the spiritual as united and never as separated from each other, he was able to define both the relationship between nationality and state and what we have called the conservative idea of the national state more clearly and profoundly than the biased politicians of the *Wochenblatt* could. We shall turn now to his justification and glorification of the German individual state.

Like the politicians of the *Wochenblatt,* he renounced the idea of a strict political unity for Germany. In this we see the persistent strength of earlier views that did not find any value in political unity for the German nation because, emerging during the decay of the old Empire, they had never known such a value. "Fortunately, the Empire was not the nation," Ranke says of this period; and his remark reminds us of Schiller's comment: "The German Empire and the German nation are two different things." But these two thinkers, separated by a generation, differ in a remarkable and instructive way in the consequences they draw from this idea. Schiller goes on to say: "The majesty of the German never rested on the head of his prince. The German has founded his own value apart from politics." But Ranke continues: "The vital forces of the nation had long since withdrawn from the Empire. They consolidated themselves in the new principalities." Schiller consoled himself with what he thought to be the indestructible ideal of the representative nation of all mankind. Ranke found comfort in the contemplation of what he saw as the indestructible political energy of the nation that, after the collapse of a tottering, unviable unity, seized on the German individual state, regenerated it, and nationalized it. "What would have become of our states if they had not drawn new life from the national principle on which they were founded?" The significance of nationality for the state was finally made clear to the general consciousness once again.

But is this nationality that is supposedly so indispensable for the state simply the nationality common to all Germans? Is it capable of permeating the individual state only to the extent that it permeated Goethe's *Faust* or the Kantian philosophy? In short, is Ranke merely applying the doctrine of the national spirit that the historical school of jurisprudence had developed, a doctrine by which the national spirit, invisible and uncompromising, reveals itself in many visible individual forms, intel-

lectual as well as political and social? Without a doubt, this is sometimes
Ranke's view, and in it we clearly see the influence of pantheism at work.
Just as the nation is for him a manifestation of human existence, so the
state, he says explicitly, is also a manifestation not only of human existence but especially of national existence, for the state is by nature much
more closely unified than the nation. He does not deny that nations tend
to form centralized national states—and this view demonstrates once
again his broader historical insight compared with the *Wochenblatt*
group—but he did not find this tendency fully realized anywhere, not
even in France and England; and he did not see it as a very strong or
promising tendency, particularly in the German nation. In his opinion,
the great political task of the German nation was rather to develop the
German individual state further in as fundamentally German a fashion
—and with as little influence from foreign patterns and theories—as
possible. "We have our own great German task to accomplish: We must
develop the genuinely German state in accordance with the genius of the
nation." The foreign patterns to be avoided were parliamentary government and the doctrine of popular sovereignty. He objected to the liberal
idea of the national state to the extent that this idea sought its authority
in a doctrine of supposedly general validity. But unlike the politicians of
the *Wochenblatt,* he did not have on hand another universal constitutional doctrine that found absolute, generally applicable values in the
feudal system. His view was that even the genuine German state could
assume a multitude of forms. He thought that the German states, like the
children of one mother, would be similar in many respects quite of their
own accord, but that it was impossible to give all German states the same
constitution. In each of them, a particular principle is at work that seeks
out its own particular form.

But at this point the originally unified nationality from which these
states emerge becomes manifold. The national basis on which Ranke
wants to build the German individual state is not just the German national spirit as such. For him, the entire German cultural nation divides
itself, in an almost imperceptible way, into as many political nations as
there are vital and independent individual states. There are statements
of his in which he must have had the cultural nation as much in mind
as the political. We find, for example: "We can only meet the threat of
dominance from another nation by developing our own nationality. I do
not mean an imaginary, chimerical one but the actual, extant nationality
that finds expression in the state." At another point, referring to Prussian
reform legislation, he has only the political nation in mind: "This legislation was based on the legal will of the prince who was solely concerned
with the interests of the whole and of the nation." Ranke's essay entitled
"Politisches Gespräch" probably offers more of both theory and personal

views than any other of his works. Here for the first time and with startling lucidity occurs the image of the cultural nation, that "mysterious power" that precedes every constitution and permeates all its forms. The state emanates out of these obscure depths. But the emanation of the state is a different thing from the emanation of individuals from the heart of nationality. In the latter case, as we saw, desire or lack of desire was of no consequence. Predetermination, not self-determination, held sway here. But in the genesis of the state, both are involved from the very beginning: "Circumstances and opportunity, genius and good luck all work together"; and "moral energy," a rich and meaningful concept in Ranke, stands high among the forces that elevate the state to universal significance. From this point on, the reader breathes only the atmosphere of the state and of the particular spirit that is alive in it. We no longer feel the strength of the nation forming the state but rather the strength of the state forming the nation, the "moral energy" at work in the state and emanating from it. The "particular state" becomes the "spiritual fatherland" of the individual; and the "spirit of communal life" that accompanies us to the end of this discussion is a political national spirit, more limited but also clearer, better defined, and more personal in character than that "mysterious power" that we left behind in the profound depths. For the state, to be imbued with nationality is to be imbued with moral strength.

In this way, the course of development that leads from the impersonal to personality and from predetermination to inner self-determination is completed. Ranke conceived of this inner self-determination of the nationalized state in a much broader fashion than the advocates of the doctrines of 1789 had. His concept of the national state is so elastic that it can take in the national state of the older as well as that of the modern stamp. The important thing for Ranke is not whether the political nation participates in the government in a representative and deliberative way. The essential point is its spiritual and moral role in the state in general. He does not regard pure power states, states dependent on soldiers and money, as national states at all, and he questions their capacity to survive.

Everything is drawn together, then, in the idea of the individuality of the great states, an individuality that emanates from their own unique and spontaneous life. We see how different this is from the ideal of progress that Humboldt had put forward in his early work of 1792. "The human race," he wrote then, "is at a level of culture now from which it can only advance through the education of individuals. Consequently, all measures that hinder this education and that press men together into masses are more harmful than before." At first glance, Ranke and Humboldt seem to be going completely separate ways. Of culture as the central task to be achieved in world history, Ranke said: "The sole essential meaning of history is not found in the often very doubtful advance of culture." And nothing pressed men together into masses more than the great power state and national state that Ranke favored. However, we cannot simplify this contrast so crassly. Ranke is not interested in the formation of great masses as such but in the spiritual personality that emerges from this formation. Individuality is the key word for both Humboldt and Ranke, but in Ranke the concept of personality includes the great collective personalities as well. We have seen the role Humboldt himself played in the explorations of the realm of individuality that the German spirit had eagerly undertaken, and in the course of time these explorations had also begun to reveal the individuality of everything that joined individuals together into masses. When Ranke says of states and nations, "True harmony will come from separation and individual development," the basic tendency of Humboldt and classical individualism is still audible in the remark; and we should not see a complete denial of the classical *Humanitätsideal* in Ranke's skeptical comment on "culture," either, particularly since the term itself is so equivocal. If we understand the concept of "culture" in an intellectual sense, then Ranke's national power state represents a genuine and noble culture. Its power and its claim to personality are not granted to it to be used arbitrarily or merely for the purpose of artificially extending its life. "The justification of its existence is that it give a new mode of expression to the human spirit, proclaim it in new appropriate forms, and reveal it anew. That is its mandate from God."

We see here again a universal commandment poised over the life of great state personalities, but the epoch-making advance in Ranke's concept of the national state is that this commandment applies to the individual development of state personalities but in no way limits or weakens it. Just as Ranke did not drive the metaphysical element out of history altogether but placed it where it belonged, namely, on the vague periphery of experience, so also he did not reject the universal element in the life of the great states but located it where it no longer inhibited their free movement. Their origin in the profound depths of nationality and their telos blend into the universal, but their life itself is simply the realization of their own being. Historical research, which observes and describes their life, is necessarily universal in that nothing human can be alien to it; but it can only understand the object of its study, the individual states, if it grants them the unlimited right to act in accordance with their own nature and needs. A remarkable antithesis results from this. The actions of states themselves do not derive from universal motives, but from egoistical ones. However, their meaning is universal, and the mirror that reflects them must be universal, too.

As we saw, Hegel put forward this antithesis, but he had exaggerated the universal study and evaluation of history so much that empirical history became a phantasmagoria. Ranke gave back to history the blood that had been drawn from it and treated it generally with more care and respect. He was content to contemplate and intuit the universal meaning that Hegel proposed to grasp. A proper definition of limits was finally achieved here; and because of this, the ideal and the concrete, the observed object and the observing subject, were separated in such a way that justice was done to them both. We could almost call it a definition of limits in a Kantian sense, although the limits were defined only in a fluid and blurred fashion. But this flowing of the particular into the universal, of experience into speculation, was founded in the very nature of the matter itself. The important thing on which all else depended was that the realm of experience was liberated and the realm of universal and speculative attempts at interpretation was relocated further away from the center of interest.

Let us turn again to Ranke's consideration of "Die Grossen Mächte." Who is not familiar with these massive forms as Ranke sketches them for us, rapidly, but in such a way that they are indelibly impressed on us as they gather strength in themselves, clash together tempestuously, and grow in stature through battle itself? Novalis and especially Adam Müller had had an inkling of this spectacle, but it was more a vision than a clear image because their subjectivity still injected too many universalistic tendencies into it. Here we encounter the true, unobscured image of the life of these powers. Lenz has rendered the basic idea of this sketch very well: "Each of these powers wants to assert its own character, the principle that informs its every organ and manifestation of life, wants to develop all its powers and strengths, both internally and in relation to the outside world. Similarities between the powers, no matter how closely they may bind states to each other, must give way to this deepest of instincts. It even forms the basis for the alliances that the powers form among themselves, and it defines the limits for every friendship." The individuality and autonomy of a state are the same thing; and in Ranke's thought, this identity of individuality and autonomy is reflected in the idea that the state must be based on "special principles of existence," on nationality, on moral strength, in order to be able to assert itself and its nature. As Ranke shows, the great powers of the West had gained this nationality, individuality, and autonomy almost as a matter of course, and in what we might call a naïve fashion, as early as the *ancien régime*. But at the time of the Revolution, they were threatened by an enemy both within and without. The external enemy was the conquering French national state, which, nourished on universal, cosmopolitan ideas, tried to bring states and nations under its universal domination. The internal

enemy was those universal ideas themselves which urged uniform political institutions on all nations and ingratiated themselves with these
nations by an appeal to the individual's desire for equality and freedom.
States threatened in their autonomy rose against such cosmopolitan oppression and leveling. They took stock of their own profound national
roots, those of the political nation no less than those of the cultural
nation, and called on them for aid. But the intellectual forces that Germany in particular infused into her threatened states were, as we have
repeatedly seen, themselves permeated with universal ideas; and because of this the internal ally of the state was also the internal enemy of
its unlimited autonomy. We saw in the cases of Stein, Gneisenau, and
Humboldt how this plethora of directly or indirectly universal ideas and
presuppositions invaded the sphere of practical politics. We saw how the
political situation that brought the different states and nations together
called the universal idea to life, and how the idea of a European community and the idea of state and national self-determination mutually supported each other and were partially congruent, but only partially, so that
here again an ally could become an enemy and an act of good will an
annoyance. The special political and social interests of the Restoration
governments subsequently appeared as a third factor in addition to the
intellectual legacy of universalistic views on the one hand and of the
experience of the Wars of Liberation on the other. The adherents of the
patrimonial state, as they themselves said, fought against absolutism in
any form, the monarchistic absolutism of the past and the democratic
absolutism of the present. As we would say, they fought against the
autonomous state personality in any form, the national state of an earlier
as well as of a modern type. They could not and did not want to draw back
from the national movement entirely, and they tried to render it harmless by developing a conservative idea of the national state that glorified
the feudal state as the genuine product of the spirit of the nation and of
the cultural nation. It is completely understandable that they also held
to universalistic ideas of a European community of legitimate Christian
powers, although these ideas were already diluted to a certain extent. In
both states and nations, this concept of community checked the desire for
power that was dangerous for the fixed forms of the old feudal life, and
it also limited the autonomy of the state personality. The concept of
community gained a positive character through the establishing of supreme legal and moral commandments that had precedence over all the
egoistical power interests of states and nations, and these commandments in turn gained a religious consecration because they were honored
as the law and revelation of God.

The historical significance and the greatness of Ranke's conception
become clear to us only when his conception is compared with this sys-

tem based on both interests and ideals. Ranke's conception retained what was fruitful in this system. It also retained—not from this system but from the Classic and Romantic movement before it—the idea of the cultural nation, of the national spirit, of a unique spiritual nationality that in turn created new spiritual individualities. However, the conservative idea of the national state that he derived from this did not lead him to a limitation of autonomy in the national state but to a justification and reinforcement of it. His national state steps into the world confidently and follows only the voice of its inner genius in all things. The ultimate origins and goals of its personality doubtless reach into depths and heights where universal forces are at work, but in the bright light of its daily life Ranke's national state pursues universal ideas only to the extent that they correspond to its own needs. Ranke knew very well, as did Hegel, that there was a "European community" in the life of states among themselves, but this community was the natural result of fundamental kinship and of a common life together. It is interesting that he found the idea of a European community alive again in the period of the revolutionary wars. But in contrast to those who wanted to make a permanent universal principle of this idea, he immediately limited his view of it by emphasizing how difficult its development had been and how "the states had come together only when threatened by virtual destruction." His main statement on this reads: "Every state was, however, in the midst of its own particular development; and every single one will, I have no doubt, return to this development as soon as the aftereffects of the revolutionary wars abate." Ranke has illuminated the heart of the matter with sure and brilliant insight. The era of the revolutionary wars appears here as a kind of intermezzo of universalistic politics in Europe by which the normal development of state life, which is based on the autonomy of individual state personalities, is temporarily diverted. But he predicts with complete confidence that this development will return again to its original course. His theory rejected the universalism of both the liberal and the legitimistic doctrine. He was not at all willing to concede that Europe might fall permanently into two camps of good and bad principles, for he knew that the same era that had evoked this dualistic view had also infused the great powers and state personalities of the *ancien régime* with new life. The future belonged to the autonomy of the regenerated national state, not to the universalistic principle. Thus, all the mists of universalistic ideas in which his generation had grown up dispersed here before his eyes, and the historian became a prophet who saw far into the future.

To see what lay ahead required more genius than to propose ideals of unification for Germany. Anyone who proposed such ideals, who demanded a national state for the entire German nation, had to be animated by a political passion that was not natural to the contemplative historian. For this reason, Ranke looked much further ahead into the life of the national state in general than did his limited contemporaries; but he greatly underestimated the forces in Germany that were pressing toward a closer unification of the cultural nation into a national state. We know today that the foundations of the cultural nation were capable of carrying more than the German individual states and more than the loose federal union that even Ranke had advocated. We can also easily see that this entire conservative idea of the national state, which was satisfied with the individual state nourished by the German spirit, was a reflection of the actual division of Germany and an attempt to justify this division intellectually before the forum of German national consciousness that was now irrevocably present. But all such ideas are derived from some kind of reality. They must be so derived; they must have as much lifeblood in them as possible if they, as an intellectual force, are to affect reality again in turn. The most palpable fact in the development of German national consciousness was simply that, in the process of passing from an awareness of spiritual unity to the desire for political expression of German nationality, this national consciousness first called a halt at the limits of the individual state; and in the course of centuries, this state had created its own particular political nationality as a territorial state. Deeply rooted sentiments would have been denied if the nationality of the individual state had not been put into the scales along with all other national values. This fact does not require proof, but it gains a more profound meaning if we recall here that both Humboldt and Bismarck pointed it out—Humboldt, the statesman who was most influenced by ideas, and Bismarck, the statesman most influenced by facts.

Ranke stands between them both in time and in his views. He, more than any other, performed the task of uniting ideas and facts. This connection between the three men, a connection we might call symphonic, shows that truly idealistic and truly realistic thinking are always bound to come together again. This is also the ultimate reason why Schiller's representative nation of all mankind could create Bismarck's national state. We shall consider that state now in our concluding remarks.

The striking similarity between the political program that Ranke developed in the thirties and Bismarck's mode of political thinking has already been elucidated by Max Lenz, an important scholar who has done much work in both fields. He writes of the influence of these two men on the political thinking of the nation: "For us Germans, it was they who first completely overcame natural law and Romanticism in history and politics." Lenz himself would want us to take this judgment *cum grano salis,* for where have intellectual impulses of such strength and fruitfulness ever been completely overcome? They live on in what supplants them. Ranke, Bismarck, the new Germany, and we, too, have all taken our intellectual life from them. The idealistically true and the realistically vital elements they contain remain preserved for us even if we turn away from what is now only the empty shell of their former life. Ranke and Bismarck's achievement was to dispense with such empty shells and to overcome paralyzing dogmas and ideals. But in emphasizing their achievement, we must also note the continuity between the new ideas for which they cleared the way and the old ideas whose withered branches they pushed aside.

The bridge that leads from Romanticism to both Ranke and Bismarck is primarily the conservative idea of the national state. This relationship is perfectly clear in Ranke, but I expect that it will not seem so obvious in Bismarck's case. We could cite his later ideas, where he finds the specific character of German national consciousness functioning effectively only through the medium of the "particular nationalities that have developed among us on the basis of dynastic family possession." But this still does not exactly constitute what we have called the conservative idea of the national state. It is closely related to it but not identical with it. This thesis, like the conservative national idea, unites the nationality of the individual state with an overall German national consciousness; but it serves only to point out the result of national development as Bismarck saw it toward the end of his life and to impress on the coming generation what a peculiar dualism of national motives underlay the new German Reich. In the years before the March Revolution, however, the conservative idea of the national state did not recognize and did not demand a German Reich. It demanded at most, like Ranke, Radowitz, and Friedrich Wilhelm IV, a consolidation of the federal constitution; and in all other respects, it was content with the German individual state. It recognized, however, that remarkably dualistic national impulses were at work in the individual state—the particular political nationality of the individual state and the spiritual nationality of the German people. We see, then, that the forces taken into account are identical with each other or at least resemble one another but that the point of view and the interests involved are different. Bismarck made the political nation of the new Reich conscious of the forces of the individual political nationalities at work within it. In this way, the conservative national idea confronted the advocates of a German political nation with the idea of the German cultural nation and of the individual political nationalities as well.

The more general historical connection between the two points of view is immediately obvious. First, the forces of the German cultural nation and of the individual state had just created the new German political nation. Second, the conservative national idea was itself one of the spiritual means for preparing the German individual state for assimilation into the future German national state. This idea had justified the existence of the German individual state but with reasons that pointed toward a still higher level of unification than the individual state itself. In this way, it had helped to keep alive the idea of an inner national community even in circles that had no confidence in the external political unity of the nation. This kind of justification of particularism resulted in the overcoming of particularism within the nation to the extent necessary for the creation of a larger German national state.

The conservative national idea, of course, not only prepared the way for the German national state but also retarded its progress. It retarded this progress intentionally, but unintentionally prepared the way. This double effect becomes obvious in the movement of 1848, in which the inhibiting impulse is more evident than the assisting one. The opponents of the Frankfurt constitution, both the advocates of particularism and those of a Greater Germany, presented arguments clearly derived from the conservative idea of the national state, and we have already seen in the case of Stahl how the Prussian conservative opponents in particular raised this idea as a banner and used it to appease their German consciences over the fact that they were leading a struggle against German unity.

But we can ask with some doubt whether Bismarck even had a German conscience at that time. Did he not carry on his battle purely as a Prussian particularist? His biographer Lenz says, "Everything that lay outside the black and white border posts was foreign soil for him." When a Prussian peer once countered Bismarck's passionate reactionary effusions by saying there was a truth in the "national idea" that should be recognized, Bismarck answered scornfully, "Then you too have been bitten by the German dog?" In the second part of this study, we shall show what dangers the German movement of the time represented for the Prussian state and for the maintenance of its particular personality and nationality. That was reason enough for a man like Bismarck, in whom the Prussian nationality and—to use his own words—its most outstanding characteristic, the warlike element, were personified, to strike out at the "German dog" and deny recognition to the German idea that endangered his native state. However, the conservative idea of the national state lay on his side of the abyss that separated him from the Frankfurt delegates, and the acknowledgment of German nationality that this idea contained was so harmless that even a dyed-in-the-wool Prussian like Bismarck could advocate its tenets without scruples of conscience. There are, in fact, many statements of Bismarck's from these years that reflect a certain German sentiment along with the emphatically Prussian one.

They have never been completely disregarded, and they have usually been interpreted as reminiscences of his youthful athletic and Burschenschaft days. The persistence of such impulses cannot be denied, but all these statements can be easily placed within the framework of the conservative idea of the national state, too. This immediately raises the question of whether these statements, to the extent that they express this idea, were a genuine reflection of his true feelings or a superficial, adopted opinion, perhaps only a tactical utilization of ideas that his party had formed without him and before him.

This question is also raised by the nature of the position Bismarck held in the Christian-Germanic circle, which was also the inner circle of the Prussian conservatives. He was never completely absorbed into it. He accepted the religious and political system offered to him here only insofar as it concurred with his own personal experience. He probably never spoke the language of his new friends in a purer form than in his speech on the Jewish question delivered in the United Diet on June 15, 1847. In that speech, he candidly designated the realization of the Christian doctrine as the purpose of the state. But his ideas on the possibility of achieving this are sober and practical. He betrays a mode of thinking both personal and typical of the Brandenburg nobility when he speaks of the prejudice he had possessed from the cradle and when he declares that his feelings of joy and honor would leave him if he were required to obey a Jewish official. We can thus see how every element of the Christian-Germanic doctrine that he takes up is transformed in his mouth and loses, entirely or almost entirely, its theoretical or doctrinaire tone. We are therefore justified in doubting from the outset that his statements tinged with German feelings really derive from his friends' theory on the relationship of Prussian and German nationality. As we saw earlier, this theory was developed from the Romantic conception of a creative national spirit that gave rise to the personal but never developed into a visible personality itself. This conception in turn was derived in part from the pantheism and panindividualism of early Romanticism and in part, too, perhaps, from the ideas of a cultural and universal nation of the spirit that Fichte, the early Romantics, and the Classical Idealists had held. We need only mention this lineage of the conservative national idea to see that it was meaningless for Bismarck. All these delicate and profound ideas could become vivid experiences for a mind inclined to contemplation but not for one, like Bismarck's, inclined to action. But were not these ideas themselves always derived from the experience of the nation, and was not the concept of a German national spirit in particular the reflection of a forceful reality? This concept was itself only reflection and speculation, but behind it lay the long, spontaneous, and natural growth of the nation. During this growth, the nation created a great deal unconsciously and only became conscious of itself when its pride, its capacity to hate, or its will was stimulated. Bismarck's account of his impressions during a trip in southwestern Germany in his youth is particularly interesting here. The account was written much later, but it contains the kind of memories that are not easily affected by later events. "In looking at the map, I was annoyed by the French occupation of Strasbourg; and a visit to Heidelberg, Speyer, and the Palatinate put me in a vengeful and bellicose mood." Such basic feelings have nothing to do with that "phase of theoretical consideration" in which, according to Bismarck's own report, he experienced his first youthful awareness of German nationality. They are even more fundamental than the "Prussian officer's outlook during the Wars of Liberation," an outlook which, again according to Bismarck's own report, he also held at that time. This account of his immediately reminds us of the first speech he gave in the United Diet in 1847, in which he refused to believe that any motives other than the basic human feelings of "shame at having foreigners command in our country," of "humiliation," and of "hatred toward the foreigners" had a part in the national rebellion of 1813. But there can be no doubt that we have here a sample of the basic ore of national sentiment that lies still deeper than a specifically Prussian or German nationality. This is the spiritual world of the folk epic, of the heroes of *Gudrun* and the *Iliad* who cannot endure the rule of foreigners. This is a need not just for national or political autonomy but, in the last analysis, for heroic autonomy. This impulse was alive at the heart of Bismarck's plans during his entire life. It gave all his political goals their particular character and was an important contributing factor in his greatness.

It was an important factor, but not the only one. He felt along with this impulse a natural, powerful attraction to the great, historically developed spheres of influence in which he grew up, an urge to assume a position in them, to make their life his, to fuse his autonomy with theirs, to rule as a great man and to serve greatness. Growing to manhood, he found three major spheres of influence open to him: the social milieu of the Prussian nobility, the monarchical Prussian state, and the German nation. He never renounced the first, but it was deeply united with the second, which surrounded him and appealed to him most forcefully. Obliged to make a choice between the second and third, between Prussia and the German nation, he chose Prussia with all the energy and passion of his character. But the German nation was not necessarily identical with the Frankfurt assembly's national-political ideal, which was based on the liberal-democratic idea of nationality. There was, however, another concept of the German nation that he was able to accept. The idea of a German cultural nation was, as we have seen, out of the question for him. As a nobleman and Prussian, he would have nothing to do with

German popular sovereignty, nor was he interested in the German national spirit of his Romantic friends. But behind popular sovereignty and national spirit lay, as historical ore, the power of the German nation, and it was to this power that he turned.

"I would have found it understandable," he wrote on April 20, 1848 to the editors of the *Magdeburger Zeitung*, "if the first expression of German strength and unity had taken the form of demanding Alsace from France and planting the German flag on the cathedral of Strasbourg." No knowledgeable person will interpret this remark to mean that he wanted to incite a national war of conquest against France. But it is not just another bold statement either. It indicated the kind of strength that was latent in him and the kind that he admired. This is still no thunderstorm, but, like similar remarks that we have already examined before, it is a distant flash of lightning. This is still not German sentiment of a political nature or even of an intellectual or ethical nature, but rather of a clearly voluntaristic nature. If we read between the lines, we find Bismarck saying: If you must have your German zeal, if you are not satisfied with the sense of well-being that your state can offer you, then I will show you what German character is when it has some force behind it. I can only be convinced by that kind of German character.

The immediate purpose of the letter to the *Magdeburger Zeitung* was to make it clear to his German and Prussian compatriots that they were suicidally foolish in granting Polish demands in Posen. We could perhaps object that he wanted to promote Prussian interests by an appeal to German feelings that he did not necessarily share himself. But we would be deaf to the natural voice of emotion if we did not recognize it even in the calculated form in which it finds expression here. He favored a purposeful, not a blind, development of German national strength, and at that point he could only find hopes of such development in the power and greatness of his own Prussia. Thus he considered German nationality a great potential force, but it had reality for him only in the power politics of his own native state, not in a centralized state that had not even been created yet.

Did he have similar feelings about the other major German states? In the same letter and in his speech of December 3, 1850 on the Treaty of Olmütz, he expressed the satisfaction he felt about all the conquests by German arms in the course of the centuries and therefore about the rule of Austria in Slavic and Italian territories. We may well doubt the genuineness of his satisfaction here, but we must also admit that it was characteristic of his thinking to grant Austria's claim to the title of a German power because of her extension of German dominance and her military strength.

We must also note, finally, that his concept of the German nation at the time had some points of contact with that of his political associates Leopold and Ludwig von Gerlach. Leopold wrote in his journal on April 24, 1848, perhaps under the influence of Bismarck, with whose ideas of this same period he might have become familiar: "How hypocritical this Germanomania is and what grave wounds it has already inflicted on Germany. Prussia had spread German customs and German law to the Niemen, the Netze, and the Prosna. The Revolution is making the greatest possible effort to drive the Germans out of all these conquered territories." The situation was similar in Bohemia, Tyrol, and Austro-Italy. "There is no mention whatever in all this of reuniting Alsace, Lorraine, the German provinces of the Netherlands, and the genuine German portion of Switzerland with Germany or of protecting German nationality in Transylvania." But in the following year, Ludwig von Gerlach agreed with Wolfgang Menzel's view that the only possible German national policy would have been to declare Austria's struggles in Hungary and Italy a German affair, to send German troops there, and to prevent altogether the armed intervention of the Russians. We see immediately how the same ideas that have a national heroic aspect to them in Bismarck threaten to wither into a somewhat extravagant doctrine in the Gerlachs. In the case of the Gerlachs it is difficult, indeed impossible, to separate doctrine and sentiment. In Bismarck it is equally difficult to separate interest and sentiment. If the historian wants to find the middle way between excessive criticism and naïveté, he can do nothing but follow his instinct for what is alive and take cognizance in both cases of the two tendencies that coexist side by side.

Our assumption is confirmed. Bismarck accepted the conservative idea of the national state to the extent that his nature and his role as an autochthon allowed and to the extent that the potential of the German nation and the interests of the Prussian state coincided. When he went beyond this and concurred with the national theory of his friends, he did so primarily for immediate tactical reasons but also because of a component of heroic sentiment that rose up in him. But it would never have occurred to him to convert the pleasure he took in Austria's military actions in eastern Europe into actions of his own and thereby pursue a German national policy in Gerlach's terms. Let every German state clear a path for itself with its own sword: Austria against its Slovaks and Magyars; Prussia—this idea came to him in these years too—by telling the Germans what their constitution should be. A few days before the Olmütz speech, he said openly in an intimate circle of his political friends that Friedrich II of 1740 was a model for emulation; and in the Olmütz speech itself, similar desires can be inferred. He held them under firm control because he saw too many dangers threatening his state on all sides at the time. With Bismarck we are always aware of sentiments that hark back to the soldier-king and that delight in boldness, but we are also aware of a modern, practical realism that utilizes circumstances to achieve a goal and that practices self-control in order to achieve self-determination.

In this same Olmütz address he spoke that great and simple truth that swept away all the mists of political Romanticism: "The only sound foundation for a major state—and in this it is fundamentally different from a minor state—is political egoism and not Romanticism. It is not worthy of a great state to fight for a cause that does not touch on its own interests."

At another point during these same years, Bismarck also called such an autonomous policy a "Prussian national policy." We would have to call this autonomous major state that he has in mind a genuine national state in the political sense even if he had not done so himself, letting all the emotional values of a "specific Prussianness" shine vividly through, for this state derives its principles of action from the internal and external needs of a politically united national community. The Prussia that Friedrich Wilhelm IV and his Romantic friends had in mind was not a national state in this sense because they did not, like Bismarck, consider the state's political egoism the only sound foundation for its policies. They subjected it to the highest ethical commandments, even in its foreign policy, and thereby limited the objectives of its power as well as its freedom of movement and even its possibilities of alliance. With the nonpolitical goals that they set for the state, they transformed the means with which the state was to work; and they also transformed political thought completely, transformed ideas of what was politically possible and feasible and thus created a source of political errors, mistakes, failures, and humiliations.

We are near the end of our discussion. Before we make our final observations, let us consider once again the two views that struggled with each other at the threshold of our era. Every student of Bismarck is familiar with the letters he exchanged with Leopold von Gerlach in May 1857 and with the memorials he submitted to his government in May and June 1857. With these documents, we feel we are in a cool dawn, and we see the moon fading.

In Gerlach's letter of May 6, 1857 the universalism of Romanticism, of the Wars of Liberation, and of the Restoration emerges again, claiming to offer a valid operating principle for European politics and to prove the validity of this principle by historical example. Charlemagne's principle was, Gerlach begins, the expansion of the Christian church. He held to this principle in his wars against the Saxons, Saracens, and others, and he was rewarded for it. But his successors fought among themselves in an unprincipled manner. The great princes of the Middle Ages, however,

adhered to this old principle once again; and the founding of Branden-
burg-Prussian power rests on this principle, on the wars fought against
nations that would not submit to the emperor, the vicar of the church. In
the later period of the decay of church and Empire, only the old principle
had repeatedly brought the states success, as the case of Austria and
Russia in their battle against the Turks shows. The wars of the Great
Elector and the first three wars of Frederick the Great also maintained
the old principle, despite interests in territory and the balance of power,
because they had a Protestant character; and the wars against Louis XIV
were really wars against the Revolution. The worst period of Prussian
politics was from 1778 until the French Revolution. That was a time
dominated by the "politics of interests, of so-called patriotism." Because
of the Revolution, the states were obliged to learn the old principle again,
a principle that necessarily does battle with, or at least stands in direct
opposition to, the Revolution in all its forms, right down to the France of
Napoleon III. Prussia and Germany fared well as long as this principle
was in effect. No foreign power had interfered in German affairs from
1815 to 1840.

Gerlach thought that he too was practicing *Realpolitik,* because his
ideal politics allegedly always found their actual reward on earth, a point
he could not prove, of course, without the most violent distortions and
oversights. He also seems to advocate the autonomy of the nation, but this
is not a genuine autonomy because it is conceived of only as the result
of incorporation into the Holy Alliance, that is, as a reward for renunciation of the true autonomy of power. Gerlach's principle of political action
led to a certain unity and firmness that lent the appearance of integrity
and that also lent the state some credibility in times of peace. "It cannot
be overlooked," Gerlach claimed, "that only he is reliable who acts according to definite principles and not according to shifting concepts of
interests etc." But like all heteronomous principles for action, this
brought with it monotony, rigidity, incapacity to adapt to changes of
circumstances, suppression of natural life forces and of historical development. He looks for laws of motion not in the forces that are actually
in motion themselves but in a universal, absolute, transcendent context
in which his faith sees them.

Bismarck is just the opposite in all respects. His politics begin at the
center of the active forces themselves. Their essence is individuality,
development, and worldliness. Seen from one aspect, his policies oscil-
late from moment to moment because they are determined by "all the
nuances of possibility, probability, or intention, so that he could remain
free to form this or that alliance in the event of war, to belong to this or
that group." But this kind of determinism belongs to true inner autonomy
just as the external world belongs to the internal world. The one can grow

and develop and assert itself only in battle with and in opposition to the other. Thus, Bismarck's view of the interaction between states is by no means lacking in constant and persistent forces. These forces are the "native and natural interests" of individual states. They are not as vacillating as Gerlach claims but are in fact much stronger than the principles that Gerlach regarded as firm and immovable. They continue to break through all changes of governmental form and make themselves felt whether the state is committed to revolutionary or antirevolutionary principles. Bismarck went into no greater detail than necessary with his friend in justifying his policy of autonomy that sought "to open every door, to keep every option unrestricted." He did not concern himself much with the question of whether the opposition of revolutionary and antirevolutionary, of good and evil principles that Gerlach had submitted was correct or not, and he did not feel any need to revise his own inner position on liberalism and revolution. He behaved in this controversy the way the state as a whole must behave if it obeys its own nature. He cleared the way for the most pressing and vital needs, for the greatest and most important expressions of life in states; and all the rest he left to the course of development.

He fought his friend's errors primarily by demonstrating their historical limitations. Like Ranke, he saw the era of the Revolution and Restoration as a kind of intermezzo in the life of states and in the principles of their leading statesmen. If there were a principle that formed the foundation of all politics, he thought, how could it have evaded the Christian and conservative politicians before 1789? "I do not see that any politician, even the most Christian and conscientious one, would ever have hit upon the idea, before the French Revolution, of subordinating his entire political activity and his attitude toward domestic and foreign politics to the principle of opposing the Revolution, nor would he ever have examined the relationship of his country to other states purely on the basis of this touchstone." He also tried to explain his older friend's error in psychological terms. "It seems to me," he said to him on May 2, 1860, "that the impressions of our youth never leave us. Overwhelming hatred of Bonaparte was a major element of your youthful experience. You call him 'revolution incarnate,' and if you knew a viler term, you would christen him with that."

He thus sought out the most concrete and most vividly felt reasons behind this error. We should never forget these reasons, but our task here should be to show the wider intellectual context of this error. In our study of Stein and Gneisenau we tried to reconstruct the profound experiences of the Wars of Liberation that split the European constellation of states into two camps, but we saw how these experiences came up against certain categories of thought and feeling, particularly against the still operative eighteenth-century spirit, which had also tried to apply its universal principles to political life. The autonomous state had to fight the same battle with these heteronomous principles that the ethical autonomy of the individual had to fight with all heteronomous moral systems. The rigid power state of the eighteenth century opposed them by its very nature, and even the enlightened rulers of the eighteenth century were careful not to let themselves be overwhelmed by these principles, particularly in their foreign policy. The Revolution and the Wars of Liberation first opened gates in the life of the state through which a strong wave of universal and nonpolitical ideals rushed into politics. These ideals found particularly fertile ground in Germany because intellectual training there was especially nonpolitical and had developed the universalistic element to a particularly high degree. Romanticism summoned up the spirits of the past against the despised rational and cosmopolitan spirit of the eighteenth century, but because Romanticism itself was still rooted in that spirit, it retrieved something related to it from the past. Thus the ancient idea of a universal community of Christian states was revived, and the political aspect of Romanticism became cosmopolitanism with a religious-ethical character. In the ideas of the Revolution and in the ideas of the Holy Alliance, we said, two universalisms clashed. The robust nature of the state doubtless struggled against this alien element that imposed itself on the state and that tried to bind its limbs. As a result, universalism was not wholly victorious anywhere, but it swayed the minds of leading personalities in the period of Friedrich Wilhelm IV so strongly that it had fateful effects on practical politics and on the power of the state. In the last analysis, it was a poison that the body had to cast off if the body was to function naturally again. Bismarck was the doctor who drew off this poison.

Originally, however, it had been not only a poison but also a medicine.

Let us look back again at national resistance against Napoleon. Here the nations appear in their manifold types and phases of development. Some of them, like the Spaniards, Tyroleans, and Russians, were based on an ancient nativistic foundation. They did not need any particular stimulus to erupt in enmity and hatred against the Napoleonic world empire. There was still something of the fanaticism of half-civilized nations in them, a fanaticism that rejected the modern cultural elements of this world empire. Ranke made the profound observation that Napoleon's dominance could spread more easily "where the mind was prepared for it," where the social ideas that had emerged in the Revolution and that Napoleon himself had advocated were known. We might add that not only the social but also the cosmopolitan aspect of the ideas of the Enlightenment had prepared the way for him. These ideas first weakened the national resistance of Germany in particular, but they then helped develop and encourage it. We are speaking here only of the higher, leading classes of the nation, because the national feelings of the Brandenburg or Pomeranian peasant with his militiaman's rifle were not much different from those of the Tyrolean or Spanish citizen-soldier. But in the intellectual leaders of the nation, the national impulse had come awake in a much more complicated way. We saw how it was permeated and entangled with universal ideals from the outset. The higher levels of German culture at first found it impossible and insufferable to acknowledge the blatant egoism of nations. The national emotions of this culture crept upward on the traditional cosmopolitan trellis. Universal and spiritualized national ideas invaded the state simultaneously and in the closest contact with each other. The national ideas gave the universal ones strength and warmth and helped them to enter the state. Later, the universal ideas had to be put aside to permit the Prussian national state to develop into the German national state. But they had not been superfluous. Nothing is superfluous that carries intellectual continuity forward between two great epochs. Nothing is superfluous, either, that can animate historical action in crucial moments. Could Stein, at the end of 1812, have persuaded the czar to carry the war beyond Russia's borders if he, as the European statesman that he was at the time, had been able to appeal only to national and state interests and not to universal ideas that went beyond such limited concerns? The cause of the nation was also the cause of European man at that time. Thus the idea of the Holy Alliance performed its greatest concrete service when the Alliance was still unwritten. For the universal idea in the life of states belongs to the spiritual elements that can only become a blessing if they remain intangible breaths of life.

Eckart Kehr

3

Eckart Kehr broke with the so-called Prussian or Rankean school of German historiography, of which Meinecke's work is so representative. He analyzed events in German history from a new perspective, studied sources hitherto regarded as irrelevant or unimportant, and launched a new interpretation of the nature and mechanics of German (and by implication *all*) historical development. Kehr's immediate influence was slight, but since World War II his reputation has grown and he is now recognized as the most influential precursor if not the founder of a new, neo-Marxist approach in German historiography.

Kehr was born in Brandenburg in 1902. His father was a high government official and the Director of the Brandenburg Academy, a strictly run preparatory school for the Prussian aristocracy. Kehr was thus born into the "ruling class" of Imperial Germany; his later radical views were to earn him the sobriquet "aristocratic bolshevik" *(Adelbolschewist)*. Kehr naturally attended the Brandenburgische Ritterakademie, but throughout his career there he quite unnaturally (in his father's eyes) protested against the school's rigid and anachronistic discipline. The "conflict of generations," that eternal tension between parents and children, was exacerbated by the stresses of world war; Kehr's father looked upon his son as a rebel, opposed to all he himself stood for. "At an early age, protest was his life element," Hans-Ulrich Wehler writes of Kehr; the struggle against the father foreshadowed his rebellion against the fathers of German historiography.

In 1921, Kehr began his studies at the University of Berlin. History was his major field of study, an interest perhaps nurtured by the fact that his father was a trained philologist and his uncle a medievalist. At Berlin, Friedrich Meinecke was his official mentor, but Kehr participated in Hans Rothfels' first seminar and he later studied with such historians as Troeltsch, Marcks, and Harnack. In the bitter years following Germany's defeat, political and ideological passions ran high. Kehr gravitated to the left of the political spectrum.

Instead of adopting the comforting escapist "stab-in-the-back" explanation for the German plight, Kehr deemed it necessary to re-examine Germany's historical relationships and the internal deficiencies that had led her down the road to disaster. It seems clear, as Wehler observes, that Kehr's political views lent support to his methodological principles of historiography.

In his dissertation on the expansion of the Imperial navy (published in 1930 as *Schlachtflottenbau und Parteipolitik, 1894 bis 1901*), Kehr methodically examined archival sources and the relevant published literature, parliamentary debates, newspapers, and periodicals. (Friedrich Meinecke commented on his "extraordinary assiduousness" and his use of "unusual and voluminous materials.") His dissertation, Kehr later observed, had a "revolutionizing effect" on him: "My studies began under the influence of political history and philosophy. I was increasingly led in the course of my work, however (and this was especially felt in the preparation of my book on the Navy), to place in the foreground the problem of the influence of economic factors and social structure on pure politics. The study of the relations between the two became the central consideration of my historical interests."

What Kehr showed in his dissertation and in the articles he published during the 1920's was that earlier diplomatic and political histories had missed or ignored the impact of economic and social interests on Germany's historical development. He attacked the orthodox school of diplomatic and political history as a fanciful exercise in the working out of "Ideas"; he rejected the Rankean emphasis on "the primacy of foreign affairs" and stressed instead the view that internal pressure and interest groups used foreign policy for their own purposes. (His posthumous editor has appropriately entitled his collected essays *Der Primat der Innenpolitik*.) Kehr persuasively argued that the German naval policy adopted during the years from 1894 to 1901 (which frightened Britain and drove her closer to France) had less to do with imperial expansion per se or with Germany's supposed "mission" in the world than with the needs and interests of German heavy industry. Hence his subtitle to the book: "An Essay Exposing the Internal Political, Social, and Ideological Presuppositions of German Imperialism." He brought the same methodological and interpretative canons to bear on such subjects as the origins of the Prussian bureaucracy, the sociology of the German army, and, as the selection below demonstrates, the social and financial bases of Tirpitz' naval propaganda.

It hardly needs to be said that Friedrich Meinecke had little to do with this aspect of Kehr's development. Kehr criticized Meinecke's "neutral" position vis-à-vis historical and political controversies. His position of "to-understand-is-to-forgive," Kehr wrote, "is one that in fact gives political justification to the status quo." Meinecke judged Kehr's dissertation to be "very good, very interesting . . . but terribly radical. And how shall the young man proceed if he does not question his own conclusions?" Kehr in turn judged Meinecke's entire *corpus* when, in a 1928 review of the latter's *Geschichte des deutsch-englischen-Bündnisproblems, 1890–1901,* he wrote, "Meinecke's whole life work is pervaded by a deliberate and disciplined self-limitation of the questions he asks." The questions Kehr asked prompted Meinecke to warn him against becoming "a complete Nihilist" who believed that "to understand all is to criticize all." Therein lay the difference between the two: for Meinecke, the historian's task was to hold up to the past *"ein schaffender Spiegel"*— a looking glass informed by the shaping, creative effects of intuition and empathy; for Kehr, the historian's task was to hold up *"ein kritischer Spiegel"* —to view events empirically, in conjunction with critical, analytical social theory.

Meinecke disagreed with Kehr but continued officially to supervise his researches; Kehr looked to other mentors for his philosophical and methodological principles. (It should be stressed that Meinecke never attacked Kehr's motives in the fashion of Ritter and Oncken, who saw him as, among other things, a tool of the Jews.) Kehr learned much from Karl Marx's writings, especially Marx's "scientific-critical" technique of unveiling the social and economic motives and forces hidden behind ostensibly "pure" political acts.

Max Weber's historical and socio-economic works were perhaps even more important an influence on Kehr, especially Weber's transcending of "vulgar Marxism," which he defined as little more than a self-satisfied, positivistic materialism. By utilizing social theory and the social sciences, Kehr believed he could more closely and accurately grasp historical reality than had the practitioners of traditional historiography with their researches on narrowly defined political and diplomatic topics, informed, somehow, by *Verstehen.*

Thus proceeding, Kehr opened to question the Rankean tradition that emphasized political and philosophical ideas, state actions, and warfare, at the expense of social and economic factors. He contributed to the critical reassessment of German Idealism and the ideal of *Bildung;* both, he argued, were in a sense defense mechanisms and psychic compensations evoked to supply the deficiencies inherent in the political impotence of the German masses and professors, and in the failure to integrate all social groups and classes into the social and political structure. The function of *Ideengeschichte,* he believed, was to provide solace for Germans, and especially for the liberally educated but politically powerless middle-class professoriate whose ambiguous position Kehr enjoyed exposing. In opposition to this historiography, Kehr sought to introduce "social history" as the most fruitful (if not the only legitimate) type of history; basing itself on sociological, economic, group, and structural analyses, and on the insights of such as Marx and Weber, social history would enable historians scientifically to perceive the general laws which shaped historical development. This was, of course, to reject the "individualizing" approach of Historicism and to adopt the "generalizing" approach of the social sciences. Finally, Kehr dramatically emphasized the necessary role of critical social theory both in probing historical events and in illuminating for contemporaries the lines of historical continuities into the present.

These are impressive accomplishments for a man who died at the age of thirty-one. Few historians have managed so much so early in life. Kehr was not without defects, to be sure. He did not succeed in clearly establishing in all cases the supposed primacy of domestic over foreign policies; he never decided whether economic and social factors were all-powerful or whether well-placed individuals of strong will (e.g., Tirpitz) could maneuver to gain their own ends; he tended to simplify socio-economic relations and to treat too mechanically the nuances, subtleties, and complexities that inhere in the interplay of men and institutions, of ideas and society. In his reaction against the tyranny of "ideas," he sometimes fell prey to social and economic reductionism; his political views too often colored his interpretations. There is a potentially crippling effect latent in Theodor Mommsen's injunction, which Kehr followed: "Whoever writes history, but especially contemporary political history, has the duty to be a political teacher." Few scholars can be sure they possess the unyielding integrity and iron self-discipline that Max Weber manifested in his analyses of contemporary society. These faults, however, were not ruinous and were perhaps inherent in the task of historical reconstruction that the young, passionate historian set for himself.

Kehr's works fell on barren soil in Germany, resisted by the historical establishment and buried, along with many other valuable cultural contributions, during the long night of the Nazi regime. Kehr himself died of a heart attack in 1933, and it was left to German émigrés to America to introduce his works and interpretations to the English-speaking world—Franz Neumann, for example, in his *Behemoth: The Structure and Practice of National Socialism, 1933–1944* (1942, 1944), and Alfred Vagts, who, as the son-in-law of Charles Beard, drew the professional attention of American historians to Kehr's views (See Charles Beard, *The Navy* (1933) and *The Economic Basis of Politics* (1957 edition). Hans Rosenberg and Hajo Holborn, among others, also preserved and transmitted the essence of Kehr's work. Since 1945, Kehr's works have been reissued and his originality and importance recognized. German historiography today, and all inquirers into the human condition, owe much to Kehr's pioneering efforts.

Selected Bibliography

There is as yet little in English concerning Kehr's work. James Sheehan's fine review article "The Primacy of Domestic Politics: Eckart Kehr's 'Essays on Modern German History'," *Central European History*, I:2 (June, 1968), 166–174, provides an excellent introduction to Kehr's work and influence. Peter Gay includes a concise account of Kehr, his work, and his relationship to German society in *Weimar Culture: The Outsider as Insider* (1968), which sees Kehr as "a lonely operator, the *Steppenwolf* of the German historical profession."

Hans-Ulrich Wehler has done more perhaps than any other historian to make Kehr widely known. His essay in *Deutsche Historiker,* I, is a comprehensive survey of Kehr's career and influence; it formed the basis for the above headnote. See also Wehler's introduction to his collection of Kehr's essays, *Der Primat der Innenpolitik: Gesammelte Aufsätze zur preussisch-deutschen Sozialgeschichte im 19. und 20. Jahrhundert* (1965). Wehler includes bibliographic references for further study. In his review essay on Wehler's *Bismarck und der Imperialsmus,* Hans Medick offers some interesting observations on Kehr's work, stressing its Weberian rather than the Marxian elements (*History and Theory,* X:2 [1971], 228–240).

Pauline R. Anderson and Eugene R. Anderson have edited and translated Kehr's *Schlachtflottenbau und Parteipolitik 1894 bis 1901* as *Battleship Building and Party Politics in Germany, 1894–1901* (1973); they include a helpful introduction. Finally, *Moderne deutsche Sozialgeschichte* (1968), edited by Wehler, offers analyses and essays representative of the "social history" Kehr advocated.

THE SOCIAL AND FINANCIAL BASES
OF TIRPITZ' NAVAL PROPAGANDA

"Party finances are understandably the most difficult area of party history for research, but one of the most important." (Max Weber.) The writing of German party history is only just begun, and these beginnings pertain more to the intellectual history of parties than to the history of their concrete operations, to their tactics and to their dependence upon the social or financial powers which stand behind them. But precisely for this reason, only a politically motivated self-restraint of research can prevent us from going further and observing the financial aspect which lies behind party history.

Now, to be sure, it will be a long time before there is any prospect of studying the financial history of a great German party. Little as the modern state can refuse (theoretically, at least) to make its budget public as the parties demand, the parties themselves still hold to the system of the absolutist state, to secret finances. They are the more secretive the less they can count on continuous, regular "taxation" of their subjects, i.e., on membership dues, and have to rely upon one-shot random contributions which depend on the adroitness of their Minister of Finance and on the favorable situation of the donor. There is a chance that we may catch a glimpse through a crack in the door at the financing of single political operations. Documents have only recently been found on the financing of Bismarck's newspaper propaganda through the so-called reptile funds, but they have not yet been published. Aside from this, the nineties of the last century were in Germany the first decade of great, far-reaching propaganda activities which required extensive financing.

The social propaganda activities of the Social Democrats after the fall of the Anti-Socialist Law, and of the Agrarians during the second agrarian crisis, depended financially upon membership dues. Of the Social Democrats, this was true exclusively. Of the Farmers' League [*Bund der Landwirte*], it was true insofar as the extraordinary contributions of

From "Soziale und finanzielle Grundlagen der Tirpitzschen Flottenpropaganda" include title of collected essays: from H.-U. Wehler, ed., *Eckart Kehr: Der Primat der Innenpolitik,* 1965. (Berlin: Walter de Gruyter & Co.), pp. 130–148. Translated by James W. Moore. Translated by permission of the publisher.

East Elbian Junkers did not form a special category separate from other contributions; they only paid higher dues, and, e.g., the 492,000 marks which the League took in in 1897 came from what was in this sense a uniform source. On the other hand, Bismarck's newspaper propaganda in the 'nineties no longer had a financial side. It was purely personal agitation by the former Chancellor, and money payments were not necessary to make the *Hamburger Neueste Nachrichten* amenable.

In the early 'nineties, the Imperial Government also began to take an interest in newspaper propaganda—the agitation of the 'eighties had been essentially Bismarck's private agitation. As Chief of the Admiralty, Caprivi had emphatically forbidden any involvement of Navy officers with the press. But as Chancellor he very soon noticed the importance of the press, and he called Otto Hamann to be Press Director of the Imperial Government. Beyond creating a semi-official atmosphere, this new press activity became important to the Imperial Government in the question of armament increases, first in enlarging the Army in the four great Bills of 1887, 1888, 1890 and 1893, then later in the naval building program in 1896 and 1900.

After the 'eighties, armament increases drove the German military budget, in part relatively, in part absolutely, higher than those of the other great powers. In the financing of these increases we find an interesting contradiction. The state itself was not able to make the larger expenditures which the enlarged military establishment required in an orderly way. Costs could no longer be pushed off on the federal states in the form of matricular payments, and instead of being paid out of taxes they were charged against the coming generation. The Empire's overheated borrowing policy began with the armament increase of 1887. Until State-Secretary Wermuth intervened, warships were also reckoned to be "interest-bearing investments" whose construction was to be undertaken on credit.

But for financing the agitation which preceded the armament increases, and which accompanied the struggles in Parliament, an increasingly solid foundation was developed. It is still not possible to know in detail the financial basis of the armament agitation of 1893, which the then Major Keim directed. But it was clearly too extensive to have been carried out without considerable funding. It is all the more possible— even without the secret documents—to know the character and the details of Tirpitz' naval agitation and of the means by which it was financed.

Naval propaganda had begun a great deal earlier than one could have guessed until now. The first instructions of the Emperor—who had seen the results of the Army agitation in 1893—date from January 1894. But this propaganda was a small thing. The Supreme Naval Command was indeed able to make contact with the national liberal press, and through an editor of Stumm's *Post* it could plant articles in the party's provincial newspapers. It was also able to found a correspondence service. But there was no life in the agitation. Tirpitz, then still Chief of Staff of the Supreme Naval Command, tried in vain to make the *Naval Review* livelier. It remained subject to the directions issued when it was founded, with their characteristic provision that it discuss the German Navy and foreign navies "only insofar as the public will not be led to make idle comments on the German Navy."

The thesis of Tirpitz' memorandum IX of 16 July 1894 would later become the ideological basis for naval construction. It concerned the profitability of expenditures on armaments: "Money spent on the Navy can already accrue indirect interest in peacetime, while expenditures for the Army are in essence only a sort of insurance premium in case of war." However, for now, it remained a theory which no one cared about. And it typifies the zeal with which the Navy promoted its cause, that they considered their task as completed if "anyone who is interested in naval matters" could inform himself about some technical question in the *Naval Review.* Admiral Hollmann, the State Secretary of the Imperial Navy Office, was absorbed in daily routine. He ignored on principle questions of agitation; he had expressly delegated them to the individual sections of the office.

Agitation was a failure, and this—insofar as the failure was one of technical execution—was true not only because of the complete lack of interest of those charged with carrying it out. There was no financial basis for it. The problem here was not that the directly interested circles in heavy industry would not have been ready to make propaganda for their interests. Although the changeover by the shipping lines to larger ships had substantially increased the number of orders, shipbuilding firms were already bemoaning their "lack of orders" as a "national disaster." Krupp, whose firm had just developed the new method of hardening armor—a method which was soon sold to all the foreign navies—and who would shortly develop the Germania Wharf in Kiel for construction of extremely large ships, showed his displeasure—harmlessly enough at first—by publishing a booklet with the title *What Has the Reichstag of 1893–4 Done for the Navy?* which was filled with blank pages. But until 1897 the Hanseatics were still opponents of naval building. The representatives of the Hansa cities in the Bundesrat could not see why a fleet should be constructed against the English free traders. Adolf Woermann, who after 1879 had brought Hamburg around in favor of colonial expansion, was encouraged by Count Dürckheim. But as president of the Chamber of Commerce and as chairman of the Association of Hamburg Shippers, he could get nothing more than a few lame petitions to expand the fleet.

Agitation could not get moving, because naval building had no sounding board. The Navy was a technical matter, like the post office or like highway construction. As yet it had no chance to play a part in the social development of the Empire and thus to become "popular." No one had clear technical ideas about construction; they wavered helplessly between cruisers and battleships. Even strategically the Navy had no value in itself. At best it could be the seaborne wing of armies marching victoriously against France. The melancholy memories which a few old liberals cherished of their Navy of 1848 no longer meant much.

From the beginning, Tirpitz worked to free the Navy from its isolation and to put it in the context of "Germany's economic development since 1871." It is this which brought him his success. That he should thus casually have identified development since 1871 with the economic boom which began in 1895 is a problem in itself. But until this identification was established in the public's mind, and until the naval question was integrated into an economic and social context, industry contributed no money for agitation.

The lack of a social basis brought the quick failure of further attempts at naval propaganda. Karl Peters, who hoped by running for the Reichstag and through a naval agitation which had the Emperor's approval to escape prosecution for his African crimes, began a campaign at the end of 1895. But he was as unsuccessful as was the former leader of the Poles in the Reichstag, von Kosciol-Koscielski, who was such a naval buff that he bore the nickname Admiralski and helped to subsidize the printing of a propaganda brochure by the Imperial Navy Office. Or than the Chief of the Naval Cabinet, Admiral von Senden, who in connection with the broader plans for naval building begun in January 1896 "sought to enlighten the Reichstag and to build enthusiasm throughout the country." Aside from the lack of support from the Ruhr and from the Hanseatics, the Navy had in 1895–6 to face the positive opposition of the Agrarians. In February 1895 von Werdeck-Schorbus coined the slogan "No subsidies, no boats," and in January 1896 von Levetzow explained Conservative opposition to the Emperor's naval plans with the classical words: "The farmers scarcely have their daily bread."

Since 1892 Tirpitz had prepared the way for naval building, tactically, strategically, technically and ideologically. But the daydream of one officer could be realized only because of the two great shifts which occurred in Germany's political and social structure in the second half of the 'nineties. First, the Center Party, defeudalized and democratized by the election of 1893, was led by Lieber out of opposition and into the government's camp. The second shift was the reconciliation between agriculture and industry, until now locked in mortal combat, a reconciliation brought about in reaction to an ever-expanding Social Democracy and to the economic boom which began in 1895 and which undercut the resistance of the farmers.

In mid-1897 Miquel introduced his coalition policy, and new State Secretaries of Foreign Affairs, of the Interior and of the Navy were appointed. The "New Course," which had borne the mark of the struggle between industry and agriculture for power over the legislative machine, was succeeded by the coalition of industry and agriculture against the proletariat. Beyond transient and faulty measures like the anti-trade-union bill, this coalition reached its zenith with the Tariff of 1902 and the Naval Laws. "Every successful imperialistic policy abroad normally strengthens, at least for the time being, the prestige and therefore also the power and the influence 'at home' of those classes, parties or estates under whose leadership the success is won." (Weber.) Naval building was meant to provide the power basis for a successful foreign policy, and this was in turn supposed to stabilize the position of the ruling strata against the Social Democratic threat.

It is in this context that we must consider the naval enthusiasm of Wilhelm II. It was not because he intervened as monarch on its behalf and "preached its necessity to those oxen in the Reichstag every day for ten years" that the Emperor was able to realize his liking for warships in the naval building program. He succeeded because the bourgeois element of the nation—which before 1897 had viewed the Emperor's naval enthusiasm with a mixture of anger and resignation—suddenly discovered in imperialism [*Weltpolitik*] and in the Emperor's naval building a promising social weapon against the proletariat. "Too much has been said about the Emperor's 'impulsiveness' and about his personality in general. The political structure is to blame." (Weber.) The idea of a decisive influence of Wilhelm II upon the realization of naval building does not explain why the Emperor could put his plans through only after 1897, and precisely after that year. His victory was the consequence of the social consolidation of the ruling classes in coalition politics.

The new situation makes it understandable how the large scale naval propaganda which began in mid 1897 suddenly began to work. The agitation of the Pan-German League and the German Colonial Association in early 1896 had proceeded along theoretically very usable lines, but had never gotten off the ground. Now they brought up extensive propaganda apparatuses. The Hanseatics learned to like the Navy. At a dinner at the Rathaus in Hamburg, Tirpitz, Heeringen—the new Propaganda Director of the Imperial Navy Office—and Adolf Woermann discussed how to proceed. On the next day Woermann tried to win over the German Trade Congress by surprise. But here he met with the opposition of the Berlin banks, which, since all chief clerks in the great banks were entitled to a vote, were decisive in the Merchants' Guild of Berlin. The bankers still held politically to the two progressive parties. They took a very dim view of the coalition and had no wish to be its stooges. But this opposition was weak to begin with. In public, the only reason which the elders of the

Guild dared to give for their refusal was "that the matter is of a political nature and its discussion could easily break up the Congress," and "that the Guild as such had taken no position on the matter, but had only advised its representative on the steering committee of the Congress against taking any position in this political question." Only in a letter to the Congress did Max Weigert express the view that "opinions may also differ, whether at just this time of commercial treaties the Navy is to be represented as an especially effective means to increase German exports, and also whether the present size of the German Navy is not to be considered adequate for the protection of German commerce—insofar as it can be protected at all in this manner—and to enhance the reputation of our fatherland."

The opposition did not continue for long. If—so far as can be seen—only the Banking House of Mendelssohn took an active interest in the Navy Association, then at least, at the time of the second Naval Bill in 1900, the other Berlin banks no longer opposed the naval demonstrations of the Trade Congress. As late as June 1897 the Hamburg section of the German Colonial Society still protested against its participation in naval agitation. But the dinner of 26 September brought the Hanseatics over as good as completely to the side of the naval supporters. Precisely the Hamburg Chamber of Commerce became the headquarters of interest-group agitation for the first Bill. The intellectual director of agitation in the Imperial Navy Office, the Privatdozent Dr. Ernst Levy of Halle, kept permanent contact with it, and he had the data collected in Hamburg and Bremen which he used in his official memoranda as evidence of "German maritime interests." So that the opposition could not accuse them of collaboration with private concerns, official letters from the I.N.O. to the Chambers of Commerce in Bremen and Hamburg were sent only to the appropriate state deputations. The letters were then passed on to the Chambers of Commerce. These then determined in the appropriate manner, by questionnaires sent to the firms in their districts, what their overseas interests were, and these were returned by way of the (municipal) Senate commissions to the I.N.O.

If the overseas interests were found to be too small, then they were appropriately padded. To be sure, Hamburg was annoyed when the I.N.O. "improved" its figures. It was also annoying that it tried to construe an increase in foreign defense budgets where they had actually been reduced or where the increase had been less than that in the German budget. But there was no lagging for that reason in propagandistic zeal. When the attempt at agitation through the German Trade Congress had failed, in Hamburg at least the entire "honorable merchant" class was mobilized. A committee was quickly formed. It gathered the leading German businessmen, who could not be assembled at the Trade Congress, for an independent demonstration at the Kaiserhof on 13 January 1898. Its resolutions were framed in closest collaboration with the Chief of the Naval Cabinet, and it shook even the opposition of the *Frankfurter Zeitung.*

After this the importance of the Hanseatics declined relative to that of heavy industry. In the agitation for the second Bill, the Hanseatics intervened only through a petition of the Chambers of Commerce of all the coastal towns. This petition has an interesting background.

At the end of December 1899 some German steamers were seized near Delagoa Bay by an overzealous English captain on suspicion of carrying contraband of war to the Boers. In Germany this called forth great excitement among the anti-English bourgeoisie against the arrogance of "perfidious Albion." The captitalist press had only a contemptuous shrug for this ideological indignation. For them, the incident was irrelevant to practical politics. However, the Hanseatics utilized the national ideology adroitly to execute a private business coup. In early January 1900 a meeting was held of the Board of Directors [*Aufsichtsrat*] of the German East Africa Line to discuss the raising of ten millions for the construction of new steamers. Here the five bankers involved declared "that before the question of compensation for the injustice which has been done us is decided, no one could and would think of putting more money into the operation."

Adolf Woermann held only one out of six millions of stock in the G.E.A.L., but now he undertook—in his own primitive and bullying manner—to get rid of the obstacles through the construction of a German Navy, which would in the future prevent these English excesses. A combined petition by all Chambers of Commerce engaged in maritime trade was to put the necessary pressure on the Reichstag. Precisely by public mention of the problems which Delagoa Bay had created for the G.E.A.L. in getting money, he hoped to make an especially powerful impression on the German people and the German Reichstag—a piece of clumsiness, but one which people were later ready to excuse. Actually, the petition distinguished itself by contradicting the doctrine propagated by the Imperial Navy Office, which made naval building a function of capitalist expansion, and declared it to be a pure necessity of state, of power politics.

Aside from this isolated maneuver, propaganda for the second Bill was made not by the Hanseatics but by heavy industry. Of course, even the Kaiserhof manifesto had been agreed to by the Central Association of German Industrialists, but at that time the Central Association was quite happy to leave the directing—and with it the attacks of the opposition—to Woermann. Krupp had recommended discretion to the gentlemen of the Central Association. He had not taken part in the invitation to the gathering; only an unpolitical fire-eater like Emil Kirdorf had signed it.

But this discretion did not mean refraining from agitation on behalf of industry. They only bided their time. When in March 1898 the cod-liver-oil manufacturer Strohschein tried to found a naval association on the basis of a worthy petit-bourgeois patriotism, and the Berlin banks declined to finance him, Krupp intervened through Victor Schweinburg, publisher of the *Berliner Neueste Nachrichten*. Strohschein was not to be had, directly, for industrial purposes, so a counter-committee was set up. It was directed by Schweinburg and by Landtag deputy Bueck, the Secretary-General of the Central Association. Since the heavy-industrial content had to be covered with an idealistic veneer, the Free Conservative leader, Baron Octavio von Zedlitz-Neukirch, was added, and Prince Wied was made president of the agitation bureau that was christened "German Navy Association" and founded on 30 April 1898.

At first this maneuver succeeded very imperfectly. To be sure, Strohschein could be brought to join the new association. But when Schweinburg approached professors at the University of Berlin, he encountered an icy mistrust of his "interest-group of Conservatives, big business and financiers." The antics of Baron Stumm, who had wanted to correct Adolf Wagner's economic theories with a revolver, were still too fresh in the professors' minds. In influencing public opinion, the psychology of heavy industry was still too crude to be effective. They operated in the primitive manner which they continued up to Stinnes' purchase of the *DAZ,* and which was only finally transcended by Alfred Hugenberg, who allowed some independence to the newspapers he controlled and in his propaganda itself did not mix politics with business in a manner obvious to every peaceable citizen. Stumm's *Post,* as well as the *Berliner Neueste Nachrichten,* which because of its bad finances Krupp was able to influence and which he had Schweinburg reorganize, were, like the Navy Association, distinctly one-sided company organs for very definite, very narrow big industrial interests. As they soon discovered to their cost, they failed to consider the ideological and patriotic sensibilities of wide circles.

Just twelve months after it was founded, the new heavy-industrial agitation bureau stood its baptism of fire. Beginning in March 1899, an angry quarrel had erupted between Germany and England concerning the possession of Samoa. Tirpitz began to regret that in 1897 he had contented himself with so small a naval increase, and that in December 1898 he had still vigorously denied having further ambitions. Now he negotiated with Hohenlohe for a new Naval Bill, and he carefully inspected private dockyards to determine their capacity for building and for expansion. The inspection had the immediate result that, beginning in early May, the two industrial newspapers and the Pan-Germans began a lively agitation. The agitation was based on the Samoa affair. It did not press the Imperial Navy Office to violate the Naval Law—the attempt was considered hopeless—but it did demand of the Reichstag that as proof of its patriotism it shorten the six-year period for naval building. But the I.N.O was disturbed when the agitation became too lively, although they themselves had encouraged it. This was because they had no bill ready for the winter, and because they observed that this agitation, which was financed by heavy industry and which "placed business interests higher than practical considerations," would be harder to control than had been the zeal of the Hanseatics in 1897–8.

This first sally by industry against the Imperial Navy Office and the Reichstag failed completely. There remained a tension between the Navy Association and the naval administration. Shortly after the Emperor's speech of 18 October 1899, when he remarked that Germany's future lay on the water and unveiled the second Naval Bill, the scandal broke around Schweinburg. On this occasion, the I.N.O. remained quiet and failed to intervene on behalf of the Navy Association. It permitted Heinrich Rippler's violent attacks in the *Tägliche Rundschau* against the interest-group politics of the Association.

Despite the violent opposition of Prince Wied, and despite the Kaiser's anger, these attacks led in November and December to the resignation of Bueck, Schweinburg and von Zedlitz. The professors in Berlin founded a counter-committee to oppose the Navy Association and to foster the new Bill in an ideologically and morally irreproachable manner. But as they lacked money, the "Free Society for Naval Lectures" had only a very limited effectiveness. They spoke to half-empty halls; even the most famous speakers would not compensate for the fact that admission was charged. Meanwhile, the popular cliché-ridden but cost-free gatherings of the Navy Association drew ever-growing crowds. And when in February 1900 the speakers of the "Society" who spoke up in nineteen of the demonstrations which the Social Democrats had called against imperialism [*Weltpolitik*] were a conspicuous failure, Stumm's *Post* loudly proclaimed its delight.

They were all the freer to do so, because meanwhile it had become clear that the politicians of the coalition no longer needed the professors for their Navy propaganda. It was also clear that the dumping of Schweinburg had not in the least diminished the covert influence of heavy industry over the Naval Association, and that the stock of the iron and steel industry, which had been falling, had been at least temporarily rescued by the announcement that the Navy would be enlarged. . . .

The great success of agitation for the second Bill, surprising even to the I.N.O., did not stem from any especially profound recognition of "the necessity of a strong naval power" by the broad masses of the bourgeoisie. Rather, it was helped by the general feeling that a favorable diversion was needed after the one defeat of the anti-socialist coalition with the failure of the *Zuchthausvorlage,* and after the other defeat which the Agrarians had handed their Prussian government with the rejection of the Canal Bill. The second reason was the organized work of a well-financed agitation bureau outside the I.N.O., the propaganda of the heavy-industrial Navy Association, which remained in Krupp's hands even after its compromised founders had resigned.

Here again we see the contrast between the bad financing of armaments increases and the splendid private financing of armaments agitation. The incompetent Imperial Secretary of the Treasury Thielmann was no less unscrupulous on this occasion than he had been on that of the first Naval Law. He fell back on the tried method which had so often had to serve to quiet social crises and to stave off the danger of revolution. Imperial finances, already headed toward an era of deficits, were painted in the rosiest possible colors; one just didn't know what to do with all that money, and the good intentions of the Reichstag, financially to consolidate the naval building program, foundered on the passive resistance of the government.

Just how well financed the agitation was, we can determine if we avoid the errors of the Americans and do not look for the substructure of imperialist propaganda in the Pan-German League. The Pan-German League has clearly doctored its financial records. Then, too, the Pan-German League was a kind of political and ideological holding company which provided "intellectual" weapons to the other propaganda groups —the Colonial Society, the Navy Association and later the Defense Association [*Wehrverein*]. The slight capital of the Pan-German cover organization tells us nothing whatever about the real financial strength of imperialistic propaganda. It was rather the "German Navy Association" which was founded to lead the naval agitation, and we can know the financing of propaganda at the turn of the century only from the finances of the real fighting organization. According to the accounts which the Navy Association published in its reports for the years 1900–3, there were in rounded numbers:

	Membership Dues	Special Contributions
1900	348,000 marks	412,000 marks
1901	225,000 marks	170,000 marks
1902	247,000 marks	410 marks
1903	262,000 marks	23,000 marks

The Association did not say who made the special contributions. The Banking House of Mendelssohn, whose director was treasurer of the Association, served as controller. A little scene from the directors' meeting of 24 January 1901 tells us where the money came from. Dietrich Schäfer sought to limit further contributions from interested parties as unworthy of the national Navy Association. This naïve proposal the assembly answered with Homeric laughter and with the cry "Non olet." It would have meant the end of the Navy Association.

The lack of accounts for the initial year 1898 and for the year of its first large operations in 1899 leaves us in the dark regarding the ratio of membership dues—which were for the most part surely given for ideological reasons—to the "special contributions" of interested parties, during precisely the initial years. The year 1900, in which the second Naval Bill was considered, shows the contributions, at 412,000 marks, as outweighing membership dues at 348,000. Both figures are extremely problematic. It seems by no means impossible that about 100,000 marks in contributions were listed as membership dues, and that even so the contributions are set too low, for the expense of public lectures is inexplicably small. The figures for 1903, with 23,000 marks in special contributions and 262,000 in dues, indicate an apparently normal ratio. One is struck by the years 1901, immediately after the passage of a law doubling the Navy, with 170,000 marks in contributions, and 1902, in which contributions sink abruptly to 410 marks. An episode from December 1901, hitherto unknown, casts an interesting light on these figures. It gives us a brief but highly instructive glimpse into the connection between business cycles and the arms race.

In the spring of 1900, in the same weeks in which the fate of the second Navy Bill was decided, the year-long economic boom collapsed. The boom had developed at the turn of the century, growing out of a mood which combined the gray fear of proletarian revolt with the simple and superficial enjoyment of new profits. As is well known, the crisis placed the German economy in a critical situation.

Two ways were open in which the crisis might be overcome. As one course, Emil Rathenau suggested that "the stronger enterprises, through purposeful organization and rational division of labor, reduce the costs of experiment, of manufacture and of selling to a minimum," and that good commercial treaties "keep open the market for our goods in friendly nations." But on the Ruhr they remembered how stocks had risen in a period of general decline after the second Navy Bill was proposed. They decided mechanically to repeat this development through pressure on the Imperial Navy Office. In January 1900 Maximilian Harden had already cited the impending crisis as the main reason for the lively industrial propaganda for the Navy. At the time, he was wrong. So far as can be seen, the outbreak of the crisis in April took industry completely by surprise. The connection between crisis and naval building can be established only for 1901. In a series of articles between mid-October and mid-November, Krupp's *Berliner Neueste Nachrichten* demanded of the Imperial Navy Office that the construction plan, which spread the process of naval building fairly evenly over the period up until 1917, be altered so that a larger number of ships should be begun at once. Fourteen days later Prince Salm-Horstmar—who had meanwhile replaced Prince Wied as president of the Navy Association—wrote the following letter to the State Secretary of the I.N.O.:

Schloss Varlar, 3 December 1901

Your Excellency:

Gentlemen of a variety of party affiliations have requested of me that I begin a movement which should cause the Reichstag to petition the government that, in view of the present hard times and of the unfavorable condition of commerce and industry and of the resulting unemployment of thousands of workers, the construction of warships, now planned to extend over a longer period of time, should be undertaken at the fastest tempo possible.

If the construction of the ships authorized in the last Navy Bill were accelerated to the maximum rate which German wharves could achieve, many branches of industry would receive new orders. Thus, they would not only be kept afloat, but also enabled to employ their workers and to hire back those whom they have already discharged. However, one of the most important factors which is being discussed here is this, that because of the demand for new ships and the resulting animation of commerce and industry, *the stocks affected would rise on the Bourse, many values would be rescued and the market would be consolidated.* (My italics. E.K.)

No single party may make such a request of the government, for this might easily be attributed to selfish or partisan motives.

It is therefore believed that the appropriate stimulus should come from a neutral quarter. For this reason the German Navy Association, in which all parties are represented, is considered to be the most appropriate ground on which the parties can join together in order to move the Reichstag to petition the government to this effect. Although I am firmly convinced that a petition by the Reichstag to this effect will be highly welcome to the government, I do not wish to neglect to act in agreement with your Excellency. I request that your Excellency make this letter known to the Imperial Chancellor, so that I may learn what the government's attitude would be to my actions in the direction indicated. In the affirmative case, I would try to get the matter moving immediately after Christmas, and would begin agitation through the organs of the G.N.A.

If the Chancellor wishes it, I gladly make myself available for a preliminary discussion. I undersign, with expression of the deepest respect,

Your Excellency's most obedient
Otto, Prince of Salm.

To this suggestion that the most serious military matters could be settled offhand in terms of "whether the stocks affected would rise," Tirpitz answered the President of the G.N.A.:

Berlin, 14 December 1901

Your Highness:

I receive with the sincerest thanks your letter of the 3d. inst. Following your wishes, I have brought it to the Chancellor's attention.

Were it possible to gain a majority of the Reichstag for a resolution requesting the acceleration of ship construction, then this would indeed be of the very highest value to our national defense.

However, your Highness will recognize that an acceleration of ship building would not in itself be enough. Naval wharves and port facilities would also have to be enlarged, more personnel trained and more ships kept in commission.

If, in the long run, only one battleship more were constructed each year, as the Navy Law now specifies, this involves, with the additional costs mentioned above, a yearly additional expenditure of 30–35 millions of marks. But if, as your Highness suggests, the German wharves were to be kept occupied at their maximum capacity, then one ship more would not be enough. It would be a question of building 2–3 more large ships each year, and thus of an added yearly expenditure of 65 or 100 millions of marks.

With the present constellation of parties, and in the existing difficult financial situation, it would unfortunately seem to be impossible to gain a majority in the Reichstag for such a resolution. Under these conditions the government must most regretfully decline to promote, directly or indirectly, any agitation for the speeding of the rate of construction. The time has not yet come for such an acceleration.

With the profoundest respect, I am honored to be,

Your Highness' most obedient
Tirpitz.

To the public, only two small newspaper items indicated what had gone on behind the scenes—a fine example, by the way, of the methodological possibility of reconstructing reality, at least in its general outlines, from indirect remarks in the press. On 28 December 1901 the Munich *Allgemeine Zeitung* published a report that the naval increase which a part of the press had called for "to mitigate the economic crisis" had been rejected in high places. On 11 January 1902 the *Rheinisch-Westfälische Zeitung* closed with its regret at the government's lack of daring "in the interest of industry, of the labor force and of the German Navy."

Special contributions to the German Navy Association fell from 170,000 marks in 1901 to 410 marks in 1902.

Henri Pirenne 1862–1935

4

Henri Pirenne was born in 1862 in Belgium, a small nation but a richly historical country. His father was a rich manufacturer and a decent nineteenth-century Liberal. Pirenne grew up in a cultured and comfortable family atmosphere, in an economic and social environment marked by industrialization, labor agitation, and political unrest. His later historiographic concerns largely reflect that environment. In 1880, he entered the University of Liège intending to study law, but he soon turned to history. His masters there (Godefroid Kurth and Paul Fredericq) were specialists in medieval and early modern history, and Pirenne himself became primarily a medievalist. Under their direction, he discovered the frustrations and rewards of exact scholarship, minute analysis of sources, and imaginative synthetic construction.

His doctoral dissertation, published in 1889, concerned the governance of the medieval industrial town of Dinant (Namur). During his student years, he attended courses elsewhere than at Liège: he learned much from Gustav Schmoller's lectures at Berlin on the growth of medieval towns; he studied diplomatics with Harry Bresslau, paleography at Leipzig with W. Arndt, and medieval history at the École des Chartes and the École des Hautes Études in Paris with such luminaries as Monod, Thévenin, and Giry. In both France and Germany, Pirenne made lasting friendships with young students, a reflection of his native cosmopolitanism ("For fifteen centuries Belgium had been the meeting-point of Latin and Teutonic influences," Carl Stephenson aptly notes) and an early indication of the catholicity of his historical views.

In 1885, after a temporary setback during one of Belgium's chronic political-confessional conflicts (Catholic-Protestant, Flemish-French, Liberal-Conservative) which spilled over into the universities, Pirenne, a Liberal, secured a teaching position at the University of Liège. In 1886, he transferred to Ghent, where he taught medieval and Belgian history. He was appointed to a full professorship at Ghent the next year and remained there until his retirement in 1930, five years before his death.

Pirenne's early historical studies manifest a concern for methodological exactness. Among his first publications were the *Bibliographie de l'histoire de Belgique* (1893) and scholarly editions of medieval texts (e.g., *Histoire du Meurtre de Charles le Bon, comte de Flandre, par Galbert de Bruges,* 1891). This concern with method remained prominent in Pirenne's work throughout his career. His essay "De la méthode comparative en histoire" (1923) influenced the thought of Marc Bloch, among many others, and his article "La tâche de l'historien" (1931; translated as "What Are Historians Trying to Do?") is both representative of Pirenne's methodological standpoint and a valuable introduction to general historiographical method. Pirenne's fame, however, rests less upon his high and exact professional standards than upon the strength and sweep of his conceptual and interpretative generalizations about vital developments in European history, especially urban and economic phenomena. A colleague described him as "an architect, not a carpenter," but he well served his apprenticeship.

Pirenne came to scholarly maturity in an age of quiet but spirited debates, often nationalistic in tone, over the problem of the transition from Roman Empire to medieval feudalism and the related problem of the emergence of free towns in a presumably closed and unfree feudal-agrarian setting. On the matter of urban evolution, scholarly opinion fell into a number of categories, the most important of which stressed the view that towns evolved from the self-governing Teutonic village, the *Mark,* which preserved the seed of Europe's free institutions throughout the medieval period. In a series of studies (1885–1891), the German historian Georg von Below accepted and expanded the *Mark* theory to include the vital influence of the expanding trade and industry of Europe after the tenth century. A sound historian and vigorous controversialist, von Below thus rejected the episcopal, manorial, guild, and market theories of town origins and pushed to the fore the "Germanic" thesis instead. Pirenne established his professional reputation when he entered into this debate. In a series of brilliant, incisive essays (1893–1898), he surveyed the controversy and analyzed, appraised, and then rejected all of the contending theories. He offered in their stead a more catholic or, rather, a relativistic view. Beyond the essential and apparently universal characteristic, namely, that all towns form an economic unit contrasting sharply with the rural environs, he found no single pattern applicable to the evolution of towns. Above all, Pirenne stressed, there is no apparent essential difference in the origins and development of either Latin or Teutonic towns. One subordinate lesson was clear: nationalism is no aid to the correct interpretation of historical facts.

In these essays, the mature Pirenne manifested the qualities which made him a great historian: a comparative perspective, a firm command of relevant facts, a gift for synthesis, and an elegant, penetrating style—Voltaire was his model. What marked him as a "modern" (or twentieth-century) historian was his awareness of and constant concern with social and economic realities with which he enriched the traditional political and juridical emphases of nineteenth-century historiography. Pirenne devoted much of his scholarly attention to such matters as the revival of commerce in medieval Europe, the origin and expansion of industries such as the manufacture of cloth, the composition and rise of the merchant class and that even more elusive group the "middle class," and the consequences of cultural conflict and assimilation: Flemish and Walloon, Franco-German and Belgian, European and Asian, Christian and Moslem.

In 1914, he published an essay, translated as "The Stages of the Social History of Capitalism," which Charles Verlinden has described as "one of the most stimulating essays ever written in the field of economic and social history." Pirenne was among the most active advocates of the use of social scientific methods and insights in historiography—especially those of economics, sociology, and psychology—without ever losing sight, however, of the historian's narrative function: "To construct history is to narrate it." It was Pirenne's comparative, economic, and social history along with his receptivity to the social sciences that made him so congenial and revered a companion and colleague to the younger innovators, Lucien Febvre and Marc Bloch. "He loved Henri Pirenne as I did," Febvre wrote of Bloch, "for his rich and overflowing vitality—for the historical sense of life which permeated his spirit."

Pirenne's career was interrupted during World War I by the German invasion of Belgium. Most of the faculty of the University of Ghent refused to resume classes under German conditions, which included the deliberately divisive order that lectures must be in Flemish instead of French; in retaliation Pirenne and others were arrested and imprisoned. Pirenne conducted vastly popular lectures on economic and Belgian history for his fellow prisoners. "I never had more attentive pupils nor did I ever teach with such pleasure," he later recalled. He also undertook to master Russian, becoming by the way one of the few Western European historians familiar at first hand with Russian historiography. Discomfited by Pirenne's work in the prison camp and smarting from international criticism, the German authorities transferred him to the solitude of an isolated German town. There, officially described as "extremely dangerous," Pirenne continued his Russian studies and wrote without any of the historian's customary Hilfsmittel an impressive and enduring *History of Europe, 400–1500*. The war's end brought him back to Belgium and to the University of Ghent.

From 1919 to his death in 1935, Pirenne maintained his scholarly activity and a cosmopolitan's involvement in the progress of historiography. He returned to direct the Belgian Royal Commission on History and was the first president of the postwar International Historical Congress (1923). Despite the death of his son in combat and his own wartime experiences, he insisted that German scholars be allowed to participate without disabilities. Pirenne also encouraged Marc Bloch and Lucien Febvre to initiate the *Annales d'histoire économique et sociale* (1929) and served as an editor for the review. He also taught at many foreign universities in the course of the postwar decade and was active in the work of numerous scholarly societies. His seminars were always crowded, and he trained scores of students, many of whom became eminent historians.

All the while, however, he was carrying on the work begun in 1899: his masterpiece, the monumental *Histoire de Belgique.* The fourth volume of the work had appeared in 1911; after the war, Pirenne resumed the series, publishing the last three volumes in 1921, 1926, and 1932. The *Histoire de Belgique* was undertaken as part of a series of national histories, and the first volume was published in German (1899); a French version (Pirenne's original) appeared in 1900; and a Flemish translation followed in 1902. As the volumes succeeded each other, Pirenne's work was recognized not only for its impeccable scholarship but for its political and national significance. No one before Pirenne had attempted to write the history of Belgium on a national scale. Pirenne's *History* had the effect of reducing parochial pride, which was no simple task in a state marked by ethnic, linguistic, and religious disunity and devoid as well of any "natural boundaries." But Pirenne's conception of the Belgian nation allowed him to trace a line of development from Roman times and to disentangle "Belgian" elements from the overlapping histories of France, Germany, Spain, Austria, England, and the Netherlands.

"Despite the difference of time and milieu, modern Belgium is indeed the continuation of the ancient Low Countries," he wrote in 1899. "It has not been given to us by diplomacy; we hold it as a very old heritage from our ancestors." This conception shines through the pages of his *History,* and it armed him against German wartime propaganda which held Belgium to be an "artificial nation" (and thus, presumably, fit to be annexed). Pirenne's response in 1925 as he carried on the work was apt:

> In a certain sense, indeed, the Germans were right in saying that Belgium is an "artificial" nation. It is indeed, if one understands by this that both geographical unity and linguistic unity are equally lacking. It has neither natural frontiers nor a language common to all its inhabitants. It is not a product of nature; it is a work of history, that is to say, a work of man. And note, I pray you, that all that man has done is artificial. Law, art, morals, civilization itself, as it has developed since the age of the cavemen, are artificial. It is in that respect that Belgium too is artificial.

This being said, let it be noted that Pirenne himself denied that a nationalistic or patriotic motive impelled his work: "I have written the history of Belgium as I would have written the history of the Etruscans, without sentiment or patriotism." Certainly no one has ever been able to refute Pirenne's claim to historical objectivity. Marc Bloch, to whom biased history was anathema, called him a "national historian" in the best sense of the term: "The *History of Belgium* has nothing of the *livre à thèse*. It is in the most rigorous sense of the term a book of good faith—like its author."

To the end of his long life, Pirenne maintained both his rigorous personal life and his stimulating scholarship. His last published essay was a minute analysis of a medieval document, but he left behind a challenging interpretation, *Mohammed and Charlemagne,* which has exercised and beguiled medieval historians ever since its posthumous publication in 1936. Its thesis, that "without Mohammed, Charlemagne would have been inconceivable," has been subjected to much searching criticism. This would have delighted Pirenne: "Every effort at synthesis, however premature it may seem, cannot fail to react usefully on investigations, provided one offers it in all frankness for what it is." Pirenne, like Bloch and Febvre, was not afraid to answer imaginatively the bold questions he put to history. He himself wrote his historiographical epitaph: "My sole end has been to seek to understand and to explain." It was adherence to that professional credo that made him, in Febvre's words, "a master historian to whom we are indebted."

Selected Bibliography

Bryce Lyon's *Henri Pirenne: A Biographical and Intellectual Study* (1974) will no doubt stand as the definitive work on our historian. James L. Cate's "Henri Pirenne, 1862–1935," in *Some Twentieth-Century Historians,* edited by S. William Halperin (1961), is a good introduction to Pirenne's work; and F. M. Powicke includes a helpful essay on Pirenne in his *Modern Historians and the Study of History* (1955). Perhaps the most informative essay on Pirenne's contributions is that by Charles Verlinden, "Henri Pirenne," in *Architects and Craftsmen in History: Festschrift für Abbot Payson Usher* (1956), 85–100. Lucien Febvre's review essay, "Henri Pirenne à travers deux de ses oeuvres," in *Combats pour l'histoire* (1953), is a warm tribute to Pirenne's methods and concepts. Jan-Albert Goris has an excellent introduction to the English version of *A History of Europe* (1956; translated by Bernard Maill), and Jacques Pirenne describes in his preface the circumstances in which his father wrote and he himself published the book.

The essay "What Are Historians Trying to Do?" is included in *Methods in Social Science: A Case Book,* edited by Stuart A. Rice (1931), 435–445, as is Carl Stephenson's analysis of "The Work of Henri Pirenne and Georg von Below with Respect to the Origin of the Medieval Town," 368–382. Pirenne's influence may be gauged by reference to the collections of essays dedicated to him: *Mélanges d'histoire offerts à Henri Pirenne* (2 vols.; 1926); *Études d'histoire dediées à la mémoire de Henri Pirenne par ses anciens élèves* (1937); and *Henri Pirenne, hommages et souvenirs* (2 vols.; 1938).

HISTORY OF BELGIUM

The Economic Movement

... During the Burgundian period, the economic and political movements in the Low Countries were similar. In both can be noted the passage from a state of things which were becoming obsolete to a state of things which were slowly emerging and would dominate the future. The histories of the state, commerce, and industry were so intertwined that they are reciprocally enlightening and explanatory. Bourgeois resistance to princely power was overcome because the fifteenth-century cities were in the process of losing their former dominance in the economic realm. The state began to show the first effects of the urban economy which started replacing the domainal economy in the twelfth century. New forces were revealed which demanded a new type of organization. Large communes sought in vain to resist this conquering new wave. They exhausted themselves fighting for franchises and monopolies, both of which were incompatible with the social and economic phenomena arising at the end of the fourteenth century.

When Philip the Bold ["le Hardi"] arrived in Flanders, the country presented a disheartening sight, for it had been ravished by war for six years. The Hanseatic merchants had left Bruges to settle in Dordrecht; Ghent had lost the better part of its population; Ypres was half destroyed; Bergues was in ruins; and Ostende was silting up. Many polders had been flooded; wolves and wild boars infested the countryside. In certain villages, the population was so reduced that the aldermanry system could not be revived. Even though less harshly put to task, most of the other territories were also suffering. In the province of Brabant, Louvain and Brussels saw the disappearance of their former prosperity. Holland and Zeeland were stained with blood resulting from struggles between the Hooks and Kabbeljaws. War was everywhere—war between Flanders and Brabant, war between Brabant and Gelderland, permanent civil war in the land of Liège.

Fifty years later, on the other hand, the Low Countries once again

This selection from the *Histoire de Belgique,* III, pp. 380–386, 405–425, was translated for this volume by Professor James Tedder of George Mason University.

became the richest region in Europe. In comparison with France, which had been devastated both by foreign and civil wars, and with England, which had been victimized by the horrors of the War of the Roses, the inhabitants of the Low Countries "could more justly consider themselves in the promised land than could the inhabitants of any other kingdom on earth." In rather pompous terms, the chronicler Chastellain admired the region's "inhabitants without number, riches and powers, use of commerce, and abundance of all manner of material possessions." Cities there were adorned with monuments, and the fertility of the fields amazed foreign travelers. This region was overflowing with well-being in comparison with Burgundy, which "had no money and smelled of France." The air was filled with buoyant enjoyment of life and that rich, luxuriant sensualism which has been a national characteristic ever since. Foreigners marveled at the luxurious clothing, "bigger and more lavish parties and banquets than in any other place, splendid and extravagant common baths and diversions with women."

It would certainly be going too far to attribute all this astounding prosperity to the intentional accomplishments of the Burgundian dukes themselves. Rather, one should attribute it to the following essential factors: the Low Countries' industrious people, admirable geographical location, and favorable circumstances. One must also recognize that the combination of territories into a single state, the profound peace enjoyed for thirty consecutive years during the reign of Philip the Good ["le Bon"], and the eventual establishment of regular, perfected civil administration incontestably hastened the advent of prosperity. In short, the fifteenth-century dukes succeeded in establishing the program which since the middle of the preceding century had only been a vague dream of the Flemish cities. Their political efforts resulted in monetary unification, free travel between provinces, and the kind of law and order which are indispensable for trade. They were not ignorant of the fact that their personal power and riches stemmed from the region's wealth. Like Chastellain, they certainly knew that "all the glory in the reigns of princes lies in the abundance of material possessions, wealth, and money, and not in the dignity and nobility of names. Princes, when prodigal in spending, vanity, and unnecessary things, and who furthermore are avaricious and tyrannical toward their subjects, show themselves to be generally weak in important matters and find their subjects cold and powerless for their own needs."

Words like these already adumbrate the mercantile theories of the sixteenth century. In any case, from the Burgundian period on, it was the prince himself, agent of the common good, who was seen occupying himself with the economic interests of the country. He sought both to conserve and augment its resources. On behalf of Flemish industry, he adopted a prohibitionist policy with regard to the English textile trade. Philip the Good left no stone unturned in his efforts to find a remedy for Ypres' decline. Charles the Bold ["le Téméraire"] took measures to revive the commerce of Vilvorde. Despite the particularist opposition of Ghent, Ypres, and Franc, in 1470 he ordered that vast work projects be undertaken to retrieve Zwin from encroachment by silt and sand and, if possible, to maintain the prosperity of Bruges. With support and encouragement from the dynasty, Antwerp became the largest northern market in the fifteenth century, and Holland laid the foundations for its maritime power. Shortly after taking possession of Luxembourg, Philip sent Liège miners in search of gold and silver deposits. And finally, his crusading plans probably included the creation of markets for Low Country goods in the Mediterranean basin.

Without a doubt, the economic policies of the House of Burgundy do not present a perfect continuity of views. They contain both contradictions and incoherences. But since the interests of the separate territories were not the same, it sometimes happened that a measure established for the benefit of one would sometimes turn to the detriment of its neighbors and, sooner or later, called for a countermeasure. For example, when it was decided as a result of a decline in the Flemish textile trade to prohibit the importation of English textiles, the trade in Antwerp suffered a considerable blow. The prohibition could therefore not be maintained. In addition, local policy considerations often kept the dukes from applying their principles systematically. To avoid a break with Ghent, they eventually began to neglect the interests of other cities in Flanders. In 1433, Charles the Bold bought the approval of the citizens in Bruges both by sacrificing the foreign merchants to them and by granting them 500,000 crowns.

The economic role of the dukes is most evident in monetary matters. Not only did they establish the kind of agreement on the circulation of metals toward which the provinces had been tending during the twelfth century, but they also had coins struck which were remarkable both for excellence and stability. In 1433, Philip the Good could brag with good reason about his coin, "which is so good that there is none better in worth as everyone knows." From 1430 on, golden crowns called *vierlanders* were circulated in the Low Countries, as were other new coins later on. The many monetary edicts in the fifteenth century give evidence of economic ideas which were already quite advanced. They affirm "that one of the main points of all good policies on which the public good is founded, both for us and for the common people, is to have and maintain good, solid, durable coin both in gold and silver." The dukes took measures to prevent the Low Countries from being invaded by weak foreign coins which could drive out the good ones if the situation were not remedied. They prohibited taking gold or silver bullion from the country, and in the cities they set up inspectors who would weigh and verify the coin of individuals without cost. They established a meticulous surveillance of minting operations. Finally, they decided that minting houses would no longer be sold surreptitiously, that is, by adjudication, and "that they would be leased by us to notable, powerful, and rich people who can provide our said cities, lands, and seigneuries with gold and silver coin which can dispatch and pay for trade goods immediately upon the presentation of bullions in the said coins." The government was already seeking to establish monetary agreements with neighboring states. In 1469, King Edward IV of England and Charles the Bold "agreed to convene a conference in Bruges on extending their legal tender as far as possible and on suppressing counterfeiting." The excellence of the fifteenth-century monetary system in the Low Countries is proved by the beauty of the coins, their great variety, and the imitations made of them in neighboring countries. While in Burgundy, the dukes struck only silver coins; but for their rich Netherland provinces, they minted an admirable gold coinage. Philip the Bold and John the Fearless maintained the kinds of Flemish coins held during the reign of Louis de Male. But, from the reign of Philip the Good, there were new coins of unusual weight. Beginning with the reign of Charles the Bold, coins came to be dated in Arabic numerals. This happy innovation was later adopted in France.

Even despite their salutary consequences, the economic activities of the Burgundian dukes have often been judged unfavorably. And strange as it might seem on first sight, one can easily find in fifteenth-century texts lamentable testimonials on the land's misery and impoverishment. Here there is an illusion, however, and we must be wary of it. Even though the fifteenth century provides the spectacle of astounding economic vigor, it was, in fact, also the period when the textile industry declined. And it was the textile industry which had made the fortune of Flanders and Brabant during the Middle Ages. Hence, it was simultaneously a period of renaissance and of crisis; the past and future are contained in it. To understand the period, one must consider both what it ended and what it inaugurated.

IV

Even though they may have produced crises of greater or lesser intensity in many cities, the social and political transformations of the Burgundian period were universally beneficent for the rural population. When the communes lost their omnipotence, the peasant was freed from the economic and political subordination into which he had fallen in the fifteenth century. He could freely devote himself to industry, and in the

Justice Councils he possessed an appeal against the urban aldermanry. Moreover, the last traces of the domainal regime disappeared in the Low Countries at the time. The nobles stopped further meddling in the exploitation of their lands and contented themselves with merely collecting the revenues from them. What was left of the rights of forced labor and mortmain was replaced by simple taxation. The leasing of land, which had been introduced into the Low Countries at the end of the twelfth century, became widespread. The purchase of numerous properties by wealthy bourgeois and royal functionaries began to cut into the monopoly on the land which the nobles and the Church had held until then. The diffusion of transferable capital and increasing mobility of money permitted land to become an item of trade. And finally, the long peace enjoyed during the reign of Philip the Good, improved assessment of taxes, cessation of private wars, increased security, and greater facility in communications were benefits which the farming classes enjoyed perhaps even more than the rest of the population. We know, moreover, that since the second half of the fourteenth century they had defended the prince's monarchical policy against the large cities, and from then on, under the Burgundian regime, they were to be the first to benefit from royal supremacy. Thus, with the exception of a revolt by the inhabitants of the domain of Cassel in 1430, whose causes are still unknown, not the slightest trace of discontent is detected among the peasantry in the fifteenth century.

Personally free since the end of the thirteenth century, the peasants of the Low Countries remained so from then on. It is only because of the most bizarre of interpretative aberrations that some scholars have believed an attempt was made to restore serfdom during the reign of Philip the Good. Yet, it seems that the number of small rural landholders greatly diminished toward the end of the Middle Ages. A number of them certainly turned into leasees and salaried agricultural workers, at least in the most advanced parts of the country, in Flanders and Brabant. Rich capitalists such as Bladelin—citizen of Bruges and treasurer of Philip the Good—had dikes built around enormous polders at their own expense. Hence, the power of private capital substituted for the power of free association or monastic work projects to which we owe the first reclamations of land through drainage. Bladelin's fortune enabled him to found a new city, named Middelburg, on his lands. To it he summoned a host of citizens from Dinant, which had been sacked in 1466. Their Walloon names are still to be found in great numbers in the region even today.

From the beginning of the fourteenth century, important progress was made in farming. The system of triennial crop rotation, in which a third of the land lay fallow each year, gave way to improved methods. The fallow land was planted with legumes or turnips. The use of artificial meadowlands became widespread. These improvements appeared in Flanders long before other territories. That is doubtless due both to the density of the population and especially to the raising of cattle which provided the peasants with an abundant source of fertilizer. Even though cattle raising was already important in the region during the first half of the Middle Ages, it became even more widespread there in the fourteenth and fifteenth centuries. The Englishman Glanville wrote that Flanders was filled with "pastures and cattle." It was the same in Holland and Zeeland, where, from the beginning of the Burgundian period, butter and cheese production became very important commercially. Cereal grains came in either by sea, or especially from Brabant, Hesbaye, Namurois, Hainaut, and Artois. In French Flanders, Douai was the great market for grains shipped to the north, and as a result, could make up for the decline in its textile industry. Less favorably situated than the other provinces, Luxembourg participated less actively in the general prosperity. Its annexation to the Burgundian domains, however, had some fortunate consequences. We know from the chronicles of Floreffe that numerous farming and land-clearing projects were initiated. Philip the Good even dreamed of exploiting its mineral resources; in 1431, he ordered a search for gold and silver mines there.

At the other end of the Low Countries, along the coasts of Holland and Zeeland, maritime fishing underwent an extraordinary phase of development during the same period. Herring fishing, whose center until then had been in Gravelines, moved off toward the north, and the barrel process, which was discovered at the beginning of the fifteenth century, gave it an unexpected impetus. Not only was the catch sufficient to nourish the national market, but it soon provided a very active export trade. Until then, the Low Countries had imported quantities of salted fish from Germany. But now they reversed the trend and, to the great detriment of the Hanseatic League, sent more and more important cargoes of fish to Germany.

When we add to these resources the benefits the peasants derived from weaving cloth and linen, we can easily see that, on the whole, the situation of the rural classes in the fifteenth century was highly satisfying. There were some dietary crises in the century, but only one of them was truly serious. In 1438–1439 the excessive cost of wheat, the result of a poor harvest, produced a famine which, when aggravated by plague, devastated all the Low Countries and caused thousands to die.

At first sight, the general well-being of the population seems incompatible with the law designed to combat the progress of mendicity which was promulgated in Brabant (1459) and applied in Flanders (1461). It would be a mistake to interpret this law as proof of the country's misery. It simply bears witness to the state's ever-increasing intervention in police matters. Beggars, who until then were relegated to the care of the Church and private charity, now attracted the attention of the government. Even though vagrants had been numerous in the Middle Ages and aroused no reprobation, they now came to be considered a cause of social ills and had to be combated. It wasn't that the state was taking it upon itself to provide for them; it intended only to submit them to administrative control and, as much as possible, to force them to work. The only beggars to be allowed were children under twelve, old people over sixty, and persons who could not exercise a trade because of having to care for children who demanded all their attention. The poor over sixty had to wear a lead disk around their necks which gave their address. All those found without this insignia would be condemned either to the galleys or to prison.

We must recognize that the changes which took place in the social constitution of the fifteenth century were bound to increase the number of vagrants rather considerably. Increasing exclusivism in the trades and a decline in the textile industry forced a host of individuals to leave their native regions in order to seek a living elsewhere. The fate of these outcasts of fortune was eased by private charity from an early period. Before 1453, a rich bourgeois from Ghent, Gerard De Stoevere, founded an almshouse for poor foreign children who devoted themselves to peddling [*mesmankins*].

As we end this rapid survey of the economic situation in the Low Countries in the fifteenth century, we would like to be able to establish with some certainty the number of residents there at the time. In the total absence of studies on the subject, the following data will doubtless be of interest. After a census taken in Brabant in 1435 on the occasion of levied benevolences, the region—excepting the city of Malines—included about 89,500 households. Similar counts taken in 1469 give 41,175 households in Flanders, 9,681 in the bailiwicks of Lille, Douai, Seclin, and Orchies, 28,724 in Hainaut, 1,688 in Namurois, 12,828 in Picardy, 27,933 in Artois, and 5,014 in Ponthieu. We must note that cities are not included in the figures of 1469. By supposing that their population formed about a third of the total population, we arrive at the number of 169,300 households for the territories counted in 1469. If we adopt an average of five persons per household, the number of residents in Brabant in 1435 would be 449,750, and in Flanders and neighboring territories, constituting therewith the province of the Chamber of the Counts of Lille, 946,950 in 1469, or in total, for a territory equivalent to almost two thirds of the Burgundian domains "on this side of the border," 1,396,700 inhabitants. We are probably not far from the truth to estimate a population of two million in the lands owned by Philip the Good in the Low Countries. Recently discovered documents would assign 700,000 to the land of Liège. We can obtain more precise results by studying population movements. We possess, in fact, counts of the households in Brabant for the years 1435, 1464, 1472, and 1492. The evident conclusion to be derived from them is that, after increasing slightly from 1435 to 1464, the number of households slowly decreased in 1472 and then diminished with frightening speed during the following twenty years. However summary this data may be, it corresponds exactly with the progression of events. In its own way it confirms the continued development of prosperity in the Low Countries up to the end of the reign of Philip the Good, and then shows us the first symptoms of recession from the beginning of Charles the Bold's military expeditions. And, finally, the data bear witness to the frightful crisis brought on by the civil troubles which broke out after the Nancy catastrophe. Already in 1469, it was noted that the villages in Hainaut had lost two to three thousand families as the result of wars and "the billeting of soldiers."

THE INTELLECTUAL MOVEMENT

Civilization in the Low Countries in the fifteenth century had the same character as that of the political situation. When these frontier regions became detached from Germany and France, which had shared them for such a long time, and when they joined together to form a distinct state, the intellectual movement—manifested in literature and especially in art and religious ideas—took its inspiration less from the outside, and bore the mark of clear-cut originality. Independence of minds goes hand in hand with national independence. For this reason, it is highly instructive to note that at the very moment national independence occurred, the history of Flemish painting opened so gloriously.

The dukes of Burgundy were not merely witnesses to this splendid efflorescence. We must bestow upon them the honor of having facilitated its progress with all their power. Like the Italian dynasties of the time, they made their court a rallying point for artists. Their luxury, which was so bitterly criticized by the middle class, attracted writers, musicians, and especially painters. The name of Philip the Good is as inseparable from that of Van Eyck as the name Leo X is from those of Raphael and Michelangelo. This brilliance which shone in the reigning house, however, was taken directly from the Low Countries themselves and was not imported from the outside as the monarchical institutions had been. In its role as art patron, the royal house was content to hasten into full bloom a culture which had sprouted long before Burgundians came to the region. Here again, as in political unification, one sees the fulfillment of an evolution whose origins can be dated back to the beginning of the fourteenth century.

I

Beyond this date, in fact, there was a decline in the French influence which had been so powerful in all Belgian provinces since the end of the twelfth century. Flanders' permanent hostility with regard to the French crown, the merchants' abandonment of the markets in Champagne, the increasing independence of territorial dynasties vis-à-vis the House of Valois, the weakening of the monarchy during the Hundred Years War, the decline of literature and the arts noted at the time in the French kingdom, and the eventual loss of Artois and subsequently of Walloon Flanders—all of these things gradually freed the Low Countries from the political and intellectual hegemony exercised by their southern neighbors.

Without doubt, the French language was far from disappearing in Flemish regions. It was maintained at the royal court and by nobles and the richest bourgeois families, who continued to send their children to learn it in Walloon cities. In all provinces, it was used with Latin for external affairs, and the princes continued to use it in their correspondence with their bailiffs and advisers. But even if it remained in some places, it was not adopted by any new ones. Along with it, on the other hand, Flemish played a more important role. In almost all cities, Flemish was substituted for Latin in current administrative acts, the keeping of land records, and the establishment of accounts. The democratic revolution which brought artisans into political life naturally favored the progress of the Flemish language. Increased relations with the Hanseatic merchants of lower Germany made it the language of business *par excellence.* Multiplication of small schools in the cities even started people of the communes to reading and writing it. Moreover, when raised to the dignified level of a literary language by the poet Maerlant, Flemish henceforth provided the people with intellectual nourishment. There are texts to inform us that simple artisans owned manuscripts of the *Rijmbijbel* and the *Leeken Spiegel.*

The co-existence of two languages in different portions of the population, each of which had an independent literature, made administrative measures indispensable from an early period. Bilingualism was officially sanctioned from the end of the fourteenth century. At Louis de Male's Tribunal, judges handed down their verdicts in the language used by the litigants. In Brabant, the chancellor had to know Latin, French, and Flemish, and the Peace of Saint-Jacques imposed the same requirement on ecclesiastical notaries. In Flanders, as we have already noted, John the Fearless ordered, on the demand of his subjects, the use of two concurrent idioms; and Philip the Good generalized in the administration of his southern provinces the application of the rules sanctioned by his father. In Holland and Zeeland, where French had barely penetrated, people hardly used anything but Flemish. It was only after Charles the Bold that French tended to become the only language officially recognized by the prince, and the result was a state of discontent which in 1477 produced the language guarantees sanctioned by the privilege granted by Marie of Burgundy. Yet, we must note the fact that the expansion of French usage which took place during the reign of Charles was in no way intended to make the Low Countries more French. Rather, it can be explained quite simply by the absolutist tendencies of the prince, who, in the same way as he extended the jurisdiction of the central government, generalized the use of the only language employed by his government. Beyond that, one cannot find in the dukes' conduct any act of hostility with regard to the idiom used by the majority of their subjects. It is true that the dialect of the Thiois region was considered a barbaric tongue by the Burgundian entourage, who, themselves, took no delight in it. Yet, they didn't stop learning it. Philip the Good and Charles the Bold spoke it. For their library they acquired a certain number of Flemish manuscripts, and it is known that Charles granted a pension to the chronicler De Roevere.

The House of Burgundy did nothing to hinder the diffusion of Flemish or the success of Flemish literature in the Low Countries. It was well aware that "its power was far more Flemish than Walloon" and, hence, prudently took great care to avoid any linguistic persecution. Flemish, which had already begun to spread in the Walloon provinces in the fourteenth century, made great progress there in the fifteenth. Froissart from Hainaut knew it. Even though it was already prevalent beforehand, Flemish became generalized in Liège from the day the county of Looz was annexed and brought into the princely territory a considerable number of inhabitants who spoke Dutch. Among the popular leaders guiding the course of events during the reign of Louis de Bourbon, a good number —like Raes de Heers, Jean de Wilde, and Vincent de Buren—were of Thiois origin. There were also many chroniclers whose names clearly reveal their nationality—Corneil Zantfliet, Adrien d'Oudenbosch, etc. They are the ones who have preserved for us the memory of the heroic struggle sustained by the country against the Burgundian princes. In addition, many Flemish expressions were introduced into the Walloon language of Liège during this period, and examples can be found on almost every page in the writings of Jean de Stavelot. The economic superiority of the Germanic parts of the country forced all who engaged in business with them to learn their language. Walloons who went to market in Antwerp had to learn it, just as the Flemish had had to learn French in the thirteenth century because of trading with the markets in Champagne. It was certainly widespread among Dinant's industrious middle classes, and from the beginning of the fifteenth century, it was even introduced into Walloon cities of mediocre importance such as Namur. The reciprocal penetration of two national languages doubtless contributed in large measure to bringing the diverse provinces closer together. Towns on both sides of the language frontier invited each other to the grand archery tournaments which had been so extraordinarily fashionable since the end of the fourteenth century. And, in the theatrical performances which accompanied these merrymakings, French

plays were performed in the Flemish communes, and Thiois actors performed *Abelespeelen* for the French cities to the south.

In such circumstances, Flemish literature developed rapidly. During
the fourteenth century, the *dietsche dichters* who were disciples of Maerlant continued to produce moral and didactic works. Yet, the school of the
Damme poet attained its greatest luster in Brabant rather than in Flanders. The latter was agitated by continual civil strife, troubled by social
demands of the weavers, occupied with its wars against France, and was
eventually dragged into the kind of political life which was too intense
to permit that leisure and tranquillity indispensable for cultivating an
essentially philosophical literature. The province had powerful orators
like Zannekin and the two Arteveldes and poets who, like the author of
the *Kerelslied,* were afire with social hatred, or who were motivated by
municipal patriotism, like Baudouin Van der Loren. Nevertheless, it lost
its *wijze clercken,* who placidly rhymed lessons of conduct or the rudiments of science for the bourgeoisie. On the other hand, Brabant, which
had been at peace for a long time under the reigns of popular princes and
an omnipotent patriciate, seized control of Netherlandic literature from
this point on. Its dialect was substituted for that of Flanders, and it retained its pre-eminence until the day it passed into Holland during the
sixteenth-century revolution.

From Brabant came the most remarkable Thiois poet of the time, Jean
Boendale *(ca.* 1280–1365). Like Maerlant, he was a municipal clerk who
was inspired by profoundly serious, practical sentiments. But he no
longer felt his mentor's naïve admiration for France. Because he was
living at the time of the duchy's first constitutional privilege and of the
1333 war in which his compatriots so valiantly defended their prince
against the coalition of his enemies, Boendale was thoroughly a citizen
of Brabant. His *Brabantsche Yeesten* stands out as the most characteristic monument of popular secular historiography in the Low Countries.
Both in it and in his moral and didactic writings, one can find the complete expression of ideas which dominated the upper bourgeoisie at the
time. Boendale is as hostile to urban democracy as to nobility. While he
does not hide his antipathy either for Flemish weavers or for Jacque Van
Artevelde, he feels only scorn for the nobility. He places all his confidence in the merchants and peasants. He is nevertheless filled with optimism, and prefers the present to the past. We can easily see that he was
writing at a time when the power of lineages was still intact.

After Boendale, the group of *Dichters* from Maerlant's school died out.
The anonymous continuation of the *Brabantsche Yeesten* gives evidence
of lamentable artistic decadence, and the few rhymed chronicles which
continued to be written into the fifteenth century drag along in puerile
banalities. On the other hand, however, writing in prose began to emerge

and to provide people with the edifying lessons which they used to find in the *Spiegels.* The profound religious feelings which had given rise to the lay brotherhoods of Beguines and Beghards at the end of the twelfth century continued to be strong during the following periods. The Beguine convents, where the bourgeoisie sent their daughters to be reared, formed ardent centers of mysticism and provided for a very intense spiritual life in the cities. Their influence was certainly more active than that of either the secular clergy or the monks, for the latter were more clearly separated from the people and often, at least in communes, in conflict with them. So piety developed, if not truly outside the Church, at least alongside it. At the end of the thirteenth century, Sister Hadewijch of Brussels was already composing poems which abounded with religious exaltation. But such mysticism was not to maintain its verse form for long. With Jan Ruysbroeck (1294–1381), it came to be written in prose, a medium deemed more favorable for writings designed for meditation, and more appropriate for urban people whose schools had popularized the art of reading. We do not intend here to insist on the height of inspiration and beauty of language in works by this founder of Flemish prose. But the divine love, which the poems of Hadewijch expressed by profane comparisons borrowed from ardent sensualism, is expressed in accents of exquisite tenderness and purity in Ruysbroeck's writings. If he deserves to be placed among the greatest religious writers of the Middle Ages, it is because he exerted an extraordinary influence on those around him. One of his disciples, Gerhard Groote, founded the Congregation of Brothers of the Communal Life, and by so doing, provided fourteenth-century mysticism with an organization which was as influential as the Beguine convents had been two centuries earlier. Despite the opposition of the mendicant monks—who feared that laymen meddling with the things of faith posed a threat to orthodoxy—the Brothers of the Communal Life composed and passed out among the people a host of edifying treatises written for them in their own common language. In these so-called *libri teutonici,* which are inspired by the same spirit as that in the *Imitation of Jesus Christ,* one must look for the flower of Netherlandic literature at the end of the Middle Ages.

Profane literature was henceforth stripped of the seriousness and gravity which characterized the school of Maerlant, and it became debased to the point of being nothing more than a simple amusement. It compensated by the quantity of its productions for its complete lack of art and real inspiration. Abandoned to Chambers of Rhetoric, it became for the bourgeoisie an object of dilletantism and a pastime, much like the archery tournaments and pompous pageants which revealed the people's delight in show and festivity. Theatrical works were produced, but their outer glitter was emphasized over any literary value. Every event provided the occasion for a spectacle: cities rivaled each other to see which could give the richest and longest mystery plays. With its production of the *Seven Joys of Mary*—which was to be performed successively during a seven-year cycle—Brussels could boast of having attained the supreme degree in this genre after 1444. The country's wealth favored such splendors, and the Belgian example probably influenced that "theatrical fury" which spread throughout France after the middle of the fifteenth century.

Love of theatrical diversions was no less prevalent in the Walloon cities of Artois and Hainaut than in Flemish and Brabant cities. On both sides of the linguistic frontier, the great "Rhetoricians" gave proof of the same fertility of imagination, and were as popular in French as in Thiois. On the other hand, serious literature had very different characteristics in the Romance and Germanic parts of the Low Countries. Between Ruysbroeck and his contemporaries Jean Le Bel and Froissart the difference is as great as one can imagine. While the great Flemish prose stylist was writing his mystical works for the pious bourgeoisie, the two Walloon chroniclers were writing out their histories for the nobility, and were doing so with purely secular feeling.

Therefore, as in the twelfth and thirteenth centuries, French literature in the Low Countries maintained the privilege of providing reading material for the aristocracy. In the first half of the fourteenth century, Duke John III of Brabant still gave evidence of maintaining a lively interest in Flemish poetry and even successfully cultivated it himself. But after his reign, French alone dominated the royal courts. The Luxembourg dynasty and, even more amazing, the Bavarian dynasty which had barely been established—the one in Brabant and the other in Hainaut and in Holland—gave up all intellectual ties with Germany. Jeanne and Wenceslas appeared to be princes who were purely French in language and customs. And when the French poet Eustache Deschamps joined their entourage, he scarcely noticed that he was away from Paris. At the same time, the few poets writing in High German who had followed the Wittelsbachs into their new land during the first few years soon went back home, for there was no one who understood their language there. After Duke Albert, the Gallicizing process reached the court in Holland in the same way it had reached those in Flanders and Hainaut much earlier. The accession of the House of Burgundy only caused the affirmation and consecration of French in the Low Countries; it did not create it. Both Jacqueline of Bavaria and Philip the Good had received the same education, spoke the same language, and read the same books.

French literature in the Low Countries had been provincial until the middle of the thirteenth century. In the west, it used the Picard dialect, and Walloon in the east. After the mid-thirteenth century, however, those who were ambitious to write well and to earn the praise of people with good taste turned to the French of France. The only writers who remained faithful to the rustic, naïve native speech of the region were chroniclers of Liège like Jean d'Outremeuse, Jacques de Hemricourt, and Jean de Stavelot, who were all living in an area where the poor rural aristocracy could not, as it did elsewhere, serve as an instrument for the progress of elegance or cultural education. It was quite different in Hainaut, however. Under the princes of the House of Avesnes, the territory set the example in every chivalric elegance. Count Guillaume and his brother Jean de Beaumont were considered accomplished representatives of good breeding at the time. At their château, Quesnoy, Queen Philippa of England and Empress Marguerite were educated. The "gentil sire Gautier de Mauny," a sophisticated example of feudal honor at the beginning of the Hundred Years' War, came from their entourage. So did the first great prose writer of the fourteenth century, the Liègeois canon, Jean Le Bel.

In Le Bel's writings one can find nothing which smacks of the canon or of the citizen from Liège. The son of a rich bourgeois family, he entered the Church only in order to find social status. He had nothing in common with his compatriot Hocsem, who was spiritually so close to the Chapter of Saint Lambert and to the Liègeois countryside. Le Bel's sole ideal was the feudal life style which was developing so brilliantly in Hainaut. Quite early in his life, he became attached to Jean de Beaumont, and at his side went to war for Edward III against the Scots. When he retired to Liège in his old age, he dazzled the poor knights of La Hesbaye with his luxury and elegance. It was not for them, but for the great lords to whom he had been both companion and friend, that he wrote his memoirs. His steadfast language, rapid narration, and colorful report make these memoirs one of the era's great masterpieces of French literature.

The fact that Le Bel was nothing less than French, however, clearly affirms the increasing independence of culture in the Low Countries with regard to foreign countries. His hero was "the noble King Edowart," and he did not try to hide the antipathy inspired in him by Philippe de Valois. Even though he adopted the true language of France, however, he did not totally submit to French dominance. He neither imitated nor copied its writers. His attitude about French literature was like that adopted by his intended audience, the high Belgian aristocracy, concerning French policy at the beginning of the Hundred Years War. He completely escaped being absorbed by it, remained individualistic, and was the first in a long line of writers in French who henceforth were going to give the Low Countries a literary tradition which rivaled that of France.

The essential characteristic of this French school in the Low Countries
is its taste for history. Completely lacking in talent in other literary
genres, it nevertheless included many excellent memorialists during the
fourteenth and fifteenth centuries. From Jean Le Bel to Georges Chastellain, the writers' subject matter was taken from contemporary events. If
one recalls the extraordinary richness of Belgian historiography during
the preceding period, one might be able to conclude that these works
corresponded to an undeniable tendency in the national character. The
fame and popularity of Jean Froissart's chronicles must have contributed in their own way to aiding this literature to maintain the tradition. We know that Froissart was the disciple and, up to a point, the
continuator of Jean Le Bel. But, because he lived in the fourteenth century during a period when new dynasties were being introduced into the
Low Countries, he extended his sights to broader horizons. Jean Le Bel
wrote for the d'Avesnes aristocracy and restricted his interests to the
events in which they had played a part. Froissart, on the other hand, was
the protégé of both Albert of Bavaria and Wenceslas of Luxembourg,
princes who were related to a host of other reigning houses and who were
actively involved in the high politics of the period. Hence, Froissart chose
the history of all Europe for his subject matter. Only a resident of the Low
Countries could have written those chronicles in which the terrible national conflicts of the waning Middle Ages became simply an object of
literary amusement. Like his patrons, Froissart easily maintained his
neutrality between France and England. He had no preconceived opinions, and even if his sympathies at first lay with England while he was
Queen Philippa's protégé, he did not hesitate to rewrite his works from
a different point of view at the end of his career to please his new patron,
Wenceslas of Luxembourg. The universal glory he enjoyed must certainly be explained by his total lack of national feeling in an age which
saw the awakening of the idea of nationalism in the great states. Because
he belonged to no side, he could please everybody. In fourteenth-century
historiographical literature, his works occupy a place analogous to that
which the Low Countries then occupied in Europe. Like them, his works
are completely neutral and cosmopolitan.

This much cannot be said of the many writers who gathered around
the Burgundian dukes during the following century. For example, skepticism disappeared from the works of Froissart's continuator Mostrelet. As
Burgundian power became affirmed and was opposed to French power,
there developed in the Low Countries a literature which rivaled French
literature. It doubtless had no national character; its inspiration was
purely dynastic, and only the slightest trace of patriotism can be found
in it. From both his Dutch provinces and from France, Burgundy, Artois,
and Picardy, Philip the Good attracted many writers who had no other

mission than to vindicate him and, in their own way, to try to raise his prestige in the eyes of Europe. The works which he commissioned are cold, dull, and conventional. However, one can find in this courtly literature, reserved for a select group of courtiers and great lords of letters and culture, a rather remarkable artistic effort which announces the approach of the Renaissance. Along with the painters and sculptors who formed the duke's entourage, writers were primarily concerned with stylistic pomp and majesty. In his time, Chastellain occupied the position of a kind of literary noble. It has been said of his chronicles that "the purely narrative portions are perhaps the most interesting produced in the Middle Ages, and before the chronicles of Commines, his bear the greatest stamp of independent mind, personal judgment, and true writing talent." His chronicles also display all the formal, rhetorical majesty which astounded his contemporaries. They considered him the very model of eloquence. Because his literary language was filled with words borrowed from Latin, flowing in grandiloquent periods imitated for better or worse from Cicero, he earned the distinction of being called the supreme rhetorician. "He became the founder of a Burgundian literary school whose successive leaders were Jean Molinet de Valenciennes and Jean le Maire de Belges. At the end of the century, the school achieved triumph in France itself with Guillaume Cretin and Jean Marot."

Lucien Febvre

5

"To Lucien Febvre—By Way of Dedication." Thus Marc Bloch opened his testament as a historian, *Apologie pour l'Histoire, ou Métier d'historien,* and affectionately hoped for Febvre's approval of the book. Such homage from so eminent a historian as Bloch is a tribute to Lucien Febvre's stature. By his powerful and original scholarship and through his collaboration first with Henri Berr and then, supremely effectively, with Bloch, Febvre did perhaps more than any other historian to enliven, to enrich, and finally, to transform French historiography in the first half of the nineteenth century. He was, in Fernand Braudel's opinion, "perhaps the only great French historian since Michelet."

Febvre was born in 1878 in Franche-Comté; he grew up in Nancy, in Lorraine, but the Jura, where he later maintained a country home, remained his *"vraie patrie."* His father was a grammarian, his uncle a historian, and in the family's cultured environment the young Febvre immersed himself in literature and history. He encountered Michelet, the greatest literary historian of France, in his father's library, and grew up nurtured by written history and absorbing the living history, as it were, which suffused the atmosphere of eastern France. That atmosphere was made acrid by the disastrous Franco-Prussian War of 1870. Febvre was of the generation that grew to maturity during a national mood of patriotism and *revanchisme.*

He studied at the Lycée Louis-le-Grand in Paris and in 1898 entered the prestigious École Normale Supérieure, where he concentrated on history, geography, and literature. In 1902, he began research under the auspices of the Thiers Institute for Historical Research on the history of Franche-Comté. Between 1905 and 1912, he published a geography, a short history, and essays on the Reformation in that province, and his dissertation, the magisterial "Philippe II et la Franche-Comté (1911). He also began an introduction to historical geography, which he completed only after the war (*La terre et l'évolution humaine,* 1922). These works indicate the wide range of Febvre's interests and his broad conception of historical studies. Geography, sociology, economics, social psychology, and ideas as well as politics entered into his definition of his craft.

To a great extent that definition was prompted by the influence of Henri Berr, whose *Revue de synthèse historique* began to appear in 1900. Berr had studied at the École Normale Supérieure and had been influenced by one of his teachers, Émile Boutroux, whose work centered on the increasing specialization of knowledge and on the possible methods for combating or at least mitigating the effects of the tendency. "We were a group of young historians at the École Normale who were beginning to find our studies banal," Febvre wrote in 1925, "and were just about to quit when, in 1900, our interest in history was refired by the appearance of the *Revue de synthèse historique.*" What Berr called for was a "new history," a "science of history" that would encompass and lead all of the other social sciences in a synthesis of science and philosophy. Berr judged that all previous philosophers of history, from Vico to Hegel, had been wrong, or at least inadequate: they had created laws and philosophies to understand history, but what was needed was a careful analysis of history prior to the construction of any philosophy of history. What made Berr so attractive and exciting to young historians like Febvre was his call for boldness in theory, for clarity in method, and for the incorporation of sociology, anthropology, psychology, ethnology, and other disciplines into historical analysis and synthesis. "The word 'theory,' " he wrote, "should not give alarm; it does not presuppose . . . vague, excessively general speculations put forth by thinkers who have never been working historians."

This view affronted the prevailing view of history that had been expressed by Monod in 1876: "We have understood the danger of premature generalizations, of great *a priori* systems that claim to cover everything and explain everything. We have sensed that history should be the object of a slow methodical process of investigation in which one moves gradually from the particular to the general, from details to the whole; where all obscure points are successively illuminated in order to have the whole picture and to base general ideas, susceptible to proof and verification, upon groups of historical facts." To this positivistic position Berr responded defiantly: "It does not appear that a science enjoys better conditions in being abandoned to routine and empiricism. And if, generally speaking, theory only sanctions practice, a concern to arrive at a theory can . . . lead to advances in practice." Berr's call for a new, synthetic, philosophical history reached a receptive audience. His *Revue* was, in Croce's words, "something which had been awaited for some time, and was destined to appear sooner or later." Berr's influence was deepened by the effectiveness with which he purveyed his ideas. Berr was, in Febvre's words, cordial, gracious, respectful of others' ideas, and above all an eternal optimist. In the first decades of the twentieth century, he gathered about him enthusiasts from all disciplines—"a group of active, lively, combative, conquering men," as Lucien Febvre, the most combative of them all, described them.

In 1912, Febvre began teaching at the University of Dijon. In 1914, he entered the army, where he served with distinction, demonstrated in battle how "passionately French" he was, and emerged unscathed, with the rank of captain. In 1920, he was at the newly reopened French University of Strasbourg, where he met Marc Bloch and the two began a friendship and collaboration that was to last until Bloch's death, and in a sense beyond. Febvre continued his close relationship with Berr (La terre et l'évolution humaine was published as Volume IV of Berr's series L'évolution de l'humanité) and was instrumental in starting up the colloquia Semaines de synthèse, designed to bring together scholars from all disciplines to exchange information and viewpoints. "From this concert of voices," he wrote, "normally separated and scarcely inclined to listen to one another, there emerged a harmony . . . they made everyone conscious . . . of the fundamental unity of the human spirit."

Febvre even considered taking over the editorship of the Revue de synthèse. He co-authored with Berr the entry "History" in the Encyclopedia of the Social Sciences (1932) in which they attempted more clearly to define the new history as scientific, generalizing, comparative, and universal in its perspective: "The final goal of the historian is . . . humanity in the totality of its representatives." But the new relationship with Marc Bloch henceforth commanded Febvre's primary scholarly attention. In what H. Stuart Hughes describes as "a curious game of musical chairs," Bloch, who had studied ideas and psychology in his early work Les rois thaumaturges, moved into economic and rural history, while Febvre, who had first studied provincial and rural matters, moved to the study of ideas, theology, and psychology. Thus, in 1928, Febvre published his study of Martin Luther in which he analyzed the social and psychological as well as theological elements in Luther's revolt, while at the same time Bloch was deep into the researches for his classic French Rural History.

In 1929, Febvre and Bloch initiated the Annales d'histoire économique et sociale, whose announced purpose was to provide a forum for the exchange of views from all fields that could contribute to the study of "les sciences humaines," but particularly to history. Febvre made the Annales the center of his intellectual life and, in intimate cooperation with his co-editor, Marc Bloch, made the review both successful and influential. Febvre used the pages of the Annales to carry on his "combats pour l'histoire"—the new Annales history, of course. The Annales of Febvre and Bloch adopted and transcended the program of Berr's Revue de synthèse historique. In 1931, Berr dropped "historique" from the title of his review, a tacit admission that the task of historical synthesis had passed to the *Annales.*

Caught up in his "crusade," Febvre poured his combative advocacy into the *Annales.* These were the most frenetic years of "Febvre militant," as Peter Burke describes him. He turned out scores of articles and reviews but completed no major work before 1942. In 1933, he took over the editorship of the *Encyclopédie Française,* an onerous task to which he devoted much effort; and he accepted as well a newly established chair of history at the Collège de France. In his inaugural address he made the point that Michelet had in effect been the last holder of the chair and that his own appointment signaled the end of "positivist" history and the re-emergence of the "general" historian: *"Historie science de l'Homme; . . . les textes, oui; mais ce sont des textes humains."*

By 1940, the *Annales,* fruit of the constant collaboration and deep friendship of Febvre and Bloch, was firmly established in the scholarly world and an *Annales* "school" had begun to emerge which assured the review's continued success. Febvre himself never sought to establish a school: "I have no school. Why? Because I have never stressed the importance of formulas, because I have never wished to constrain any mind. On the contrary, I wished to free them, to give them the living power to discover and to judge."

The outbreak of World War II ended Febvre's collaboration with Bloch, who re-enlisted in the army. Febvre carried on the *Annales* as best he could and found time to produce three books between 1942 and 1944: *Le problème de l'incroyance au XVIe siècle* (a selection from which is included below); *Origène et des Périers;* and *Autour de l'Heptaméron.* All three were examples of what Febvre called "psychological history," by which he understood his own particular way of grasping historical reality entire. Such an approach, Febvre maintained, would enable historians to perceive the world of "sensibility" experienced by men in the past, their "affective life," their hopes, fears, loves, hates, beliefs. To reconstitute that "affective" world, the historian had to draw upon linguistics, ethnology, philosophy, iconology, literary analysis, and psychology. Febvre added such disciplines to his own vast erudition, his mastery of theology, and his empathy for emotional "climate," in writing these three works, of which *Le problème de l'incroyance* is the chief. It is his masterpiece and his most representative work.

After 1945 and Bloch's death, Febvre stood alone, surrounded by his younger *Annalistes.* These are the years of "the Febvre Pontificate," in H. Stuart Hughes's phrase. He continued his editorship of the *Annales;* from 1945 to 1950 he served as a French delegate to UNESCO; he presided over the establishment of the now famous "Sixth Section" of the École Pratique des Hautes Études, rather like the institutionalization of his beloved *Semaines de synthèse;* and he maintained to the very end his splendid, often splenetic enthusiasm for a history that would combine the generous warmth of a

Michelet with the rigorous science of a Durkheim. It is fitting that the collection of his essays and reviews, *Combats pour l'histoire* (published in 1953, three years before his death), closes with a call for "A New Kind of History" *("Vers une autre histoire")*. There Febvre envisions the day "when people will talk about 'history laboratories' as real things, without raising a smile," when "well-trained, well-structured teams" will conduct "co-ordinated investigations." Using microfilms, maps, statistics, graphs, and linguistic, psychological, ethnological, archeological, and botanical materials, the director of the teams "will be able to map out any investigation, put the right questions, point to precise sources of information" in order "to look for solutions to the great problems of life which societies and civilizations came up against daily."

This is a noble, some would say grandiose, conception of history and historical method. That Bloch's *Feudal Society* and Febvre's own *Problem of Unbelief* were, as J. H. Hexter notes, "produced by methods wholly artisanal" did not dampen Febvre's enthusiasm for organized team efforts. Critics of the *Annales* school have charged it with mechanizing and depersonalizing if not dehumanizing history, and of transforming it into a form of cultural anthropology. Febvre was alert to these criticisms but steadfastly believed that his program was compatible with the preservation of individualistic and humanistic values: "Being a historian means never resigning oneself. It implies trying everything, testing out anything that might possibly fill in the gaps in our information. It means exercising one's ingenuity, that is the word." If he himself never succeeded in fusing art and science into a "new history," he certainly succeeded in impelling others to make the effort. It is no denigration of his achievement to stress that his "school," fruitful and important as it is today, remains but one of many mansions in the house of history. Febvre himself never lost sight of his own historically conditioned circumstances: "We may talk of the general trend of history toward other goals and other achievements, but life itself will have the last word on the details of its successes and failures."

Selected Bibliography

Certainly the best introduction to Febvre, man and historian, is his collection *Combats pour l'histoire* (1953): "Not my combats," he writes, "but combats for history; it is for history that all my life I have fought." Another collection demonstrates Febvre's wide influence: *Hommage à Lucien Febvre. Eventail de l'histoire vivante offert par l'amitie d'Historiens, Linguistes, Géographes, Économistes, Sociologues, Ethnologues* (1953); it has an informative, affectionate preface by Fernand Braudel, "Présence de Lucien Febvre."

Peter Burke has recently edited a number of Febvre's essays, *A New Kind of History: From the Writings of Lucien Febvre* (translated by K. Folca, 1973).

Burke's short introduction is excellent. Fernand Braudel's "Personal Testimony," *Journal of Modern History,* 44:4 (December, 1972), 448–467, includes many personal observations on Febvre and his work. H. Stuart Hughes has a useful section on Febvre, Bloch, and their milieu in his *The Obstructed Path: French Social Thought in the Years of Desperation, 1930–1960* (1966). Jean Glénisson, *La Recherche historique en France de 1940 à 1965* (1965), is essential. Glénisson points to the apparent paradox that a handful of individuals succeeded against institutionalized resistance in forcing the acceptance of an interpretation that was generally hostile to the role of individuals in history. But Fernand Braudel responds that "this little stream, narrow and lively, from the *synthèse* to the *Annales,* ran through a vast countryside, during a particular epoch of history. . . . Is it by chance that Henri Berr, Lucien Febvre, Marc Bloch, and myself all four came from eastern France? That the *Annales* began at Strasbourg, next door to Germany and to German political thought?" ("Personal Testimony," 467.)

Martin Siegel's "Henri Berr's *Revue de Synthèse Historique,"* in *History and Theory,* IX: 3 (1970) is an intelligent essay. Palmer A. Throop's "Lucien Febvre, 1878–1956," in *Some Twentieth Century Historians,* edited by S. William Halperin (1961), is a useful survey. An acerbic and penetrating analysis of the *Annales* and of Febvre's greatest pupil is J. H. Hexter's "Fernand Braudel and the *Monde Braudellien . . . ," Journal of Modern History,* 44:4 (December, 1972), 480–539. On the matter of "team research," see F. M. Powicke's restrained essay, "The Limits of Effective Co-operation in the Synthesis of History," *Modern Historians and the Study of History,* pp. 200–205, and Richard Cobb's unrestrained but telling view, "Historians in White Coats," *Times Literary Supplement,* December 3, 1971, 1527–1528.

It should be noted that the *Annales d'histoire économique et sociale* became the *Annales d'histoire sociale,* then the *Mélanges d'histoire sociale,* before adopting its present title, *ANNALES,* subtitled "Économies, Sociétés, Civilisations."

THE PROBLEM OF UNBELIEF
IN THE SIXTEENTH CENTURY

Were There Philosophical Bases for Irreligion in the Sixteenth Century?

Sixteenth-century philosophy does not stand in high repute among our contemporary philosophers. Even the best writers persist in finding it both chaotic and intellectually feeble: "A pullulation of doctrines," Bréhier terms it in his recent *History of Philosophy;* "a pullulation of doctrines and concepts that we may see emerging throughout the Middle Ages but which hitherto had been repressed; a confused mixture that might be called 'naturalism' because generally it subjected neither the universe nor human conduct to any transcendental law but sought only immanent laws." And it is with contempt that this historian of philosophy (Need we ask if contempt is a proper attitude for a historian?) judges the "confused naturalism" that he diagnoses in terms so disconcertingly value-laden. For after all, the historian has trouble enough understanding matters without the added task of judging their worth and value. This mass, he tells us, contains "along with quite viable and fertile concepts the worst intellectual monstrosities." *Et voilà.*

However, before posing difficult problems or embracing possible points of view on the philosophy of the men of the Renaissance, it would be preferable first to remind ourselves that the history of science, of reason itself, is constructed from pieces of patterns, from strongly contrasted tonalities, from a series of theses and attitudes which are not only distinguishable one from the other but also oppose and contradict each other. Each aspect entails some portion of truth, allowance being made for the circumstances of time, place, social conditions, and intellectual atmosphere which explain its emergence and content. To the extent that we can thus justify these contrasts and contradictions we may understand why, circumstances having changed, each thesis, each mental atti-

From *Le problème de l'incroyance au XVIe siècle: La religion de Rabelais,* a volume in the series "L'Evolution de l'Humanité" (Paris: Editions Albin Michel, 1962), pp. 383–414, 500–501. Translated by Gerald J. Cavanaugh. Translated by permission of the publisher.

tude, had to give way to others. Only this way may we evaluate the persistent effort of human intelligence reacting to the pressure of events, to the force of circumstances. That is truly the task of the historian.

I. THE INTELLECTUAL APPARATUS OF THE TIME

Let us thus begin by posing some questions concerning milieu, social conditions, and intellectual possibilities. And, getting to the essential point, let us formulate a problem, simple in appearance but whose elements in regard to the sixteenth century no one has yet cared to assemble: the problem of knowing what clarity, what penetration, what efficacy (in our opinion) inhered in the thought of Frenchmen who, in their speculations, used none of those common words which suggest themselves to us whenever we begin to philosophize and whose absence from the language implies not only a hindrance but truly a deficiency or lacuna in any thought.

1. Words Which Were Lacking

Neither *absolute* nor *relative;* neither *abstract* nor *concrete;* neither *confused* nor *complex;* neither *adequate* (which Spinoza loved, but in Latin) nor *virtual* (which Chapelain used but only around 1660); neither *insoluble, intentional, intrinsic, inherent, occult, primitive, sensitive* (all words of the eighteenth century); nor *transcendental* (which adorned Bossuet's periods around 1698). None of these words, which I draw randomly from our dictionaries and Brunot's *History of the French Language,* none of them belong to the vocabulary of sixteenth-century men, not even, to emphasize the point, to the richest vocabulary of all, that of Rabelais.

Still, these are only adjectives, a few adjectives. What of the nouns? How many of them are missing? Neither *causality* nor *regularity;* neither *concept* nor *criteria;* neither *condition* (before the *Logic of Port Royal*) nor *analysis,* nor *synthesis,* nor *deduction* (which then meant only *narration*), nor *induction* (which appeared only in the nineteenth century); not even *intuition* (used first by Descartes and Leibniz); neither *coordination* nor *classification* ("This barbarous word only recently coined" notes Férand's *Dictionary* in 1787): none of these common words, words which we find absolutely necessary to philosophy, none of them figured in the vocabulary of Rabelais' contemporaries. They did not even have the term to express what only since the middle of the seventeenth century men have called a *system;* nor, naturally, did they have words to label and to enumerate (that is, in order to be able to grasp instantly and utilize intellectually) those elements of the "systems" that most mattered to men of that time, and especially to those we label "rationalists." *Rationalism* itself only appears much later, in the nineteenth century; *deism* hardly begins its career before Bossuet, one of its first users; *theism* is an eighteenth-century borrowing from the English; *pantheism* may be found during the Regency, taken from Toland's works; *materialism* had to await Voltaire, La Mettrie, and Diderot's *Encyclopedia* before being generally accepted; *naturalism* appears in the Trévoux *Dictionary* in 1752 (after first being used by La Mettrie in 1748); *fatalism* is also found in La Mettrie, but *fatalist* had to await the publication of Diderot's novel in 1796; *determinism* is a latecomer, a Kantian term; *optimism* appears in the eighteenth century (Trévoux, 1752), but *pessimists* arrive only in 1835, in the *Dictionary of the Academy,* and *pessimism* appears even later; *skepticism,* used by Diderot, only then began to replace the venerable *Pyrrhonism,* dear to Balzac and Pascal; *fideism* emerges in 1835, out of theological controversies. And how many others: *idealism* (Trévoux), *stoicism* (La Bruyère), *quietism* (Nicole, Bossuet), *puritanism* (Bossuet), and so on. Let us always remember, before judging our philosophers, that none of these words were available to thinkers in the sixteenth century when they wished to philosophize in French for fellow Frenchmen.

Nonconformists though they were (and *conformist* is Bossuet's word), they did not even have an appropriate term to distinguish themselves and around which to rally. *Libertine* appeared late in the century and *libertinism* only in the seventeenth century (La Noue and Charron). *Free thinker* is launched only in the eighteenth century, with Helvétius, and *free thought* was conceived by Voltaire in his *Essay on Tolerance* (1763). But *tolerance* itself triumphs (thanks again to Voltaire) only in the midst of the century of *toleration,* that product of the early years of the same century; *intolerance* had already appeared, in the works of Montesquieu and d'Argenson. Again, *irreligious* is from the style of Port Royal, and *controversalist* is Pascal's; *orthodoxy* and *heterodoxy* are also of the seventeenth century (Naudé and Furetière).

Let us note incidentally that the ancestors of the Libertines of the age of Louis XIII did not have in their language such words as *observatory, telescope, magnifying glass, lens, microscope, barometer, thermometer,* and *motor.* These verbal lacunae must be emphasized because the idea which at each moment in their history presents itself to men as a valid explanation of things—and thus becomes confused with the actual truth —this idea accords with the technical means available to modify and predict the course of those same things. Thus we are justified in insisting on the vocabulary, as yet so poorly defined, of the sciences contemporary to *Pantagruel,* whether of chemistry, at that time still immersed in alchemy; or of biology, which does not attain true scientific status until the nineteenth century; or of astronomy, not yet differentiated from astrology and, before the seventeenth century or, more often, the eighteenth, devoid of such terms as *attraction, orbit, ellipse, parabola, revolution, rotation, constellation,* and *nebula.* Even the French mathematical vocabulary remains so deformed, so poor, and so vague that Pascal in 1654 was unable to formulate a problem in French and had to fall back on Latin because, as he wrote so often, "the French is useless here."

Pascal's is a serious charge. The words available to men when they reasoned in French on the sciences—or when they reasoned at all—were not words made for such reasoning, for explication and demonstration: savants' words. They were rather everyman's words, the current, living language. "Accordion words," so to speak, whose meaning could be expanded or contracted, modified or evolved with a freedom denied to truly scientific terms which must remain exact and unchanging in meaning. Charles Nicolle, for one, has criticized this practice, as he puts it, of making slaves of words, of chaining them irrevocably to a certain meaning. Perhaps it is slavery. But without such constraints how can we give to thought a vigor, solidity, and clarity that is truly philosophical?

2. Syntax and Perspective.

The vocabulary thus outlined, what of syntax? Certainly, old French, that concrete, impressionistic, and naïve French of the twelfth century in which the verb, master of the game, is enthroned in second position and from there contemplates the other elements of the sentence which revolve around it like satellites, this old French was far from the level of the sixteenth century with its anarchic liberty, the disorder of its constructions, and, so difficult for us to grasp, the continual confusion of time patterns, simple and complex:

> La dame le veut retenir
> Par le mantel l'avoit saisi,
> Que les attaches en rompit. . . .

We have an impression of eccentricity and incoherence. It reminds one of novice photographers who, faced with the scene to be filmed, ceaselessly leap and move about with their equipment; but the impression is no less disagreeable when the operator decides (as happened often in the Middle Ages) to employ one temporal scale to depict events which do not all unfold, at all times, at the same pace or moment. In a word, an absence of perspective and, thus, difficulties in interpreting the confused design of these venerable authors. They evoke in some imprecise words an object, a person, a scene. They leave it to the reader to classify, to order, and to make precise the image so presented.

Undoubtedly, great progress had been made by the end of the fifteenth century. The increasing number of forms brought under the leveling rule of analogy; the two-case system (subject-object) abolished and, consequently, the introduction into phrases of a more rigorous constructive order, permitting a sure distinction of subject from object; the verb surrendering its primacy, little by little, to the subject; in brief, and translated into grammatical terms, clear symptoms of a progressive organization of thought, an organization whose transformations both reflect and facilitate change. The same holds true for perspective, which gradually becomes a need and then an instinct for writers. Just as their entire vision of the world (and ours) was insensibly modified, so a more regular usage, more concordant with concepts of time, allowed writers progressively to introduce order into their thought and perspective, profundity even, into their accounts.

Clearly all was not perfect at the turn of the fifteenth century. Ferdinand Brunot loves to cite an example from Commines' narration of the battle of Montlhèry: "The cannon [writes the chronicler without astonishment] killed a trumpet [*sic*] bearing a plate of food up the steps." One may cite many other examples from Commines, including a phrase in which he states: "And that imagination gave them the obscurity of the times"; or this impressionistic note: "The king arrived one morning by sea close to us, abundantly horsed on the river bank." . . . But we should not conclude that all is clarified and ordered in the sixteenth century. . . . Observe Brantôme: "I came forward, when I spoke of it with Rochefoucaut, only to beg the king, in order not to be labeled traitor, by one of my friends, in order to withdraw elsewhere whither I should be happier than in his realm." The phrase does not testify to a great aptitude for logical development of thoughts.

What of chronology? It remains irregular, often quite irregular: "They said they do not go" is hardly clear. And Jean d'Auton's phrase is a maze: "The said letters that the said lieutenant of the King sent him, from which things were very angry at the Boullongnoys, saying that he will destroy them, if it need be by arms on the spot, and that, rightly, had deserved cruel punishment. . . ." One would say that a child was playing with a magnifying glass, looking through first the convex then the concave lens and continually changing his point of view. Moreover, the word order is not strictly fixed. The verb is frequently placed before the subject: "provoked him have his sons and daughters" and "there awaited the monks the abbot." Again, the object often precedes the verb: "The same shade had the dawn and the roses." Sturel's fluent translation of Plutarch may be contrasted to other of his works which show how even with the best writers sixteenth-century French retained the tendency to place both essential ideas and secondary details on the same plane, through an almost complete absence of subordination. . . .

Prolix, verbose, too often devoid of rhythm and charm, French was a language of peasants who rarely spoke—but when the occasion for speaking arose they spoke interminably, reveling in explications, incidents, details, and circumstances because they are ill-prepared to unravel the threads of their own thought; because they have time, plenty of time, all the time in the world; and finally . . . because everything in the language is charged with heavy meaning and secret magic. It is not surprising, then, that they were incapable of adopting the concision of the classical writers; on the contrary, they lengthen it, they expand it. Amyot, faced with a Greek word easily translated by one French term, always offers two: "his power and his army"; "his house and his goods." In brief, that work has only begun which will end in the style of Louis XIII that Lanson describes, with its solid sentences, slowly unfolding: the sentence showing thought working toward order, taking care above all to be rigorously connected, in which words, arranged in a logical order based on relatives, conjunctions, and present participles, evoke "the chiseled stone encompassing the bricks of the structures of the Place Royale."

Powerful constraints and heavy burdens on thought: no one escaped them. Huguet, rather naïvely, poses this question concerning Rabelais: "How is it that this great writer did not take as much liberty with syntax as he did with vocabulary?" Simply because he could not. Not because, as Huguet surmises, "it is ordinarily not in syntax that one finds originality"; syntax does not depend upon one man, even a genius. It is in its way a social institution; it is an entity itself and reflects a historical time and a social group—not an individual writer. And each epoch, each group, has, in large measure, the syntax it deserves, that is to say the syntax that accords with the level of intellectual development and scientific knowledge.

Action and reaction. The state of the language inhibits the growth of thought, but the push of thought, in spite of all, bursts the boundaries of language, breaks them, enlarges them. But even if the men of the sixteenth century had had a language better adapted to the needs of philosophical and religious speculation, what would they have done in the absence of a richer and better developed science? Some experts have recently criticized Copernicus for having impaired his system by trying to render it too precisely. Others, no less qualified, have insisted on "the benefits of imprecision," noting that "Kepler would not have discovered his laws if he had been more precise." Evidently the conditions of speculation are not the same in all epochs. There are some times when it is necessary to risk, to invent, before moving forward. Afterwards, one sees (or sees once again). Language and thought: that is the problem posed as it were to the tailor of an unusable garment, namely that he must unceasingly readjust his material on the body of a client in perpetual transformation; sometimes the garment hangs too loosely, sometimes the client is too tightly bound. They must accommodate themselves to each other, and they do, but only gradually. Language often serves as a barrier, if not a dam, whence it happens in intellectual history that much philosophical water is held back until one day it quite suddenly breaks through the dam, sweeping all before it.

3. The Objection of Latin

People may say of the above, "You are playing with words! Did not the sixteenth century have Latin? And when people philosophized, was it not in the language of Cicero, their master not only in writing but in thought?"

Undoubtedly, all men of those times who speculated (all or almost all, the "almost all" put in only as a scruple or in due regard to Bernard Palissy), all men were bilingual. Or, if they were not, they were embarrassed. Ronsard, among many others, understood this:

> Frenchmen who would read my lines,
> If they are neither Greeks nor Romans,
> Will have, instead of my book,
> Only a weight in their hands.

But, speaking Latin, did people then think in Latin? Even when they tried to resuscitate the language, to render it as living as possible, Latin thought remained dead. Insofar as they imposed it on themselves it could only inhibit their intellectual growth. It enslaved them to archaic fashions of thinking and feeling, fashions that were dead or, if you wish, obsolete and out of phase. Their civilization, we know, was saturated with Christian ideas and sentiments. They extended themselves to introduce, very laboriously, into these ideas and sentiments others which at least in part contradicted them, or if you will, others which ought to have or should have contradicted them.

Thus, let us try to translate into Latin most of the concepts that Frenchmen did not have French words with which to express themselves. *Absolute?* But *absolutus* could not suffice; it had no philosophical use. *Abstract?* But *abstractus* meant isolated or separate . . . similarly, *relative.* The Latin *pertinens ad* meant something else and the Low Latin *relativus* had hardly any grammatical sense. Nor can we speak of *transcendental* (or scarcely of *transcendent,* in the philosophical sense of superior, excellent, sublime). This is to say nothing of the whole series of names of systems marked by *ism.*

One can always maneuver a bit, I know, to seek equivalents, to use paraphrases, to translate one clear word by twenty. But, I emphasize, to translate an idea one must already possess it. Whoever has not the word in French does not attempt to render it in Latin. Finally, if we attempt to express the idea of determinism by a long paraphrase (as the good Goelzer does in his *Dictionnaire Francis-Latin: doctrina qua rerum universitas ex causus aliis ex alliis nexis necessario constant*), it is because we have had in France in the nineteenth and twentieth centuries classes in philosophy and professors of philosophy who have transmitted to us both the word and the concept it expresses. But to explicate that concept, to translate it, would have been impossible for sixteenth-century men who had neither a baccalaureat in philosophy nor one in mathematics, and from their solitary efforts the common, current, and almost vulgar notion of determinism that we all effortlessly possess from our youth would never have emerged. Such a concept is derived from more than the work of one man.

We could go on discussing innovations such as the compass, the cannon, the printing press, which the Latinizers of the sixteenth century could label in Latin only at the cost of subtle and lengthy effort, veritable linguistic contortions, involving much exaggeration and no little illusion. Granted that no one in the universities, no master would have had much difficulty in inducting the most vulgar of vulgar words into Latin —and ending up with phrases like this: *Placuit nationi remediare et obviare abusibus commissis vel committendis per nuntios nationis; vult specialiter quod fiat una distincta tabula omnium dioceseon*—which is a professor's Latin, and: *capis me pro alio; parvus garsonus bavat super sese; ego bibi unum magnum vitrium totum plenum de vino*—which is a student's Latin. Let us simply note that such practices tended to rob Latin of its character of an international language. The student in Tübingen would have been as surprised by *favat super ses* as Pantagruel hearing the oracular remarks of the student of Limousin. But the real difficulty is not here. It begins when one must "get inside of occult ideas," as the poet wrote.

The *cap* or *beret* was there; *birettus* or *birrus* in the jargon of students; *mortar* was in the language of militarists *(bombarda),* and *laced shoes (solutares ad laqueos)* and *straw hats (capellae de fultro)* were familiar terms to the dandies of Navarre College. Every common object was literally there to be named in Latin but what of words for ideas and concepts? Where were they? At the disposition of thinkers? Here we have a vicious circle. If they were really there, at least potentially, flowing over the threshold of philosophical knowledge, was Latin, a language made to express the intellectual processes of a civilization dead for more than a thousand years, capable of playing midwife to ideas trembling to be born?

Certainly Latin had served theologians and Scholastics in expressing thoughts never conceived of by Greeks and Romans—nevertheless, they applied themselves to the task of rejoining the ancient flock, as soon as they found themselves out of the fold, and of availing themselves of Aristotle's mantle whenever and insofar as they could. But new needs, needs for purity and accuracy were born; a strict notion of "barbarism" had combined with a no less strict notion of "solecism"; philologists had begun their task of captious censure, one it is easy but naïve to criticize. These men knew what they were about; I speak of Lorenzo Valla, Erasmus, Budé. And after all, in constraining their contemporaries (who did not ask for more and, nine times out of ten, were their enthusiastic accomplices) to return to the purity and correctness of classical Latin, they ended one equivocation. They placed ancient philosophy in the classical past and cleared the field for new constructions. Without wanting to, they facilitated the use of languages living and full of vigor. They opened the door to "modern" philosophies.

4. One Example: The Infinite

Of the many difficulties which sixteenth-century men encountered we select but one, a telling example, however. Malebranche's affirmation in his *Researches* (III, ii, 6) is well known: "The most beautiful, the most exalted, the most impressive, and the primary proof of the existence of God is that which implies the least of things, the idea of the infinite." The infinite: certainly, one may speak in Latin of *infinitas* or of *infinitio.* Certainly. But let us look a little closer.

At one extreme, the Greeks. Now, since the Eleates at least. They had proclaimed that the finite in space, the delimited, the perfect in itself, the completed, was the only conceivable form of being, because thought and understanding determined everything. The Latins followed in this; among all the ancients the belief prevailed that the universe was limited in time and space, since the series of causes in nature is dependent upon a first uncaused cause. The ancients similarly shared in the rejection of the infinite and the unlimited, which was also the indeterminate and, as such, marked by imperfection: the area of perfection was that of the limited. Ancient gods, to be perfect, were themselves finite and limited. In sum, for two thousand years the infinite was virtually the sign of deficiency and imperfection.

At the other extreme, the Scholastics and their idea of an infinite God —fruit of another idea, that of an unlimited Universe or of an infinite void which envelops the Universe, an idea which was not totally foreign to the first Greek philosophers but which did not win acceptance until shortly before the Christian era. It served to introduce the notion of an

Infinite Being, on which metaphysical and theological reflection unceasingly exercised itself from the beginning of the first century: a Being infinite not only in quantity but in power, surpassing all that we may ever conceive, and from the first, having an equally infinite grandeur, power, intelligence, and will. From that starting point, Scholastic thought began to sketch the argument that Kant later called the ontological argument, and which in the seventeenth century curiously gave rise to metaphysical speculations. However, skeptics also utilized the concept of infinity, stressing its obscurities in order to confound the claims of rationalism.

Now, if sixteenth-century men had continued to follow the path traced by the men of the twelfth, thirteenth, and fourteenth centuries; if they had continued to express themselves as had their forebears, with the words of a Scholastic Latin which was distancing itself more and more, in body and soul, from classical Latin; if they had not declared war, as it were, on both the way of thinking and the style of writing of their fathers and grandfathers; if they had not wished to break with their modes of reasoning and their allegedly barbarous language (leaving aside the question of how effectively they actually did break with the immediate past); if they had not ventured beyond Christianity, theology, and Scholasticism, to return to the sources, to the true sources of classical thought and especially to Cicero, more studied and emulated than ever before as a philosopher, more studied and emulated than ever before as a writer: then there would have been few or no difficulties. But, in fact, they chose otherwise. They dreamed of a total revolution. With singular verve, they declared war on their past, and by an act whose lack of logic they appeared not to have perceived, they undertook to innovate by vaulting beyond the immediate past, the Christian Middle Ages, in order to plunge directly and totally into the more distant past, pagan antiquity.

In such an embarrassing situation there was in truth only one way out, and some people did not deceive themselves about it. "If I write in French," Descartes wrote, "which is my native tongue, rather than in Latin, which is that of my teachers, it is because I hope that those who avail themselves only of their natural powers of reason will better judge my opinions than those who trust only in the writings of antiquity." With that explanation, the *Discourse on Method* concludes. Clearly, one could not do better than oppose to the fatal sterility of traditional thought, enclosed in its Latin strait jacket, the revolutionary fecundity of "pure natural reason" using an instrument appropriate to its needs. But that instrument had previously to be forged, and it is no accident that only around 1600 philosophy numbered two considerable thinkers who expressed themselves in French, Du Vair and Charron. The true philosopher followed: René Descartes. After him, there were no longer any philosophers in France who expressed themselves in Latin.

Theologians had already been alerted to this great change. The insistence with which Evangelicals and sixteenth-century Reformers claimed for each of the faithful the right to read in his native tongue, in "vulgar French," and not only in Vulgate Latin, the most sacred texts of his religion, the Bible—this insistence astonishes us. It betrays a fundamental malaise. These men dimly felt that between the Word which they saw as the Word of Life and the living souls whom they urged to receive it there interposed a screen of supplementary obstacles, a screen derived not merely from a dead language but more specifically from a language that for centuries expressed and preserved a philosophy profoundly hostile to everything preached by that same Word: a philosophy of the persecutors of Christianity, of men who had wanted, when Christianity manifested itself, to suppress it forever.

II. THE TWO PHILOSOPHIES

All that being said, we may now return with greater possibilities of understanding to our philosophers of the sixteenth century and, asking pardon for some perhaps disparaging remarks, pose some questions that are precise in their thrust. Precise, and thus without exaggerated ambitions. What is the meaning, and we do not say "of the philosophy of the Renaissance"—that would be posing a great, a much too great question —but rather, what is the common meaning (if there is one) that may be drawn from among all those "swarming and pullulating philosophers," as Bréhier called them, who appear in the West at the end of the fifteenth and the beginning of the sixteenth century? Even so restricted, denying in advance any hopes of a "synthesis," the question poses an enormous problem that is beyond solution. But it has been asked many times and we will not turn it aside without a serious examination, after which we will turn to another no less redoubtable question. Of a practical turn, it appears a very simple one, but it is nonetheless particularly difficult to resolve. It involves at one and the same time a logical and a rational problem and a problem of psychology and sentiment: to be precise, it involves the very great question of "sincerity."

How did these philosophers, whose common tendencies and principles we are trying to discover, if at all possible, reconcile themselves not only theoretically but practically to the Christianity which pervaded all men's lives at that time? And if it appears that in their principles they were not Christians, how did these men who professed and propagated such principles reconcile their philosophical speculations with their submission as believers to the Church? May one say, with brutal frankness, that they so reconciled themselves with the aid of hypocrisy, that they lied, and that their apparent submission to Christianity was only an act of cowardice, prudence, and pretense?

1. Greek Philosophy and Christian Faith: A Conflict?

Every synthesis of "Renaissance philosophy" appears uneasy, troubled. This is to be expected. As the late and regretted historian of philosophy, Leon Blanchet, wrote in his study of *Campanella* (1920), how can we summarize in one formula "the thought of a transitional age which was still seeking its way and which did not succeed in giving its ideas the order and harmony proper to ages of equilibrium and organization?" It has been tried, however, and more than once: in Italy especially, where scholars have quite naturally accorded a particular attention to the Renaissance. Thus, in a study of Pomponazzi (1868) and in another work on Telesio (1872), which preceded his two-volume *Historical Studies* on the idea of nature in the Renaissance, Fiorentino noted throughout the Middle Ages and other epochs, "a coherent effort to investigate the supernatural world: species and types beyond the individual; matter and form underneath their manifest union; God behind all things; the intellect beyond the soul—and the true virtue which broods over life." In a word, Fiorentino defined the Middle Ages as the era of transcendence and the Renaissance, on the contrary, as the age of the restoration or the establishment of immanence. In one vast perspective he delineates the whole continuum of those thinkers that may be labeled medieval, from Proclus, that forefather, to Ockham, all attempting to deny nature while extolling the spirit; after which, at the close of the fourteenth century, by an inverse movement, the Renaissance thinkers appear and attempt to affirm the spirit in the midst of nature.

These are great constructs, true and false at the same time, as are all such massive and poorly analyzed concepts: *the* Middle Ages, *the* Renaissance, not to speak of *the* Transcendent and its rival *the* Immanent. At least they have the merit in general of posing problems, of exciting reflection, of requiring a response or a further development. This is what took place in Italy itself when, in a new essay on Telesio and in a survey of the relationships of Scholasticism and the new philosophies, Giovanni Gentile maintained that in fact the conflict was not between immanence and transcendence, those creatures of reason, but rather between Greek philosophy and Christian thought.

This was a historian's view and as such could not leave us indifferent. It is a fact that the "men of the Renaissance," in employing that clichéd but fitting formula, took the ancients and especially the ancient Greeks as their master in philosophy. The Greeks, through the interpretative translations that the Romans made of original systems—for example, Lucretius, adopting and adapting the physics and psychology of Epicurus; Cicero, encompassing in brilliant and beautifully written dialogues his academic eclecticism; and Seneca, popularizing a Stoic morality whose rigor he humanely tempered. But the Greeks were also studied directly, in Greek, by men eager to expand their horizons, to return to the original sources, to read the true Plato, the true Aristotle; the Greeks, whom these men did not abruptly discover: it is superfluous to say, no doubt, that Greek thought had for a long time permeated Scholastic systems. Étienne Gilson has proclaimed that Greek thought in the Renaissance was not hostile to Christian dogma but rather, in assisting Erasmus in the writing of his *Enchiridion* and his *Paraclesis,* it helped to purify Christianity of such excessive and divergent Greek philosophies as the Platonic, Pythagorean, Academic, and Stoic. But precisely, the aim of Erasmus attests to the scope of the curiosity that spurred the bold ambitions of the humanists; a curiosity which moreover led beyond its immediate objects, because these unpolished men of our French sixteenth century—unpolished in their ferocious capacity for work, their astonishing manifestation of the asceticism of autodidacts, their triumphant fervor in their efforts, miseries, even in catastrophes—it is not Aristotle or Plato, Plutarch or Epictetus whom they seek in the *Morals* or in the *Enneads,* in the *Organon* or in the *Timeus:* it is themselves they seek to discover in these works, at once clear and difficult, obscure and brilliant; themselves and the reasons for their living, believing, and acting in a world which was created for them, before them, and by them. Hellenic thought was assimilated, yes, but in order to transcend it, to go beyond it. And let us not reproach them for having taken up as their own, for example, the synthesis of Empedocles, the theory of the four elements—air, water, earth, fire, along with love and hate—and joining to it the concept of the four fundamentally opposite qualities: the dry and the wet, heat and cold, which for centuries signified the victory of quality over quantity. Let us not reproach them, because for two thousand years those concepts were invoked in physics as in cosmology and in alchemy, and for two centuries more, until Lavoisier, they continued to inform chemistry and medicine. No, we do not reproach them: but we see that it is because of the Greeks that a Copernicus, however reluctant to innovate, could derive the first seeds of his hypothesis, the point of departure for his reflections. He went much further, yes, but others first brought him to the extreme limits of their universe.

Now this love of Greek thought among the men of the Renaissance raises an important question. It is precisely the one that Étienne Gilson posed when he depicted Erasmus suffering to see about him so many Greeks and so few Christians, angry to see the impious comparison made of Christ and Aristotle, and furious against the corruption worked by the Hellenic mind on that Christian doctrine of which Saint Paul observed that it had conquered with its foolishness the wisdom of the world. This problem was precisely the one that Gentile addressed and sought to solve in the works cited above.

Greek philosophy, he wrote, is "thought seeing beyond itself, seeing itself in Nature, in immediate sensibility, or as Idea. But among the Greeks the Idea is not the act of thinking; it is an entity on which thought fixes itself and which it presumes as eternally true, as the eternal reason of all reality and of consciousness itself, alongside of the vicissitudes of things in general; in one hypothesis after another, this Idea is a reality which is itself what it is, independent of the relations that thought establishes with it when it perceives it."

This, Gentile notes, is a tragic conception—"the saddest of all that the human soul could formulate concerning its own existence in the world" —since the soul sees in fact, or, if you prefer, in faith, the real existence of which it thinks and affirms. But, in the Greek view, truth, real truth, does not reside in man's soul; it is beyond the grasp of the man who, as in the Platonic myth of Eros, labors mightily to seize it, to embrace its true essence—only to see it escape all efforts to encompass it. Truth remains estranged from the world of man, being in its immutable perfection inaccessible to him. Consequently, Greek science, whose conditions Aristotle analyzed so marvelously in his logic, that science is not like ours, a body of knowledge acquired by man, an instrument of understanding and of domination forged by an active and conquering intelligence. No, it is not that science which is fashioned and refashioned continually throughout history; it is rather a science which uncovers first principles, encompasses them, links them together as concepts whose unity constitutes all that is knowable; it is a science which does not evolve, which neither waxes nor wanes, which excludes history—because, *ab initio,* it is in itself identical with absolute perfection.

Christianity quite clearly opposed such conceptions as false. In God's manifestation as a man in this world is implied the restitution to man of his full worth; God becoming man rendered mankind a partaker of divine nature. God Himself submitted to all of humanity's misery, including the last: death. Love was thus no longer what it had been in the Platonic myth, a fervid contemplation of the ineffable. It was the very work of man, reconstituting itself eternally. It was no longer the ecstatic celebration of a world which is, but an ongoing celebration of a world which makes and remakes man, a man who is much less intelligence and wisdom than love and will, a man who creates the truth within himself —a truth mixed with the good and which, far from being exterior to us, is made part of us when we seek after a pure heart and a good will, with sincerity and innocence. This is a great transformation: man is no longer a spectator, he is an agent. He finds himself, and within the bosom of Christianity.

Thus, what of opposition? We have two doctrines or, rather, two conceptions, and they have little in common. And is it to choose between them? No, because there are not two philosophies but only one, and it is in fact a faith. A revealed truth which did not come necessarily, by itself, and immediately, was integrated into a system of speculative thought. In such a case, compromise was essential. Instead of freeing itself from Aristotelian logic, the logic of transcendence, Christian thought throughout the Middle Ages remained linked to Greek concepts.

It was with God made man, to the Son that all thought had primarily to concern itself. But philosophers preferred to orient themselves around the concept of the Father. Very carefully, Christian thought allowed itself to take up again and again the temptations and challenges of Aristotelian metaphysics which yet maintained the very principle of reality existing beyond reality itself. It was in vain that Christian thought attempted to plumb the depths of the abyss, always open before it, which separated the unmoved cause of motion from motion which did not itself contain its sufficient cause; which caused the gulf between the principle of becoming (which never became) and that nature which found in reason neither its generation nor its corruption: let us say, in a word, between the soul and the body, and between the intelligible soul (understanding in action) and the natural soul, that possible intellect which is incapable of knowing anything by itself.

A divorce between matter, the force of everything, and form, the realization of everything; a separation between life and the life's aspiration —these were the insoluble torments of all those—whether Aristotelians or Platonists, realists or nominalists, Averroists or Thomists—who in the course of the Middle Ages were trying to grasp reality and who, frustrated by the very fashion in which they formulated and reformulated the question, did not and could not succeed in apprehending it. In truth, they all were spiritually in the position of Tantalus. Thus, in spite of its efforts, the Middle Ages never succeeded in harmonizing those mystical tendencies which affirmed the immediate presence of God and His Truth in the human mind and spirit (but which at the same time denied the knowledge and understanding that is developmental and systematic) and those philosophical tendencies which, presupposing a reality beyond the mind that seeks it, gave all their care to a construction (formally rich but substantially empty) from which truth could never be derived.

2. Greek Philosophy, Christian Faith: Exchanges

Given all this, it is easy for us to say that the task of the Renaissance was clear, if quite broad. It was to dissolve Scholastic logic, psychology, and physics and to re-establish in their rightful places, within the human soul, not only truth (that daughter of time now recognized as such) but virtue and perfection, both acquired by man and, as it were, tailored to his own measure. The task was to proclaim, to affirm the absolute value both of nature and humanity. Certainly—and we are quite correct in adding it—the Renaissance courageously undertook that task. But with what clarity of mind and purpose? To say that it did so in a modern fashion is another question. Nothing that concerns humanity is simple —let us then be on guard against being simplistic. And let us not go on saying or believing that the Renaissance girded itself against Christianity and offered itself as a self-consciously rival system of thought: that is to falsify history.

And it would be falsification not only because it would require us to believe that by some sort of prodigious miracle Renaissance man was able easily to break the thousands of links by which his thought, sensibilities, and will were connected to Christianity but also—and this is a more serious consideration—because it would make of Christianity itself and of its relations to philosophy (not Greek philosophy but certainly derived from it) a singularly elementary conception. It would be to refuse to understand the eternal play of borrowings and exchanges which link these two terms that we would like to set up as antagonists. It would mean failing to see that those grand syntheses of Ficino and Pico, which we call Hellenic, Aristotelian, or Platonic in inspiration, are all permeated by Christianity and, even if suspect in the eyes of those strict guardians of orthodox, the Church doctors, are all inspired despite their "Greekness" by the spiritual breath of the Gospels. It would be to close our eyes on the singularly illogical role (but then logic has precisely little influence in such matters) on the extremely important role played by the rebirth of Platonic thought in this history of medieval thought in decline and of modern thought in its origins, a historical role in which Rabelais was both artisan and protagonist.

Because if it is true—using a formula of Bréhier's which does not take us far beyond Gentile—that "in spite of all its divergences and diversities there was throughout the Middle Ages but one image or, if you will, one system within which was incorporated all possible images of the Universe" (which system Bréhier defines as "Theocentrism": "from God as principle to God as end and culmination, by way of finite beings"—a formula which one commentator maintains is acceptable "to the most orthodox traditionalist as well as to the most heterodox mystic inasmuch as the order of nature and the order of human conduct are placed necessarily between the principle and its aim")—if it is true there was such a unity, then the revival of Platonism which is evident in so much Renaissance philosophy could only sharpen and solidify in it the notion that "the great task of philosophy is to order matter and mind between God as principle and God as aim."

This, then, at the very moment in which their thought was joyfully nourished with new elements of singular power; at the very moment when, in order to continue the work undertaken resolutely by the Ock-hamists from the fourteenth century on, namely, the study of the facts of nature in and for themselves, a mass of new evidence derived from exploration and discovery appeared—evidence which suddenly and pow-erfully enlarged the old conceptions found in the medieval *Mirror of the World,* in the entire *Weltanschauung* of medieval man; at the very mo-ment when, being launched upon the open ocean thanks to the compass and other inventions, the contemporaries of Columbus and Magellan began to measure, or rather to examine what others among them had already measured, and to examine with a fearful and exultant astonish-ment, the extraordinary consequences of their acquisitions; this at a time when, with their technology and especially their firearms assuring them an easy, crushing, and lasting superiority over people armed only with bows and arrows, they began to exploit the riches of their conquered lands and to draw homeward over prodigious distances the flora and fauna found in them, and, further, to begin to take direct possession of so many people, of so many cultural forms whose ancient structures which had been preserved and carried forward from generation to gener-ation by tradition, were to crack, be dislodged, and finally to evaporate. This, finally, at the very moment when the nascent philological spirit began to apply itself to the exegesis of texts that were not only recovered in their literal sense but permeated by a sense, still tentative, of what we may call history.

A contradiction or, more simply, a compromise: because no one at the time saw any contradiction. It was a time when what were called docu-ments of nature were mixed with or joined to those documents of humanity which comprised the beautiful antique texts. It was a time when techniques began to appear not only as utilitarian but as instru-ments by which to manipulate reality, to capture natural phenomena, to interpret them in order to bend them to the new power of man; it was a time when people could finally, validly, begin effectively to organize the great inquiry into nature that would enable man to elaborate systems alien to the "theocentrism" Bréhier speaks of; it was then that some of the most zealous advocates of such inquiry—Rabelais among others—stubbornly continued to organize his thought around the old themes of which we have spoken: God as the principle. God as the aim and culmi-nation. And between that principle and that end everything and every soul carefully arranged. Why such a singular attitude? Why that illogical combination? Good reasons may be alleged, among which is that philoso-phy then was only opinion. A chaos of opinions, contradictory and shift-ing. Shifting because they lacked a solid and stable base, an assured base which could consolidate them. They lacked, that is to say, science.

III. THE BASES OF IRRELIGION: THE SCIENCES?

The science of that age—as soon as we say it, we smile. We make sport of the unicorn horns over here, of old wives' remedies over there, superstitions, ignorance, credulity everywhere. But we become respectful, we honor a heroic effort, we recur to the old myth of the Renaissance—and we are right so to shift our position.

1. The Old Myth of the Renaissance

An old myth that remains vital, in spite of so many criticisms. In the beginning, antiquity and the science of the ancients, the fertile invention of the Greeks creates the geometry of Euclid, the mechanics of Archimedes, the medicine of Hippocrates and Galen, the cosmography and geography of Ptolemy, the physics and natural history of Aristotle: an amazing range and depth of knowledge that the Greeks passed on to the Romans—after which a descent into night, the profound night of the Middle Ages. The ancient treasure is mislaid if not entirely lost; and then nothing for centuries except syllogistic reasoning and sterile deduction, not one new fertile doctrine, not one important technical invention.

Nothing then, until the end of the fifteenth century, when a new revolution beckoned, one in which men, taking stock of their intellectual poverty, set themselves the task of recovering lost treasures, of finding one by one the artifacts scattered over Europe. In order to use these great rediscovered riches, they taught themselves by a superb effort to read the true classical Latin, classical Greek, and even Hebrew, which was useless for scientific work but indispensable for Biblical exegesis. Then, intoxication: gorged by all of the ancient provender so suddenly placed before them, these humanists set to work. They were assisted by the newly invented printing press and by new maps which abruptly enlarged both their intellectual and physical horizons. Copernicus based himself on Pythagoras, Kepler on Copernicus, and Galileo on Kepler, while Vesalius added the fruits of experience to the Hippocratic tradition.

Thus the old Renaissance myth, in which everything seems so logical, simple, coherent—the old myth we can no longer accept. Not that we regard ourselves as satisfied in knowing that "the men of the Middle Ages" were far from being ignorant of all ancient culture. What matters most is not that Father John or Father Martin or some old Benedictine congregation could read in manuscript in the year 1280 this or that fragment of an ancient classical text; what matters is the fashion in which such scholars read, *really* read the fragment. As we do? Certainly not. Their Christianity did not merely serve to soothe the vast metaphysical anxieties which afflicted the faithful. Animating, informing the great compendiums of the era, the *Mirrors of the World, Views of the World,* and so forth, it encompassed the whole person throughout every stage of his existence, public life as well as private, religious as well as lay. It provided men with coherent notions concerning Nature, Science, History, Morality, Life. And it was in accordance with such notions that men read, interpreted, and assimilated without regard for historical perspective those ancient texts—fragments and residues—that a happy circumstance allowed them to study.

In contrast we have the revolution of humanism. But what in fact was the impact and influence of humanism in the age of the Renaissance on scientific conceptions? Many scholars, among them Lynn Thorndike, have reduced that influence to nothing, or almost nothing. They sustain the plausible thesis that humanism and science developed separately, with no direct interactions. On the one side is humanism, exclusively concerned with texts and writers. This humanism reads Pliny the Elder as it reads Pliny the Younger, citing both with veneration, extolling the knowledge of the uncle as it praises the style of the nephew, and creating, in the Scholastic tradition of Bartholomew of England and Albert of Saxony (both published and republished in emulation of each other by the best printers), a classical tradition, from the start Aristotelian, which does not ever renew itself or anything else. On the other side, there is reality itself. Discoveries, inventions, techniques with which one sets in motion intellectual qualities and reflections that later are to become the qualities and reflections that characterize authentic scientific minds.

Now, between literary and practical knowledge there were few or no contacts. In cartography, for example, we see a growing interrelationship between the precise and detailed information furnished by maps of harbors, those masterpieces of local navigation, and the maps of Ptoleme, with their networks of coordinate points. But did this example encourage emulation among men of the time? Hardly any. We are astonished and moved to admiration when in a book on the Venetian navy in the fifteenth century we unexpectedly encounter a reference to an attempt at the beginning of the century to marry Theory and Practice—and even more astonished, because it is so unusual, to read of such an attempt that succeeded. In 1525 and 1526 when the Venetian Senate was deliberating on the type of navy appropriate for the destruction of pirates, Matteo Bressan, an experienced, practical sailor suggested a certain type of round boat. But Victor Faustus, a renowned Greek scholar and humanist, a student of Greek mathematics and Aristotelian mechanics, dared to embark upon the sea of practice and to offer to the Senate well-conceived plans for the construction of five-tiered galleys. The marvel is that Faustus won the competition, the savant surpassing the "practical" man, to the great rejoicing, one should imagine, of humanists eager to exalt the new Archimedes. . . . It matters little that the ships designed by Faustus did not become popular: a tradition of interaction between theory and practice had been created. [But it was of slow growth.]

. . . One last word. To undertake to make of the sixteenth century a century of skepticism, libertinism, and rationalism, and to extol it as such is to perpetrate the worst of illusions and errors. In the minds of its best representatives it was, quite to the contrary, a century of religious inspiration, one in which all things reflected the Divine.

Consider aesthetics. What feverish secrets in the time of a Renaissance molded by Platonism! "I believe," Bembo wrote to Pico, "that just as there is in God a certain divine form of justice, temperance, and the other virtues, there is also a certain divine form of style, an absolutely perfect model that, so far as they could, Xenophon, Demosthenes, Plato especially, and, more than any other, Cicero had in view when they composed their works. With that image or model conceived in their minds, they applied their style and genius. I think we ought to do likewise: our task is to approach as best we may that image of beauty." The attempt could be made but only by anticipating a mysterious communication of that divine form. That is, without special assistance from on high, Petrarch (in the words of Despautère) would "neither have declared war on the barbarians nor recalled the Muses from their exile, nor revived the cultivation of eloquence."

Consider philosophy. Men reasoned, certainly—and sometimes transcended reason, to the point of irrationality. An exasperated Scholasticism marked all of them. They had all been formed by it in disputation and it could hardly have been otherwise. But did they remain within its bounds? In the case of Aristotle they discovered after many efforts a subtle method by which to reconcile him not only with Plato but also with Plotinus. They impregnated their metaphysics with a mysticism that conferred on pure ideas a sort of bodily solidity and warmth of life. What matter if some among them were tempted either by the confusions of a sensual idealism which added to the seductions of paganism a new touch of perversity, or by the dreams of a visionary credulity which plunged blindly into the labyrinth of occultism. Most of them inhabited, in spirit and desire, not the trivial and burning sphere of the senses, not even the purified realm of rational reason, but a third realm, that in which God resided and which enlivened His creatures, that realm wherein those who searched after Him in all purity of mind would, one less cold and less uncertain day, catch a momentary glimpse of the most high and holy illumination.

This was the source of their ineffable nobility—and also of their weaknesses, since their moral life remained enveloped in the material world.

Their spiritual effort raised them, however, these ecstatic Epicureans, to the highest level of contemplation. There were exceptions, let it be understood. The mysticism of the majority maintained them in sane and stable patterns. Almost too sane and stable when, for example, we consider the man in whom, truly, the beginning of the century is most pleasingly mirrored: Erasmus, who was a trifle Voltairean at times in his irony.

In sum, "the profound religiousness of most of the makers of the modern world": this formula which is apt for someone like Descartes remains even more applicable to those of a century earlier, Rabelais, for example, and for all those for whom he knew how to translate so superbly the "profound faith" of Christianity.

Marc Bloch

1886—1944

6

Marc Bloch was perhaps the most respected and venerated French historian of the first half of the twentieth century. He was also one of the most emulated. His own works are striking in their conceptual originality and in their empirical thoroughness; in cooperation with Lucien Febvre he helped launch French, and more than French, historiography on a new course. His scholarship, his humanity, and his heroic martyrdom at the hands of the Gestapo have combined to render his name imperishable in the annals of historiography.

Bloch was born in 1886 in Lyons, where his father was a distinguished professor of ancient history. The Bloch family was close-knit and intensely patriotic—Marc Bloch was proud to recall that his great-grandfather had fought the Prussian invasion in 1793. From his father he derived his interest in history and especially in the long evolution of French society from Roman Gaul through the medieval period to modernity. In 1905, he entered the École Normal Supérieure, where he specialized in history and geography; after his graduation he spent a year studying at Berlin and Leipzig. From 1909 to 1912, he trained as a medievalist under the auspices of the Thiers Institute for Historical Research and gathered much archival material for a work on medieval Île-de-France. He taught at lycées in Montpellier and Amiens until 1914, when he entered the infantry as a sergeant. He served bravely at the front throughout the war, emerging as a captain with four exemplary citations and the Legion of Honor. Bloch always looked upon his wartime experiences as valuable aids to his understanding of history, men, and societies. (One is reminded of Edward Gibbon's references to his years of service in the militia, 1760–1762: "But my principal obligation to the militia was the making me an Englishman and a soldier. . . . Experience forced me to feel the characters of our leading men, the state of parties, the forms of office, and the operation of our civil and military system. . . . The captain of the Hampshire grenadiers (the reader may smile) has not been useless to the historian of the Roman empire.")

In 1919, Bloch joined the French University of Strasbourg, where his colleagues included such luminaries as Christian Pfister, C.-E. Perrin, Georges Pariset, Georges Lefebvre, and, most important for his future work in rural history, Lucien Febvre. It was an exciting intellectual center in an age of scholarly ferment: "The most brilliant university our history has known," in Fernand Braudel's opinion. The turn of the century had witnessed widespread dissatisfaction with the status quo in all disciplines in Europe's academic world. In France, Henri Berr's *Revue de synthèse historique* signaled an all-out assault on the traditional academic historiography then firmly entrenched in the universities and lycées. The philosophy and methodology of that historiography was perhaps best represented in the "scientific" and unimaginative official handbook for students of history, *Introduction aux études historiques,* by Langlois and Seignobos (1894). The emphasis there was on scientifically accumulated "facts" drawn from surviving written documents which presumably would speak for themselves without the need for hypothesis or theory. Historians so nurtured, Bloch wrote, "were profoundly honest workmen, but a little short-winded. . . . My beloved teacher, Charles Seignobos, once let fall a saying that may fairly stand as their slogan: 'It is useful to ask oneself questions, but very dangerous to answer them.' Surely, this is not the remark of a braggart, but where would physics be today if the physicists had shown no greater daring?" In the two decades after the Great War, Bloch and Febvre worked together to rouse history from its somnolence; in 1929, after many years of inspired collaboration in Henri Berr's work, they founded the *Annales d'histoire économique et sociale.*

It was through their willingness to ask questions and to attempt answers, their eagerness to break out of the confines of traditional historiography that Bloch and Febvre and their allies revitalized French historiography. The essential point was both methodological and conceptual. While in no way denigrating the work of historians like Seignobos, Bloch argued that documentary evidence and written texts—the stuff of traditional historiography— were insufficient to enable the historian to encompass the past. It is the human situation in its entirety, not merely the surviving documents, that leads one to a true and full account of the past. Thus Bloch pioneered in the successful effort to broaden the range of historical evidence.

In his own work and through the *Annales,* he consistently stressed the importance and made use of such disciplines as geography, technology, sociology, archeology, linguistics, collective psychology, literature, and ethnography, among others: "Few sciences, I believe, are forced to use so many dissimilar tools at the same time. However, man's actions are the most complex in the animal kingdom, because man stands upon nature's summit." Thus he enlisted the study of folklore and myth in his work on the magical power of kings, *Les rois thaumaturges;* he studied place names as an aid in the explanation of regional differences and the extent of foreign penetrations; he drew upon his experiences of false rumors in the trenches during the war in an analysis of isolated medieval societies which were often prey to unfounded rumor; he made a specialty of the study of agrarian techniques and technology—plows, mills, crop rotation, grains, sowing and harvesting practices. Bloch criticized historians "who consider the facts of agricultural practices beneath their dignity and who hold their noses as they pass by manure heaps"; and in discussing Fustel de Coulanges's tendency to err because of his total reliance on written records, Bloch wrote, "De Coulanges was not a man on whom the external world made much impact."

Bloch's familiarity with contemporary peasant practices allowed him to elaborate a "regressive" method for the study of past agrarian arrangements. By using evidence from the present, e.g., field patterns and farming practices, Bloch was able to perceive the problems and conditions of earlier times. Rural communes especially often preserve and utilize customs and techniques formed in the distant past. In his own work, Bloch carefully but convincingly used eighteenth- and nineteenth-century land surveys to illuminate medieval rural conditions. This was to reverse the usual chronological approach, from origins to the present state. "It seems to me," he wrote, "that when one wishes to elucidate the 'origins' of a social fact there is always a danger in using as a point of departure its genesis. Embryology is an admirable science, but it makes sense only if we know something about the mature being."

Just as Bloch dissolved rigid disciplinary lines and abandoned traditional chronological approaches, so, too, he escaped from the excessive concern with one topic or one area or even one country's history, offering instead "comparative history." The comparative method, as Bloch practiced it, enabled him to perceive similarities and contrasts between areas in institutions, techniques, and economic and social developments. He followed a comparative approach in studying such disparate areas as the magical powers of kings, the movement of livestock prices ("a European-wide phenomenon"), agrarian usages ("Problems of the French rural world? Let us rather say of the European rural world"), and the transformation of feudal relationships (which in Bloch's view formed a problem in "the comparative history of European societies"). Certainly, his own comparative works and those of his emulators opened broad historical vistas and stimulated the new, fruitful questions and daring but tentative answers that were central to Bloch's conception of history. So fruitful was his method that one reviewer of his classic *Les caractères originaux de l'histoire rurale française* (1931) suspected that the work would within thirty years be totally useless and out of date—simply because Bloch had raised so many questions and stimulated so much new research. Bloch himself wished no better destiny for his works.

Such a bold, innovative approach makes it superfluous to stress that Bloch found the social sciences congenial and valuable to history. Sociology (Bloch was particularly influenced by Durkheim), geography (which Bloch thought both essential to and very much like history), social psychology, and economics—whatever contributed to the further, deeper understanding of man in society over time Bloch willingly used. His conception of *"les études humaines"* resembles Dilthey's definition of *"die Geisteswissenschaften"* in its blend of rigor and empathy. "Each science has its appropriate aesthetics of language. Human actions are essentially very delicate phenomena, many aspects of which elude mathematical measurement. . . . Between the expression of physical and of human realities there is as much difference as between the task of a drill operator [who uses precision tools] and that of a lutemaker . . . guided primarily by his sensitivity to sound and touch." While Bloch drew upon the social sciences, he avoided reductionism of any sort.

The criticism by the Soviet philosopher I. S. Kon that he had "no consistent *Weltanschauung"* would not have troubled Bloch. He merely sought to illuminate and to understand the changing conditions over time of men and women in their communities, states, and societies. It is arguable that his sociological approach led him to scant the role of individuals and to underestimate political decisions and military events; certainly, as R. R. Davies observes, "His was a history without heroes, and certainly without hero-worship." But Bloch did believe that the historian's "quarry" was man: "Behind the features of landscape, behind tools or machinery, behind what appear to be the most formalized written documents, and behind institutions, which seem almost entirely detached from their founders, there are men, and it is men that history seeks to grasp." Bloch aimed at a total history of humanity, *"l'histoire humaine."* This was in keeping with his principles and his personality, for he was above all else a humanist with a deep faith in human nature and in the equality of humankind, the subjects and makers of history.

In 1939, Bloch volunteered his services to his *patrie* once more and suffered through France's demoralizing defeat. His shock and bitterness show through the pages of his analysis of what he called that *Strange Defeat,* in which he searched for its causes and roundly criticized the failings and selfishness of those groups, including his own, the educators, who by their moral deficiencies contributed to France's fall. Because of his Jewish background he was forced by the anti-Semitic laws to leave Paris, eventually finding a temporary haven at Clermont-Ferrand. He could not accept offers of sanctuary overseas: "I was born in France. I have drunk of the waters of her culture. I have made her past my own. I breathe freely only in her climate and I have done my best, with others, to defend her interests." When the Nazis occupied the South of France, he went into the Resistance. Captured by the Gestapo, he was tortured and finally executed on June 16, 1944, not far from his birthplace, Lyons, along with twenty-six companions. In his will he wrote, "I die now, as I have lived, a good Frenchman." He was a great historian and a great man.

Selected Bibliography

English readers are fortunate in that many of Bloch's works have been translated. His seminal *Les caractères originaux de l'histoire rurale française* (1931) is available as *French Rural History: An Essay on Its Basic Characteristics* (translated by Janet Sondheimer, 1966), with an informative foreword by Bryce Lyon and an incisive preface from the second French printing by Lucien Febvre. To appreciate fully the book's impact, however, readers should consult Volume II of that second printing, *Supplément établi d'après les travaux de l'auteur,* carefully edited by Robert Dauvergne. Dauvergne shows how Bloch, with "his incessant work and new researches," would have rectified and modified the book had he lived to prepare a revised second edition. The *Supplément* ought to be translated. Bloch's *La société féodale* is also available in translation, *Feudal Society* (1961); the convenient two-volume paperback edition (1964) includes M. M. Postan's foreword. The selection below is taken from that work.

Several of Bloch's essays have appeared in *Land and Work in Medieval Europe* (1967), with a helpful introduction by F. R. N. DuBoulay. The translation is by J. E. Henderson, who recently rendered Bloch's early work *Île-de-France* into English (1971). Bloch's essay on "Feudalism" in the *Encyclopedia of the Social Sciences* (1932) is a good introduction to his style and perspective.

Among the best surveys of Bloch's life and his contribution to historiography are P. Dollinger's comprehensive essay "Notre Maître Marc Bloch," *Revue d'histoire économique et sociale,* XXVII (1948), 109–126; C.-E. Perrin's excellent "L'Oeuvre historique de Marc Bloch," *Revue historique,* CXCIX (1948), 161–188; Lucien Febvre's sensitive article "Marc Bloch," in *Architects and Craftsmen in History: Festschrift für Abbott Payson Usher* (1956), 75–84; and R. R. Davies's perceptive "Marc Bloch," *History,* 51 (1967), 265–282.

Bloch's "comparative" approach is analyzed in two valuable essays: J. A. Raftis, "Marc Bloch's Comparative Method and the Rural History of Medieval England," *Medieval Studies,* XXIV (1962), 349–368; and W. H. Sewell, Jr., "Marc Bloch and the Logic of Comparative History," *History and Theory,* VI (1967), 208–218. See also Jean Glénisson's discussion of Bloch in *La Recherche historique en France de 1940 à 1965* and H. Stuart Hughes's appraisal in *The Obstructed Path.* (Both of these works are fully cited in the headnote to Lucien Febvre's selection.) Bloch's own thoughts—dialogues with himself, as it were—on the delights and frustrations of the art-science of history may be most conveniently found in his posthumously published *Apologie pour l'histoire, ou Métier d'historien* (1948); it has been translated by Peter Putnam as *The Historian's Craft* (1953) with an introduction by Joseph R. Strayer and a "Note on the Manuscript" by Lucien Febvre.

FEUDAL SOCIETY

MATERIAL CONDITIONS AND ECONOMIC CHARACTERISTICS

The Two Ages of Feudalism

The framework of institutions which governs a society can in the last resort be understood only through a knowledge of the whole human environment. For though the artificial conception of man's activities which prompts us to carve up the creature of flesh and blood into the phantoms *homo oeconomicus, philosophicus, juridicus* is doubtless necessary, it is tolerable only if we refuse to be deceived by it. That is why, despite the existence of other works on the various aspects of medieval civilization, the descriptions thus attempted from points of view different from ours did not seem to us to obviate the necessity of recalling at this stage the fundamental characteristics of the historical climate in which European feudalism flourished. Need I add that in placing this account near the beginning of the book there was no thought of claiming any sort of illusory primacy for facts of this kind? When it is a question of comparing two particular phenomena belonging to separate series—a certain distribution of population, for example, with certain forms of legal groups—the delicate problem of cause and effect undoubtedly arises. On the other hand, to contrast two sets of dissimilar phenomena over a period of several centuries, and then say: "Here on this side are all the causes; there on that are all the effects," would be to construct the most pointless of dichotomies. A society, like a mind, is woven of perpetual interaction. For other researches, differently oriented, the analysis of the economy or the mental climate are culminating points; for the historian of the social structure they are a starting-point.

In this preliminary picture, designedly limited in scope, it will be necessary to retain only what is essential and least open to doubt. One deliberate omission, in particular, deserves a word of explanation. The

From *Feudal Society* (Chicago: University of Chicago Press; London: Routledge & Kegan Paul, 1961), I, 59–75, 79–87. Reprinted by permission of the publishers. Translated by L. A. Manyon.

wonderful flowering of art in the feudal era, at least from the eleventh century on, is not merely the most lasting glory of that epoch in the eyes of posterity. It served in those times as a vehicle for the most exalted forms of religious sensibility as well as for that interpenetration of the sacred and profane so characteristic of the age, which has left no more spontaneous witness than the friezes and capitals of certain churches. It was also very often the refuge, as it were, of certain values which could not find expression elsewhere. The restraint of which the medieval epic was incapable must be sought in Romanesque architecture. The precision of mind which the notaries were unable to attain in their charters presided over the works of the builders of vaults. But the links that unite plastic expression to the other features of a civilization are still insufficiently understood; from the little that we know of them they appear so complex, so subject to delays and divergences that it has been necessary in this work to leave aside the problems posed by connections so delicate and contradictions that to us seem so astonishing.

It would, moreover, be a grave mistake to treat "feudal civilization" as being all of one piece chronologically. Engendered no doubt or made possible by the cessation of the last invasions, but first manifesting themselves some generations later, a series of very profound and very widespread changes occurred towards the middle of the eleventh century. No definite break with the past occurred, but the change of direction which, despite inevitable variations in time according to the countries or the phenomena considered, affected in turn all the graphs of social activity. There were, in a word, two successive "feudal" ages, very different from one another in their essential character. We shall endeavour in the following pages to do justice as much to the contrasts between these two phases as to the characteristics they shared.

The First Feudal Age: Density of Population

It is and always will be impossible for us to calculate, even approximately, the population of Western countries during the first feudal age. Moreover, there undoubtedly existed marked regional variations, constantly intensified by the spasms of social disorder. Compared with the veritable desert of the Iberian plateaux, which gave the frontier regions of Christendom and Islam the desolate appearance of a vast "no man's land"—desolate even in comparison with early Germany, where the destruction wrought by the migrations of the previous age was being slowly made good—the country districts of Flanders and Lombardy seemed relatively favoured regions. But whatever the importance of these contrasts and whatever their effect on all the aspects of civilization, the fundamental characteristic remains the great and universal decline in population. Over the whole of Europe, the population was immeasurably smaller than it has been since the eighth century or even since the twelfth. Even in the provinces formerly under Roman rule, human beings were much scarcer than they had been in the heyday of the Empire. The most important towns had no more than a few thousand inhabitants, and waste land, gardens, even fields and pastures encroached on all sides amongst the houses.

This lack of density was further aggravated by very unequal distribution. Doubtless physical conditions, as well as social habits, conspired to maintain in the country districts profound differences between systems of settlement. In some districts the families, or at least some of them, took up their residence a considerable distance apart, each in the middle of its own farmland, as was the case, for example, in Limousin. In others on the contrary, like the Île-de-France, they mostly crowded together in villages. On the whole, however, both the pressure of the chiefs and, above all, the concern for security militated against too wide dispersal. The disorders of the early Middle Ages had in many cases induced men to draw nearer to each other, but these aggregations in which people lived cheek by jowl were separated by empty spaces. The arable land from which the village derived its sustenance was necessarily much larger in proportion to the number of inhabitants than it is today. For agriculture was a great devourer of space. In the tilled fields, incompletely ploughed and almost always inadequately manured, the ears of corn grew neither very heavy nor very dense. Above all, the harvests never covered the whole area of cultivation at once. The most advanced systems of crop-rotation known to the age required that every year half or a third of the cultivated soil should lie fallow. Often indeed, fallow and crops followed each other in irregular alternation, which always allowed more time for the growth of weeds than for that of the cultivated produce; the fields, in such cases, represented hardly more than a provisional and short-lived conquest of the waste land, and even in the heart of the agricultural regions nature tended constantly to regain the upper hand. Beyond them, enveloping them, thrusting into them, spread forests, scrub and dunes—immense wildernesses, seldom entirely uninhabited by man, though whoever dwelt there as charcoal-burner, shepherd, hermit or outlaw did so only at the cost of a long separation from his fellow men.

The First Feudal Age: Intercommunication

Among these sparsely scattered human groups the obstacles to communication were many. The collapse of the Carolingian empire had destroyed the last power sufficiently intelligent to concern itself with public works, sufficiently strong to get some of them carried out. Even the old Roman roads, less solidly constructed than has sometimes been imagined, went to rack and ruin for want of maintenance. Worse still, bridges were no longer kept in repair and were lacking at a great number of river-crossings. Added to this was the general state of insecurity, increased by the depopulation to which it had itself in part contributed. Great was the surprise and relief at the court of Charles the Bald, when in the year 841 that prince witnessed the arrival at Troyes of the messengers bringing him the crown jewels from Aquitaine: how wonderful that such a small number of men, entrusted with such precious baggage, should traverse without accident those vast areas infested on all sides by robbers! The Anglo-Saxon Chronicle shows much less surprise when relating how, in 1061, one of the greatest nobles of England, Earl Tostig, was captured and held to ransom by a handful of bandits at the gates of Rome.

Compared with what the world offers us today, the speed of travel in that age seems extremely slow. It was not, however, appreciably slower than it was at the end of the Middle Ages, or even the beginning of the eighteenth century. By contrast with today, travel was much faster by sea than by land. From 60 to 90 miles a day was not an exceptional record for a ship: provided (it goes without saying) that the winds were not too unfavourable. On land, the normal distance covered in one day amounted, it seems, to between nineteen and twenty-five miles—for travellers who were in no hurry, that is: say a caravan of merchants, a great nobleman moving round from castle to castle or from abbey to abbey, or an army with its baggage. A courier or a handful of resolute men could by making a special effort travel at least twice as fast. A letter written by Gregory VII at Rome on the 8th December 1075 arrived at Goslar, at the foot of the Harz, on the 1st of January following; its bearer had covered about 29 miles a day as the crow flies—in reality, of course, much more. To travel without too much fatigue and not too slowly it was necessary to be mounted or in a carriage. Horses and mules not only go faster than men; they adapt themselves better to boggy ground. This explains the seasonal interruption of many communications; it was due less to bad weather than to lack of forage. The Carolingian *missi* had earlier made a point of not beginning their tours till the grass had grown. However, as at present in Africa, an experienced foot-traveller could cover astoundingly long distances in a few days and he could doubtless overcome certain obstacles more quickly than a horseman. When Charles the Bald organized his second Italian expedition he arranged to keep in touch with Gaul across the Alps partly by means of runners.

Though poor and unsafe, the roads or tracks were in constant use. Where transport is difficult, man goes to something he wants more easily than he makes it come to him. In particular, no institution or method could take the place of personal contact between human beings. It would have been impossible to govern the state from inside a palace: to control a country, there was no other means than to ride through it incessantly in all directions. The kings of the first feudal age positively killed themselves by travel. For example, in the course of a year which was in no way exceptional, the emperor Conrad II in 1033 is known to have journeyed in turn from Burgundy to the Polish frontier and thence to Champagne, to return eventually to Lusatia. The nobleman with his entourage moved round constantly from one of his estates to another; and not only in order to supervise them more effectively. It was necessary for him to consume the produce on the spot, for to transport it to a common centre would have been both inconvenient and expensive. Similarly with the merchant. Without representatives to whom he could delegate the task of buying and selling, fairly certain in any case of never finding enough customers assembled in one place to assure him a profit, every merchant was a pedlar, a "dusty foot" [*pied poudreux*], plying his trade up hill and down dale. The cleric, eager for learning or the ascetic life, was obliged to wander over Europe in search of the master of his choice: Gerbert of Aurillac studied mathematics in Spain and philosophy at Rheims; the Englishman Stephen Harding, the ideal monachism in the Burgundian abbey of Molesmes. Before him, St. Odo, the future abbot of Cluny, had travelled through France in the hope of finding a monastery whose members lived strictly according to the rule.

Moreover, in spite of the old hostility of the Benedictine rule to the *gyrovagi,* the bad monks who ceaselessly "vagabonded about," everything in contemporary clerical life favoured this nomadism: the international character of the Church; the use of Latin as a common language among educated priests and monks; the affiliations between monasteries; the wide dispersal of their territorial patrimonies; and finally the "reforms" which periodically convulsed this great ecclesiastical body and made the places first affected by the new spirit at once courts of appeal (to which people came from all parts to seek the good rule) and mission centres whence the zealots were despatched for the conquest of the Catholic world. How many foreign visitors came to Cluny in this way! How many Cluniacs journeyed forth to foreign lands! Under William the Conqueror almost all the dioceses and great abbeys of Normandy, which the first waves of the "Gregorian" revival were beginning to reach, had at their head Italians or Lorrainers; the archbishop of Rouen, Maurille, was a man from Rheims who, before occupying his Neustrian see, had studied at Liège, taught in Saxony and lived as a hermit in Tuscany.

Humble folk, too, passed along the highways of the West: refugees, driven by war or famine; adventurers, half-soldiers, half-bandits; peasants seeking a more prosperous life and hoping to find, far from their native land, a few fields to cultivate. Finally, there were pilgrims. For religious devotion itself fostered travel and more than one good Christian, rich or poor, cleric or layman, believed that he could purchase salvation of body and soul only at the price of a long journey.

As has often been remarked, it is in the nature of good roads to create a vacuum around them—to their own profit. In the feudal age, when all roads were bad, scarcely any of them was capable of monopolizing the traffic in this way. Undoubtedly such factors as the restrictions of the terrain, tradition, the presence of a market here or a sanctuary there, worked to the advantage of certain routes, although far less decisively than the historians of literary or artistic influences have sometimes believed. A fortuitous event—a physical accident, the exactions of a lord in need of money—sufficed to divert the flow, sometimes permanently. The building of a castle on the old Roman road, occupied by a race of robber knights—the lords of Méréville—and the establishment some distance away of the St. Denis priory of Toury, where merchants and pilgrims found by contrast a pleasant reception, were sufficient to divert the traffic from the Beauce section of the road from Paris to Orleans permanently westward, so that the ancient roadway was abandoned from that time on. Moreover from the beginning of his journey to the end, the traveller had almost always the choice of several itineraries, of which none was absolutely obligatory. Traffic, in short, was not canalized in a few great arteries; it spread capriciously through a multitude of little blood-vessels. There was no castle, burg, or monastery, however far from the beaten track, that could not expect to be visited occasionally by wanderers, living links with the outer world, although the places where such visits were of regular occurrence were few.

Thus the obstacles and dangers of the road in no way prevented travel. But they made each journey an expedition, almost an adventure. If men, under pressure of need, did not fear to undertake fairly long journeys (they feared it less, perhaps, than in centuries nearer to our own) they shrank from those repeated comings and goings within a narrow radius which in other civilizations form the texture of daily life; and this was especially so in the case of humble folk of settled occupations. The result was an ordering of the scheme of human relations quite different from anything we know today. There was scarcely any remote little place which had not some contacts intermittently through that sort of continuous yet irregular "Brownian movement" which affected the whole of society. On the other hand, between two inhabited centres quite close to each other the connections were much rarer, the isolation of their inhabitants infinitely greater than would be the case in our own day. If, according to the angle from which it is viewed, the civilization of feudal Europe appears sometimes remarkably universalist, sometimes particularist in the extreme, the principal source of this contradiction lay in the conditions of communication: conditions which favoured the distant propagation of very general currents of influence as much as they discouraged, in any particular place, the standardizing effects of neighbourly intercourse.

The only more or less regular letter-mail service which functioned during the whole of the feudal era was that which linked Venice to Constantinople. Such a thing was practically unknown in the West. The last attempts to maintain a royal posting-service, on the model left by the Roman government, had disappeared with the Carolingian empire. It is significant of the general disorganization that the German monarchs themselves, the true heirs of that empire and its ambitions, should have lacked either the authority or the intelligence necessary to secure the revival of an institution clearly so indispensable to the control of vast territories. Sovereigns, nobles, prelates were obliged to entrust their correspondence to special couriers, otherwise—as was usual among persons of lesser rank—the transport of letters was simply left to the kindness of passing travellers; as, for instance, the pilgrims on their way to St. James of Galicia. The relative slowness of the messengers, the mishaps that at every stage threatened their progress, meant that the only effective authority was the one on the spot. Forced constantly to take the gravest steps —the history of the papal legates is in this respect very instructive—every local representative of a great potentate tended only too naturally to act for his personal advantage and thus finally to transform himself into an independent ruler.

As for knowledge of distant events, everyone, whatever his rank, was obliged to rely on chance encounters. The picture of the contemporary world which the best-informed men carried in their minds presented many lacunae; we can form an idea of them from the unavoidable omissions even from the best of those monastic annals which are as it were the written reports of medieval news-hawks. Moreover, it was seldom exact as to time. It is, for example, remarkable to find a person so well placed for acquiring information as Bishop Fulbert of Chartres showing astonishment on receiving gifts for his church from Cnut the Great: for he admits that he believed this prince to be still a heathen, although in fact he had been baptized in infancy. The monk Lambert of Hersfeld is quite well-informed about German affairs, but when he goes on to describe the grave events which occurred in his time in Flanders (a region bordering on the Empire and in part an imperial fief), he soon makes a series of the strangest blunders. Such an imperfect state of knowledge was a poor foundation for any large political designs.

The First Feudal Age: Trade and Currency

The life of the Europe of the first feudal age was not entirely self-contained. There was more than one current of exchange between it and the neighbouring civilizations, and probably the most active was that which linked it to Moslem Spain, as witnessed by the numerous Arab gold pieces which, by this route, penetrated north of the Pyrenees and were there sufficiently sought after to become the object of frequent imitations. In the western Mediterranean, on the other hand, long-distance navigation was now practically unknown. The principal lines of communication with the East were elsewhere. One of them, a sea-route, passed through the Adriatic, at the head of which lay Venice, to all appearance a fragment of Byzantium, set in a world apart. On land the Danube route, for a long time severed by the Hungarians, was almost deserted. But farther north, on the trails which joined Bavaria to the great market of Prague and thence, by the terraces on the northern flank of the Carpathians, continued to the Dnieper, caravans passed back and forth, laden on the return journey with products of Constantinople or of Asia. At Kiev they met the great transversal which, running across the plains and from river to river, linked the riparian countries of the Baltic with the Black Sea, the Caspian or the oases of Turkestan. For the West had missed its chance of being the intermediary between the north or north-east of the continent and the eastern Mediterranean, and had nothing to offer on its own soil to compare with the mighty comings and goings of merchandise which made the prosperity of Kievian Russia.

Not only was this trade restricted to very few routes; it was also extremely small in volume. What is worse, the balance of trade seems to have been distinctly unfavourable—at any rate with the East. From the eastern countries the West received almost nothing except a few luxury articles whose value—very high in relation to their weight—was such as to take no account of the expense and risks of transport. In exchange it had scarcely anything to offer except slaves. Moreover, it seems that most of the human cattle rounded up on the Slav and Lettish territories beyond the Elbe or acquired from the slave-traders of Britain took the road to Islamic Spain; the eastern Mediterranean was too abundantly provided with this commodity from its own sources to have any need to import it on a large scale. The profits of the slave-trade, in general fairly small, were not sufficient to pay for the purchase of precious goods and spices in the markets of the Byzantine world, of Egypt or of nearer Asia. The result was a slow drain of silver and above all of gold. If a few merchants unquestionably owed their prosperity to these remote transactions, society as a whole owed scarcely anything to them except one more reason for being short of specie.

However, money was never wholly absent from business transactions in feudal Europe, even among the peasant classes, and it never ceased to be employed as a standard of exchange. Payments were often made in produce; but the produce was normally valued item by item in such a way that the total of these reckonings corresponded with a stipulated price in pounds, shillings and pence. Let us therefore avoid the expression "natural economy," which is too summary and too vague. It is better to speak simply of shortage of currency. This shortage was further aggravated by the anarchic state of minting, another result of the subdivision of political authority and the difficulty of communication: for each important market, faced with the threat of shortage, had to have its local mint. Except for the imitation of exotic coinages and apart from certain insignificant little pieces, the only coins now produced were *denarii,* which were rather debased silver pieces. Gold circulated only in the shape of Arab and Byzantine coins or imitations of them. The *libra* and the *solidus* were only arithmetical multiples of the *denarius,* without a material basis of their own. But the various coins called *denarii* had a different metallic value according to their origin. Worse still, even in one and the same area almost every issue involved variations in the weight or the alloy. Not only was money generally scarce, and inconvenient on account of its unreliability, but it circulated too slowly and too irregularly for people ever to feel certain of being able to procure it in case of need. That was the situation, in the absence of a sufficiently active commerce.

But here again, let us beware of too facile a formula—the "closed economy." It would not even apply exactly to the small farming operations of the peasants. We know that markets existed where the rustics certainly sold some of the produce of their fields or their farmyards to the townsfolk, to the clergy, to the men-at-arms. It was thus that they procured the *denarii* to pay their dues. And poor indeed was the man who never bought a few ounces of salt or a bit of iron. As to the "autarky" of the great manors, this would have meant that their masters had gone without arms or jewels, had never drunk wine (unless their estates produced it), and for clothes had been content with crude materials woven by the wives of tenants. Moreover, even the inadequacies of agricultural technique, the disturbed state of society, and finally the inclemency of the weather contributed to maintain a certain amount of internal commerce: for when the harvest failed, although many people literally died of starvation, the whole population was not reduced to this extremity, and we know that there was a traffic in corn from the more favoured districts to those afflicted by dearth, which lent itself readily to speculation. Trade, therefore, was not nonexistent, but it was irregular in the extreme. The society of this age was certainly not unacquainted with either buying or selling. But it did not, like our own, live by buying and selling.

Moreover, commerce, even in the form of barter, was not the only or perhaps even the most important channel by which at that time goods circulated through the various classes of society. A great number of products passed from hand to hand as dues paid to a chief in return for his protection or simply in recognition of his power. It was the same in the case of that other commodity, human labour: the *corvée* furnished more labourers than hire. In short, exchange, in the strict sense, certainly played a smaller part in economic life than payment in kind; and because exchange was thus a rare thing, while at the same time only the poorest could resign themselves to living wholly on their own produce, wealth and well-being seemed inseparable from authority.

Nevertheless, in an economy so constituted the means of acquisition at the disposal even of the powerful were, on the whole, singularly restricted. When we speak of money we mean the possibility of laying by reserves, the ability to wait, the "anticipation of future values"—everything that, conversely, the shortage of money particularly impedes. It is true that people tried to hoard wealth in other forms. The nobles and kings accumulated in their coffers gold or silver vessels and precious stones; the churches amassed liturgical plate. Should the need arise for an unexpected disbursement, you sold or pawned the crown, the goblet or the crucifix; or you even sent them to be melted down at the local mint. But such liquidation of assets, from the very fact of the slowing down of exchange which made it necessary, was never easy nor was it always profitable; and the hoarded treasure itself did not after all constitute a very large amount. The great as well as the humble lived from hand to mouth, obliged to be content with the resources of the moment and mostly compelled to spend them at once.

The weakness of trade and of monetary circulation had a further consequence of the gravest kind. It reduced to insignificance the social function of wages. The latter requires that the employer should have at his disposal an adequate currency, the source of which is not in danger of drying up at any moment; on the side of the wage-earner it requires the certainty of being able to employ the money thus received in procuring for himself the necessities of life. Both these conditions were absent in the first feudal age. In all grades of the hierarchy, whether it was a question of the king's making sure of the services of a great official, or of the small landlord's retaining those of an armed follower or a farmhand, it was necessary to have recourse to a method of remuneration which was not based on the periodic payment of a sum of money. Two alternatives offered: one was to take the man into one's household, to feed and clothe him, to provide him with "prebend," as the phrase went; the other was to grant him in return for his services an estate which, if exploited directly or in the form of dues levied on the cultivators of the soil, would enable him to provide for himself.

Now both these methods tended, though in opposite ways, to create human ties very different from those based on wages. Between the prebend-holder and the master under whose roof he lived the bond must surely have been much more intimate than that between an employer and a wage-earner, who is free, once his job is finished, to go off with his money in his pocket. On the other hand, the bond was almost inevitably loosened as soon as the subordinate was settled on a piece of land, which by a natural process he tended increasingly to regard as his own, while trying to reduce the burden of service. Moreover, in a time when the inadequacy of communications and the insufficiency of trade rendered it difficult to maintain large households in relative abundance, the "prebend" system was on the whole capable of a much smaller extension than the system of remuneration based on land. If feudal society perpetually oscillated between these two poles, the narrow relationship of man and man and the looser tie of land tenure, the responsibility for this belongs in large part to the economic regime which, to begin with at least, made wage-earning impracticable.

The Economic Revolution of the Second Feudal Age

We shall endeavour, in another work, to describe the intensive movement of repopulation which, from approximately 1050 to 1250, transformed the face of Europe: on the confines of the Western world, the colonization of the Iberian plateaux and of the great plain beyond the Elbe; in the heart of the old territories, the incessant gnawing of the plough at forest and wasteland; in the glades opened amidst the trees or the brushwood, completely new villages clutching at the virgin soil; elsewhere, round sites inhabited for centuries, the extension of the agricultural lands through the exertions of the assarters. It will be advisable then to distinguish between the stages of the process and to describe the regional variations. For the moment, we are concerned only with the phenomenon itself and its principal effects.

The most immediately apparent of these was undoubtedly the closer association of the human groups. Between the different settlements, except in some particularly neglected regions, the vast empty spaces thenceforth disappeared. Such distances as still separated the settlements became, in any case, easier to traverse. For powers now arose or were consolidated—their rise being favoured by current demographic trends—whose enlarged horizons brought them new responsibilities.

Such were the urban middle classes, which owed everything to trade. Such also were the kings and princes; they too were interested in the prosperity of commerce because they derived large sums of money from it in the form of duties and tolls; moreover they were aware—much more so than in the past—of the vital importance to them of the free transmission of orders and the free movement of armies. The activity of the Capetians towards that decisive turning-point marked by the reign of Louis VI, their aggressions, their domainal policy, their part in the organization of the movement of repopulation, were in large measure the reflection of considerations of this kind—the need to retain control of communications between the two capitals, Paris and Orleans, and beyond the Loire or the Seine to maintain contact with Berry or with the valleys of the Oise and the Aisne. It would seem that while the security of the roads had increased, there was no very notable improvement in their condition; but at least the provision of bridges had been carried much farther. In the course of the twelfth century, how many were thrown over all the rivers of Europe! Finally, a fortunate advance in harnessing methods had the effect, about the same time, of increasing very substantially the efficiency of horse-transport.

The links with neighbouring civilizations underwent a similar transformation. Ships in ever greater numbers ploughed the Tyrrhenian Sea, and its ports, from the rock of Amalfi to Catalonia, rose to the rank of great commercial centres; the sphere of Venetian trade continually expanded; the heavy wagons of the merchant caravans now followed the route of the Danubian plains. These advances were important enough. But relations with the East had not only become easier and more intimate. The most important fact is that they had changed their character. Formerly almost exclusively an importer, the West had become a great supplier of manufactured goods. The merchandise which it thus shipped in quantity to the Byzantine world, to the Latin or Islamic Levant and even—though in smaller amounts—to the Maghreb, belonged to very diverse categories. One commodity, however, easily dominated all the rest. In the expansion of the European economy in the Middle Ages, cloth played the same vital rôle as did metal and cotton goods in that of nineteenth-century England. If in Flanders, in Picardy, at Bourges, in Languedoc, in Lombardy, and yet other places—for the cloth centres were to be found almost everywhere—the noise of the looms and the throbbing of the fullers' mills resounded, it was at least as much for the sake of foreign markets as for local requirements. And undoubtedly this revolution, which saw our Western countries embarking on the economic conquest of the world by way of the East, is to be explained by a multiplicity of causes and by looking—as far as possible—towards the East as well as towards the West. It is none the less true that it could not have occurred without the demographic changes mentioned above. If the population had not been more numerous than before and the cultivated area more extensive; if the fields—their quality improved by augmented manpower and in particular by more intensive ploughing—had not become capable of yielding bigger and more frequent harvests, how could so many weavers, dyers or cloth-shearers have been brought together in the towns and provided with a livelihood?

The North was conquered, like the East. From the end of the eleventh century Flemish cloth was sold at Novgorod. Little by little, the route of the Russian plains became hazardous and was finally closed. Thenceforward Scandinavia and the Baltic countries turned towards the West. The process of change which was thus set in motion was completed when, in the course of the twelfth century, German merchants took over the Baltic. From that time onwards the ports of the Low Countries, especially Bruges, became the centres where northern products were exchanged not only for those of the West itself but also for merchandise from the East. Strong international links united the two frontiers of feudal Europe by way of Germany and especially through the fairs of Champagne.

Such a well-balanced external trade could not fail to bring a flow of coin and precious metals into Europe and so add substantially to its monetary resources. This relative easing of the currency situation was reinforced—and its effects multiplied—by the accelerated rhythm of circulation. For in the very heart of the West the progress of repopulation, the greater ease of communications, the cessation of the invasions which had spread such an atmosphere of confusion and panic over the Western world, and still other causes which it would take too long to examine here, had led to a revival of commerce.

Let us avoid exaggeration, however. The picture would have to be carefully shaded—by regions and by classes. To live on their own resources remained for long centuries the ideal—though one that was rarely attained—of many peasants and most villages. Moreover, the profound transformations of the economy took place only very gradually. It is significant that of the two essential developments in the sphere of currency, one, the minting of larger pieces of silver much heavier than the *denarius,* appeared only at the beginning of the thirteenth century (and even at that date in Italy alone) and the other, the resumption of the minting of gold coins of an indigenous type, was delayed till the second half of the same century. In many respects, what the second feudal age witnessed was less the disappearance of earlier conditions than their modification. This observation applies to the part played by distance as well as to commerce. But the fact that the kings, the great nobles, and the manorial lords should have been able to begin once more to amass substantial wealth, that wage-earning, sometimes under legal forms clum-

sily adapted from ancient practices, should have increasingly supplanted other methods of remunerating services—these signs of an
economy in process of revival affected in their turn, from the twelfth
century onwards, the whole fabric of human relations.

Furthermore, the evolution of the economy involved a genuine revision
of social values. There had always been artisans and merchants; individuals belonging to the latter class had even been able, here and there,
to play an important rôle, though collectively neither group counted for
much. But from the end of the eleventh century the artisan class and the
merchant class, having become much more numerous and much more
indispensable to the life of the community, made themselves felt more
and more vigorously in the urban setting. This applies especially to the
merchant class, for the medieval economy, after the great revival of
these decisive years, was always dominated, not by the producer, but by
the trader. It was not for the latter class that the legal machinery of the
previous age—founded on an economic system in which they occupied
only an inferior place—had been set up. But now their practical needs
and their mental attitude were bound to imbue it with a new spirit. Born
in the midst of a very loosely knit society, in which commerce was insignificant and money a rarity, European feudalism underwent a fundamental change as soon as the meshes of the human network had been
drawn closer together and the circulation of goods and coin intensified.

MODES OF FEELING AND THOUGHT

Man's Attitude to Nature and Time

The men of the two feudal ages were close to nature—much closer than
we are; and nature as they knew it was much less tamed and softened
than we see it today. The rural landscape, of which the waste formed so
large a part, bore fewer traces of human influence. The wild animals that
now only haunt our nursery tales—bears and, above all, wolves—prowled
in every wilderness, and even amongst the cultivated fields. So much was
this the case that the sport of hunting was indispensable for ordinary
security, and almost equally so as a method of supplementing the food
supply. People continued to pick wild fruit and to gather honey as in the
first ages of mankind. In the construction of implements and tools, wood
played a predominant part. The nights, owing to the wretched lighting,
were darker; the cold, even in the living quarters of the castles, was more
intense. In short, behind all social life there was a background of the
primitive, of submission to uncontrollable forces, of unrelieved physical
contrasts. There is no means of measuring the influence which such an
environment was capable of exerting on the minds of men, but it could

hardly have failed to contribute to their uncouthness.

A history more worthy of the name than the diffident speculations to which we are reduced by the paucity of our material would give space to the vicissitudes of the human organism. It is very naive to claim to understand men without knowing what sort of health they enjoyed. But in this field the state of the evidence, and still more the inadequacy of our methods of research, are inhibitive. Infant mortality was undoubtedly very high in feudal Europe and tended to make people somewhat callous towards bereavements that were almost a normal occurrence. As to the life of adults, even apart from the hazards of war it was usually short by our standards, at least to judge from the records of princely personages which (inexact though they must often be) constitute our only source of information on this point. Robert the Pious died at about the age of 60; Henry I at 52; Philip I and Louis VI at 56. In Germany the first four emperors of the Saxon dynasty attained respectively the ages of 60 (or thereabouts), 28, 22 and 52. Old age seemed to begin very early, as early as mature adult life with us. This world, which, as we shall see, considered itself very old, was in fact governed by young men.

Among so many premature deaths, a large number were due to the great epidemics which descended frequently upon a humanity ill-equipped to combat them; among the poor another cause was famine. Added to the constant acts of violence these disasters gave life a quality of perpetual insecurity. This was probably one of the principal reasons for the emotional instability so characteristic of the feudal era, especially during its first age. A low standard of hygiene doubtless also contributed to this nervous sensibility. A great deal of effort has been expended, in our own day, in proving that baths were not unknown to seignorial society. It is rather puerile, for the sake of making this point, to overlook so many unhealthy conditions of life: notably undernourishment among the poor and overeating among the rich. Finally, we must not leave out of account the effects of an astonishing sensibility to what were believed to be supernatural manifestations. It made people's minds constantly and almost morbidly attentive to all manner of signs, dreams, or hallucinations. This characteristic was especially marked in monastic circles where the influence of mortifications of the flesh and the repression of natural instincts was joined to that of a mental attitude vocationally centred on the problems of the unseen. No psychoanalyst has ever examined dreams more earnestly than the monks of the tenth or the eleventh century. Yet the laity also shared the emotionalism of a civilization in which moral or social convention did not yet require well-bred people to repress their tears and their raptures. The despairs, the rages, the impulsive acts, the sudden revulsions of feeling present great difficulties to historians, who are instinctively disposed to reconstruct the past in terms of the rational. But the irrational is an important element in all history and only a sort of false shame could allow its effects on the course of political events in feudal Europe to be passed over in silence.

These men, subjected both externally and internally to so many ungovernable forces, lived in a world in which the passage of time escaped their grasp all the more because they were so ill-equipped to measure it. Water-clocks, which were costly and cumbersome, were very rare. Hourglasses were little used. The inadequacy of sundials, especially under skies quickly clouded over, was notorious. This resulted in the use of curious devices. In his concern to regulate the course of a notably nomadic life, King Alfred had conceived the idea of carrying with him everywhere a supply of candles of equal length, which he had lit in turn, to mark the passing of the hours, but such concern for uniformity in the division of the day was exceptional in that age. Reckoning ordinarily—after the example of Antiquity—twelve hours of day and twelve of night, whatever the season, people of the highest education became used to seeing each of these fractions, taken one by one, grow and diminish incessantly, according to the annual revolution of the sun. This was to continue till the moment when—towards the beginning of the fourteenth century—counterpoise clocks brought with them at last, not only the mechanization of the instrument, but, so to speak, of time itself.

An anecdote related in a chronicle of Hainault illustrates admirably the sort of perpetual fluctuation of time in those days. At Mons a judicial duel is due to take place. Only one champion puts in an appearance—at dawn; at the ninth hour, which marks the end of the waiting period prescribed by custom, he requests that the failure of his adversary be placed on record. On the point of law, there is no doubt. But has the specified period really elapsed? The county judges deliberate, look at the sun, and question the clerics in whom the practice of the liturgy has induced a more exact knowledge of the rhythm of the hours than their own, and by whose bells it is measured, more or less accurately, to the common benefit of men. Eventually the court pronounces firmly that the hour of "none" is past. To us, accustomed to live with our eyes turning constantly to the clock, how remote from our civilization seems this society in which a court of law could not ascertain the time of day without discussion and inquiry!

Now the imperfection of hourly reckoning was but one of the symptoms, among many others, of a vast indifference to time. Nothing would have been easier or more useful than to keep an accurate record of such important legal dates as those of the births of rulers; yet in 1284 a full investigation was necessary to determine, as far as possible, the age of one of the greatest heiresses of the Capetian realm, the young countess of Champagne. In the tenth and eleventh centuries, innumerable charters and memoranda were undated, although their only purpose was to serve as records. There are exceptional documents which are better in this respect, yet the notary, who employed several systems of reference simultaneously, was often not successful in making his various calculations agree. What is more, it was not the notion of time only, it was the domain of number as a whole which suffered from this haziness. The extravagant figures of the chroniclers are not merely literary exaggeration; they are evidence of the lack of all awareness of statistical realities. Although William the Conqueror certainly did not establish in England more than 5,000 knights' fees, the historians of a somewhat later time, and even certain administrators (though it would certainly not have been very difficult for them to obtain the right information), did not hesitate to attribute to him the creation of from thirty-two to sixty thousand of these military tenements. The period had, especially from the end of the eleventh century, its mathematicians who groped their way courageously in the wake of the Greeks and Arabs; the architects and sculptors were capable of using a fairly simple geometry. But among the computations that have come down to us—and this was true till the end of the Middle Ages—there are scarcely any that do not reveal astonishing errors. The inconveniences of the Roman numerical system, ingeniously corrected as they were by the use of the abacus, do not suffice to explain these mistakes. The truth is that the regard for accuracy, with its firmest buttress, the respect for figures, remained profoundly alien to the minds even of the leading men of that age. . . .

Culture and Social Classes

To what extent was the language of the educated, medieval Latin, also the language of the aristocracy? To what extent, in other words, can the group of *literati* be identified with the ruling class? So far as the Church is concerned, the answer is clear. It is of no great consequence that the pernicious system of nominations had resulted, here and there, in the appointment of ignorant men to the highest posts. The episcopal courts, the great monasteries, the chapels royal, in a word, all the headquarters of the ecclesiastical army, never lacked educated clergy who, while often of noble or knightly origin, had been brought up in the monastic and especially the cathedral schools. But as soon as we come to the lay world, the problem becomes more complex.

Let us not imagine that, even in the darkest times, this society was positively hostile to all learning. That it was commonly deemed proper that a leader of men should have access to the treasure-house of thoughts and memories to which the written word, that is to say Latin, alone provided the key is most clearly shown by the importance attached by many sovereigns to the education of their heirs. Robert the Pious, "king learned in God," had been the pupil of the illustrious Gerbert at Rheims; William the Conqueror gave his son Robert a cleric as tutor. Among the great of the earth, there were to be found genuine book-lovers: Otto III, brought up, it is true, by his mother who, as a Byzantine princess, had brought from her native country the customs of a much more refined civilization, spoke Greek and Latin fluently; William III of Aquitaine had assembled a fine library where he was sometimes to be found reading far into the night. To these examples may be added the cases, by no means exceptional, of those princes who, intended originally for the Church, had retained some of the learning and some of the tastes proper to the clerical world; such a one was Baldwin of Boulogne—a rough soldier, nevertheless—who became king of Jerusalem.

But an education of this type was possible only in the atmosphere of a great dynasty, already firmly based on their hereditary power. Nothing is more significant in this respect than the almost regular contrast in Germany between the founders of dynasties and their successors. Both Otto II, the third Saxon king, and Henry III, the second of the Salians, were carefully educated, in contrast with their fathers—Otto the Great, who learned to read at the age of thirty, and Conrad II, whose chaplain avows that he "knew not his letters." As often happened, both the fathers were thrown too young into a life of adventure and peril to have had time to prepare themselves, otherwise than by practical experience or oral tradition, for their profession as rulers. Still more was this true of the lower ranks of the nobility. The relatively brilliant culture of a few great royal or noble families should not deceive us; nor should the exceptional fidelity with which the knightly classes of Italy and Spain held to pedagogic traditions, somewhat rudimentary though these were: the Cid and Ximenes, if their knowledge perhaps did not extend much farther, at least knew how to sign their names. But north of the Alps and the Pyrenees at least the majority of the small or medium lords who exercised most authority at this time were illiterates in the full sense of the word. So much was this the case that in the monasteries into which some of them precipitately retreated in the evening of their days, the terms *conversus,* that is to say one who comes late to the monk's vocation, and *idiota,* which designated the monk incapable of reading the Holy Scriptures, were treated as synonymous.

This neglect of education among the laity explains the rôle of the clergy both as interpreters of the ideas of the great and as depositaries of political traditions. The princes were obliged to rely on the clerical element among their servants for services that the rest of their entourage would have been incapable of rendering. About the middle of the eighth century the last lay referendaries of the Merovingian kings had disap-

peared; in April 1298, Philip the Fair handed over the seals to the knight
Pierre Flotte. Between these two dates more than five centuries elapsed,
during which the chancelleries of the sovereigns who reigned over
France had at their head churchmen exclusively. It was the same elsewhere, on the whole. It is important to realize that the decisions of the
powerful of this world were sometimes suggested and always expressed
by men who, whatever their national or class allegiances, none the less
belonged by their whole training to a society by nature universalist and
founded on spiritual things. Beyond question they helped to maintain,
above the confusion of petty local strife, a concern for certain wider
issues. When required, however, to give written form to acts of policy,
they felt impelled to justify them officially by reasons drawn from their
own moral code. Thus there came to be diffused over the documents of
almost the entire feudal era that veneer of disingenuousness the evidence of which is to be seen in particular in the preambles of so many
enfranchisements masquerading as pure gifts, though they were in fact
purchased for money, or in so many royal grants of privileges, invariably
made to appear as inspired by simple piety. Since for a long period the
writing of history itself, with accompanying value-judgments, was also
in the hands of the clergy, the conventions of thought as much as the
conventions of literature combined to hide the cynical reality of human
motives behind a sort of veil which was only to be finally torn asunder,
on the threshold of modern times, by the harsh hands of a Commynes and
a Machiavelli.

The laity, however, remained in many respects the active element in
secular society. Undoubtedly the most illiterate of them were not on that
account ignorant men. Apart from the fact that they were in a position,
when necessary, to have translated for them what they could not read
themselves, we shall see presently to what an extent tales told in the
vernacular could transmit both memories and ideas. Still, we must never
forget that the majority of lords and many great barons were administrators incapable of studying personally a report or an account, judges
whose decisions were recorded (if at all) in a language unknown to the
court. Is it surprising that these leaders, who were ordinarily obliged to
reconstitute their past decisions from memory, should often have totally
lacked the sense of continuity which, quite erroneously, some historians
of today are at great pains to ascribe to them?

Almost strangers to writing, they tended to be indifferent to it. After
Otto the Great had received the imperial crown in 962, he allowed a
privilege to be issued in his name which was inspired by the "pacts" of
the Carolingian emperors and perhaps by certain historical writings;
granting to the popes, "till the end of time," the possession of an immense
territory. By thus denuding himself of territory, the king-emperor would

have abandoned to the Patrimony of St. Peter the greater part of Italy and even the control of some of the most important Alpine routes. Certainly Otto never dreamed for one moment that these dispositions, though very precise, would in fact be carried out. It would be less surprising if it were a question of one of those dishonest agreements which at all times, under pressure of circumstances, have been signed without the least intention of executing them. But absolutely nothing, save perhaps an imperfectly understood historical tradition, obliged the Saxon prince to make such a pretence. On the one hand, there is the parchment with the ink on it; on the other—quite unconnected with it—what was actually done; such was one particularly flagrant example of a typical dichotomy. A great many people in a position to direct human affairs did not understand the only language deemed worthy to record, not only the knowledge most useful to man and his salvation, but even the results of all social activity.

The Religious Mentality

"Ages of faith," we say glibly, to describe the religious attitude of feudal Europe. If by that phrase we mean that any conception of the world from which the supernatural was excluded was profoundly alien to the minds of that age, that in fact the picture which they formed of the destinies of man and the universe was in almost every case a projection of the pattern traced by a Westernized Christian theology and eschatology, nothing could be more true. That here and there doubts might be expressed with regard to the "fables" of Scripture is of small significance; lacking any rational basis, this crude scepticism, which was not a normal characteristic of educated people, melted in the face of danger like snow in the sun. It is even permissible to say that never was faith more completely worthy of its name. For the attempts of the learned to provide the Christian mysteries with the prop of logical speculation, which had been interrupted on the extinction of ancient Christian philosophy and revived only temporarily and with difficulty during the Carolingian renaissance, were not fully resumed before the end of the eleventh century. On the other hand, it would be wrong to ascribe to these believers a rigidly uniform creed.

Catholicism was still very far from having completely defined its dogmatic system, so that the strictest orthodoxy was then much more flexible than was to be the case later on, after scholastic philosophy and the Counter-Reformation had in turn exercised their influence. Moreover, in the ill-defined border land where Christian heresy degenerated into a religion actively opposed to Christianity, the old Manichaeanism retained a number of votaries in various places. Of these it is not precisely known whether they had inherited their religion from groups who had remained obstinately faithful to this persecuted sect since the first centuries of the Middle Ages, or had received it, after a long interval, from Eastern Europe. But the most notable fact was that Catholicism had incompletely penetrated among the common people. The parish clergy, taken as a whole, were intellectually as well as morally unfit for their task. Recruited with insufficient care, they were also inadequately trained; most commonly instruction consisted in casual lessons given by some priest, himself poorly educated, to a youth who was preparing himself for orders while serving the mass. Preaching, the only effective means of making accessible to the people the mysteries locked up in the Scriptures, was but irregularly practised. In 1031 the Council of Limoges was obliged to denounce the error which claimed that preaching was the prerogative of the bishops, for obviously no bishop would have been capable by himself of preaching the Gospel to the whole of his diocese.

The Catholic mass was recited more or less correctly in all parishes, though sometimes the standard was rather low. The frescoes and bas-reliefs on the walls or the capitals of the principal churches—"the books of the unlettered"—abounded in moving but inaccurate lessons. No doubt the faithful nearly all had a superficial acquaintance with the features most apt to strike the imagination in Christian representations of the past, the present, and the future of the world. But their religious life was also nourished on a multitude of beliefs and practices which, whether the legacy of age-old magic or the more recent products of a civilization still extremely fertile in myths, exerted a constant influence upon official doctrine. In stormy skies people still saw phantom armies passing by: armies of the dead, said the populace; armies of deceitful demons, declared the learned, much less inclined to deny these visions than to find for them a quasi-orthodox interpretation. Innumerable nature-rites, among which poetry has especially familiarized us with the May-day festivals, were celebrated in country districts. In short, never was theology less identified with the popular religion as it was felt and lived.

Despite infinite variations according to environment and regional traditions, some common characteristics of this religious mentality can be discerned. Although it will mean passing over various deep and moving features and some fascinating problems of permanent human interest, we shall be obliged to confine ourselves here to recalling those trends in thought and feeling whose influence on social behaviour seems to have been particularly strong.

In the eyes of all who were capable of reflection the material world was scarcely more than a sort of mask, behind which took place all the really important things; it seemed to them also a language, intended to express by signs a more profound reality. Since a tissue of appearances can offer but little interest in itself, the result of this view was that observation was generally neglected in favour of interpretation. In a little treatise on the universe, which was written in the ninth century and enjoyed a very long popularity, Rabanus Maurus explained how he followed his plan: "I conceived the idea of composing a little work . . . which should treat, not only of the nature of things and the properties of words . . . , but still more of their mystic meanings." This attitude explains, in large part, the inadequacy of men's knowledge of nature—of a nature which, after all, was not regarded as greatly deserving of attention. Technical progress—sometimes considerable—was mere empiricism.

Further, this discredited nature could scarcely have seemed fitted to provide its own interpretation, for in the infinite detail of its illusory manifestations it was conceived above all as the work of hidden wills—wills in the plural, in the opinion of simple folk and even of many of the learned. Below the One God and subordinated to his Almighty Power—though the exact significance of this subjection was not, as a rule, very clearly pictured—the generality of mankind imagined the opposing wills of a host of beings good and bad in a state of perpetual strife; saints, angels, and especially devils. "Who does not know," wrote the priest Helmold, "that the wars, the mighty tempests, the pestilences, all the ills, indeed, which afflict the human race, occur through the agency of demons?" Wars, we notice, are mentioned indiscriminately along with tempests; social catastrophes, therefore, are placed in the same class as those which we should nowadays describe as natural. The result was a mental attitude which the history of the invasions has already brought to notice: not exactly renunciation, but rather reliance upon means of action considered more efficacious than human effort. Though the instinctive reactions of a vigorous realism were never lacking, a Robert the Pious or an Otto III could nevertheless attach as much importance to a pilgrimage as to a battle or a law, and historians who are either scandalized by this fact or who persist in discovering subtle political manœuvres in these pious journeys merely prove thereby their own inability to lay aside the spectacles of men of the nineteenth and twentieth centuries. It was not merely the selfish quest of personal salvation that inspired these royal pilgrims. From the patron saints whose aid they went to invoke, they expected for their subjects as well as for themselves, not only the promise of rewards in heaven, but the riches of the earth as well. In the sanctuary, as much as on the field of battle or in the court of law, they were concerned to fulfil their function as leaders of their people.

The world of appearances was also a transitory world. Though in itself inseparable from any Christian representation of the Universe, the image of the final catastrophe had seldom impinged so strongly on the consciousness of men as at this time. They meditated on it; they assessed its premonitory signs. The chronicle of Bishop Otto of Freising, the most

universal of all universal histories, began with Creation and ended with
the picture of the Last Judgment. But, needless to say, it had an inevitable
lacuna: from 1146—the date when the author ceased to write—to the day
of the great catastrophe. Otto, certainly, expected this gap to be of short
duration: "We who have been placed at the end of time . . ." he remarks
on several occasions. This was the general conviction among his contemporaries as it had been in earlier times, and it was by no means confined
to the clergy; to suppose so would be to forget the profound interpenetration of the two groups, clerical and lay. Even among those who did not,
like St. Norbert, go so far as to declare that the event was so close that
the present generation would witness it no one doubted of its imminence.
In every wicked prince, pious souls believed that they recognized the
mark of Antichrist, whose dreadful empire would precede the coming of
the Kingdom of God.

But when in fact would it strike—this hour so close at hand? The
Apocalypse seemed to supply an answer: "and when the thousand years
are expired . . ." Was this to be taken as meaning a thousand years after
the death of Christ? Some thought so, thus putting back the great day of
reckoning—according to the normal calculation—to the year 1033. Or
was it rather to be reckoned from his birth? This latter interpretation
appears to have been the most general. It is certain at any rate that on
the eve of the year 1000 a preacher in the churches of Paris announced
this date for the End of Time. If, in spite of all this, the masses at that
time were not visibly affected by the universal terror which historians of
the romantic school have mistakenly depicted, the reason is above all
that the people of that age, though mindful of the passage of the seasons
and the annual cycle of the liturgy, did not think ordinarily in terms of
the numbers of the years, still less in figures precisely computed on a
uniform basis. How many charters lack any trace of a date! Even among
the rest, what diversity there is in the systems of reference, which are
mostly unconnected with the life of the Saviour—years of reigns or pon-
tificates, astronomical indications of every kind, or even the fifteen-year
cycle of the indiction, a relic of Roman fiscal practices! One entire country, Spain, while using more generally than elsewhere the concept of a
definite era, assigned to it—for reasons that are somewhat obscure—an
initial date absolutely unrelated to the Gospel, namely the year 38 B.C. It
is true that legal documents occasionally and chronicles more frequently
adhered to the era of the Incarnation; but it was still necessary to take
into account the variations in the beginning of the year. For the Church
excluded the first of January as a pagan festival. Thus, according to the
province or the chancellery, the year designated the thousandth began
at one or other of six or seven different dates, which ranged, according
to our calendar, from 25th March 999 to 31st March 1000. What is worse,

some of these initial dates, being essentially moveable since they were linked with a particular liturgical moment of the Easter period, could not be anticipated without tables, which only the learned possessed; they were also very apt to lead to permanent confusion in men's minds by making some years longer than others. Thus it was not unusual for the same day of the month, in March or April, or the feast of the same saint to occur twice in the same year. Indeed, for the majority of Western men this expression, "the year 1000," which we have been led to believe was charged with anguish, could not be identified with any precise moment in the sequence of days.

Yet the notion of the shadow cast over men's minds at that time by the supposed imminence of the Day of Wrath is not altogether wrong. All Europe, it is true, did not tremble with fear towards the end of the first millennium, to compose itself suddenly as soon as this supposedly fateful date was past. But, what was even worse perhaps, waves of fear swept almost incessantly over this region or that, subsiding at one point only to rise again elsewhere. Sometimes a vision started the panic, or perhaps a great historic calamity like the destruction of the Holy Sepulchre in 1009, or again perhaps merely a violent tempest. Another time, it was caused by some computation of the liturgists, which spread from educated circles to the common people. "The rumour spread through almost the whole world that the End would come when the Annunciation coincided with Good Friday," wrote the abbot of Fleury a little before the year 1000. Many theologians, however, remembering that St. Paul had said: "the day of the Lord cometh like a thief in the night," condemned these indiscreet attempts to pierce the mystery in which the Divinity chose to veil his dread purpose. But is the period of waiting made less anxious by ignorance of when the blow will fall? In the prevailing disorders, which we should unhesitatingly describe as the ebullience of adolescence, contemporaries were unanimous in seeing only the last convulsions of an "aged" humanity. In spite of everything, an irresistible vitality fermented in men, but as soon as they gave themselves up to meditation, nothing was farther from their thoughts than the prospect of a long future for a young and vigorous human race.

If humanity as a whole seemed to be moving rapidly towards its end, so much the more did this sensation of being "on the way" apply to each individual life. According to the metaphor dear to so many religious writers, the true believer was in his earthly existence like a pilgrim, to whom the end of the road is naturally of more importance than the hazards of the journey. Of course, the thoughts of the majority of men did not dwell constantly on their salvation. But when they did, it was with deep intensity and above all with the aid of vivid and very concrete images, which were apt to come to them by fits and starts; for their

fundamentally unstable minds were subject to sudden revulsions. Joined
to the penitent mood of a world on the verge of dissolution, the desire for
the eternal rewards cut short more than one leader's career by voluntary
withdrawal to the cloister. And it ended for good and all the propagation
of more than one noble line, as in the case of the six sons of the lord of
Fontaines-lès-Dijon who eagerly embraced the monastic life under the
leadership of the most illustrious of their number, Bernard of Clairvaux.
Thus, in its way, the religious mentality favoured the mixing of the social
classes.

Many Christians, nevertheless, could not bring themselves to submit to
these austere practices. Moreover, they considered themselves (and perhaps not without reason) to be incapable of reaching heaven through
their own merits. They therefore reposed their hopes in the prayers of
pious souls, in the merits accumulated for the benefit of all the faithful
by a few groups of ascetics, and in the intercession of the saints, material-
ized by means of their relics and represented by the monks, their servants. In this Christian society, no function exercised in the collective
interest appeared more important than that of the spiritual organizations, precisely in so far—let us make no mistake about this—as they
were spiritual. The charitable, cultural and economic rôle of the great
cathedral chapters and of the monasteries may have been considerable:
in the eyes of contemporaries it was merely accessory. The notion of a
terrestrial world completely imbued with supernatural significance
combined in this with the obsession of the beyond. The happiness of the
king and the realm in the present; the salvation of the royal ancestors and
of the king himself throughout Eternity: such was the double benefit
which Louis the Fat declared that he expected from his foundation when
he established a community of Canons Regular at the abbey of St. Victor
in Paris. "We believe," said Otto I, "that the protection of our Empire is
bound up with the rising fortunes of Christian worship." Thus we find
a powerful and wealthy Church, capable of creating novel legal institutions, and a host of problems raised by the delicate task of relating this
religious "city" to the temporal "city"; problems ardently debated and
destined to influence profoundly the general evolution of the West. These
features are an essential part of any accurate picture of the feudal world,
and in face of them who can fail to recognize in the fear of hell one of
the great social forces of the age?

Georges Lefebvre 1874—1959

7

That Georges Lefebvre is widely recognized as the leading historian of the French Revolution tends to obscure the broad foundations of his high reputation. He was a complete historian. In his insatiable curiosity, in the scope of his historical views, and in the new perspectives he opened, Lefebvre transcended his own special field and earned a place among the great social historians. Enormous erudition, historical imagination, and concern for theory informed Lefebvre's historiography throughout his long career.

Lefebvre was born in Lille in 1874 in the Department of Nord. His family background was working class (*"Il sortait du peuple,"* writes Albert Soboul); he knew poverty as a child and straitened circumstances well on into maturity. It was only through scholarships provided by the newly established Republican school system that Lefebvre was able to proceed on to the University of Lille. He never forgot the debt he owed to his *"chère école Laïque."* From his youth, Lefebvre was attached to Republican traditions, especially Jacobin ones (Robespierre was a hero to him), and although he was a professional cosmopolitan in the languages and foreign histories he read, he remained intensely French, a patriot through and through. In 1898, he attained his *agrégation,* in history and geography, preparatory to the work on his dissertation for the doctorate.

For the next quarter-century, obscure and impecunious, he taught at various *lycées,* with few connections in fashionable or prestigious intellectual circles. Lefebvre, however, knew how to work and, what is more, thoroughly enjoyed historical research in primary sources. *"J'ai poursuivi des recherches par curiosité d'esprit,"* he wrote; and Richard Cobb notes, "At 85, Lefebvre had the curiosity of a boy of 16, and he has described the supreme satisfaction of untying the strings on a bundle of papers in the attic of a village *mairie."* He ransacked the archives of hundreds of Flanders villages in preparing his great thesis, *Les paysans du Nord pendant la Révolution française* (published in 1924 at his own expense). Henri Pirenne, reviewing the book

161

and commenting upon the enormous amount of research that went into it, called it "a model of scientific conscientiousness or, rather, of scientific abnegation." Albert Mathiez, in high praise, likened Lefebvre's labors to those of a Benedictine monk.

Between 1907 and 1932, he produced three other substantial works that testify to his erudition and historiographical range. At the request of his mentor, Charles Petit-Dutaillis, he translated in three volumes Stubbs's *Constitutional History of England,* to which he added an original essay on the English Parliament in the thirteenth and fourteenth centuries (1907, 1923, 1927). He wrote a long introduction to a collection of *Documents relatifs à l'histoire des subsistances dans le District de Bergues pendant la Révolution (1788-an IV)* (1914). The work remains authoritative and must be read by any student of the period. And he completed a pioneering essay in social psychology, which is also a significant work of social history, *La Grande Peur de 1789* (1932). These works were accompanied by scores of articles and reviews in the *Annales historique de la Révolution française* and the *Revue historique.* By 1932, Lefebvre had "arrived." After Mathiez' death that year, he assumed the editorship of the *Annales historique de la Révolution française* (a post he held until his death); and in 1937, after teaching at the Universities of Clermont-Ferrand (1924–1927) and Strasbourg (1928–1936), he attained the chair of History of the French Revolution at the Sorbonne, where he remained active to the end of his life.

The first edition of his synthesis, *La Révolution française,* appeared in 1930 (a collaborative effort with Raymond Guyot and Philippe Sagnac; the 1951 edition is Lefebvre's entirely). His *Napoléon,* a probing and comprehensive study, followed in 1935. In 1939, he published what has become a minor classic, *Quatre-Vingt-Neuf,* as part of the sesquicentennial celebration of the Revolution (the Nazis suppressed the book in 1940). At the close of World War II, during which he stubbornly continued to teach in order to prevent a "traitor" from being appointed in his stead, Lefebvre's reputation as one of the great historians was unchallengeable.

Like most historians who matured about the turn of the century, Lefebvre fell under the influence of the "New History" then being expounded, at least as an ideal, throughout Europe. Lefebvre read and accepted much of the sociological work of Durkheim, Le Bon, and Halbwachs; he contributed to Henri Berr's *Revue de synthèse* and collaborated with Marc Bloch and Lucien Febvre in their *Annales d'histoire économique et sociale.* More important, as a Guesdean socialist, Lefebvre maintained a "Marxist" perspective, derived from Marx's writings, of course, but rather more influenced by the nuanced historiographical approach of the socialist Jean Jaurès. "If I had any one master, it was he," Lefebvre wrote. From Marx, Lefebvre learned to stress the importance of economic matters, and he adopted the Marxist notion of a dialectical evolution of societies. He drew upon Marx's idea of "contradictions," which he readily enough discovered in his researches on the complexities of old-regime society. From Jaurès, he learned to appreciate ambiguities, to avoid economic reductionism, and to concentrate on the actions of societies, of groups of people rather than on individuals, in his historical studies.

Such influences contributed to the formation of Lefebvre's new and fruitful approach not only to the French Revolution but to the analysis of old-regime society in general. Lefebvre took up Revolutionary historiography where Mathiez had left off. Previous historians, including professionals like Alphonse Aulard and *littérateurs* like Taine, had treated the Revolution "from above," as it were. They concentrated on the actions of the great political figures— Lafayette, Mirabeau, Danton, Robespierre—in the Paris arena; they omitted any discussion of economic and social matters and they ignored the masses, when they did not caricature them as the "Mob" or the "People." Jaurès, in his *Histoire socialiste de la Révolution française* (1901 *et seq.*), and Mathiez, in such studies as *La vie chère et le mouvement social sous la Terreur* (1927), showed how the Revolution could and should be treated "from below," as a social movement involving classes, groups, strata of people with collective interests, aims, and desires. Hence Lefebvre's *Paysans du Nord,* the first major study of the role of peasantry, the first major study of a non-Parisian phenomenon during the Revolution. Traditionalist, purely "political" historians were a bit nonplussed by the work when it appeared; it seemed more the production of a geographer than a historian. But Lefebvre's *thèse* represented the wave of the future; social and economic analyses of the French Revolution threatened until quite recently to overwhelm the political aspects of that historical process.

With new perspectives came new methods and new sources. Lefebvre was among the first historians to substantiate his views with statistical tables—200 pages of them in *Les Paysans*. He was one of the first to emphasize quantitative as well as qualitative analysis: *"Pour faire de l'histoire, il faut savoir compter,"* he wrote; and that is why he made the *archives hypothécaires,* fiscal rolls, and notarial records—those rich sources which outline property ownership, profits, and transfers—a special field of study. His work on *The Great Fear* and his "Revolutionary Crowds" (among others) drew upon both social psychology and an appreciation of collective mentalities, which in turn presuppose a knowledge of economic, social, and political conditions. In what has been judged as perhaps his most original contribution, he appears to have been the first historian to suggest that what has actually happened is not as important as what people *think* has happened. ("He is the first of a group of historians of popular myths," Cobb writes.) His analyses of urban and rural social structures and stratification demonstrated for the first time how complex and fluid French society was before the Revolution, how difficult it is to speak of separate "classes" or even of clear divisions between town and county; he was very critical of Soviet historians in this matter and roundly rebuked them for their failure to understand the complexities of either the French land system or the French social system.

Yet Lefebvre's enthusiasms for theory and for the social sciences sometimes led him astray. His own definition of social class was rather rigid, based solely on wealth and income, even though he recognized that social status requires an elaboration of that definition. In emphasizing archival research, Lefebvre disdained literary sources and thus often missed important evidence. He advocated a "sociological history" that "aspired to scientific status," but he read social scientists like Le Bon rather too uncritically and was not very familiar with German sociology. He was fascinated by biology and thought that there would perhaps one day be a way to enlist that science in the cause of historical explanation, although he did not know precisely how. His "Marxism" inclined him to the "grand synthesis," the general plan of history by which all is explained, all events and developments "reduced" to reactions stimulated by the "basic" economic forces at work in history. He sometimes slipped into a dogmatic position on the role of the "revolutionary bourgeoisie" and into a mechanical dialectic of class conflict. Hence he could respond with an acerbic *ad hominem* assault when Alfred Cobban suggested that the "bourgeois Revolution" with all of its ideological and interpretative baggage was a myth.

And yet, much of the time his scholarship and common sense precluded dogmatism. His desire for a clear "scientific" quantitative history never overcame his professional honesty when his researches showed him ambiguity, flux, and contradictions that could be grasped only qualitatively, almost by intuition. *"L'esprit de géométrie,"* he wrote, recalling Pascal, "does not embrace all of life, and the spirit of *finesse* retains its rights." Prejudiced as he was in favor of Robespierre, he dealt fairly and definitively with Danton. Much as he sought for "laws" in history, he recognized that the best that historians could come up with were certain "constants," which, however, had no predictive value. Although he stressed economic and social factors in history, he did not deny all power to ideas, and he insisted that men make their own history, though constrained by natural and social forces. And despite his affinity for the work of Berr, Febvre, and Bloch, he nevertheless distanced himself from their heavily "social-scientific" or cultural-anthropological stance, and from what he judged to be their tendency toward hasty or overly ambitious generalizations. Perhaps most revealing, he refused to surrender either the narrative line or "political history." The *Annales* school derisively labeled the study of political events *"histoire événementielle ou historisante,"* terms which Lefebvre described as "dreadful neologisms." To the historian of the French Revolution, *"la longue durée,"* so appealing to certain *Annalistes,* posed a threat to historical understanding.

"Il faut travailler," Lefebvre wrote, and he worked to the last. His revision of *La Révolution française* appeared in 1951, to be followed by a third edition in 1957. He continued to work with the *Annales historique de la Révolution française* and in the archives. At the age of seventy-nine, he set out on what he called his third honeymoon, to explore the local archives of the Orléanais. The rough draft he left of the results of those researches was published posthumously in two volumes as *Études orléanaises:* I, *Contribution à l'étude des structures sociales à la fin du 18e siècle;* II, *Subsistances et Maximum (1789-an IV)* (1962–1963); the work is typically erudite and exhaustive. It is also provisional in certain of its conclusions and suggestive of further researches; for Georges Lefebvre, the historian's work was one of continued inquiry and could never be complete. That lesson is part of his enduring legacy.

Selected Bibliography

Perhaps the most engaging and affectionate appraisal of Lefebvre is Richard Cobb's "Georges Lefebvre," which appeared first in *Past and Present,* 18 (November, 1960), and is included in his collection of essays and reviews, *A Second Identity: Essays on France and French History* (1969). Beatrice Hyslop, who knew Lefebvre well, contributed a moving essay, "Georges Lefebvre, Historian," to *French Historical Studies,* I (1960), 256–282. Gordon H. McNeil's "Georges Lefebvre, 1874–1959," in *Some Twentieth Century Historians,* is an informative essay; and R. R. Palmer's preface to his translation of *Quatre-Vingt-Neuf: The Coming of the French Revolution* (1947) is a helpful analysis of Lefebvre's contribution to Revolutionary historiography. Very much worth reading is Palmer's review essay, "Georges Lefebvre: The Peasants and the French Revolution," *Journal of Modern History,* XXXI (1959), 329–342. Albert Soboul's introduction to the second edition of Lefebvre's *Études sur la Révolution française* (1963) is a testimonial from the master's best-known student. It should be followed up by Lefebvre's review essay *"Avenir de l'histoire"* in that collection. Volume I of the English version of *La Révolution française* (translated by Elizabeth Moss Evanson, 1962) includes a short foreword by Paul H. Beik; and *The Great Fear of 1789* (translated by Joan White, 1973) is introduced by George Rudé, another of Lefebvre's students. Worth reading are Marcel Reinhard's appreciations: "Un historien au XXe siècle: Georges Lefebvre," *Revue historique,* CCXXIII (January–March, 1960), 1–12; and "Georges Lefebvre, 1874–1959," *Revue d'histoire moderne et contemporaine,* VII (1960), 5–10. Finally, students should refer to Alfred Cobban's penetrating critique of the position of the Lefebvre "school," *The Social Interpretation of the French Revolution* (1965), which opened a debate still under way.

STUDIES ON THE FRENCH
REVOLUTION

*The Distribution of Landed Property and of Cultivated Holdings at
the End of the Old Regime*

The distribution of landed property at the end of the old regime is a
subject which from the beginning has aroused passionate debates. Supporters of the Revolution claim as one of its results the creation of free
peasant smallholdings through the sale of nationalized land. [*Biens na-
tionaux:* ecclesiastical property and, later, confiscated émigré land.] Opponents of the Revolution argue that long before 1789 a large portion of
the land had already passed into the hands of the peasants; they base
their assertion on the testimony of such sources as Arthur Young, the
grievance lists [*cahiers*], oral traditions, and local examples. Over the
years, however, scholars have debated the question without considering
whether archival researches in fact settle the matter. The Revolutionary
administration, it is true, did not systematically record and preserve the
acts of sale of nationalized land, but it usually preserved the old leases
[*terriers*] and documents concerning land taxes. Tocqueville was aware
of the lists of the 5 per cent income tax [*vingtièmes*], and he noted the tax
accounts of 1791. He himself, however, only made a random sampling of
these documents. Historians have produced numerous monographs on
the condition of the rural masses in the eighteenth century, but they
contain only vague generalizations concerning the distribution of property and have thus cast little light on the matter. Not until the twentieth
century did scholars evaluate with reasonable certainty the extent of
ecclesiastical property. The contributions of certain Russian historians,
for example, Kovalewsky and Kareiev, only muddled the issue, as we
shall see. After 1885, French historians began the serious study of the sale
of nationalized land, but the distribution of property before 1789 remained a neglected question.

It was another Russian historian, Loutchisky, whose valuable efforts

From *Études sur la Révolution française* (Paris: Presses Universitaires de
France, 2nd ed. 1963), pp. 88–92, 279–298. Translated by Gerald J. Cavanaugh.
Translated by permission of the publisher.

cleared the air of gratuitous and contradictory affirmations. Loutchisky initiated the study of tax roles and demonstrated how the matter might be clarified by a *quantitative* evaluation of property distribution, even if it were only an approximation. His own work indicated that the task was immense and could only be brought off by scholars resigned to writing rigorously formulated monographs. In 1912, he published an excellent study of Limousin. Camille Bloch had already studied the *vingtième* lists of Loiret (1900); Laude, drawing upon lease records, published his essay on Artois in 1914, while Donat analyzed the leases and land surveys of Larrazet, in Tarn-et-Garonne (1926). At the same time, historians most concerned with the sale of nationalized land began to see that their own conclusions would take on added interest if they knew the distribution of property before 1789. Schmitt's study of Bar-le-Duc (1907) was helpful and it was followed by the works of Porée, Martin, and Nicolle on, respectively, Sens, Toulouse, and Saint-Gaudens (1912, 1916, 1924). I myself have tried to resolve the question for the department of Nord (1924).

II

It seems that we are now agreed on the method to follow: as complete a utilization as possible of pertinent documents, with the necessity of extracting from them quantitative data.

Little needs to be said concerning the value of these documents, especially the rolls of the *vingtième* and the *taille* [the major land tax, paid mainly by peasants], which Loutchisky used so well and which are quite accessible and easy to exploit when well drawn up. The debate over the worth and reliability of such documents was a long one but is now ended. However, the value of documents relative to the *vingtièmes* and the *tailles* ought not to be decided on principle. It is always a question of type, time, and place. The registers established by the directors of the *vingtièmes,* especially in the case of a surveyed village, offer a base for approximating the total area of the place. The same is true for documents such as the *pieds de taille,* but in this case the land of privileged owners (nobles, churchmen, wealthy commoners) might not be included. This may also be true of the *vingtième* rolls; there the situation is not yet clear. Often quite inferior to these documents are the tax lists established in villages for collection purposes. In principle these were drawn from the official register, but more often they derived from older and therefore less accurate lists. Researchers must always consider changes over time. Lists were often drawn according to "occupations" without distinguishing the entire patrimony, of which only a part may have been leased out. In such a case (and in the Nord it is frequent) the documents preclude the study of the distribution of property, but we must note they are still

valuable as indications of lands under cultivation which previously escaped the historian's notice and which are of capital interest. Finally, in
all these documents important information concerning the residence
and status of named individuals may very well be missing. In brief, each
document requires a preliminary critical examination and frequently
corroborative evidence. There is no longer any justification, however, for
ignoring them *a priori.*

If the tax rolls of the old regime were useless, however, we should not
be without recourse. There exist a large number of leases and contracts
[*terriers*] regulating the church tithe [*dîme*] and feudal dues and fees
[*droits féodaux*]. It is true that many of these relate to mere fragments of
a parish and they usually fail to indicate the names of lessees and the
changes which must have occurred over time. But they were carefully
drawn up and often include a land survey. Their principal defect as
sources is their relative rarity: they are altogether lacking in maritime
Flanders, and in Puy-de-Dôme only a few eighteenth-century leases remain. In Artois, however, Laude was able with their help to study twenty-
seven parishes very closely.

Is this all we have? By no means. The Revolution bequeathed to us
many documents on landholding. The Consituent Assembly (1789–1791)
ordered tax lists and registers drawn up in each commune. More to the
point, the operation was in fact carried out in subsequent years. Most
notable were the results of governmental decisions in 1805–1806 which
ordered in each commune the evaluation of revenues proportionate to
total cultivation. These were followed in 1807 by the initiation of a general land survey [*cadastre*]. These documents are in general more precise
and more detailed than those of the old regime. We may at times doubt
their accuracy concerning estimates of total land in cultivation, and
there is also the question of types of land. But a comparison with survey
documents does allow for the resolution of ambiguities. By means of
documents drawn up in 1791 or shortly thereafter we may easily reconstitute the distribution of landed property as it was when the sale of nationalized lands began. Nevertheless, it remains true that scholars have used
such documents only in the study of Nord and the Vire region. The
evident reason for such a gap in our historical knowledge is that research
must be begun in communal archives which ordinarily have not yet been
inventoried: only the departments of Calvados and Aube have published
repertories of their communal landholdings before 1800. That date, incidentally, demonstrates that in undertaking the task of compilation, researchers did not consider the question we are considering, otherwise
they would have begun their repertories from the time of the first land
survey registers (1791). Very numerous in Calvados, the tax lists and
registers are already rare in many other regions, for example Nord and

Puy-de-Dôme. Because they are of no use to present-day administrators, they are gradually disappearing through neglect or deliberate destruction. It is to be hoped that departmental committees of the economic history of the Revolution will note the existence of such documents and take the necessary steps to integrate them into departmental archives where they will be preserved and made more accessible.

In sum, we may now hope that scholars will in the future refrain from ignoring or treating with preconceived skepticism these valuable documents which are often difficult to discover and whose study, always long and wearying, does not arouse much public enthusiasm. For this type of research there are not many devoted scholars, especially among our students. It would be helpful if even that potential few were not further discouraged by being assured that their efforts are doomed in advance to be fruitless.

III

The studies mentioned above are few in number; however, we may already advance certain conclusions whose principal worth is, for the moment, to indicate the subject's intrinsic and great interest.

Let us note immediately that the existence in France at the end of the old regime of a propertied peasantry is now beyond dispute. We should hardly have to emphasize this fact if Kovalewsky and Kareiev had not reopened the discussion by advancing the view that only the freeholders [*alleutiers*] ought to be considered proprietors. Now, there were indeed very few freeholders and we can even say that there were no proprietors in France because the King claimed the right of eminent domain over all land. In regard to the peasants, it is clear that the possessor of a tenure laden with quit rents, field rents, and feudal fees [*cens, champarts, droits casuels*] was not a freehold proprietor. Those who received such rents and fees were presumed to have only conceded the use of the land and thus retained "eminent" rights to the property. This is the interpretation adopted by the Constituent Assembly when it declared certain feudal obligations redeemable for a money payment. But the tenant could bequeath, give, sell, or rent his land, which moreover was heritable. Thus the experts in feudal land contracts recognized the "useful domain" of the peasants (as contrasted with "eminent domain"); and it is precisely because he in fact exercised all the rights of a modern proprietor that the "feudal" rents and fees he paid seemed to the peasant an unjustifiable and intolerable abuse. It is thus necessary to label as proprietors all those peasants who possessed a heritable tenure. Loutchisky undertook laborious researches to establish this point, which we trust will no longer be contested. For certain areas, especially lower Brittany, some difficulties remain. The *"tenure en quevaise"* was not freely heritable; the *"tenure convenancière"* was revocable. Like many other feudal relationships, they were very likely servile in origin. Depending on how one views them, these types of tenure could be assimilated among the other types. The Legislative Assembly and the convention differed from the Constituent and Directory Assemblies in such views, and the agrarian question thus varied considerably from time to time. But for most of France this situation did not apply. The sale of nationalized land thus did not create peasant property; it merely extended it, and because of the way the sales were organized, the extension was quite restricted. The great Revolutionary work certainly accelerated an evolution which had for centuries been working itself out in various ways, but the new impetus was integrated into the old process and thus lost its potentially catastrophic character. From the nineteenth-century perspective, only the exact rate and extension of the transformation had to be determined; the principle itself had been established. We must note that our researches would lose their value if the distribution of property and of cultivated holdings in relation to population movements was not slowly emerging, in the light of recently published works, as an essential element in the agrarian crisis which so powerfully contributed to the success of the Revolution.

That crisis had many causes: the burdens of taxation, tithe, and feudal levies; the archaic agricultural technology; the increasing restrictions being placed on peasants' collective rights, gleaning, open pasture, use of the forests, and other communal rights. We are thus not studying the entire question here. But the distribution of land played a more important part than heretofore realized. Land was lacking among the peasants: this essential fact is often forgotten because it is not always mentioned in the *cahiers,* precisely because the poorest peasants could not or dared not express their views. In studying the sale of nationalized land, scholars implicitly maintain that the legislation of the various assemblies satisfied the wishes of the rural population. Sometimes they even deny that the feeble efforts of the Jacobins [*Montagnards*] to render the sales more democratic originated as a response to the demands of the rural proletariat. The agrarian crisis manifests itself clearly, however, when historians study the distribution of property and relate it to such documents of the Revolutionary era as the inquiry into begging (1790), the reports on communal lands, and the innumerable petitions which swamped the committees of the Assemblies and the local administrations right up until 1794.

IV

From evidence already assembled, we know that an extreme variety marked the agrarian map of France in 1789. From region to region, the percentage of land held by nobles might fluctuate from 9 per cent to 44 per cent; rarely did church lands exceed 20 per cent of the total and in some areas was only 1 per cent; bourgeoisie holdings ranged from 12 to 45 per cent; peasant holdings from 22 to 70 per cent. The Nord department with its naturally diverse regions remarkably resembles a great portion of the distribution spectrum of varying landholdings. In the southern part of the department the aristocracy dominated: the church in the plain of Cambrésis and Hainaut, the nobility in the forested areas along the Ardenne, church and nobility together in the Ostrevent section and the plains of the Scarpe. Peasant property, rather developed and sometimes quite extensive in the grasslands of the Sambre, progressively decreased as one moved northward and was minimal in the region of the Scarpe. In the north, in maritime Flanders, the aristocracy owned but a fifth of the land. Bourgeoisie and peasant property dominated there, the first group owning one half of the maritime plain, the second group one half of the area of Bois. Around Lille, the situation was very complex and in a state of transition. The clergy were relatively poor in land, the nobility remained very powerful; compared with the south, the bourgeoisie were increasing their holdings, and the peasants too were expanding. This diversity, as Loutchisky has well demonstrated for Limousin, characterized each region of France, from village to village.

Can we discern any dominant traits? Certainly for ecclesiastical property, which has been subjected to the most careful study. We know that the extent of such property has been exaggerated. In Nord it was considerable only in the plain of Picardy: 30 per cent in the Laonnais area, 40 per cent in Cambrésis. As we move into Flanders and into the forested *bocage* area of the Sambre, it plunges to 12 per cent and often below; moving on to the Caux area, it drops to 6 per cent. In all of France it did not exceed 10 per cent, and Lecarpentier's estimate of 6 per cent may be correct. In countrysides whose geographic features resemble those of the Picardy plains, ecclesiastical property never reaches the same levels: 20 per cent in Brie, 12 per cent in Sénonais, but only 5 per cent in the Eure area and 4.5 per cent near Loiret. It is even lower in the other sections of the department. For historians, it is perhaps most noteworthy that it gets progressively lower as one moves south. Such a situation must have deep roots in our ancient history.

For the nobility, many points remain obscure. Noble lands dominated in the west of the department. Areas of waste and marsh favored noble holdings, for example in the north, in the Avesnes area, and in the Scarpe plains. But it was also extensive around certain large towns: Toulousain, Lille, Brie: it is evident that rich bourgeoisie were recruited into the nobility, ennobling themselves and thus their property. Naturally, bourgeoisie property predominated in the environs of the larger towns.

As for peasant property, its variations are sometimes more apparent than real. For example, in lower Brittany its extent was mediocre; but in fact, as noted above, the major portion of the land was cultivated there under the system of tenancy at the will of the landlord [*domaines congéables*]. If these holdings are defined as peasant property, and the Legislative Assembly and the Convention so defined them, the area then becomes comparable to others. Moreover, the narrow extent of land held by the peasants is explainable by the vast extent of forest, waste, and marsh lands, for example, in east Avesnes and in the valley of the Scarpe. If we measure only cultivatable land, the disproportions attenuate or disappear. But there nevertheless remain important differences, especially if we recall that much peasant property consisted of regions that were originally forested or that were mountainous, where clearing was left to individual initiative (Bois in Flanders: 50 per cent; Vire: 60 to 70 per cent; Limousin: 55 per cent). In contrast, peasant proprietorship was weakest in those areas where clearings were carried out by wealthy abbeys or rich concessionaires, who alone had the capital necessary to undertake such tasks (maritime Flanders: 20 per cent). It was also weak around the larger towns where bourgeoisie property abounded (around Lille and Toulousain, for example, peasant holdings were, respectively, 28 and 22 per cent of the total); similarly, around Versailles peasants owned only 1 per cent of the land at most, because the royal domain was particularly preserved to insure an area for the hunt. It may yet be said, however, that in many cases the existence of ecclesiastical and noble property appears to be the sole obstacle opposing the expansion of peasant holdings, and thus explaining these regional variations.

Finally, the extreme division of property was a universal trait. The very great majority of peasants owned only tiny plots. In Limousin, of 5,314 peasant proprietors, 23 per cent possessed less than an acre [*arpent:* about four-fifths of an acre]; 35 per cent held from one to five acres. That is to say, 58 per cent of the peasants owned less than five acres of land. In Laonnais, the respective percentages were 49 and 26: a total of 75 per cent. In the fifteen communes of Loiret, of 1,968 proprietors, 22.76 per cent had less than an acre, 81.45 per cent had less than ten acres. In the Nord department, south of the Lys, 75 per cent of the peasants had less than one acre. Not only did peasant proprietorships exist, then, but the number of proprietors was considerable. Another perhaps even more important fact is that the property of privileged groups and of the bourgeoisie, although naturally concentrated in the hands of many fewer individuals, was portioned out in a mass of parcels of land of more or less mediocre size: large farms are relatively rare in France. This resulted in important consequences for France's economic evolution and for the sale of nationalized lands: in the absence of large farms, agricultural progress was hindered; and since the sale of secularized and confiscated lands concerned mainly land under cultivation and therefore small plots, the existing practices facilitated peasant acquisitions.

With these two characteristics, the multiplicity of peasant proprietorships and the dispersion of the landed estates [*domaine proche*] of the privileged groups, the agrarian regime of France contrasted sharply with that of eastern Europe and of England. Loutchisky was particularly struck by this contrast, which he made the cornerstone of his studies.

V

We know the type of agrarian organization which begins as we move into Saxony and Bavaria and which predominates once we cross the Elbe or enter Hungary. Instead of being distributed in any number of tenures, almost the entire domain [*seigneurie*] remains in the hands of the lord [*seigneur*], who cultivates it himself by means of labor [*corvée*] his peasants, mainly serfs, owe him. We know also that, in contrast, serfdom, *corvées,* and feudal usages had disappeared from England by about 1500. Certain fees and dues drawn from the land remained, but between 1500 and 1700 most of the tenants who paid them left the land, their lords having dispossessed them by various expedients, including violence, in order to create large enclosed farms. The English peasants were thus free, but the majority of them were reduced to the condition of propertyless day laborers. According to Loutchisky, France offered a third agrarian type, which moreover was representative of most of western Europe, including Rhineland Germany. Peasants there were almost all free, as in England. But almost all of them, even day laborers, also owned some land, tiny as it might be. There was, then, in Loutchisky's view, no rural proletariat yoked to the *corvée* or living exclusively by means of day labor. Loutchisky notes the lords' failure to exploit their estates in a way comparable to that practiced in eastern Europe and the habit of leasing or renting land in plots that were always quite small, mainly because labor was scarce. Consequently, French agriculture remained backward and unable to produce much for export. The French rural system was thus characterized by the peasant who farms for himself and at best for the neighboring village.

There is much truth in this thesis that Loutchisky defended so brilliantly in his study of Limousin, a work based on minute investigations. The uniqueness of western Europe's agrarian structure cannot be called into doubt. There were serfs in France, and propertied peasants themselves often were subject to the *corvée.* But their *corvée,* while servile, was never arbitrary and most often had either been abolished in favor of a money payment or was simply never invoked, the lords often having neither land nor residence in the area. There was no such thing as the

Gesindedienst, which in eastern Europe obliged the peasants' children to work solely for the *seigneur.* Moreover, as we have seen, the French peasants owned a substantial part of the land, and large farmers were a small minority.

However, Loutchisky was swept along in a polemical debate and was perhaps too wedded to his own opinions. It was not that he neglected to offer necessary qualifications. He himself noted the presence in Limousin of landless peasants and established that France indeed contained rural proletarians. He even indicated that there were many such peasants in lower Normandy. Nor did he deny that there was an agrarian crisis: "If Limousin was miserable," he wrote, "it was only because the peasants had not enough land." But this implicit recognition of the crisis may easily escape the reader, and the general view in Loutchisky's book is that there was no crisis. We must look at the matter more closely.

VI

By means of the lists of the *taille* we may most readily establish the proportion of propertyless peasants, because those lists carefully distinguished between the *taille* on property, the *taille* on cultivation, and the *taille* on industry or the *"naturel taillable."* Such research is much more easy than that which concerns itself with the accounts of land areas; it is however much less advanced. At the same time, we must note that such tax lists do not exist everywhere; in that case, and it applies to the Nord, scholars are forced to compare the number of proprietors with the hearth counts and lists of heads of families. We may also consult the census of taxpayers drawn up in 1790 to determine the "active citizens" [i.e., those awarded the franchise had to pay a minimum tax]. The approximation so obtained is less satisfactory, but it may suffice to settle the question at least in principle. Finally, when we have the list of personal property taxes of 1791, we may utilize it as a valuable corroboration of the state of things at the end of the old regime, providing, of course, that the municipality has observed article 12 of the January 13, 1791, law requiring the naming of all citizens incapable of paying the necessary amount of taxes (equal per year to three days labor). Given this record, no documentary *lacunae* remain.

In the district of Sens, of 12,256 households [*feux*], 815 were exempt from taxation. Of these, 380 were of the town of Sens and the other 435 thus represent for the rural areas a total of 3 per cent. This is the lowest total we know of, but it should be noted that those who paid the equivalent of only one or two days' labor might in fact have been propertyless. The examination of leases confirms the case at Sens, however. In contrast, the thirteen communes of Loiret, not far from there, had a total of

24.05 per cent propertyless peasants; while in Limousin, Loutchisky counted 17.6 per cent of the total as propertyless in the parish of Tulle. In the Nord, 15 to 20 per cent of the peasants on the plain of Cambrésis were propertyless; the percentage was lower in the grasslands of the Sambre, where in certain villages every family had at least a cottage and a garden. At Larrazet (Tarn-et-Garonne) in 1763, the percentage of non-propertied was 16.14. But there were areas where they were much more numerous. For lower Normandy, Loutchisky put the figure at 40.2 per cent; around Vire, sixteen communes counted 29 per cent; at Monnain, in Orne, a tax roll of 1790 listed 27.17 per cent. In the Nord, there were 30 to 40 per cent propertyless peasants between the Scarpe and Lille; 70 per cent in Ferrain (the area of Roubaix and Tourcoing being over-populated); 60 to 65 per cent in the plains of the Lys; 55 per cent in the Bois area; 75 per cent in the maritime plain. Clearly, Flanders resembled England more than Sens, and it was not the only such area. From the Versailles region we have similar figures: 55.5 per cent for Saint-Cyr, 70.5 per cent at Viroflay, 73.3 per cent at Vélizy. Quite probably Brie was in the same situation, and we need to examine other regions where peasant proprietors appear numerically weak, in Toulousain, for example. Thus, we discover here the extreme diversity which marked France, and if we accept Loutchisky's thesis we should only do so in the sense that the condition distinguished France from eastern Europe and England but not that it expressed in its totality the real situation. There were many more propertyless peasants than Loutchisky inadvertently led us to believe. And we cannot oppose the purely agricultural areas to those that were already endowed with rural industries, as Loutchisky did in referring to the examples of Limousin and lower Normandy. If the district of Sens confirms his conclusion, Cambrésis, where the fabrication of muslin prospered and where there were fewer than 20 per cent propertyless peasants, and the Flanders maritime plain, purely agricultural and with a total of 75 per cent propertyless peasantry, ruin that thesis completely.

But it is not enough to demonstrate a more or less considerable number of propertyless peasants. Loutchisky ought to have insisted that the great majority of rural proprietors did not have enough land by which to live; they had to work for others or practice an auxiliary trade. That is why rural industry prospered even in Cambrésis, where nine of ten peasants owned at least their cottages. In order to understand this situation clearly, it is useful to know the rural economy and especially to determine approximately how much land it took to maintain a family. When we have studied the numerical distribution of farms, we may take as a point of comparison the dominant type of farm or sharecropping situation. In Limousin, Loutchisky indicates that the usual domain was from 14 to 28 acres [arpents]. From this we see that among 5,314 proprietors not more than 1,000, or 18 per cent, could live independently. Of the propertyless, only 15 per cent figured as heads of families; and all of the rest, if they could not rent a piece of land or if they could not find work assisting the sharecroppers, had to beg their bread or migrate. Further, the standard of living assured by this independent proprietorship in Limousin differed greatly from what was judged acceptable in Flanders, because there it was estimated that twelve acres sufficed to maintain a family, the land there being more fertile. Thus, 16 per cent of the proprietors and 5 to 6 per cent of the heads of families attained or surpassed this minimum. In Brittany, where Henri Sée studied twenty-eight parishes, 81 per cent of the peasants owned less than three acres; in Monnain, 87 per cent had less than twelve acres; and in these areas of fallow land, such lots were very small. It was even worse around Versailles and most likely in Brie as well. Thus, when the revolutionaries proposed to increase the number of proprietors through the sale of nationalized land, they neglected the most important part of the problem, that which at least most interested the majority of peasants in so many areas: they were already proprietors and wished to expand their tiny domains. The laws of June 5 and September 13, 1793, did nothing for them, and that is one reason they were dead letters.

VII

At the same time, it is desirable that future researches be not limited to the study of the distribution of property. It is important in effect to verify whether the distribution of cultivated holdings did not in some measure attenuate the agrarian crisis. Just as an artisan may live if someone rents him a workshop and tools, so the peasant may live either as a lessee or sharecropper. This is one of the reasons so many eighteenth-century peasants were attracted to the areas of unenclosed small farms and sharecropping; it is also the reason why of all the demands of the peasants until 1794 the most obstinate was the call for the break-up of large farms.

Unfortunately we have no quantitative information on this matter except for the Nord. Scholars might also draw some indications from the *taille* lists of the Vire and Versailles regions. Loutchisky sought to demonstrate that the number of cultivated holdings in the Limousin was not very high, but he did not count them. He did not seek to discover whether the number of peasants exceeded that of proprietors and how many "mixed" peasant proprietors there were who had to add a leased farm to their own land in order to survive.

Regions in which a few large farmers engrossed almost all of the land put to lease, for example around Versailles, were probably few in number. In the plain of Picardy, however, the large farms predominated, and this may not have been a unique instance. People complained bitterly about the same situation in Beauce, and the known extent of privileged property in Brie might have had the same results. We must repeat concerning cultivation what we noted about distribution: regional diversity was extreme. In the Nord, for example, Flanders was an area of peasants who leased land [*fermiers*] and of "mixed" occupancy [owners who were also lessees]. These two categories together made up 87 per cent of the cultivators in the maritime plain: 83 per cent toward the Lys, from 70 to 65 per cent moving toward the Scarpe. In several of these areas peasant proprietorship was rather important: it was particularly there that the proprietor found it most easy to round off his holding and that others most easily succeeded in leasing land as *fermiers*. Flanders also possessed a "rural bourgeoisie," if we may so speak, that was quite distinct from the proletarian day laborers. In the south area of Nord, on the contrary, where the peasants owned tiny plots of land and experienced a greater need to add to their holdings by leasing land, where cultivation was much less advanced and the fallow system was still followed, the land was let out to great masses of peasants, and the number of larger lessees [*fermiers*] was less by half.

To what extent was the agrarian crisis mitigated by the renting of privileged and bourgeoisie land? Around Versailles, it was of little matter; in Cambrésis, where there were from 15 to 20 per cent non-proprietor peasants, the proportion of peasants who had no land whatsoever dipped to about 10 per cent. In Flanders, however, the proportion rose considerably. About 15 to 20 per cent of the heads of family in Walloon Flanders had no land as opposed to at least 30 to 40 per cent non-proprietors; one third in maritime Flanders against at least 55 to 60 per cent. (This is to say that, in general, the more non-proprietor peasants there were, that is, those who depended upon leased lands to survive, the more propertyless peasants. Put another way: The more the land was leased out to peasants, the less land there was available for peasants to buy.) In the north of Vire, the increase was lower because land was not leased out ordinarily; however, in fifteen communes, 20.73 per cent of those subject to the *taille* were *fermiers* [lessees], so those inhabitants who were taxed only on the basis of their produce [*taille naturel*] made up only 8.29 per cent of all those taxed. In twelve of these communes, 19.38 per cent of the proprietors worked leased land as well as their own.

But when we examine in detail the distribution of cultivated lands in relation to their extent, we arrive at a result analogous to that concerning the distribution of property. In the Nord, between the Lys and the Sambre, 60 to 70 per cent of the occupants farmed less than two and a half acres; 20 to 25 per cent worked from two and a half to twelve acres. The numbers improve in maritime Flanders and south of the Sambre, but those farming less than twelve acres compose at least three-quarters of the total, except in the maritime plain, where the figure is at least 60 per cent. At Monnain, the only other example we have, forty-seven cultivators worked less than two and a half acres, fifty-three from two and a half to twelve; together they made up 74 per cent of the total, working less than 12 per cent of the land.

Undoubtedly we would have an exaggerated idea of the agrarian crisis if to the study of property distribution we failed to join that of the distribution of cultivation. But we see clearly that to explain the hostility of the peasants toward large farms it is not necessary to discover whether such farms were increasing in number. Those that already existed constituted a sufficient attraction for all those peasants who could not establish themselves or who could not find enough land to lease in order to round out their own property.

VIII

It need hardly be said that in order to appreciate the seriousness of the situation we must know how the distribution of property and of cultivated holdings was evolving at the end of the old regime. To attain that end we must double our efforts in order to compare the two factors parish by parish, unless the registers regularly note the pertinent changes, such as Loutchisky was fortunate to discover in Limousin, Laonnais, and Toulousain. Notarial records also furnish valuable evidence.

According to Loutchisky, the peasants acquired 4,718 *sétérées* of land from 1779 to 1791 in seven parishes of the *élection* of Tulle, almost entirely at the expense of the nobility. [A *sétérée* was a local measure of land equivalent to the amount necessary to grow twelve bushels of grain.] From 1782 to 1791 they acquired 1,610 *sétérées* in eighteen parishes of the *élection* of Brive, at the expense of bourgeoisie and nobility. M. Schmitt affirms that a similar property shift, from nobility to peasantry, occurred in the Bar-le-Duc district and that it involved a great amount of land. In Toulousain and Laonnais, peasant expansion was much slower: 75 acres in sixty parishes of the former, from 1760 to 1787; 264 acres in seventeen parishes of the latter, from 1750 to 1785. In the Nord, the case was similar to these last two regions. We might also ask whether some of these gains resulted from the clearing of communal lands that were merely defined previously as *seigneuriale;* this may be asked particularly of Limousin. It also remains to be shown that the number of proprietors increased because of these purchases, something Loutchisky failed to do. The increase in peasant property might have benefited mainly those peasants who were already proprietors, and as the division of the patrimony proceeded in each generation the agrarian crisis would in no way have been mitigated. The dissociation of the rural masses by the formation of a class of wealthier peasants might have been the principal result of these acquisitions. This seems to have been the case in the Nord. There, the very small proprietors increased in numbers, and divisions at each new generation were the principal cause of that increase.

As for the cultivated holdings, we should not of course accept without question all the complaints against the expansion of large farms. We do have some incontestable evidence, however. In Cambrésis, the tendency toward concentration was not uniform; in maritime Flanders it is undeniable. On the other hand, if the middling farms increased in Walloon Flanders, there is evidence that in maritime Flanders especially the small and tiny farms multiplied rapidly without however increasing their size. This is the consequence of the increasing parcelization of the small properties. By comparison, then, the large farm appeared even larger, even if it did not expand.

Finally, it remains essential to investigate the demographic question. This could in fact be the key to most of the relative problems—but on this point we are least informed. It is true that we have no census worthy of the name, but we ought at least to have statistics on births and deaths, inasmuch as the church recorded them. It is not the number of inhabitants at a given date that we need but the tendencies of the changes. There is also the problem of migrations, but the number of births and deaths could throw light on this as well. Messance, for example, did such a study for the first half of the eighteenth century (1766), but his excellent work has not been emulated in our time, although it requires no technical knowledge to pursue the subject up to the Revolution. The population certainly increased. But once again we discover regional diversity: in Messance's time, Normandy was already marked by low natality. Around Orléans, however, Marc Bloch has discovered an excess of deaths over births—and this was opposite to the situation in the Nord. Complaints relative to the shortage of day laborers, which then easily shift into lamentations on depopulation, ought to be handled with great care. For farmers to begin complaining, there needed only to exist rural industries which drew off their day workers. There were also areas of heavy emigration, such as Auvergne and Limousin. If there were relatively few propertyless peasants in Limousin, it was because the "limousinants" were already numerous residents of Paris, employed in the building trades. In short, the demographic factor must be seriously studied. In the Nord, the inquest of 1790 defined one-fifth of the population as indigent in normal times; in hard times a more or less considerable number of families responded to the stressful conditions by sending their children out "to seek their bread." Manufacturing was well established in this area, however; and if it could not provide employment and thus bread for the population, it was because the population was growing and the number of propertyless peasants was increasing too rapidly. It is at least probable that this case was not exceptional.

IX

The old regime was thus exposed to grave troubles in the event of food shortages and manufacturing crises. Both of these occurred toward the end of 1788 and paved the way for the agrarian revolt which broke out in July 1789 and which flared intermittently until 1793. But if the lack of land was one of its causes, how is it that the peasants who had been united in their demands for the abolition of the tithe and feudal fees and dues were not similarly united in calling for the distribution to them of at least the nationalized lands? Why did the peasant masses lose their unity as soon as the destruction of the aristocracy had been assured? We may find the several reasons for this state of affairs in the facts outlined above.

In the first place, a class or stratum of wealthy peasants—one may perhaps call them the "peasant or rural bourgeoisie"—had over a long period come into existence. It comprised the large farmers [fermiers], the proprietors of middling farms, proprietors of their own "occupations," and all economically independent farmers. The proportion of such wealthier peasants was always small, but they formed a solid stratum and were very influential because all other peasants were dependent upon them for work, for use of their plows and teams, for grain after poor harvests and before any harvest, and for charity (which was given more out of fear than of pity). The old regime had no way of winning their support, short of instituting real equality of taxation and of organizing the commutation of the tithe into a land tax while abolishing or otherwise providing for the end of feudal dues and fees. In desiring these things, the wealthy peasants were in accord with the poor. But the wealthy peasants had no reason to desire the distribution of church lands to those peasants who had no land; quite the contrary, they could only lose by the division of the larger farms. Thus, the system set up by the Constituent Assembly—sale to the highest bidder—favored them.

Furthermore, a majority of the peasants were already proprietors, already won over, that is, to an individualistic notion of private property and habituated to the idea of acquiring property by individual effort, without concern for one's neighbor. Even though the specter of the "agrarian law" was often invoked during the Revolution, there is evidence that many peasants manifested repugnance at the thought of buying the land of émigrés because it was patrimonial property that was being confiscated; similarly, the peasants rarely demanded that the church lands be appropriated without payment. If they called for the breaking up of large ecclesiastical farms, it was only to multiply the number of farms, and they never demanded the expropriation of large non-church holdings. When church lands were auctioned off, no peasant resisted the temptation to buy what he could. Those who did so increased the ranks of the "peasant bourgeoisie"; the further dissociation of the rural masses was thus precipitated.

That noble, ecclesiastical, and bourgeoisie holdings varied from one village to another was also a fact that exercised a great influence. Where the clergy had no land, or where there were no émigrés, or where the bourgeoisie dominated, the peasants had no way of obtaining land, and even the Jacobin laws could have no effect. But the preponderant fact appears to be that the privileged groups—nobles, clergy, wealthy bourgeoisie—did not work their own lands as the lords did in central and eastern Europe. They rented them out in sections that were usually small and often tiny parcels. To expropriate the large landowners would have been to place in question not only the fate of the more important lessees [grands fermiers] but also that of a great number of humbler peasants. Thus, the agrarian "movement," properly speaking, which tended toward the acquisition of land could only occur in areas of large ecclesiastical or royal properties, such as the plain of Picardy or the environs of Versailles. The movement, then, was sporadic.

We may thus understand why the agrarian problem was held to be of secondary importance by the leaders of the Revolution, even the Jacobins, and why the French Revolution was able to maintain a "bourgeois" character. When we compare the sale of nationalized lands with the agrarian transformations occurring today (1928) in a number of eastern European states, the contrast is startling. Assuredly, the bourgeoisie and the aristocracy itself in those countries have yielded to the logic of circumstances. A part at least of the great landowners were foreigners, and the national interest required that the peasants be freed from their authority. Thus the "agrarian law" has ceased to be a mere phantom, at least in that area. But the contrast has profound roots that are no other than those which already existed at the end of the eighteenth century between the agrarian organization of France and that of central and eastern Europe. . . .

Danton's Character

In his polemical analysis of Danton's career, Albert Mathiez did more than merely return to and specify the charge of corruption made against Danton. He also tried to demonstrate that, even leaving aside his venality, Danton was a vile politician, a trimmer who sought only his personal advantage. We cannot deny . . . that Danton's words and actions are replete with contradictions. Here we will recall but a few examples.

After the King's abortive flight to Varennes [June 1791], Danton plunged into the Revolutionary movement. On July 16 he was at the Champ de Mars assembly; but on July 17 he is lost from view. The people had rejected the Orléans regency petition, and Danton began to have second thoughts about his involvement. Martial law had also been declared; he abandoned his colleagues to their fate and went into hiding.

At the end of 1791, he at first opposed the war, in accord with Robespierre. The war spirit became dominant, however, and he ceased opposing it and joined with the Girondist war party. By March 1792, he was being considered for a ministerial position, but his ambiguous convictions and past associations barred his advancement. Thus checked, Danton became hostile to the Girondists and the Court.

After Valmy on 28 September [1792], he was in favor of a propaganda war against France's enemies, and yet in October he proposed a decree stating that the nation was no longer in danger. He then advocated an annexationist policy while secretly hoping for peace. He wished to save the King, and yet he voted for his death.

His relations with General Dumouriez [who later defected] have many suspicious traits that Pariset, following Mathiez, has stressed, without his concluding that Danton was in complicity with the general: "We shall never have proof of it." Barthou, in defense of Danton, emphasizes that everyone had praised and trusted Dumouriez. True, but it is no less true that in the first months of 1793 nobody was closer to Dumouriez than Danton. Without mentioning the ninth and tenth of March, which dates coincide with the time Dumouriez adopted an arrogant attitude toward the Convention, Danton on March 15 opposed the decree of accusation against Dumouriez and hastened to Belguim, promising the Convention he would bring the rebel to repentance. He returned from Brussels on March 21 bearing but an equivocal letter and did not remit it to the Committee of General Defense until March 26. He alone defended the mutinous general until the last extremity.

On May 31, 1793, in agreement with the Mountain, he extorted from the Convention the decree suppressing the Committee of Twelve, his aim surely being to reduce the Girondists to impotence. But desiring this aim, he loathed the means, because—and here I agree with Barthou—he did not wish to exclude the "Twenty-Two," who were his allies, from the Convention.

After leaving the Committee of Public Safety, he helped to increase its powers; he fought hardest to save it when it was under attack in the Convention in September 1793; he spoke in menacing terms against its critics, even against the Girondists. But, after all, he refused to enter the Committee, where he would have been able, in cooperation with Robespierre, to regulate and to moderate the Terror. Rather quickly, he became an opponent but with such subtlety that people scarcely knew it. He succumbed without even having led the assault on the Committee in person.

In his study of Danton, Barthou attempts to bring order to this chaos by describing his man as a realist. Danton was not uncultured, but he had little taste for general ideas; his political and social ideas were rather narrow. He had no inclination to order his thoughts coherently, he spoke and acted according to the circumstances, and he would have shrugged his shoulders had anyone disputed his right so to behave. But he nevertheless had a goal (otherwise the realist would only have been an adventurer): he wished to save the nation which he never distinguished from the Revolution.

There is much truth in this portrayal. I am not disposed to reproach Danton too harshly for having engaged in violent denunciations in order to maintain his ascendancy over the *sans-culottes* and to lead them whither he wished. It was not a noble tactic, but are there many politicians absolutely free of any cause for reproach? We must be especially prudent in whatever concerns foreign affairs. Mathiez wrote a book to show that Danton, publicly the man of "audacity," never stopped thinking of peace and of bringing on negotiations. Such a policy may be dangerous in certain circumstances but cannot be condemned in principle. A statesman may evoke the defensive passions of the nation while he labors to spare unnecessary bloodshed; theoretically, there is no logical contradiction and it appears that Danton admitted this double purpose. But in fact he would have realized neither aspect had he proclaimed that effort and sacrifice were not necessary. We may be inclined to forgive Danton's speeches in favor of Dumouriez and the many coincidences that render them suspect, as powerfully as they may work on our feelings, because the destitution of a general for treason in the face of the enemy is always disastrous for the morale of the army.

This being said, I do not believe that all the twists and turns in Danton's behavior may be explained satisfactorily by appealing to the "realism" in his policies. I cannot judge as disinterested his conduct in the Champ-de-Mars affair and at the beginning of 1792; there is a startling contradiction between his words of 28 September 1792 and his proposal of October 4; it was not preoccupation with the public good that led to his retiring from politics in October 1793. In the first of these examples, I perceive with Mathiez a prudence not at all noble and a desire always to be found on the strongest side. But such weaknesses are very common—and do not prevent a man from being a hero at other times—thus, no crime may be imputed to Danton. The very words he addressed to Theodore de Lameth, after having promised to do his utmost to save the King —"If I lose all hope, I declare to you, not wanting to lose my head along with his, I will be among those who condemn him"—these words would seem only too human to me if the suspicion of venality did not throw its sinister light over his vote. But what he said was what many others were thinking and dared not aver, and this includes the Girondists. Moreover, prudence and ambition do not seem to me capable of explaining away the other two examples I cited above.

In truth, both portraits—the realist and the adventurer—conform in various ways to reality, without exhausting its possibilities. To call him simply a hero is to reduce Danton's complexity; to call him a villain is to suppose he always coldly calculated his words and actions. To combine hero and villain would create a portrait a little too nuanced. We must consider in some measure his temperament. His contradictory words are less surprising when we recall that he often improvised and that he seems to have been sensible to the excitement unleashed by impassioned crowds or by an agitated assembly. He inflamed his audience, and their applause intoxicated him. We should be less astonished by certain aberrations in his conduct were we to reflect on his nonchalance, his laziness. He was a colossus, bigger than life, but whose profound and spontaneous concern was to enjoy life without reference to ideological or moral ends, holding himself as close as possible to nature, careless of the morrow. We understand him better when we see him proud of his strength, proud of the abuse he could withstand, proud of his sexual prowess. As strong as he was, he had moments of depression which aggravated his laziness and degenerated into debilitation. Finally, it seems to me that he was truly "magnanimous," as Royer-Collard said. If he was unscrupulous, he was also without hate, bitterness, and the thirst for revenge which contributed so much to deform and make bloody the Terror. If he resigned himself too easily to the spilling of blood when it seemed to him inevitable, I do not conclude that he desired it or loved it. There were political maneuvers behind his opposition to the Terror at the end of 1793. There was also the desire to save his compromised friends, as well as personal concern. But we can equally admit a political preoccupation: the system called for a reaction and, in any case, there was a threat to the Revolution if the Jacobins continued to decimate each other. Finally, why not believe he was sincere when he asked that "we spare the blood of men"? Did not Robespierre constantly maintain that it was necessary to punish only the leaders of factions and the counter-revolutionaries? Did he not save the seventy-three condemned members and regret the death of Elizabeth? With Robespierre it was a matter of politics and humanity; with Danton it was quite the same.

Self-interested subtlety, crafty prudence, venality: I admit all these in the measure I stated above. But sometimes also the true realism of a statesman, followed by ungovernable passions, careless negligence, sudden renunciations in fits of a violent temperament that no moral or intellectual discipline could hope to master. And yet again, adventure, impetuous recurrences of conciliatory generosity and humane pity which also explain his temperament, too avid for pleasure to tolerate the somber reflections of suspicion and hatred. What a rich complexity—and yet even that is not enough.

Mathiez implicitly denied to Danton any true attachment to the cause of the nation, to the revolutionary *patrie.* It seemed impossible to him that a bribed and venal agitator could participate in the generous enthusiasms and passions of those he is charged with deceiving. In my opinion, it was not so impossible, and here we touch upon the psychology of the agitator, a subject that has barely been studied. It is a question of knowing whether one may retain for a long time one's ascendancy over a crowd by deceiving it in cold blood, as it were. Between the real demagogue and the crowd, an exchange occurs: the crowd confers authority on him because he inspires it. He receives because he also gives, and without sincerity on his part I doubt that the game could long continue. Now the ascendancy of Danton over men has been profound; it continues to this day. So many moving orations improvised on the spot, so many striking phrases—too often of doubtful authenticity, unfortunately, but which nevertheless give the same impression of having been thrust up from the depths of his being—I cannot persuade myself that a depraved skeptic, a pure villain, a Talleyrand, could ever have uttered them.

Élie Halévy

8

Élie Halévy ranks among the most distinguished of modern historians for many reasons. Two of them are especially compelling. The first is that in his two greatest works, *The Growth of Philosophical Radicalism* (1901–1904) and *England in 1815* (1923), he was dealing with a society to which, as he put it, "I am foreign by birth and by education." With his scholarship, sensitivity, and historical imagination, Halévy brilliantly overcame this formidable obstacle. "No foreigner," observed G. P. Gooch, "has combined in the same degree a knowledge of every aspect of modern English life and thought with a sympathetic analysis of our character and outlook." The second reason flows from the first. In a discipline that defines its scholarly results as for the most part merely "interim reports" which undoubtedly will be superseded, Halévy's two masterpieces are yet unsurpassed. *The Growth of Philosophical Radicalism* is still the definitive work on the subject, while in the judgment of E. P. Thompson, *England in 1815* "remains the outstanding general survey of early 19th century British society." Few works of history have for so long retained so high a place in scholarly opinion.

Halévy was born in 1870 into a rich and cultured family of Jewish background. His father was a scholar and musician, a composer of libretti for Offenbach, among others. The Halévy household was noted for its liberal politics, its encouragement of the arts, and its intellectual atmosphere. Élie Halévy received an excellent education, first at the Lycée Condorcet and then at the École Normale Supérieure, where he majored in philosophy. He graduated in 1892; that same year he helped to found the *Revue de métaphysique et de morale* and he began lecturing at the École des Sciences Politiques. (After 1900, he customarily lectured each year alternately on English history and on socialism.) His thesis, "La Théorie platonicienne des sciences," appeared in 1896 and received favorable critical attention. It is a study in pure philosophy but already manifests that analytical approach Halévy was to use in his historical works. As C. C. Gillispie observes:

Except that he was never mystical, his own cast of mind was Platonic: austere, analytical, and logical, always seeking to penetrate to the central idea or conception, moral or intellectual, which gave form not only to bodies of doctrine but also to concrete political and social movements. Halévy always accorded primacy to systems of values, ideas, beliefs, and morals rather than to material interests in explaining human motives and social actions. This note runs through all his work. The issue does not arise as such in *La Théorie platonicienne des sciences,* but he never had any sympathy for crude economic determinists, although later he gave great weight to the importance of objective social and economic circumstances in shaping ideas and opinions—which is to say that he himself was not a crude idealist. But his idealism was not of the romantic variety. He was, if anything, even less sympathetic to Hegelians that to Marxists.

Working dialectically, Halévy would unfold his subject analytically, layer by layer, until he came to a core of basic attitudes and assumptions, discovering along the way the inevitable inconsistencies and antinomies which inhere in any complex system of thought. "Man is not governed by interest but by beliefs and passions," he wrote.

Halévy's emphasis on the primacy of ideas, beliefs, and values in explaining human motives and actions led him easily from philosophy, although he always remained a philosopher, to intellectual history. Hence his analytical inquiry into *The Growth of Philosophical Radicalism,* which he had touched upon in his doctoral thesis. His philosophical approach perhaps best explains why he remained aloof from the campaign for a "New History" then being waged by Henri Berr and others. He set out to explain by his analysis of the Benthamite school just how the dichotomies of individualism and state intervention, of hedonism in theory and stoicism in practice could be so neatly resolved or reconciled in one philosophical doctrine. Halévy thus analyzed the utilitarians' emphasis on the artificial identity of interests—that is, the role of the legislator in blending individual and societal interests harmoniously— and their concomitant emphasis on the natural identity of interests—that is, on the natural impossibility, because of "the invisible hand," of individual interests harming society. Implicit in this is Halévy's concern over the problem of the relationship of private interests to the interests of society and of the individual to the state. This concern might be labeled the hallmark of the liberal. In any event, Halévy traced the evolution of utilitarian philosophy from its "origins and principles," through the youth of Bentham, to its emergence as a full-fledged doctrine, "philosophic radicalism," one of the dominant intellectual influences in nineteenth-century English social thought. This was an enormous intellectual undertaking, involving the study of numerous and difficult works, most especially the prolific output of the master, Bentham himself. Halévy was the only scholar of his time to have worked through all of Bentham's manuscripts. He succeeded in demonstrating that although the principles of natural and artificial identity of interests were *logically* irreconcilable, both were *historically* applicable—the one encouraging economic liberalism, the other political reform. Halévy thus established how even strong intellects may be unaware of contradictions and shifting assumptions in their philosophies.

One of Halévy's attributes is that he has the capacity for handling ideas in relation to their circumstances. He shows Bentham, affected by a liberal atmosphere engendered by the struggle against Napoleonic despotism and by the accidental encounter with the liberal James Mill, transforming himself after 1808 into a radical democrat—a position not logically inherent in his pragmatic utilitarianism. Concomitantly he shows the relation of the antinomies in utilitarian doctrine to free trade currents and to the impetus for political and social reform. Above all, Halévy makes manifest his convictions that ideas, beliefs, and opinions are important in history, not so much for their intellectual content, but for their social results in the behavior of groups of people. Skill in abstract analysis, shrewd judgment, wide-ranging learning, and sympathy for his subject enabled Halévy to compose that rare intellectual study, "a secondary work so perceptive and so clear," as Gillispie has put it, "that it provides the reader more illumination on its subject than a study of the sources would do."

It was these qualities that Halévy brought to bear in the first volume of his massive *History of the English People in the Nineteenth Century,* again with certain antinomies in mind. Like most French liberals of the late nineteenth and early twentieth century, he pondered the basis of English social tranquillity in an age of general turmoil. Looking at England, Halévy perceived liberty *and* stability, inequality *and* social solidarity. How, he asked, was it possible for England to have evolved with a relative absence of strife? How have English representative institutions been built up and modified? What laws governed the process? What were the causes, what the forces which allowed parliamentary government in the state, the factory, and the church to become an almost sacred tradition to nineteenth-century Englishmen? Approaching this English society as a Frenchman with a "valuable capacity for wonder" (as he put it) and a viewpoint that was "perhaps more objective," because more external, Halévy proceeded both to analyze English institutions and customs and to narrate the course of English history from 1815.

His interpretation was based on an exhaustive study of both primary and secondary materials. He first examined the machinery of government—legal, administrative, military, and political—and discovered that "England was a museum of constitutional archeology where the relics of past ages accumulated." English freedom, he concluded, derived more from certain "accidents" and from the inadequacy (in a modern bureaucratic sense) of English institutions than from providential design or from inherent institutional strengths. Decentralization; informal rather than bureaucratic organizations;

a ruling family without prestige; the central military importance of the navy; an imperfect but nonetheless responsive representative House of Commons jealous of its prerogatives; rights of assembly and petition; freedom of the press—all of these acted in a negative fashion, preventing tyranny from developing. But they promised little by way of future stability or further extension of well-ordered liberty, and they did not answer the question with which he had begun: How, in an age of revolutions had England been spared revolutionary upheavals? Halévy thus turned to other areas: "We must . . . seek elsewhere, in the character either of the economic organization or of the religious life of the nation, the secret of this progressive regulation of liberty."

Halévy thus proceeds by his favorite method, analysis, to eliminate explanations which while "not wholly worthless . . . are insufficient." In his study of the English economy, he finds great wealth being produced and new, effective economic institutions being introduced but also growing disequilibrium between agriculture and manufacturing, institutionalized economic crises, and heightened social tensions and class conflicts. He concludes:

> If the materialistic interpretation of history is to be trusted, if economic facts explain the course taken by the human race in its progress, the England of the nineteenth century was surely, above all other countries, destined to revolution, both political and religious. But it was not to be so. In no other country of Europe have social changes been accomplished with such a marked and gradual continuity. The source of such continuity and comparative stability is, as we have seen, not to be found in the economic organization of the country. We have seen, also, that it cannot be found in the political institutions of England, which were essentially unstable and wanting in order. To find it we must pass on to another category of social phenomena—to beliefs, emotions and opinions, as well as to the institutions and sects in which these beliefs, emotions and opinions take a form suitable for scientific inquiry.

Here, in beliefs, emotions, and opinions, and in the institutions which embody them, Halévy found the roots of English social stability.

The "Methodist" or "Evangelical" revival—"the last Protestant movement which has given birth to permanent institutions"—yielded in Halévy's interpretation the secrets of English ordered progress and expanded freedom in the nineteenth century. Analyzing Methodist and Evangelical beliefs and institutions, and narrating their evolution through the eighteenth century, Halévy determined the pervasive moral and social influences they exerted on nineteenth-century England. Emphasizing duty, probity, personal restraint and independence, as well as (in the Evangelical strain, especially) humanitarianism, social reform, and the urge for improvement, Methodism channeled the vast forces of potential unrest into constructive patterns. It also inevitably engendered new sects, e.g., the New Methodist Connection, which moved even further toward democratic organization and ordered participation by the laity, being implicitly political and social in consequence: "The free organization of the sects was the foundation of social order in England." Above all, Methodism was a widespread social phenomenon. It was an obstacle to political revolution because it both satisfied intense human longings and offered the masses a secure place in the scheme of things—it was itself, in Halévy's phrase, "a popular revolution." Methodism and Evangelicalism thus "imbued English society with their *ethos.*" They raised the moral tone and improved the social behavior of the people; they tempered the excesses of the aristocracy and the greed of the new capitalists; they taught Englishmen how to organize and to agitate within the law for desired changes; they prescribed philanthropy for the successful and resignation with trust in self-help for the less fortunate.

Halévy notes the defects of the Methodist and Evangelical virtues: their baleful effects on the fine arts, not least obvious in the ugliness of the period's architecture; their excessive concern with public and private morals and behavior, reflected in campaigns against sabbath infractions, "immoral" plays, and "dangerous" literature. Yet his conclusion stands: religious currents in England had carried with them self-discipline, moral rectitude, and individual responsibility, all within a context of order. The phrase "England is a free country," Halévy wrote, "means at bottom that England is a country of voluntary obedience, of an organization freely initiated and freely accepted." No historian has yet offered a more persuasive interpretation of the basis of English liberty.

In succeeding volumes of his *History of the English People,* Halévy continued his narrative down to 1841 with *The Liberal Awakening, 1815–1830* (1912) and *The Triumph of Reform, 1830–1841* (1923). World War I interrupted his work. Too old to enlist as a combatant, Halévy volunteered and served with distinction as an ambulance driver. Resuming his studies after the war, Halévy shifted his attention to a more contemporary period of English history and published two more volumes as "Epilogues": *Imperialism and the Rise of Labour, 1895–1905* (1926) and *The Rule of Democracy, 1905–1914* (1932). These volumes sustained the distinction of the first; the "Epilogues" were hailed as "the most completely satisfying contemporary history of any state."

Halévy's last scholarly publications focused on socialism, a subject with which he had always been concerned, both as a historian and as a liberal. Again he noted antinomies, the "double aspect" of modern socialism: "It is a doctrine of emancipation, which aims at abolishing the last traces of slavery remaining in industrialization, and it is a doctrine of organization, which to protect the freedom of the weak against the strong, needs a restored and strengthened social power." The experience of world war taught "the men of revolution and the men of action that the modern structure of the state placed almost unlimited powers at their command." Once the next war began, Halévy predicted in 1936, nationalism and socialism would "consolidate the 'tyrannical' idea in Europe." Hence the title of his book, *L'ère des tyrannies*. Writing in the aftermath of World War I, with the example of the totalitarian regimes before him, it is perhaps understandable that Halévy underestimated the strength of democracy and democratic socialism, and exaggerated the powers of fascism. He saw in the end of nineteenth-century liberalism the probable end of those liberties he cherished; certainly the institutionalized socialism of Saint-Simon would have absorbed the individual into the state as effectively as had the totalitarianism of Stalin and Hitler. Whatever his shortcomings as a prophet, Halévy manifested to the end those scholarly attributes which raised him to the highest rank among historians. He applied to socialism, nationalism, the origins of the war, and the emerging European society those same analytical and descriptive skills which had informed his earlier masterpieces.

Selected Bibliography

Charles C. Gillispie, "The Work of Élie Halévy: A Critical Appreciation," *The Journal of the History of Ideas*, XXII: 3 (September, 1950), 232–249, is an excellent study, comprehensive and penetrating. We drew heavily upon it for the above headnote. Ernest Barker, "Élie Halévy," *English Historical Review*, LIII (1938), 79–87, is informative and helpful, as are C. H. Smith, "Élie Halévy," *Some Historians of Modern Europe*, edited by E. E. Schmitt (1942), 152–167; and Léon Brunschvigg, "Élie Halévy," *Revue de métaphysique et de morale*, XLIV (1937), 679–691. R. K. Webb's short preface to his translation *The Era of Tyrannies* (1965) is perceptive and enlightening. R. B. McCallum's introduction to the 1961 edition of *England in 1815* (translated by E. I. Watkin and D. A. Barker) is helpful. For a short account, with bibliographic references, of the present state of Halévy's thesis on Methodism and modern England, see Bernard Semmel, *The Methodist Revolution* (1973), pp. 3–5 and *passim.*

ENGLAND IN 1815

Prologue to Part I

*1748. Montesquieu, in his "Esprit des Lois," proposed the political insti-
tutions of England as a model to the Governments of the Continent. At
that time the Whigs held office in England. The feature of the British
Constitution which excited Montesquieu's admiration was the guarantees it provided for the liberty of the subject. For Montesquieu the best
and freest type of Constitution was the "mixed" or moderate Constitution, which combined the distinctive principles of monarchy, aristocracy, and democracy. Such a Constitution was to be found in England.
And again the best and freest type of Constitution was that in which
there is a clear-cut separation between the three departments of government—the legislature, the executive, and the judicature. This also was
to be found in the British Constitution.*

*1815. We now find the Whigs defeated and demoralized, reduced to the
condition of a permanent Opposition. With scarcely an interruption for
over thirty years past the Cabinets have been Tory, supporters of the
royal prerogative. Aboukir and Trafalgar, Salamanca and Vittoria,
Waterloo, the two Treaties of Paris have bestowed upon the Tory pro-
gramme the irrefutable consecration of success. What, then, has taken
place since Montesquieu wrote? Has England passed through revolutions and coups d'état? Far from it.*

*In England itself Montesquieu's theory continues to be the classical
interpretation of English constitutional law. Blackstone, the great Tory
jurist, in his "Commentaries on the Laws of England," is generally content to follow in the steps of the "Esprit des Lois." An examination,
therefore, of the political institutions of England, as they existed in the
opening years of the nineteenth century, raises a very delicate problem.
That problem is to understand the development by which a theory elaborated to defend a Constitution regarded by the Whigs as essentially a free
Constitution serves fifty or sixty years later to defend a Constitution*

From *England in 1815* (Tonbridge, England: Ernest Benn Ltd., 1923), pp, 3–17,
383–387, 389–401, 588–591. Reprinted by permission of the publisher. Translated
by E. I. Watkin and D. A. Barker.

*denounced by the Whig Opposition as oppressive and reactionary. Is it
that the constitutional forms, without being directly violated or abolished, have been worked in a manner foreign to their true intention and
thus perverted? Or is it rather that the reactionary movement has
affected not the Constitution itself, which remains intact, but the public
opinion of the country, freely expressed through the forms of this very
Constitution? Perhaps the Liberalism of 1748 no longer satisfies the demands of the Liberals of 1815. Or is the Constitution after all freer than
would be imagined from the Opposition complaints? The very ease with
which these complaints find expression, together with the fact that the
Government is compelled to meet the grievances of the Opposition with
a host of partial concessions, proves how hard it is to arrive at an adequate definition, a definition that will do justice to all the complex
factors at work, of the period known to historians as the Tory Reaction.*

THE EXECUTIVE, THE JUDICATUREL, AND THE ARMED FORCES

I

When George III ascended the throne he was not satisfied, as had been
the first two monarchs of his dynasty, to be merely a German prince, well
paid by the English aristocracy for acting as a figure-head in London. He
wished to effect in his personal interest a restoration of the royal authority, which had been so weakened of late, and to govern England as the
other European sovereigns governed their countries, as he himself governed his electorate of Hanover. The Tory Reaction dates from his accession. But what, after all, had been the success of this new policy of King
George? His personal popularity in 1815 is certainly beyond dispute. The
gentry had always admired in him his tastes for country life and sport,
and was not scandalized by his indifference to literature, science, and art.
The middle classes prized his strict virtue, even his bigoted Protestantism. The vast majority of Englishmen shared his prejudices against
Catholic emancipation, his stubborn determination to carry on the war
with France.

We must not, however, forget that the monarch and his Court were
marked by a German pedantry and formality which had given frequent
offence. Moreover, he had been for a long period the victim of intrigues
among parliamentary cliques, exposed to the insults of London journalists, to hostile demonstrations by the mob, to the attempts of assassins. It
was, in fact, only in 1810, when King George, who had already several
times been deprived temporarily of his reason, became permanently

insane, that he won the unbounded veneration of his people. His misfortunes won him sympathy as his virtues had won him respect: monarchy in England became a harmless fetish. The King George of 1815, blind, deaf, and insane, exactly realized the ideal of a puppet king, so dear to the eighteenth-century Whigs, and the puppet became the popular idol. Thus at the very moment of triumph for the party, which is commonly believed to represent the principle of autocracy, the cause of constitutional government won a brilliant victory. The insanity of the King of England made not the slightest change in the Government of the country. The same Cabinet, supported by the same majority, remained in office. In fact, if we were to confine our attention to the proceedings of the Government, we should be unable to distinguish between the time when England possessed a monarch and the time when she possessed only the shadow of a monarch.

But perhaps the royal family boasted a member sufficiently intelligent, energetic, and influential to assume the government of the country, when the King himself had become incapable of rule? No; among the numerous sons of King George not one was fit to govern. With the exception of the sensible but insignificant Duke of Cambridge, and the Duke of Sussex, a Liberal and a friend of reform, who had, however, lost caste by his marriage with Lady Augusta Murray, all the Princes were objects of universal hatred or scorn. Even when they had inherited their father's virtues, they made those very virtues odious. Their love of discipline was tyrannical, narrow, stupid. The Duke of Clarence, who served in the Navy, drove his subordinates to exasperation. In 1798, despite the flattery he received from Nelson, the King was forced to recognize his unfitness for command. The Duke of Kent, a religious man and a philanthropist, caused a mutiny at Gibraltar by his excessive zeal for the repression of drunkenness in the Army. He also was compelled to resign. The Press was on the watch to expose and exploit the scandals caused first by one then by another of the Princes. When Mrs. Jordan, the celebrated actress, lived with the Duke of Clarence as his avowed mistress, rumour declared that he was supported by her earnings. The Duke of York, the favourite son of King George and the Commander-in-Chief of the Army, was considered a man of virtue and a good administrator. Then it was discovered that he kept a mistress, and that she had organized with his connivance a regular trade in commissions. The affair caused widespread scandal, a parliamentary inquiry was instituted, and the Duke had to retire into private life for two years. The Duke of Cumberland, perhaps the most intelligent of the King's sons, made himself particularly unpopular by his unbending Toryism. One morning he was found by his bedside wounded, while in an adjoining apartment his valet was lying with a fatal wound. Despite the verdict of an impartial jury, report accused him of murder and infamous vices. To hide himself from popular view he withdrew to the Continent, to return in 1815 married to the Princess of Salm, a lady of doubtful reputation. To support his new establishment he asked Parliament for a higher grant in the Civil List. The House of Commons, after a most insulting debate, refused his request. And what, finally, can be said for the weak and contemptible Prince of Wales, who from 1810 onwards exercised the functions of Prince Regent?

Before his regency he was known to the public only by his constant squabbles with his father and his equally constant requests to the nation for money. One of the regular occupations of Parliaments for many years was the payment of the Prince's debts. By a promise to put his finances in order, pay off his creditors, and increase his income, the nation at last secured his marriage. He had one daughter by his wife, Princess Caroline of Brunswick. After the child's birth the couple separated and the wretched story of their quarrel began. The Prince of Wales considered himself an unofficial leader of the Opposition. The Whigs therefore took the part of the husband, the Tories of his wife. But later on, when the Prince became Regent, he became at the same time a Tory. Henceforward he found his supporters in the Tory ranks, while the Whigs espoused the cause of the injured Princess. And the Prince brought discredit on both parties in turn, as he joined first the one, then the other. To be sure, he was no country squire like his father and brothers. He had pretensions to intellectual culture. Sheridan had been his intimate friend. At their first meeting he won the heart of Thomas Moore, the poet. Scott, whom he entertained at luncheon, left his presence intoxicated with delight and loyalty. But that was not the way to become popular in England. The public forgave his drunkenness, his quarrelling, his immorality, for these were manly vices. The public could not forgive his effeminacy, his cowardice, which had become a byword, and his persistent desire at the age of fifty to be not only the most fashionable but the most handsome man of his time, the Adonis of European aristocracy. Four hostile Courts: such was the sight presented by the English royal family at the beginning of 1815. In a small and simply furnished house at Windsor the old Queen was watching over the last years of her husband, a mental and physical wreck. The Prince of Wales kept up a royal establishment at Carlton House, where he entertained lavishly. His morganatic wife, Mrs. Fitzherbert, a woman universally respected, to whom he had been secretly wedded according to the rites of the Catholic Church, had been forsaken. The Marchioness of Hertford was now the favourite, and she and her set—the Marquis of Hertford, the Marquis of Yarmouth, and the Marquis of Headfort—led the Prince and distributed his patronage. Kensington Palace was the headquarters of the Princess of Wales. She was a poor, brainless creature, whose head had been turned by the court paid to her by the men of letters, statesmen, and leaders of fashion, who wished to annoy the Prince Regent. Meanwhile, at Warwick House, Princess Charlotte, the daughter of the Prince and Princess, led a dreary and commonplace existence. Her father loathed her and in his jealousy tried to get rid of her. He decided to give her in marriage to the Prince of Orange, who would remove her to Holland. The Princess resisted the scheme and took shelter with her mother. To fetch her home the Prince had to send a regular embassy of ministers, headed by the Lord Chancellor. The middle class and the populace of London joined in the quarrel, and not on the side of the Regent.

When the allied sovereigns visited London after the victories of 1814, the English were not slow to show them how little they respected their rulers. Whenever the Prince drove out in his carriage, whenever he appeared at the theatre, the mob either kept a complete silence or booed. Whenever Princess Charlotte appeared there was an outburst of applause. When these monarchs attended a sitting of the House of Commons, the Opposition raised a full debate on the Regent's behaviour to the two Princesses, in which his vices were denounced, their sufferings deplored. Such were the facilities afforded by the institutions of Great Britain to the open and legal expression of public contempt for the disorders of the royal family. Despite fifty years of the Tory Reaction, England was not governed by a Court. Whether the head of the State were popular like George III or unpopular like the Regent was in England a matter of less importance than might be expected. For he could not exercise the control over the Government that was exercised by the head of the State in every other European country.

II

Of what grievance, then, since the Tory Reaction began, did the Whig leaders complain? They feared lest the King should, to use the phraseology of the time, compensate for his diminished "prerogative" by the increase of his "influence." By prerogative we are to understand the King's constitutional rights, derived from legislation or custom, by influence the King's indirect action upon Parliament by his employment of the means of corruption at his disposal—distribution of money and especially distribution of places. According to the theory of the division of powers, while Parliament makes the laws, it is the office of the King to carry them into execution, or more accurately, to choose the executive. It would seem, therefore, from the very nature of the Constitution, that the state departments, the government offices, must be under the immediate control of the head of the executive. Such departments were the Treasury, the Exchequer, the Secretaryships of State, the Board of Trade, the Board of Control, and the Military Departments. All the offices through which the revenues were collected, Customs Duties, Excise, and Direct Taxes, were subordinate to the Treasury. The First Lord of the Treasury was usually the Prime Minister. The Exchequer, at the head of which was the Chancellor, was also a dependency of the Treasury. Immediately the Budget had been passed, the audit of the national receipts and expenditure took place in the Exchequer. The three Secretaries of State were the Home Secretary, the Foreign Secretary, and the Secretary of State for War. The Board of Control supervised (controlled) the administration of India. The Military Departments were the Admiralty, the War Office, and the Artillery Office, also the Military Treasury or the Paymastership of the Forces. The most coveted offices were by no means always those which from their functions were in a position to exert the most direct influence on the national policy. They were the offices which disposed of the greatest number of places, possessed the most extensive "patronage." The Treasury and the Admiralty had richer prizes to bestow than the Foreign or the Home Office. According to the Whigs, all these offices and places constituted the sphere of royal influence. Moreover, a host of abuses which had grown up in the government departments made the possession of administrative posts even more lucrative, and thereby increased the power of the Government in whose hands lay the nomination to these places.

The system by which government officials were remunerated was nothing less than a scandal. In addition to their fixed salary they received additional emoluments and fees, which were in some cases determined by the amount of money passing through their hands. Hence it was to their interest, in direct opposition to the interest of the taxpayer, that the State should receive and expend the largest possible sums. Equally scandalous was the management of accounts in the public offices at the end of the eighteenth century. Each department possessed its departmental treasury, and these treasuries were mutually independent. Between the time when a government official received money from the Treasury and the time when he paid it out to his subordinates, or again between the time when he received the taxes and the time when he paid them into the Treasury, he could make whatever use of this money he pleased; he could even deposit it in a bank at interest. It was, therefore, to his profit to keep the money in his hands as long as possible, a procedure by no means for the advantage of the national finances. Nor was this all. There were a very large number of posts which were considered not as entailing on their holders any obligation to perform, in return for a reasonable salary, any function of social utility, but as positions of power which carried with them a pension and were purely a reward for services rendered in other spheres, either to the country as a whole or to a party. The administration had thus, as all the world knew, become choked with offices, officially classed as sinecures, posts without any useful service attached, posts whose remuneration was out of all proportion to the service performed, posts whose salary was taken by one man while a deputy did the work at a lower rate. By a judicious distribution of "places" the King was able to create dependents, to buy a body of supporters, and with their help to prevent the free expression in the House of Commons of the national will.

All this formed the burden of Whig complaints. Very different was the language of the Tories, the party which at the end of the eighteenth century was known as "the King's friends." According to them the working of representative institutions, as they operated in England, was a source of danger to the prosperity, indeed to the very existence, of the country. It was by no means the case that foreign policy and home government were subject to the control of the people; they were, on the contrary, the sport of aristocratic cabals, determined by the intrigues and caprices of a handful of noble families. The King had become the head of a new party—a party superior to contending factions—whose sole aim was to defend the permanent interest of the entire nation. "To check as much as may be possible the spirit of party appears to be one of the first duties and noblest employments of a King." Thus wrote the Tory, Thomas Gisborne. Who could blame George III for seeking the aid of new men to resist the heads of the great "connections" (the Cavendishes, the Russells) and bestowing his patronage on these supporters? "The House was not of that aristocratic spirit," said Lord Castlereagh, "that would deprive men of humble birth but of great talents of any participation in the administration of the State." On this interpretation—an interpretation, moreover, by no means indefensible—administrative posts were the stake in a contest between the King and the great Whig families. A severe and an unfair contest, the Tories might well add, so great was the preponderance in the British Constitution of the power of Parliament and the aristocracy over the power of the Crown.

According to the constitutional division of powers, replied the Whigs, it was part of the royal prerogative to choose the Officers of State, and this right enabled the King to exercise an illegitimate influence which endangered the balance of powers. This would certainly have been the case had the division between the executive and the legislature been carried out in practice as strictly as the theory demanded. But a mixed or complex Constitution like that of Great Britain is unable from its very nature to define with mathematical accuracy the sphere of each of the powers of government. Each of the powers encroached on the spheres of the others. The question was whether or no these encroachments were favourable to the royal prerogative.

Blackstone regards the King as not merely the head of the executive, but also as "a constituent part of the supreme legislative power," and ascribes to him in this capacity the right to reject any measure passed by Parliament which failed to meet with his approval. That is to say, he ascribes to him a right of veto on the joint decision of both Houses. And this veto would be a clear gain for the prerogative. But, as a matter of fact, the Tory monarch never had occasion, after his accession to the throne, to put into practice the doctrine of Blackstone. Whenever there arose a difference of opinion between the King and his Cabinet about a Bill adopted by the latter, one of two things always happened. Either the majority in Parliament shrank in the disturbed condition of Europe from a constitutional crisis, and therefore consented to postpone the issue to avoid a conflict, or the King dissolved Parliament, and on his appeal to the country the electors returned a majority favourable to the royal wishes. George III never encroached on the functions of the legislature, nor did he ever attack directly the established constitutional customs that secured the independence of Parliament against the Crown, nor even those customs which constituted a perpetual encroachment of the legislature upon the functions proper to the head of the executive. It is true that, despite repeated attempts, the eighteenth-century Whigs never succeeded in placing the government departments under the control of committees of Parliament, and in thus achieving the complete subordination of the executive to the legislature. But it is equally true that the heads of these departments, the Cabinet Ministers, were Members of Parliament, and responsible to Parliament for the measures they took, the appointments they made, and for the way in which they carried out the presumed wishes of the national representatives. In the Cabinet both powers, the legislative and the executive, were confused, but a separation also was made, unnoticed by Montesquieu—a separation, namely, between the agents of the executive, who carried on the actual work of government, and the head of the executive, who was by a fundamental principle of the Constitution irresponsible for the acts of his agents. Such had been the working of government under the first two Georges, and despite the personal interference of George III in politics it had changed little, if at all, since. As much as King George, indeed more than the King, William Pitt, the Prime Minister, embodied the new and victorious Toryism. Pitt's parliamentary dictatorship, which covered the last fifteen years of the eighteenth century, did not differ materially from the dictatorship of his father, thirty years earlier. And his father had been a leader and tribune of the Whigs.

Further, the Whigs accused the King of underhand and indirect attempts to undermine the Constitution. By these very accusations, however, they bore testimony that the King was too weak to attempt its open violation. In fact, not only had the prerogative not increased during the reign of George III, it had actually decreased. On his accession King George had renounced, by an act of grace, the revenues derived from the hereditary possessions of the Crown, and had expressed his desire that these revenues should henceforth be collected in the same fashion as the other national revenues and included in the Civil List. Later he had been obliged to acquiesce in a limitation of his right to grant pensions. Henceforward the amount disbursed in pensions might not exceed a definite figure, separately fixed for England, Scotland, and Ireland. Impeachment was a quasi-judicial procedure employed by Parliament to secure the responsibility of the executive officials. In 1791 the Crown lost the power to stop proceedings by dissolving Parliament. On two occasions, in 1788 and in 1811, when the King had become incapable of government, Parliament refused to proceed by way of address, and invite the Prince of Wales to assume the regency by right of birth. On both occasions Parliament took upon itself to nominate, by a special Act, the head of the executive and to define the limits of his authority, and on both occasions it was the Whigs who supported the hereditary principle, because they favoured the claims of the Prince of Wales and because the Prince was considered their leader. It was the Tories who secured, in opposition to the Whigs, the triumph of the old Whig doctrine of the supremacy of Parliament.

The Whig opposition also denounced the management of the government departments. Here, certainly, they had good cause for complaint: the abuses were scandalous. But these abuses dated from the period of Whig rule, and the only complaint that could fairly be brought against the Tory Ministries was that they had failed to abolish them when they succeeded to power. And these abuses, it might be argued, far from favouring the despotic aspirations of the Crown, were, on the contrary, calculated to perpetuate the supremacy in the executive of the Whig aristocracy.

A body of officials, drawn from the middle or lower classes and poorly paid, would be animated by feelings of jealousy towards the aristocracy. On such officials a monarch, greedy of power, could rely for support in a struggle against the arrogant pretensions of the heads of the great families. But it was to satisfy the claims of this aristocracy that those offices of wealth and influence, those sinecures of which we have spoken, had been instituted. And these high officials, securely entrenched in their bureaus, bid the Crown defiance. The English aristocracy had laboured, and with success, to establish the rule that permanent civil servants were irremovable. Every office conferred for life was deemed, by the lawyers and by Parliament, the freehold of its occupant; therefore no government post could be taken from its occupant or suppressed, nor even could its character be changed without violating the right of private property. It was even an established custom to grant certain posts in reversion. The patent which conferred the post provided that on the holder's death it should revert to his son or to some other person specified. Sometimes the patent even nominated three successive holders of the same office. Thus was constituted in the government departments of England a species of mortmain. We must add that by 1813 the higher officials had lost their former right to sell the subordinate posts. The result of all this was that even in the departments where, as head of the executive, we might have expected to find him absolute, King George was no sovereign, but merely an overlord. In many respects the bureaucracy of London presented the characteristics of an hereditary feudalism.

"It is our purpose," contended the Opposition speakers, "by a reform of the administration, to prevent the establishment in our midst of a powerful bureaucracy under the control of a despotic monarch." "Your contention is absurd," replied the supporters of the Government. "These very abuses, at which you exclaim, effectively limit the royal prerogative and protect the aristocracy against the Crown." We cannot be surprised that public opinion watched with an ever-increasing scepticism a dispute in which both parties were obviously fighting for their own interests. When in 1784 the issue had been whether the East India patronage should be entrusted to a parliamentary commission or to a Minister nominated by the Crown, the country had plainly declared in favour of the King and against the great parliamentary families. Quite recently, in 1812, when the Whigs were about to take office, they had attempted to prevent the Prince Regent from choosing the officers of his household without consulting the Cabinet. The attempt failed; victory rested with the Regent, and the leaders of the Opposition realized, to their disgust, that public opinion did not support them. The nation's one desire was the reform of abuses, whoever might benefit by them, and the middle classes were delighted that, in part owing to the pressure of the new democratic ideas, in part to the exigencies of party warfare, the reform had already begun. ... If the materialistic interpretation of history is to be trusted, if economic facts explain the course taken by the human race in its progress, the England of the nineteenth century was surely, above all other countries, destined to revolution, both political and religious. But it was not to be so. In no other country of Europe have social changes been accomplished with such a marked and gradual continuity. The source of such continuity and comparative stability is, as we have seen, not to be found in the economic organization of the country. We have seen, also, that it cannot be found in the political institutions of England, which were essentially unstable and wanting in order. To find it we must pass on to another category of social phenomena—to beliefs, emotions, and opinions, as well as to the institutions and sects in which these beliefs, emotions, and opinions take a form suitable for scientific inquiry.

Prologue to Part III

The religious institutions of the United Kingdom were no less intricate and confused than the political. The Established Church in England and Ireland was Episcopal, in Scotland Presbyterian. Of the subjects of the British Crown the majority were Protestant, but there were 4,000,000 Irish Catholics. Of the Protestants the majority were adherents of the Established Churches, but 2,000,000 belonged to free groups, whose organization was more or less republican. In the seventeenth century this diversity had been a source of disorder, even of anarchy. Was it the same during our period? Or amid so many conflicting currents was one influence predominant, and did it make for peace? If so, what was that influence?

England was not only remarkable for its intense religious life. It was also a country which could boast a high level of culture—artistic, literary, philosophic. It possessed a school of first-rate painters, and the greatest poets the age produced anywhere in the world. Dalton, Davy, and the Herschells were scientists of world-wide renown. The English philosophers and economists amazed Europe by the boldness with which they applied to the study of Man the accepted methods of the natural sciences. Did this development of culture take place in the teeth of the dominant religion? Or here, too, can we discover a conciliatory influence at work? Had the opposing forces concluded a compact of peace, tacit or express; and if so, on what terms?

During the eighteenth century England had been the scene of a great religious movement, unparalleled on the Continent—the last Protestant movement which has given birth to permanent institutions. This was the "Methodist" or "Evangelical" revival. To this movement, in combination on the one hand with the old Whig political traditions, on the other with the new ethos produced by the industrial revolution, British Liberalism of the opening nineteenth century owed its distinctive character. We shall witness Methodism bring under its influence, first the Dissenting sects, then the Establishment, finally secular opinion. We shall attempt to find here the key to the problem whose solution has hitherto escaped us; for we shall explain by this movement the extraordinary stability which English Society was destined to enjoy throughout a period of revolutions and crises; what we may truly term the miracle of modern England, anarchist but orderly, practical and businesslike, but religious, and even pietist.

Religion

I

It was in the year 1739 that John Wesley and George Whitefield began to preach Methodism. It was a period of general disturbance. A political was aggravated by an economic crisis. On all sides there were strikes and riots. Similar conditions a half-century later must have given rise to a general movement of political and social revolution. In 1739 the revolt assumed a different form. The discontented workmen flocked to the sermons of three clergymen and their disciples. The popular ferment took shape as an outburst of enthusiastic Christianity. But what doctrinal novelty did the two Wesleys and Whitefield proclaim to the English people? Anglican clergymen deeply attached to the Established Church, their sole aim was her defence and regeneration. This they sought to attain by reviving the venerable Protestant dogma of justification by faith. Despite the radical depravity of his nature, man was capable, since his Saviour's death, of sudden illumination by grace. It was for the Christian preacher by his eloquence to make himself the instrument of the Divine Will, to stimulate "conversions" in the sense that Protestant theology understands the term, to procure for his hearers an immediate sense of holiness, a certainty of salvation. At first the founders of Methodism preached in the churches, at Bristol, at Newcastle, in London. Later, when the clergy alarmed by their eccentric style of preaching and by their doctrinal extravagance forbade them the use of their churches, they preached in marketplaces and in the open fields. Their audiences numbered ten, fifty, even eighty thousand. Driven from the Anglican Church, and carried away by the enthusiasm they had themselves excited, they drifted almost unconsciously into the sphere of the dissenting sects. It was on the frontier of the Church of England that Wesley founded the vast organization of Methodism. Thus the old establishment and the existing Free Churches constituted the double environment in which the new spirit was developed. And it is only when we are acquainted with this environment that we can understand the character and estimate the importance of the Methodist revival.

I I

The Church of England, or, to call it by its official title, the "United Church of England and Ireland," was a complex institution, a patchwork. Her apologists might say of the Church what Bishop Jebb said of her liturgy—that it "is not the work of one man, of one society, or of one age: it is like the British Constitution, a precious result of accumulative and collective wisdom." The ritual of the Church of England had retained many features of Catholic ritual; but in obedience to long-established prejudices her unwritten constitution prescribed for the national worship the nakedness of Lutheranism or Calvinism. Moreover, her creed as formulated in the thirty-nine articles is to all appearance unadulterated Protestantism. At first sight the organization of the Church conformed to the Catholic type. In England there were two archbishops and twenty-six bishops, in Ireland four archbishops and twenty-seven bishops. But these princes of the hierarchy and their subordinates had alike discarded celibacy. Monasteries and convents had disappeared, as it seemed, forever. Archbishops and bishops were direct nominees of the Crown: capitular election was a legal fiction, a mere registration of the royal choice. The ordinary clergymen, the parochial representatives of the archbishops or bishops, were for the most part nominated, not by the episcopates, but by the Crown or lay patrons. Convocation, a species of ecclesiastical parliament, with an archiepiscopal president, an Upper House of bishops, a Lower House of representatives of the inferior clergy, after losing under Henry VIII the right to revise the canons of the Church, under Charles II the right to fix clerical taxation, for a century had ceased altogether to meet. The King, acting on the advice of Parliament, was the supreme head of a religion in which, to employ the accepted terminology, the "Erastian" principle was scrupulously respected, a religion essentially national whose source was the will of the secular government.

Of what character should we expect to find a clerical body thus constituted? England was probably the sole country in Christendom where no proof of theological knowledge was exacted from candidates for ordination. These were all drawn from the universities of Oxford and Cambridge; and neither of these universities possessed a special organization for the teaching of Christian doctrine. At Oxford theology was reduced to one single question asked of all candidates for examination. At Cambridge no theology whatsoever entered into any of the examinations for a degree. The entrance examination once passed, and it was elementary in the extreme, not to say childish, students, who were not the eldest sons of gentle families, and did not possess sufficient industry or capacity to face more difficult examinations, could proceed without further delay to the clerical status. It is true that to hold any benefice, episcopal ordination was indispensable, and that ordination involved a preliminary examination by the bishop or his chaplain, whose object was, or was supposed to be, to discover the candidate's intellectual and moral endowments. But, as all the world knew, this examination was a mere formality. "A few minutes' conversation or examination, which either good nature or pity or interest or carelessness, or all together, may render very slight, can never make the diocesan thoroughly acquainted with the literary, much less with the moral, character of the intended minister."

It is, therefore, no matter for surprise that the clergy of the national Church of England were intellectually inferior to the clergy of the Established Churches of Protestant Germany. How could any serious criticism of the Scripture text be expected from men who did not even know their Bible? At the beginning of the nineteenth century Marsh brought back from Leipzig some results of the German Higher Criticism, a theory of the composition of the Gospels, namely the hypothesis of a lost Protevangelium, from which our Four Gospels have been derived. Jebb was contemporaneously engaged in the study of Hebrew prosody, discovered as a result new rules of rhythm, and utilized his knowledge of these to elucidate a few obscure passages in the New Testament. And this was all, or almost all.

If, however, the Anglican clergymen lacked scientific curiosity, neither were they possessed by a fanatic zeal for orthodoxy. In the eighteenth century the High Church party was far more a political than a theological party. The High Churchmen were Tories who supported the royal prerogative and denounced rebellion as sinful. To be sure they inclined to Arminianism, to the doctrines of free will and justification by works, but this was due to their abhorrence of the republican opinions held by the Calvinists. For their part, the Low Churchmen, in their antipathy to the Church of Rome, might oppose to the Catholic doctrine an orthodox Calvinism. But in the eighteenth century the Low Church tradition, which dated from William of Orange and his Whig bishops Burnet, Tillotson, and Stillingfleet, was latitudinarian. Throughout the century the sermons of Anglican preachers, whatever their party, though most markedly among the Whigs, kept the miraculous character of Christianity as far as possible in the background. Their religion was a liberal and rationalistic Christianity, a system of humanitarian ethics in which the supernatural was left out of sight. The goal of this direction of Anglican opinion was the book published by Paley in 1785 in which he identified Christian with utilitarian ethics, and presented Jesus Christ as the first teacher of the greatest happiness principle. Nevertheless, the members of the Church continued with little scruple to subscribe the thirty-nine articles which formulated the fundamental articles of Anglican belief. Those who in 1772 petitioned Parliament for release from this obligation merely betrayed a doctrinal scrupulosity of very doubtful taste. The attempt failed; and why regret its failure? The material point was that nobody was obliged to believe the thirty-nine articles or even to read them.

The remedy that should have been applied was to reform, or more truly to organize, the theological education of the clergy. But Anglican opinion was opposed to this step. In 1809 Cockburn proposed the introduction of Christian theology into the Cambridge course of studies. But he was content to ask for the adoption of the system in force at Oxford, namely a theological question in every examination. For, he adds, "that divinity should not be the exclusive, nor perhaps the principal, employment of such young persons is reasonable, because men of all professions and ranks are at that period educated together; future Peers, future senators, lawyers, physicians, clergymen, etc., are all fellow students at the same lecture; and, as it would be absurd to make them all study physic exclusively, so it would be wrong to make divinity the sole object of their common attention." As for making theology the special study of the minority of students destined for orders, Cockburn does not even contemplate the idea. Above all things clergymen must be gentlemen; and to secure this it was of the first importance that they should receive the education which all English gentlemen received. The Anglican clergy was, and was anxious to remain, a branch of the aristocracy.

Consider first the higher clergy. It was universally admitted that the choice of archbishops and bishops must be political. For the last thirty years the Tories had enjoyed an almost uninterrupted tenure of power. Consequently the two archbishops and almost all the bishops were Tories. Eleven in 1815 were of noble birth, among them the Archbishop of Canterbury, a Manners and a cousin of the Duke of Rutland, and the Archbishop of York, a brother of Lord Vernon. Ten had been tutors or schoolmasters of a prince, a duke, or a statesman. The Bishop of Lincoln, Tomline, successively tutor, secretary, and biographer of Pitt, was typical of these men. Two prelates, Thomas Burgess, Bishop of St. David's, and George Huntingford, were Lord Sidmouth's personal friends. And the see of Sodor and Man was actually a benefice in the hereditary patronage of the Dukes of Athol. It was but the natural result that the present occupant, George Murray, should be a member of the family. The Irish episcopate was equally aristocratic. Three archbishops and eight bishops belonged to influential families. One family alone, the family of Beresford, occupied three sees.

Let us now turn to the lower clergy—the deans, the canons, the archdeacons; and the ordinary parish priests—the parsons. Wherever their appointment was in the hands of the archbishop or the bishop, he was careful to distribute his patronage among his clients and relatives. And first among the latter, since the Anglican hierarchy was married, were his sons and his sons-in-law. But the extent of the patronage exercised by the episcopate was inconsiderable. Out of the 11,700 benefices of England and Wales, the patronage of scarcely 1,500 belonged to the bishops or cathedral chapters. The English reformation found the religious orders predominant among the clergy, and in the vast majority of parishes a religious order was perpetual rector, and enjoyed the exclusive right to appoint the "vicar," who was the actual parish priest. With the dissolution of the monasteries their parochial patronage was transferred either to the colleges at Oxford and Cambridge, to the public schools of Eton and Winchester and to the cathedral chapters, since all these bodies were the direct heirs of former religious houses, or to the Crown, or to the families of the great landowners. To this latter class belonged 5,700 benefices. Hence in one-half of the parishes the appointment of the vicar was in the hands of the landlord, his legal and incontestable right. And even when the appointment lay with the Crown the Government often found it difficult to resist the pretensions of the gentry. The landowner of the parish whose vicar was to be appointed demanded that the Crown should give effect to his choice.

Thus did the ecclesiastical constitution of the country harmonize with the political. The landed gentry were masters equally of the ecclesiastical as of the civil administration. Nepotism, the vice of aristocracies, found full scope, and was aggravated by pecuniary interest. The sale of benefices by public auction was a normal occurrence. The highest bidder could purchase either the immediate enjoyment of the benefice, if there was then a vacancy, or the right to the next presentation. The sums offered were advertised in the newspapers, which informed the public of the value of the benefice and the age of its present occupant. For the older the clergyman in possession the higher was the sum that could be obtained for an advowson whose enjoyment could not be long delayed.

Whether he owed his living to favour or had purchased it in the open market, there was nothing whatever of the "priest" about the English clergyman. Should a young man of good birth, or simply the son of a respectable or wealthy family, enter the Church or the Army? Circumstances, parental caprice, often chance decided his choice. While the war lasted, the Army offered a better opening. Peace came and the Church beheld once more a stream of candidates for ordination. Crowds of military parsons, as Cobbett termed them, descended on the country parsonages, and combined the stipend of their living with the half-pay of retired officers. Only too often, apparently, the scion of a good family regarded a vicarage as the means of closing an irregular youth. We hear, for instance, of a gentleman who on leaving the university squandered in town a considerable portion of his estate: he married a clergyman's daughter and took orders. And we are told of another who, when plunged in debt, disembarrassed himself by a living in Suffolk. "Here he became a great favourite with the country gentlemen, by whom his society was much sought; for he kept an excellent hunter, rode well up to the hounds, drank very hard. He sang an excellent song, danced remarkably well, so that the young ladies considered no party complete without him." After further vicissitudes and further pecuniary difficulties we find him possessed of a substantial benefice—"by which he was enabled to launch again into the gay world." The utmost that could be expected of clergymen thus recruited was to avoid scandal and to behave as honourable gentlemen. In any case, it was essential that they should be well paid. They belonged to good society, and usually possessed a wife and family. Even if their stipends were considerable, it was all they could do to support their social position. It is certain that the Anglican clergy were a heavy charge on the nation. But an exact estimate of their cost is difficult to reach. It is not easy to arrive at a fixed or an accurate valuation of incomes composed of the rental value of the parsonage, the rent of glebe land, and the tithe. In 1810 Cove estimated the total annual revenue of the Church as exceeding £2,900,000. But the *Black Book* of 1820 estimates it at £5,000,000, and later around 1832 there were critics of the system whose estimate was £9,000,000. We may adopt the official figure reached in 1833 by a commission appointed for the purpose, the figure of £3,500,000, intermediate between Cove's estimate and the estimate of the *Black Book*. But no total valuation of this kind can give a sufficient idea of the stipends actually received by individual clergymen.

The bishops of England and Wales, inclusive of the Bishop of Sodor and Man, enjoyed a total income of £181,631. But whereas the income of the Archbishop of Canterbury and of the Bishop of Durham exceeded £19,000, and the income of the Bishop of London exceeded £15,000, the Bishop of Rochester had to be content with £1,500, and the Bishop of Llandaff with a bare £900. The total income of the parochial clergy was £3,250,000. But it would be of little use to attempt to form a notion of the English parson's income by simply dividing this figure by the number of livings. The average so attained would mean very little. For the income of 4,000 livings, over a third of the whole number, did not exceed £50, and of these 4,000 poor livings there were 1,726 where the income ranged between £100 and £150, 1,061 where it did not exceed or fall below £150. Must we draw the conclusion that the organization of the Anglican Church was chaotic, or even stigmatize it without qualification as a system that favoured some of the clergy at the expense of their fellows? In reality, these official figures are often deceptive; for the clergy, to eke out stipends admittedly insufficient, had built up an entire system, which custom had sanctioned, of accumulative benefices, or pluralities.

One incumbent could hold simultaneously two, three, four or even more benefices. There is an instance of a single ecclesiastic in possession of eight. How, then, were these combined parishes served, since they were thus dependent on the spiritual care of a single man? The rector or vicar (for the vicar of one parish could be rector of another and vice versa, and either, indeed, might even be a bishop or archbishop) appointed a curate at a low stipend, and took the rest of the income for himself. From the parishes of Wetherale and Warwick the Dean and Chapter of the see received tithe to the value of £1,000 per annum, and an equal sum in rents. They paid a curate £50. From Hesket in the Carlisle diocese the Dean and Chapter received annually between £1,000 and £1,500. They paid their curate £18 5s. or a shilling a day, that is less than the pay of a workman paid by the day. These curates were in the true sense the inferior clergy of the Church of England—her plebs. To gain a livelihood for wife and family they were often obliged to become farmers, and apologists of the system sought to console them for the extremity to which they were reduced by classical allusions and quotations from Cicero: *nihil agricultura homine libero dignius.* Occasionally they sought their bread and butter from occupations even more "illiberal." A speaker in Parliament mentions in 1806 the case of a curate turned weaver. Thus was reproduced in the administration of the Church an abuse we have already witnessed in the civil government of the kingdom. Every position is regarded as its holder's sinecure. The actual duties are performed by a deputy—paid with a portion only of the emolument.

When the pluralist was not a corporation but an individual, and when the parishes from which he derived his income were not too far apart, he would not even appoint a curate. Alone he provided as best he could for the spiritual needs, to be sure extremely simple, of the faithful of his two or three parishes. Every Sunday morning he would gallop from church to church and hurry through a service shortened by himself for the purpose, and which he would make even shorter on days when he was more than usually pressed for time. If it was raining too hard, he did not put in an appearance. No one was the least surprised. Dr. Drop, they said, was taking the service that Sunday. If he noticed that one of his churches lacked a congregation, he shortened his Sunday round by omitting the service. But he did not omit the stipend. In country parishes Holy Communion was celebrated only three or four times a year—at Easter, Christmas, Whitsun, and Michaelmas. In the dilapidated churches, no better than empty barns, the children of the village played their marbles, the beadles hatched out their chickens. Even the pocket boroughs of the political franchise were paralleled by pocket rectories. Cobbett, in the course of one of his rural rides, remarked a Wiltshire parish which was simply an ecclesiastical Old Sarum. The parson's income amounted to £300 a year. There was neither church nor parsonage. Whenever a new parson was to be inducted, a tent was erected on the site where the parish church had once stood, and in that tent the ceremony of induction was performed. So scandalous had the abuse of non-residence become that public opinion was roused, and a series of official inquiries were made which enable us to measure its extent. Out of 11,000 livings there were over 6,000 where the incumbent was non-resident. Of the 3,998 livings whose income did not exceed £150, in 2,438 the incumbent was non-resident. These inquiries, it must be remembered, were confined to England and Wales. In Ireland the vast majority of livings were obviously sinecures; for scarcely a sixteenth part of the population was Protestant, and by no means all Protestants were members of the Established Church. Nevertheless, that Church was established on precisely the same footing as if the entire population made use of its services. Here the scandal was not that the parsons neglected their flocks, but that the country was burdened by the expense of this enormous ecclesiastical establishment devoid of adherents.

The churches actually in existence were empty; and a clergy devoid of conscientiousness or zeal had an interest in their remaining empty. Their work was the easier. But even had they been all filled, they would certainly have been insufficient to hold even a small minority of the population of England. Since 1688 neither bishops nor parsons had given a thought to the need of adapting the system to the increase of population and its altered distribution. Therefore the distribution of bishoprics and parishes was treated in the same fashion as the distribution of constituencies. Formerly but half the province of York had been inhabited; now great centres of industry were being rapidly multiplied. But it still counted only six bishops as against twenty in the province of Canterbury, and 2,000 parishes for 10,000 in the Southern province. Bath, Chichester, Ely, and Hereford possessed their bishops; Manchester, Leeds, Birmingham, and Liverpool had none. The total church accommodation in Liverpool amounted to but 21,000 seats. The population was 94,000. In Manchester there was accommodation for 11,000 of the 79,000 inhabitants. In London the Established Church provided about 150,000 seats for a population that exceeded a million.

An Act of Parliament had indeed been passed in the reign of Anne to provide for the erection of fifty churches in London; but its execution had been neglected. During the entire course of the century, despite the unexpected increase of the population, only ten churches were erected in the capital. To be sure any Englishman who chose might open a place of worship; but the Anglican service must not be used. If he wished to erect an "episcopal" chapel, he was faced with endless difficulties. Tithepayers were apprehensive of an increase in their burdens on the appearance of a new clergyman. The noble patrons of the existing churches had no desire for a new church which by its competition with the other livings would reduce their market value. The Duke of Portland compelled the parish of Marylebone, with a population of 40,000, to be content with a village church with accommodation at the utmost for 200. But if the

Church of England could neither obtain for her faithful a more diligent clergy nor a better provision of churches, what must be the inevitable result? Either the population would be exposed to revolutionary influences, anti-clerical and hostile to religion (fear of this result was an increasing preoccupation in conservative circles towards the end of the eighteenth century: they could not fail to remark the rapid dissemination of Tom Paine's deistic and "Jacobin" writings in the poor quarters of the large towns) or the inertia of the Anglican clergy would be a valuable asset to the preachers of dissent. But from the professional standpoint of the Anglican clergy this latter prospect—a country religious indeed but alienated from the official worship, the established religion threatening to become the creed of a minority, the nation disposed to adopt the American system of free churches—was a prospect as little reassuring as the former.

The abuses were crying. Yet public indignation was slow to awake. And even when in the opening years of the nineteenth century there grew up a powerful movement of democratic opposition directed against governmental abuses, administrative scandals, the unfair system of parliamentary representation, the oppressive taxation, critics displayed an amazing forbearance towards the Church. Already for the past fifteen years the system of tithes had been the subject of severe criticism in Parliament. It was now a question freely discussed whether the tithes should not be "commuted" for a fixed money payment. But it was in Ireland, not in England, that the population revolted against the tithe. The Irish complained that their tithes were payable on arable land only, not on pasture, with the result that the entire burden rested on the poor cotter, while the wealthy cattle-breeder paid nothing. They complained that they were levied by middlemen, that the proctors who farmed the tithe paid the clergymen a lump sum and made their fortune by squeezing the peasants dry. And Catholics and Presbyterians complained of their obligation to support the episcopal worship. In England these abuses did not exist. No doubt the farmers had reason to complain of an impost which discouraged agriculture, was levied solely on land, and bore indiscriminately on Anglicans and members of other religious bodies. But it was equally true that the vast majority of English farmers belonged to the Established Church, that in England every species of land was equally subject to tithe, and that the proctors were non-existent. And as we have already seen, the English farmers were not, like the Irish tenantry, members of the proletariat. They were capitalists leagued with the landlord against the labourer, in a position, moreover, to dictate their terms to their landlord, and when the leases were renewed to shift the payment of tithe on to his shoulders.

The other abuses, non-residence of vicars, the miserably inadequate stipends of curates, were already being remedied, not under the pressure of a party in arms against clerical oppression, but, as we shall see, to satisfy the demands of that section of the Church which under the influence of Methodism was seeking to strengthen the hold of the clergy on the masses. Take it all in all, the nation was tolerant of a clergy, apathetic indeed, and worldly, but little disposed to play the tyrant. Statesmen of both parties were agreed in their appreciation of a system under which the priests did not constitute an order marked off from the rest of the nation, but were men of their own class, their relatives and friends, intimately bound up with the life of county society. Even a democrat like Cobbett, an avowed enemy alike of the Crown and the aristocracy, and a violent opponent of the Methodists, had not yet in 1815 declared war on the parish clergy.

Conclusion

From whatever point of view we study the institutions of Britain we are brought back to the same formula. England is a free country. But language is not a perfectly accurate instrument, and the same word can bear many meanings. What then are we to understand by British freedom?

After thirty years of Tory reaction, England was a free country. Such was the conclusion of our study of her political institutions. And we meant by this that England was a country in which the executive was systematically weakened in every direction. It would not even be true to say that government was based on the division of powers and that in this division the province of the executive was narrowly limited. On the contrary, the several branches of administration were confused in such a way that all the others encroached on the executive, and the powers of its nominal head were reduced to a minimum. The actual executive consisted of the group of persons which composed the Cabinet, all members of the Legislature, and responsible to it. The Justices of the Peace, men of good family, scattered up and down the entire country, united judicial functions with administrative duties of the first importance. A free Press and the right of rebellion, ultimate guarantees of popular liberty against the encroachments of any department of government, were a very real part of the British Constitution. And the jury system in turn guaranteed the liberty of the Press. The weakness of the Army, a weakness which survived even the large increase of numbers necessitated by a long war, made rebellion a serious possibility. Montesquieu was not wrong in describing the British Constitution as a mixed Constitution equally composed of monarchy, aristocracy, and democracy. But it would perhaps be more accurate to term it a blend of oligarchy and anarchy.

We also pointed out that the economic system of England was a free system, and by that we meant that England was the country in which capitalism had developed more rapidly than in any other country in Europe, and therefore the country in which the system of free contract had superseded most completely the system of custom, corporate trading, and state regulation. Mechanical inventions had multiplied until men had come to regard a continual transformation of technical methods as the normal condition of industry. The guilds had disappeared, or had become mere social groups wholly devoid of compulsory powers. The State indeed still protected the nation's manufactures and agriculture against foreign competition. But as far as the former were concerned this protection had been rendered unnecessary by the enormous technical superiority of English methods of manufacture over those in use abroad. And agrarian protection had become inefficacious and unpopular: for it raised the cost of subsistence above the "natural" level. Therefore the principle of Free Trade was continually gaining ground. Moreover, the progress of capitalism involved the accumulation of vast wealth in the hands of a few, and this in turn stripped increasing numbers of their property and reduced them to the condition of wage-earners. No legislation regulated the relations between the employer and his hands. The old statutes bore no application to the novel conditions of manufacture. And it was no easy task to build up the new system of laws demanded by the complexity of economic life. Alike in country and town the proletariat formed a disorganized and turbulent mass. The old political Whiggery of the noble families was gradually replaced or overlaid by the economic individualism of the commanders of industry. The political riot which from 1688 to the French Revolution had been the traditional expression of popular feeling in Great Britain gave way to the strike, the riot of the workers, the revolt of the hungry. England was the country of economic freedom, unbridled competition, and class war.

And finally, if we consider the religious, moral, and intellectual conditions in England, we must still term England a free country. For England was a country in which the Established Church, whatever privileges it might enjoy, left the sects outside her borders entire liberty of organization, full power to form a host of little States within the State. Atheism and Deism alone were excluded from this toleration, as anti-social systems. But sects whose doctrine was practically indistinguishable from Deism had obtained a legal status and had just been secured by Act of Parliament from the bare possibility of persecution. Of official protection of art, literature, or science there was little or none. Although the Tory monarch, George III, had shown signs of a desire to put an end to the traditional inaction of the Crown in this sphere, had founded the Royal Academy, and had encouraged the reorganization and rejuvenation of the Royal Society, all that was best in the intellectual life of Britain developed apart from royal interference. The absence or insufficiency of royal patronage was supplied by the patronage of the aristocracy. And the patronage of the new industrial class counted for even more. Throughout this youthful British society, free from all Court ties, free even from any connection with the governing aristocracy, independent thinkers were at work, who carried on their experiments and made their discoveries unguided and uncontrolled. Did this lack of organization in the religious and in the scientific world produce the same anarchy we have observed in the political and in the economic? Certainly not, and for the following reason.

The religious bodies whose freedom was respected by the State were societies which, because they lacked the power of legal coercion, were obliged to direct their efforts to the establishment of a powerful moral authority alike over their own members and over society as a whole. And their efforts were successful. They exercised the influence they sought. Not only did they encourage the growth in every sphere of a spirit of free association, and occasion directly or indirectly the mass of voluntary institutions both philanthropic and scientific so characteristic of modern England. They disturbed the torpor of the Government and even of the Established Church. They occupied themselves with the regulation of public morality, compelled the application of existing laws, revived laws which had fallen into abeyance, demanded new legislation. Uniting their influence with that of industrialism, they fashioned the character of the English middle class, dogmatic in morals, proud of its practical outlook, and sufficiently powerful to obtain respect for its views from the proletariat on the one hand, from the aristocracy on the other. The ruling classes watched the growth of this new power, whose nature they could not comprehend. They knew that the British Constitution did not give them sufficient strength to repress a general rebellion. And they perceived that the development of industrialism was rendering the social order more unstable and multiplying industrial and political crises. So they called to mind the French Revolution and the American War of Independence and feared "Methodism" almost equally with Jacobinism. Had they understood the situation better, they would have realized that Methodism was the antidote to Jacobinism, and that the free organization of the sects was the foundation of social order in England. "England is a free country": this means at bottom that England is a country of voluntary obedience, of an organization freely initiated and freely accepted.

Jaime Vicens Vives

9

True historiography is difficult of accomplishment even in the best of social and intellectual circumstances. Jaime Vicens Vives, however, wrote outstanding works of history under conditions which hindered both his research and his interpretative and methodological innovations. His greatness as a historian must be appreciated as well by the environing obstacles he was forced to overcome as by the superior and enduring quality of his works. Almost singlehandedly he initiated the process, still incomplete, of bringing Spanish historical studies into the mainstream of modern historiography.

Vicens was born in Gerona (Catalonia) on June 28, 1910. His family was prosperously middle class, and Vicens grew to maturity enjoying the advantages of Catalonian culture, progressivism, and openness to European (as opposed to merely Spanish) influences. In 1926, he entered the University of Barcelona, where he specialized in history. He began his graduate studies in 1930, a period of hardship for him, his parents having died and left him in relative poverty. On the basis of his manifest abilities, he was awarded an instructorship in history at Barcelona in 1934. His mentor at the university, Antonio de la Torre, was a renowned specialist in fifteenth-century Spanish history, and he imparted to Vicens an abiding respect for archival research, bibliographic exhaustiveness, and methodological exactitude.

Vicens chose as his thesis topic the relations between Barcelona and Ferdinand II (published in Catalan in 1936–1937 as *Ferran II i la ciutat de Barcelona, 1479–1516.*) The three-volume work already manifests those qualities that would make Vicens an innovative historian. As one of his colleagues, Soldevila, wrote: "In this doctoral thesis it can be said that one already finds the whole Vicens, both in essence and in potential, with his great capacity for work, his zeal for reinterpretation, his eagerness for polemics, his substantial documentation, his [intellectual] aggressiveness." The book forced a revision of the widely held view that the Castilian Ferdinand II had somehow betrayed and despoiled Catalonia. Vicens, himself a Catalonian, demonstrated that the true historical picture was quite different, that Ferdinand had been restrained in his dealings with Catalonian liberties and instrumental in assisting the region to get through an economic depression. A polemic inevitably ensued over this interpretation; to this day, relations between Catalonia and Madrid remain explosive. Vicens, however, valued historical truth above the myths dear to his Catalonian homeland, and in 1940 he published an expanded defense of his views, *Politica del Rey Católico en Cataluña.*

By that time, however, Vicens had experienced the agonies of his country's civil war. Drafted into the Republican army in 1937, he managed to avoid combat duty but served in a medical unit until the end of the war in 1939. His prewar involvement in university reform and his service in the Republican army combined under the repressive Franco regime to force his exile to an obscure and insignificant outpost in the university system, and it was not until 1948 that he was allowed to return to the University of Barcelona. But those years of intellectual exile were fruitful. Vicens redoubled his resistance to orthodox schools and interpretations and happily explored new approaches to Spanish history. Cut off from university grants and from contact with like-minded scholars, he made a virtue of necessity and turned to textbook writing in order to advance his views and to earn money. He was successful, financially and intellectually, at the task, and in 1942 he established with a relative the publishing house Editorial Tiede, devoted to the publication of textbooks and educational materials. The house gained international respect and made respectable profits, thus allowing Vicens an outlet for scholarly works and surcease from financial worry.

Between 1943 and 1960, he wrote or collaborated on twenty-eight manuals on history and geography. He later observed that a well-written, solidly based textbook often advanced historical studies more than a volume of pure research. Many of his textbooks were so successful that he had the satisfaction of seeing his historiographical ideas and innovations purveyed at a profit in schools and universities whose leaders generally resisted those very influences. Vicens published only one work of pure scholarship before his return to academic respectability: *The Historia de los remensas en el siglo XV* (1945), a study, now regarded as definitive, of the peasantry, social structure, and economy of fifteenth-century Catalonia. In 1947, he was finally allowed to return to the center of university life, not without first making some compromises and being compelled to maneuver past the shoals of academic politics. He competed for and won a professorship at the University of Zaragoza, and then in 1948 he gained by unanimous vote of the examiners the chair of Modern History at his alma mater, the University of Barcelona.

From his new and relatively secure position, Vicens was able both to continue his own scholarly productions and to advance his program for the reform and renovation of Spanish historiography. Throughout the 1950's, he published major works on fifteenth-century Spanish and Catalonian history and on his other primary field of interest, nineteenth-century Spanish economic and social history. (Vicens was also very much interested in recent Spanish history but, as Stanley G. Payne observes, "The twentieth [century] was still too dangerous a theme to invite research.") Those works, masterfully researched and vigorously argued, were themselves extraordinarily influential, but Spanish historians were further exercised by Vicens' methodological and interpretative innovations expressed in his works and advanced as well through the work of the Centro de Estudios Históricos Internacionales, which Vicens established in 1949.

Perhaps the most critical element in Vicens' crusade to hasten the emergence of Spanish historiography from "its dreams of rhetorical grandeur," was the influence of the French *Annales* school. In 1950, Vicens attended the Ninth International Congress of Historical Sciences in Paris and there encountered at first hand the methodologies, enthusiasms, and programs of the new school of socio-economic historiography centered in France and Belgium. He was immediately impressed by the methods and productions of the *Annalistes,* with their stress on economic and social history, on the "structure" of societies, and on quantification and the use of statistics. As he later wrote: "Unless we resort to statistical method as our primary instrument, collective life cannot be deciphered. . . . Statistics is essential for the determination of values, fortunes, and mentalities; unless these matters are approached through a minute analysis of prices, salaries, political trends, and cultural tendencies, it is possible to understand nothing." These were elements and tendencies already present in his own work, and the Paris experience confirmed their importance for him and generated in him a further enthusiasm for the new historiography. (It might be noted that only the high cost of the graduate training had prevented the young Vicens from pursuing his first love, engineering. This inclination and aptitude no doubt predisposed him to the quantitative, structural approach of the *Annales.*)

The last decade of his life was dedicated to the reorientation of Spanish historiography. His spirit, as it were, brooded over what he called "a period of transition."

> In one way this period is characterized by the liquidation of a series of anachronistic positions (in general, those of the scholarly and philological school of Castilian nationalism), and in another way by the birth of a new concept of writing history, responsive to real life and pulsing with human blood, and incompatible with great abstract themes and with those political and ideological drugs that have poisoned Hispanic historiography.

Returning to Barcelona in 1950, he announced to his students and to those of his colleagues willing to listen that the quantitative, socio-economic methods of the *Annalistes* with their quest for a total and comparative history had to be applied to the study of Spanish history. Vicens himself later summarized the controversy over the nature of Spanish history and outlined the factors needing elucidation *à la les "Annales"*:

> The dimensions of the controversy aroused by these [contemporary] historians (which has involved all of us who cultivate this science on the Peninsula) lead one to suspect that it will be productive. It will be particularly so if in its resolution, stereotypes and platitudes are abandoned, and the basic factors of Peninsular history are set forth: men, misery, and famine; epidemics and death; land owner-ship; the relations between a lord and his vassal, between a government official and the citizen subject to his jurisdiction, between an employer and a worker, between a monarch and his subject, between a priest and a believer, between one municipal government and another, between town and town, between national capital and province, between individual production and national income, between a soul and God. These factors do not differ greatly from those that underlie the experience of neighboring Mediterranean nations; for this reason it is very doubtful that Spain is "a historic enigma" as Sánchez Albornoz believes, or that it is "un vivir desvivién-dose" as his opponent declares. This is too much anguish, Unamuno style, for a Mediterranean community with very concrete and compact "epoch-making" prob-lems of procuring a modest but dignified livelihood for its thirty million inhabitants.

To broadcast his message, Vicens initiated the publication of the *Estudios de historia moderna,* in the first number of which (1951) he noted: "We [in Spain] are a full half-century behind in making documentary preparation for our scientific activities." After describing and castigating the propensity of Spanish historians to find refuge in metaphysical flights rather than engage in serious, sustained empirical investigations, he concluded: "It is necessary, then, that the present generation sacrifice itself in so far as it is able . . . and that it struggle in the hard task of carrying out the greatest labor of erudition that has been seen in the country since the eighteenth century." Vicens certainly sacrificed himself to that task.

In 1953, and drawing upon the financial resources of Editorial Tiede, he started another journal, the *Indice histórico español,* whose dual function was to point out the superficiality of most of the contemporary Spanish historiography and to introduce Spanish historians to modern methods and current works on Hispanic history. These organizational efforts, guided by Vicens and assisted by a growing number of colleagues and students, led to the gradual formation of what came to be known as the "School of Bar-celona." The group's program and achievements aroused enthusiasm but, especially from traditionalists, resentment and adverse criticism as well. Vic-ens had always to work on the periphery of the professional establishment, with little or no help from conservative or reactionary educational authorities; inevitably, because he was a true historian, neither did he receive support from romantic *catalanistas* or ideological Leftists, whose positions he analyzed as clinically as those of the Right.

Nothing daunted, Vicens continued until his untimely death in 1960 to expound the necessity of an innovative historiography and to publish works that incorporated and displayed its virtues and advantages. In the five-volume *Historia social y económica de España y América* (1957—1959), which he edited, he prefaced the credo of the Barcelona School:

> We fundamentally believe that history is life, in all its complex diversity. Therefore we do not feel bound by any a priori limitation with regard to method, hypothesis, or conclusion. We scorn materialism for being one-sided, positivism for being artificially schematic, ideologism for being shallow. We hope to capture the living reality of the past and, above all, the interests and passions of the common man.

His own contribution to that compendium, on the nineteenth and twentieth centuries, constitutes, in Stanley G. Payne's view, "the best commentary on the Spanish nineteenth century yet written in Spain." His last major works, *An Economic History of Spain* and *Approaches to the History of Spain,* set the seal to his high reputation as "Spain's first truly modern historian." His works will long remain a standard of excellence, and his methods and inter-pretations will impel historians so long as Spanish history is written.

Selected Bibliography

Perhaps the best introduction to Vicens is by way of his own prologue to the second edition of his *Approaches to the History of Spain* (1960; translated and edited by Joan Connelly Ullman, 1967). José Ferrater Mora's foreword to the translation offers helpful insights on Vicens' work, as does Gabriel Jackson's review article, "The Historical Writing of Jaime Vicens Vives," *American Historical Review,* LXXXV: 3 (February, 1970), 808–815. Stanley G. Payne, "Jaime Vicens Vives and the Writing of Spanish History," *The Journal of Modern History,* XXXIV: 2 (June, 1962), 119–134, is an excellent study, particularly informative on Vicens' intellec-tual and academic environment. Payne includes many bibliographic references for further study.

AN ECONOMIC HISTORY OF SPAIN

Infrastructure of Spanish Economic History

Geological Formation of the Hispanic Peninsula. The basic infrastructure of Spain's economic history is determined by the nature of the land masses which appeared in southwestern Europe as the result of an extremely long tectonic process. What are the chief stages in this geological history, and what have their consequences been for the Spanish economy?

In the Paleozoic era a gigantic land mass *(Hesperia)* appeared which formed the southern boundary of a large continent. This mass took on its definitive shape during the Silurian, Cambrian, and Hercynian periods. It was during this last period that the principal axes of the Meseta's structure were established, in a northwest-southeast direction, forming high mountain ranges now worn down by erosion. When, as a result of various folding actions, geological upheavals submerged the accumulations of lush vegetation created by the warm climate of the epoch, the foundation was laid for the rich carboniferous deposits of some Spanish coalfields, notably those of Asturias and Puertollano. At the same time, the Hercynian upheavals cracked the initial nucleus, and through these cracks important mineral layers appeared, such as those found throughout the southern lip of the Meseta, or Sierra Morena (copper in Huelva, lead and silver in Sierra Morena, mercury in Almadén, etc.).

The important consequences of this Paleozoic movement, therefore, were (1) establishment of the Meseta, the essential nucleus of the Hispanic Peninsula, (2) northwest-southeast direction of the principal topographical alignments and of the hydrographic system, (3) relative abundance of soft and hard coal formations, and (4) presence of mineral layers in some mountain sectors.

During the Mezozoic era the structural lines of Hesperia were maintained, despite the fact that several times during this period the region was flooded by seawater. The result was the deposition of large quantities of calcareous alluvia around its edges. There was no essential change, except for the rather unfavorable role which these deposits later exercised on Spanish agricultural soil. In the strictly mineralogical sphere, the marshy system which followed the Cretaceous sea resulted in numerous lignite deposits. These, apart from the typical calcareous and marble formations, are the only manifestations of the Mezozoic which have economic importance in Spain.

In the Tertiary period the tectonic process was more important. As the continent of Gondwana, or Africa, advanced against the northern continent, in the process destroying the geosyncline which separated them, its deep folds came into violent contact with the edges of the primary Spanish and French land masses. This collision, known as the Alpine, produced a number of tectonic upheavals which have given the Peninsula its shape: in the south, the Baetic system; in the north, the Pyrenees. Simultaneously, it produced the elevation of the old calcareous sediments on the edges of the Meseta, giving rise to the Iberian System and the Cantabrian mountains at the same time that a series of fractures and mountain resurgences brought about the present configuration of the Central System and Sierra Morena.

After the Alpine mountains were formed, the Meseta became covered by a series of lakes connected with the shallow seas covering the valleys of the Ebro and Guadalquivir; these slowly became filled in by sediments from the great Tertiary mountain chains. Also, the phenomena of compression and decompression gave rise to numerous mineral deposits (iron in Biscay, lead in Cartagena).

At the end of the Tertiary, and after the opening of the Strait of Gibraltar, the Peninsula took on its present outlines. Only the plains of the Levant and the Andalusian and Portuguese coastlines continued to be partly submerged.

In the Quaternary era the superficial coverings of alluvia, clay, and sand were laid down. At that time huge glaciers covered the Pyrenean region and the high peaks of the Cantabrian, Iberian, and Baetic systems. The most fertile agricultural lands date from this period.

It should be kept in mind that the Tertiary compressions and decompressions took place in a generally northeasterly-southwesterly direction; that is, in a direction diametrically opposed to that of the Hercynian period. This fundamental texture is still to be observed in the hydrographic network and natural routes of the Peninsula.

Spanish Soil. Two sets of facts can be observed from the tectonic process we have just described, one which has to do with the general structure of the Spanish land mass, the other with the quality of its agricultural soil.

Geographers point out the presence of four main structural elements in the Peninsula: the Meseta; the mountains which surround it; the depressions adjoining it on the northeast and south; and the outer mountain ranges. The surrounding mountain systems are the Cantabrian to the north, the Iberian to the east, and the Sierra Morena to the south, although the last is less a mountain range than the result of erosion of the Meseta's southern edge, graded down by the fault which opened up early in the Tertiary. The adjoining depressions are the Iberian, or Ebro, valley to the north, and to the south the Baetic or Guadalquivir valley. The exterior mountain ranges are the Pyrenees to the north and the Baetic to the south. This geographical structure determines, at first glance, the specific characteristic of the Hispanic Peninsula: its natural unity, modified by marked regional compartmentation.

Modern research has revealed that the soil of the Peninsula can be separated into two great subdivisions which we shall call, following Hernández Pacheco, "siliceous Spain" and "calcareous Spain." This important difference arises as much from the geological nature of the soil as from the climatic and physiographic accidents which have taken place in recent times.

In this regard, a work of Lucas Mallada's entitled *The Evils of Our Country and the Coming Spanish Revolution (Los males de la patria y la futura revolución española),* published in 1890, is still of some interest. He divides the national territory into the following types of soils: bare rock, 10%; low-yield land, 35%; moderately productive, 45%; and highly productive, 10%. These figures substantially alter the eulogy usually made of the fertility of Spanish soil, derived from the *Laudes Hispaniae* written by St. Isidore in the 6th century and repeated by Alfonso X, "the Wise."

In fact, only 55% of Spanish soil is suitable for agriculture, which in comparison with the European average is a disappointing proportion. Fernando Martín Sánchez-Juliá has recently taken issue with these figures in an article entitled "Fundamental Truths About Spanish Agrarian Economy" *(Verdades fundamentales sobre la economía agraria española),* in which he has attempted to dispute the pessimistic theory of Spanish agriculture. But if we examine his figures we see that his conclusions are similar to those of Lucas Mallada, for the truth is that the Hispanic Peninsula cannot be compared with countries like France or Holland, but rather with other Mediterranean countries such as Italy or Greece, whose agricultural shortcomings are well known.

Morphology of the Peninsula. If we are to understand the economic infrastructure of Spain, the study of its relief is essential. It is well known that Spain occupies the second place in Europe, after Switzerland, for the ruggedness of its terrain. But this fact is still more important if we keep

in mind the blocked-off and compartment-like arrangement of this relief. To use Salvador de Madariaga's happy phrase, the whole Meseta is
like "the citadel of a Spanish castle," indicating that the plateau occupies
the position of a castle in relation to a block of territory which separates
it, like a bastion, from the European continent.

If we examine a hypsometric, or altitude, table of the Hispanic Peninsula, we will observe the following: 15% of the territory has an altitude
between 0 and 200 meters; 17%, between 200 and 500; and the rest, 68%,
more than 500 meters. And 42% falls between 100 and 500 meters. Such
a geographical structure gives rise to unfavorable conditions for agricultural and commercial life, all the more so when the extreme abruptness
of the relief is an additional complicating factor. If we leave out the Ebro
and Guadalquivir valleys and some few highlands in New Castile, León,
and Old Castile, the mountain ranges cross the territory of the Peninsula
like barriers, and sometimes like actual walls. If the Pyrenees rise like
a mountain frontier between Europe and Spain, access to the sea from
the Meseta is no less difficult, on the Cantabrian side as well as on the
Mediterranean or the Atlantic.

To sum up, then, we should keep in mind three chief facts about the
tectonics and morphology of the Peninsula: (1) geographic cantonalism;
that is, division of the territory into separate compartments not easily
accessible among themselves, (2) the unconnected nature of the hydrographic system, which confers geographic reality on the tectonic division, and (3) the abnormal relief picture. The constant and enormous
differences in altitude offer great difficulties to the development of communications.

Hispanic Climate. The study of climate is of prime importance in any
consideration of economic history. Our point of reference must necessarily be that of the present-day climate. However, when we study the
possibilities of the Spanish economy in the past, we must keep in mind
that our climate is not necessarily that of former times. There is a dearth
of data on this subject, but we do know that ever since Neolithic times,
that is, since about 4000 B.C., there has been a prolonged period of desiccation in our peninsula and in general all over the tropical zone. This
phenomenon has given rise to the steppe-like character so typical of the
country. It is possible that this desiccation became more pronounced at
the beginning of the 14th century, as certain changes which took place
in the southernmost regions of Spain (in Almería, for example) seem to
indicate. But we cannot trace its development exactly. On the other hand,
modern studies indicate that during certain periods in modern times
Spain experienced long periods of drought. One of them probably occurred at the beginning and toward the middle of the 16th century. Oth-

ers took place in the course of the 17th and 18th centuries. The economic history of Spain would make great progress if we could learn the exact nature of these oscillations between humidity and aridity, which constitute the essential problem for proper comprehension of our agricultural past.

At the present day, a major part of the Hispanic Peninsula is arid. The French geographer Brunhes divided it into two regions, *humid Iberia* and *dry Iberia.* To do so he used the 500 mm. isohyetal line, which runs, approximately, to the north of Barcelona, follows the southern slopes of the Pyrenees, extends almost to the Picos de Europa, surrounds the Cantabrian System and the mountains of Zamora and León in a great arc, descends toward the southwest, penetrates deeply into the Meseta by way of the Central System, and then, returning to its northeasterly-southwesterly direction, disappears in the Algarve, in southern Portugal. To the north of this dividing line humid Iberia receives more than 500 mm. of precipitation yearly, and dry Iberia, to the south of it, less than 500 mm. This division is rather rough, for what really matters is not the quantity of rain but its distribution over the course of the year and its retention in the soil. Two geographers, Dantín and Revenga, have established a map of the mean annual dryness of the Peninsula, which corrects Brunhes's and makes it more accurate. Humid Iberia is composed of three zones: one in the North which includes the Pyrenees, the Cantabrian System, the mountains of León and Zamora, Galicia, the Central System, and northern Portugal as far as the Tagus; and two in the South, that of the Sierra de Cazorla (sources of the Guadalquivir and Segura rivers) and that of the Sierra Grazalema in the province of Cádiz. The rest of Spain is included in dry Iberia, which has four zones of extreme aridity (Ebro valley, the middle basin of the Duero, the plains of New Castile, and the lower Guadalquivir basin) and one almost desert zone (the southeastern coast from Murcia to Almería).

It is said that humid Iberia comprises less than 32% of the Spanish territory, while the dry zone makes up more than 68%. Actually, the most accurate figures are the following: the arid region contains 314,000 sq. km., of which 66,000 receive from 500 to 600 mm. annual rainfall, 180,000 from 400 to 500 mm., and 68,000, less than 400 mm. If we keep in mind that these last two portions have a total area of 248,000 sq. km., or almost half of the territory, we will realize the extraordinary importance of the problem of aridity in Spain.

The causes of this situation are to be found in the excessive evaporation characteristic of regions situated along the 45th parallel latitude north, and also in the lack of moisture resulting from the climatic mechanism. Three climatic centers influence Spain: to the northeast the Siberian low-pressure area, which is cold and dry; to the northwest the

Icelandic low, which is damp and temperate; and to the southwest the Azores high, which is hot. The rains produced by these two low-pressure areas, which are responsible for the fertility of Western Europe, rarely reach our latitudes; the Azores high-pressure area keeps them away from the Peninsula. Only in very favorable circumstances, especially during equinoctial periods, when the Azores high approaches the equator, do rains from the Atlantic lows reach the Peninsula. The success of a given harvest depends on these rains, and so, consequently, does the prosperity of the country.

As a result of this climatic situation, steppes (or rather, those regions which have been rendered barren by man) occupy 7% of the peninsular territory. The Spanish steppes can be classified in the following groups: (1) southeastern, from Cape Gata to Cape Nao, (2) the Baetic steppes, (3) those of New Castile (from Albacete to Madrid, including La Mancha), (4) the region around Valladolid, and (5) the steppes of the Ebro valley.

There is no doubt that these steppe-like zones have played a decisive role in the evolution of Spanish economic history.

Hydrography. As can be deduced from the foregoing, the arrangement of the hydrographic network derives from two factors, (1) the course of the great tectonic lines which form the northwest-southeast pattern, caused by the movements of the Hercynian period, and the northeast-southwest pattern formed by the Pyrenean movements, and (2) the geographic cantonalism arising from tectonics in general.

These two phenomena, together with the factor of humidity, act to determine the three essential characteristics of Spanish hydrography. In the first place, rivers have little volume. We need only compare a few statistics of Spanish rivers with other European rivers to realize how little water flows into the former (the largest Spanish river, the Ebro, flows at the rate of 700 cubic meters per second at its mouth, while the rate of the Po is 1,800 and the Rhône, 1,880, not to mention the great rivers such as the Rhine, Danube, Volga, etc.). In the second place, there is variation of flow: because of the unpredictable character of the rainfall, the volume of Spanish rivers is extremely irregular. This variability, ranging from double volume to fifteen times, reaches enormous proportions during high-water periods and leads to catastrophic floods. This is especially true of the rivers and streambeds of the Mediterranean littoral, where water volume can rise from almost nothing to 3,000 and 4,000 cubic meters per second. This fact presupposes great difficulty in the natural exploitation of rivers. Only at the price of enormous effort has man been able to reduce these wild variations partially and make use of river water for irrigation.

The third characteristic is the abruptness of the hydrographic contour.

No Spanish river presents a gentle course between its source and its mouth; on the contrary, a number of steep drops occur. The rivers of the Meseta usually have two, one when they emerge from the mountains where they originate and another at the place where they encounter the change of altitude between the Meseta and the Portuguese zone. The Ebro is still more complicated, for it experiences three drops: the first when it reaches the Meseta, the second when flowing out of the Meseta through the Pancorbo passes, and the third when it encounters the gorges of the Catalan shoreline system.

With rare exceptions, then, Spanish rivers are not suitable for irrigation because their waters are confined between steep banks. Some have been used along part of their course, and are still being used, for navigation; but this is not common. To utilize them for hydroelectric or agricultural purposes necessitates huge regulatory systems such as reservoirs and dams, and even in these cases there is a problem with the large volume of mud and sediment deposited in them because of their great tendency to flood.

Plant Cover. Spain's plant cover corresponds in general to that of other Mediterranean steppes. Lack of forests is characteristic, although in this regard we should not base our opinion entirely on present figures, for it is evident that before the 19th century—that is, before large areas of communal and mortmain land were brought under cultivation—there were more forested zones in Spain than there are today. Descriptions which have come down to us from the 13th, 14th, and 15th centuries speak, in fact, of large forested zones where today we find only steppes or moorland.

Generally speaking, meadow land is found in humid Iberia and steppes and subtropical plants in dry Iberia. Forests of characteristic mountain type exist in the Pyrenees, the Cantabrian System, the mountains of León and Zamora, in the Central System, the Sierras of Moncayo, Oca, and Demanda, and in the Montes Universales and similar chains.

In this connection the limits of the spruce and beech tree and the esparto plant are important. The southern limit of the European spruce takes in all of the Pyrenees region and extends toward Catalonia, including the Montseny massif. The southern limit of the beech tree is also significant; it covers almost all of Catalonia, then turns to the north of the Montes Universales, runs along the entire crest of the Central System on its western side and reaches as far as the Sierra de la Estrella in Portugal. The northern limit of esparto grass is typical of a large part of the steppe regions, for it begins near Tarragona, crosses the Ebro region to the north of Saragossa, curves toward the south of the Central System, and takes in a large part of La Mancha and the whole northern portion of the Baetic System.

Throughout these zones we can observe a considerable difference between the plant cover of Spain and the rest of Europe. But in addition to this natural plant cover, there exists another which is manmade. We refer here essentially to the *vega** and the *huerta,*** both creations of man in the face of Nature. We shall speak of these later, when we discuss man's reaction to the unfavorable soil of Spain.

Natural Communications. Even though we admit that Spain's geographical relief has always made collective life difficult, we can easily see that mountain defiles and passes must have had great influence as natural means of communication, for such passes have been used from earliest times for travel and commerce.

Our mental picture of the present communications network is a radial one, branching out from Madrid; but in fact the natural routes of communication in the Peninsula run from north to south and divide it into four great zones. The first joins Galicia to Portugal, especially by means of the Atlantic coastal plains; the second joins Asturias to León, Extremadura, and western Andalusia, through the pass of Pajares and the valley of the Alagón; the third connects the province of Santander with Old Castile, New Castile, and Andalusia by means of the passes of Reinosa, Guadarrama, and Despeñaperros; the fourth, much more limited, connects Catalonia with Valencia and Murcia by means of the passes along the Mediterranean coast.

Among these four zones, there are a number of centers of connection which correspond to the isolated compartments into which the Peninsula is divided. Between the first and the second zones there are few important connections, and this explains up to a point the political division of Spain and Portugal. However, between the second and the third, numerous points of connection exist, especially in the north between Castile and León. Aragon occupies a prominent place between the third and fourth zones and serves to connect Castile with Catalonia by means of the Jalón valley and the passes of Fraga. And finally we must stress the role of general correlation played by the territory to the south of the curve of the Central System, that territory whose capitals have been successively Toledo and Madrid. It is in this region that the routes of communication of all four zones come together.

Geophysical Position of Spain. The geophysical position of a country is determined by its location in respect to the great mercantile, trade, or political routes in any particular period. In this regard it must be realized that the Hispanic Peninsula enjoys a wholly favorable geophysical posi-

---

*Intensively cultivated flatland, often a river valley.
**A plot of irrigated land, intensively cultivated.

tion, for it is at the center of the crossroads formed by the two great lines of communication of Western Europe and the Mediterranean, from France to North Africa on the one hand, and from the Atlantic to the Near East on the other. This axis of communications has meant that the Hispanic Peninsula always exercised a very important role in all periods of history, and that in consequence its situation in regard to large-scale international commerce has been preponderant at times, enabling the Peninsula to benefit from outside stimuli or influencing its economic and financial life. . . .

Demographic, Agricultural, and Industrial Decline of Spain in the 17th Century

The Problem of Spain's Economic Decline. The subject of Spanish economic decline has aroused debates of the most impassioned kind, from the time it was first broached by the *arbitristas* of the 17th century to the present. Legions of Spanish and foreign authors have dedicated themselves to studying it, often with open prejudice, as the American historian Hamilton has pointed out repeatedly. Thus, German writers have exaggerated the magnitude of the collapse, wishing to glorify by contrast the figure of Charles V, whose ancestry was partly German; the Italians have done the same out of a desire to put the blame for the downfall of their own country on someone else, a downfall which was coincident with and related to Spanish domination of Italy; French and Spanish authors have done so because they wanted to extol the Bourbons' economic policy; finally, the "liberals and Protestants of every country, to stigmatize the Inquisition and the persecution of racial minorities."

However, these exaggerations should not make us forget the coincidence of extremely abundant evidence pointing to a decline in herding, agriculture, industry, and trade in the Spain of the 17th century. "Aridity, deforestation, insufficient harvests, emigration, expulsions, spread of mortmain, alms-giving and ecclesiastical vocations, vagabondage, disdain for work, mania to acquire titles of nobility, *mayorazgos,* high prices, upward movement of wages, taxes, wars, weakness of royal favorites and of the sovereigns themselves . . ." are all terms used over and over to depict the country's disastrous economic situation. Nevertheless, we must point out with Pierre Vilar that "these causes of decadence" are too numerous for us not to suspect in them the presence of stronger reasons; that is, the general economic crisis of the 17th century, in which converged (in the case of Spain) political impotence, incapacity for production, and social disintegration. The origins of this crisis went back a long way, though it did not become clearly apparent until Philip II's death in 1589. As Hamilton writes: "In broad terms one can say that it took Spain only a century (from the union of Castile and Aragon in 1479, to the annexation of Portugal in 1580) to attain political pre-eminence and only a century (from the death of Philip II in 1598 to that of Charles II in 1700) to fall into the rank of a second-rate power."

Demographic Stagnation and Depopulation. We lack data which would permit us to draw up a general balance-sheet of Spanish demography at the end of the 17th century, like the one made by Ruiz Almansa for the last years of the 16th. In the case of Catalonia, for example, no census was taken during the entire century. Under such circumstances it is not surprising to observe the divergent figures given by different authors: while Ruiz Almansa holds that the population of Spain remained stationary throughout the 17th century, varying only slightly from the figure of 8 million inhabitants, Hamilton assigns to it a loss of about 25% of its total population and concludes with von Beloch that by 1700 Spain probably had only about 6 million people.

Stagnation or depopulation, the one certain fact is the break in the ascending curve of 16th-century Spanish demography. On the other hand, there was a growing tendency toward a new distribution of the country's human potential: the centripetal tendency of the previous period gave way in the 17th century to a relationship which placed the population of the Peninsula's periphery in an ever more favorable situation. This tendency was also apparent within the smaller area of Catalonia, where settlements along the coast grew with extraordinary rapidity at the expense of population centers in the interior.

Now that we have come down to the regional level, let us give a few cases in detail. As for Castile, Domínguez Ortiz points out as probably closest to the truth a number given in a memorial of 1623 which, basing its figures on the books of the Treasury of Papal Bulls, gives Castile some 6 million inhabitants. If we compare this figure with that of approximately 1600, it would mean that in thirty years the kingdom had suffered a decline of 25%. But what happened during the seventy-seven years between 1623 and 1700? Domínguez Ortiz does not attempt to answer this, but describes the exodus from rural areas and the consequent "demographic concentration which, in certain extreme cases, reached the point in some parts of La Mancha or Andalusia where towns of many thousands of inhabitants were separated by 15 or 20 kilometers of desert," as the characteristic feature of Castilian demography in the 1600's. He finds specific causes for this phenomenon in the terrible tax demands which fell most heavily on the villages, levies of soldiers, absenteeism of rich landowners, and the oppression of hamlets and chief towns in certain districts. (For example, he says, the miserable state of the people of Las Hurdes is in large part a legacy of jurisdictional abuses originating in La

Alberca.) And he points out as general factors in the population decline the decadence of the monarchy, sale of real property and of council positions, excessive number of clergy, attraction of the Indies, etc.

In the territories of the Crown of Aragon, the expulsion of the Moriscos, decreed by Philip III, occasioned the most spectacular drop in population. A memorial of 1638 states that of the 453 Valencian hamlets occupied by Moriscos up to 1609, 205 were still abandoned, while the resettlement of the remaining 248 had required the transfer of 13,000 households of Old Christians. In the Kingdom of Valencia the expulsion affected 23% of its inhabitants; in Aragon, 16%; and in Catalonia, where the Moriscos were concentrated along the course of the Ebro and Segre rivers, only a little over 1%. As for the Principality of Catalonia, recent studies have emphasized the influence of the same factors pointed out by Domínguez Ortiz for the Castilian rural exodus. Parish registers and much other subjective evidence coincide in placing the maximum population around 1615–1620; at that time, which coincides with the final stages in the great current of French immigration, the country probably had about half a million inhabitants. Later, especially from 1630 to 1660, the tendency was one of stagnation if not regression.

One more reference to the demographic trend in 17th-century Spain: in general, two great phases can be distinguished, one of depression during the first half of the century, and another of recuperation following the end of the great period of plague (1648–1654) which, concentrated in the Western Mediterranean area, affected not only the Levant—from the Roussillon to Andalusia—but also invaded the Meseta from the south and from Aragon. We must make perfectly clear, however, that our information is inconclusive, and consequently so are any generalizations we may necessarily have drawn. In the case of Galicia, for instance, a study by Ruiz Almansa, whom we have quoted so often, has revealed that population loss was moderate during the first few years of the 17th century and became progressively greater after the revolt in Portugal and subsequent war. In this area, therefore, we cannot speak of recuperation during the second half of the 17th century.

The Plagues. Those specialists who have pointed out the demographic stagnation of the 17th century, while they have been concerned with its causes, have generally passed over the most important of them: incidence of the plague factor on population development. Contagious diseases, which periodically intervened in the demographic process (no generation in the 17th century escaped their impact), decisively influenced the tendency toward decline.

The survival of a medical system which still considered Galen the supreme authority, and the persistent state of undernutrition in most of the country, caused by economic decline in general and agricultural decline in particular, explain the extraordinary virulence of 17th-century plagues. At that time there was a very close relationship between harvests and population figures, and the inadequate system of land transport could not cope with large-scale shipment of grain. In a closed economy, as Hapsburg Spain still was, a district's food supply was reduced to what its agricultural resources could produce. Only the coastal towns could resort to importing grain in case of an insufficient harvest. Under these conditions mortality was closely linked to the ups and downs of local agricultural production. People made considerable efforts to soften the effects of these, such as storing the surplus harvest in good years, or simply resorting to biological measures. Nonetheless, a time would come when a series of bad harvests made all these efforts insufficient, and the specter of famine stalked the land. Then, when the disproportion between the number of men and the amount of available food became intolerable, the always latent factor of plague caused terrible ravages among the undernourished people. Jean Meuvret, in France, has demonstrated with statistics and graphs the exact coincidence in times of famine between the mortality curve and the price of wheat; when grain is lacking the curve shows a dizzying rise. There are no analogous studies for Spain, but we do have documents and proofs of the solid connection between demographic development and economic conditions.

As for the results of the plague itself, there is much evidence from persons and institutions of the period concerning the loss of one-third or one-fourth of the inhabitants of a given locality or region due to plague. That these figures are not so exaggerated as might be thought is proved from counts of deaths listed in parish records, or those which cities occasionally ordered made. Thus, the minute-book of the old Council of Barcelona permits us to follow very closely the impact of the epidemic on the Catalonian capital over a period of time. To sum up, and taking into account the fact that we do not have reliable figures for the whole country, we can at least state that the population loss in the Spanish Levant during the 17th century was due, more than anything else, to the constant incidence of contagious diseases, notwithstanding the counterfactor of a booming birthrate, on the order of 40 or 50 per 1,000.

Now that we have noted the importance of the plague factor in demographic development, we need to pinpoint its appearance in time and estimate its periodicity. As on so many other occasions, we find ourselves in an area where nothing has been published, where ground has not yet been cleared, insofar as the greater part of Spanish territory is concerned. On the other hand, studies made by Emilio Giralt and Jorge Nadal have succeeded in reconstructing the complete picture of the great plagues of the 1600's in Castile: 1589–1591, 1629–1631, 1650–1654, and 1694. That is, in the space of one century there were four appearances of plague, with a mean periodicity of twenty-five years; this was what we meant when we said that no generation could have escaped its effects. Generally speaking, these plagues affected the entire country, producing population losses that were difficult to overcome. The most serious of all was produced by the great epidemic we have mentioned before, that of 1648–1654, which came at the end of a series of catastrophic events and placed Spain in one of the most dangerous moments of her history. For the rest, the study of these plagues has corroborated the theory concerning a close relationship between undernourishment and rise in the mortality rate. When things were going badly in one region, the others, where circumstances were identical, soon saw themselves attacked as well. A good example of this is the path taken by the plague about the year 1650; it began in Andalusia in 1648, spread into Murcia and Valencia, spilled over into Catalonia and then Aragon through the passes of the Maestrazgo region, into France, and finally to Majorca, Sardinia, and Naples, where it still persisted in 1656.

Now that we have established the principle that plague depended on food supply, we would not be wrong in attributing the high incidence of plague to the long drought of the last few decades of the 16th century and the early years of the 17th. Aridity meant the failure of many harvests, hence undernourishment, triumph of plague, and depopulation. In this respect the 17th century, like the 14th, was a fateful one for Spanish demography.

The Spaniard and Labor: The Hidalgo Mentality. We have already seen how, in the last years of the 16th century, the twin spectacle of a bourgeoisie ruined by its own enterprises and an inactive, though prosperous, aristocracy, had had a most unfortunate effect on the mental attitude of the Spanish working classes. Survival of the economic factors which caused this bitter paradox and the subsequent polarization of the country's social structure into two antagonistic groups—the active and the inactive—found confirmation in the 17th century by means of customs and laws which placed a stigma of social dishonor on the mechanical occupations, as they were called at the time.

Any number of examples, foreign as well as domestic, could be adduced to corroborate this thesis, and many authors have defined the attitude of the 17th-century *hidalgo* as the expression of a theory of leisure. In *Lazarillo de Tormes,* the 16th-century picaresque novel, just one step removed from the crisis that was to usher in the new century, we read that, "any no-good wretch would die of hunger before he would take up a trade." This aversion to work was accompanied by a puerile pride in indolence: "Let London manufacture those fine fabrics of hers to her heart's content; Holland her chambrays; Florence her cloth; the Indies their beaver and vicuña; Milan her brocades, Italy and Flanders their linens . . . so long as our capital can enjoy them; the only thing it proves is that all nations train journeymen for Madrid, and that Madrid is the queen of Parliaments, for all the world serves her and she serves nobody." This absurd defense came from the pen of Alfonso Núñez de Castro during the dark days (1675) of Charles II's minority, on the eve of the financial disaster of 1680.

Groaning under the weight of all the disadvantages (direct taxes fell exclusively upon him) and none of the advantages, it is not surprising that the poor commoner of the 17th century should have pinned all his hopes on changing his status and going over to the other camp by purchasing a patent of *hidalguía,* or minor nobility. The consequences of the first step—changing his status—are well known: "People of the plebeian class disdain to work in factories, workshops, and manufactories, and steer their children into other careers in which, for one person who wins, a thousand lose"; and as a final result, "idleness, depopulation, and an increase in the crime and indigence which are found everywhere."

The second step was the acquisition of a patent of nobility. Literature is full of examples of the mania to attain the category of knight or *hidalgo* which obsessed the Spaniards of the 17th century. Let us take a look at the consequences of this mania. Traditionally the *hidalgos,* like the lesser nobility in general, had made up for the tax exemption they enjoyed by giving military service: while the plebeian paid taxes to the Crown, the *hidalgo* defended it by force of arms. However, the creation of professional armies and the discrediting of the military profession in the 17th century ("the people are so convinced that all those who exercise the soldier's profession are wicked, that there is no tailor or cobbler who would not consider it a great dishonor were his son to take it up") deprived the *hidalgo* of his function; and he often used his social position "not in order to go to war, but in order not to go." On the other hand, the Crown's financial needs, which required the collaboration of all citizens, leaped the barrier between commoner and noncommoner and extended taxation to those privileged persons who had not paid it previously.

Thus, though the 17th-century Spaniard's mania for nobility continued to gain ground, the boundaries between the status of commoner and *hidalgo* grew more and more imprecise. What difference could there be between a plebeian and a *hidalgo* if, as Prieto Bances assures us, the latter was hardly a noble (since he had no power), nor necessarily free (since it was possible to be one and yet be in a state of servitude), nor a soldier by obligation (*hidalgos* formed a large part of the knightly group, but could be excused from all military service)? In reality the difference was purely formal. The *hidalgo* belonged to a higher estate in society and accepted everything on cóndition that his rank would not be affected. The example given by Domínguez Ortiz is significant: obliged to pay taxes by the Crown, the Castilian *hidalgo* defended his immunity as such with more fervor than he did his pocketbook, which in any case was slim. The medieval idea associating taxation with dishonor and servitude was still alive in Castile, and when the *hidalgos* of the 17th century were forced to pay taxes, they did not recognize the poll tax, which they felt to be an unworthy levy; they resigned themselves, however, to paying taxes of a general nature, "provided that, in defense of principle, a rebate or small quantity should be returned to them, given by the State or municipal government as indemnification for the part of the *sisa* corresponding to their personal consumption. Many paid taxes until they were ruined, but always insisted on observing the legal fiction that they need not be included in the list of taxpayers."

Conclusion: the Castilian *hidalgos* of the 17th century deprived the Spanish economy of an enormous human potential, which went into other, completely unproductive professions: "Church, royal household, or the sea."

Destitution and Vagrancy: Indiscriminate Charity. Though he did not entirely eschew work—as has been repeated so many times by those interested in presenting him as an archdrone—we will have to agree at least that the Spaniard of the Golden Century refused to put any effort into tasks which he considered plebeian (Carande). The same man who spared no effort to preserve his honor, win fame and achieve glory in Italy, Flanders, Germany, or the Indies, was quite willing to live, even under the best of circumstances, on some modest income from property, or, in the majority of cases, from some other form of parasitism, turning the country into "an idle and vicious republic," as Cellorigo puts it. This Spanish attitude toward life, which often displayed spectacular traits, coincides in any case with the development of the mania for nobility and the insufficient recompense given to sound work. This situation progressively decreased the needs of the poor and caused their stoicism to increase. In this respect, the literature of the period undertook to reflect faithfully the subterfuges of a society sunk in destitution and at the same time eager to hide its difficulties. On this point it is interesting to notice how closely the best literary witnesses to the crisis followed it: the two parts of *Guzmán de Alfarache,* the most important of the "black" novels, were published in 1599 and 1604, and the first part of *Don Quijote,* the liveliest satire on the society of the time, appeared in 1605.

Destitution reached a peak during Philip IV's reign. The king himself has left proof of his concern over general food supply in his letters to

Sister María de Agreda, but he was as impotent to solve this problem as the others with which he was faced. There were moments when the situation became so desperate that it resulted in dangerous popular uprisings—for example, one in Seville in 1652, known under the name of the "Green Banner," a classic mutiny brought on by famine which kept the Feria quarter in a state of revolt for twenty-one days and had repercussions in Cordova and other Andalusian cities.

The cure proposed by the State to avoid similar movements was worse than the disease. Its supply policy was dictated by the simplistic mercantilist idea then in vogue (Viñas Mey): imposition of a price ceiling—"cheap bread"—on staple articles, without taking into consideration that a simple price war, ignoring any compensation to the poor laborer, would merely swell the army of unemployed who had had to abandon trades that did not give them a living wage. Nor did the attitude of the clergy, who stubbornly denounced the state of destitution, respond to a more intelligent view of the problem. The free soup of the convents, distributed indiscriminately to every sort of vagabond and needy person, raised begging to the status of a *modus vivendi,* was a contributing cause to "that sort of religious aura with which Spaniards invested the act of giving or receiving alms," and stripped beggars of "their shamefaced appearance, for they lived in a well-organized manner and turned begging into a lucrative business" (Pfandl).

Foreigners in the Spanish Economy. Ever since the middle of the 16th century, in the wake of the discoveries and colonization of America, Spain had been the gathering place for many European businessmen. At the end of the century, to the influx of precious metals was added as a further inducement the industrial decline of the country, which made provisioning of the Indies fleet dependent on foreign imports.

During the 16th century the most favored merchants had been natives of countries allied with the Crown: Genoese, Flemings, and Germans. We have already spoken of the advantages obtained by the former, beginning with the treaty of 1528. Their supremacy lasted exactly one century, for after 1629 they were dislodged from their Spanish positions by the Portuguese, who, thanks to their African establishments, could open or close at will the supply of Negro slaves so necessary to the Indies. In fact, in 1640 there were 2,000 Portuguese traders—the majority of them Jews or *conversos*—in Seville, and to judge from the obituaries of the cathedral, their number was growing. The Portuguese *conversos*—or *marranos,* as they were called—could count on very favorable positions in the court itself and in the principal port cities on the Cantabrian Sea. Their central offices were in Hamburg, the city where they had taken refuge after the Spanish *tercios* captured Antwerp in 1585. Portugal's separation from the Spanish Crown put an end to Portuguese expansion in Spain and her colonies.

The Flemings, for their part, had relied upon the favor of Charles V. Export trade from the Low Countries to Spain was very active until the insurrection there. This event obstructed mercantile dealings. On the one hand, the Dutch became bitter enemies of Spanish shipping and commerce. Between the capture of La Brielle in 1571 and the Peace of Westphalia in 1648, Holland carved out a colonial empire at the expense of Spain and Portugal. On the other hand, the Walloons of the south, who were Catholics, and the Flemings remained loyal to Spain; but the war paralyzed industry and commerce in their country, with the natural repercussions on trade with Spain. It survived, however, and even experienced a period of considerable prosperity after 1621, when Holland again went to war with Spain after the Twelve Years' Truce. The Flemish colony in Andalusia was large. We need only recall that in 1596 whole companies of Flemings could be formed to defend the city of Cádiz against English attack.

Last, the Germans, the great bankers of the Crown during Charles V's reign, appeared on the Spanish coasts as merchants and sailors beginning in the last years of the 16th century. This was an action carried out by the Hanseatic cities (members of the medieval German Hanseatic League). These cities took advantage of the Dutch provinces' rebellion to bring to Spain wood, grain, tools, metals, and munitions supplied by the rebels. As neutrals, the Hamburgers and other Hanseatic merchants were favored by the governments of Madrid and Brussels and made a great success of this trade, especially at moments when England and France found themselves at war with Spain. The great risks taken by Hanseatic shipping, which, pursued by the Dutch and other adversaries of the Hapsburgs, often had to sail around the north of Scotland and Ireland, were amply compensated by the large profits to be gained. During the truce of 1609–1621 Spanish-Hanseatic trade fell off considerably but later managed to recover, until recognition of the United Provinces in 1648 reestablished the former situation.

The lure of profits from the Indies trade was so great that even countries who were enemies of the Spanish Crown lost no opportunity to enter the country and swell the colonies of foreign merchants in every port. The French were prominent among them. Traders from Nantes appeared in Seville, Málaga, and the Canaries under the protection of those of Bilbao, whose privileges they shared because of the trade agreement existing between those two cities. Merchants from Vitré developed their contacts with Cádiz, Sanlúcar, and Puerto de Santa María after 1560. Finally, the Normans, who already thought of Seville and Cádiz as way stations on the Canaries route, stopped in those cities more frequently after the 16th century. We do not know the number of French citizens established in the Spanish seacoast cities, but the presence of French consuls in Cádiz (1575 or 1581), Seville (1578), Barcelona (1578), and Valencia (1593) attests their importance.

In regard to the French, we must mention the continuation of the great stream of peasants, herdsmen, and small artisans which had begun at the end of the 15th century. While immigration into Catalonia dropped sharply about 1620, it grew more intense in the rest of Spain. In Aragon and Valencia, French farmers assured continuation of the crops after the Morisco expulsion. In the Castilian cities, the French carried out the humblest trades, those which repelled the minds of the natives. By the end of the 17th century, French pressure in the large cities and towns of Spain was so considerable that there were even violent popular outbreaks against them.

The last to arrive in the deteriorating Spain of the 17th century were the English and Dutch. And this is understandable. Not only had they been the Spaniards' bitterest adversaries, but their Protestant status was also a barrier between them and Spain. It was necessary to seek a *modus vivendi,* however, for although the Spanish Crown owned the Indies, Amsterdam and London had the industries necessary to supply them. This fact was translated into a special regime enjoyed by Protestants in Seville, Cádiz, Málaga, and Puerto de Santa María. By the end of the century Santander also tried to obtain this same privileged situation. But the Crown did not give its authorization.

In the second half of the 17th century the enormous Dutch trade with Spain, in particular with Cádiz, changed Amsterdam into Europe's chief money market: the stock of currency concentrated in the city became so considerable that it permitted, against the rules of the mercantile system, export of precious metals and coins not only to India for its own trade, but even to a number of Western countries. Already active during the Thirty Years' War, this trade reached its apogee after the peace of 1648, when Hispano-French rivalry induced the Spaniards themselves to favor the business dealings of their late enemies, the Dutch. In the last decades of the 17th century Dutch and English merchants appeared in Catalonian ports as active buyers of the brandy made from Panedés and Maresme wines.

Owing to Spain's weakness in the 17th century, the activity of these foreigners was prejudicial to the country's interests. When we take up in detail the matter of trade we shall see how they monopolized almost all the great maritime traffic, especially that carried on with the Indies. Contemporary Spaniards were well aware of this process, and there were a great many complaints by *arbitristas* and even literary testimony to the situation. Both coincided in repeating *ad infinitum* the "desubstantization" of Spain through its effects. We shall conclude by quoting the opinion of Sancho de Moncada, who alleged that foreigners enjoyed the largest incomes in the nation: "more than a million in *juros* (bonds on public revenue), an infinite number of *censos* (bonds on private debts), all the funds of the Crusade, a great number of prebendaries, *encomiendas,* benefices, and annuities."

Decline of Agriculture: Expulsion of the Moriscos. Early in the 17th century the Spanish soil, always so neglected because of the traditional predominance of herding, received a rude blow. The expulsion of the Moriscos (former Mudéjares forced to convert in 1502 in the Crown of Castile and in 1525 in the Crown of Aragon), decreed in 1609–1611, deprived agriculture of the most skilled manpower it possessed. (Article 5 of the expulsion decree exempted 6% of the Moriscos "so that dwellings, sugar mills, rice harvests, and irrigation systems may be preserved, and so that they may give instruction to the new settlers.") How was such an unfair decision arrived at? We shall quote Pierre Vilar's reply to the question: "They (the Moriscos) were a residue of the conquered Moors, converted by force but not assimilated; sometimes shopkeepers, more often farmers, formed into closed communities at the service of the great lords of the Reconquest: a colonial problem on home soil which Spain had borne for two centuries without solving. About 1600, after so many revolts, repressions, expulsions, and mass displacements, the danger of a general uprising was probably only a myth. But suspicion toward the crypto-Christian, 'bad blood,' the spy, the marauder, the businessman who laid his hand on too many ducats, turned the Morisco into an all-too-obvious scapegoat in a moment of crisis. He was considered too prolific and too frugal: those were the real charges."

Let us examine the results of the expulsion. In the demographic sphere a new loss occurred which was difficult to recoup. . . .

In other words, the number of expelled persons came to nearly 300,000 persons altogether, equivalent to about 3% of all Spaniards. But the expulsion did not affect the different regions equally, so that those composing the Crown of Aragon, especially Valencia, were much more seriously damaged. In these regions the problem of resettlement became extremely urgent; but this does not mean that it was always solved. In Valencia, for example, almost half the Morisco villages abandoned in 1609 were still uninhabited in 1638. In Aragon, conversely, French immigration succeeded in "filling in," as the expression of the period was, the void left by the expelled Moriscos.

In the economic sphere the consequences were even more important. Essentially, disappearance of the agricultural *élite* (as early as May, 1610, the *Audiencia* of Valencia lamented the "scarcity of laborers caused by the expulsion of those very Moriscos who were so extremely hard-working") meant the disappearance of the *revenues* with which these vassals' lords paid their interest charges, or annuities obtained from mortgage loans *(censos* and *censales),* contracted with the speculators of the cities *(censalistas).* If we recall the extraordinary enthusiasm of moneyed people to invest their capital in *censos al quitar,* or annuities, we will easily understand the collapse produced in this parasitic society by the departure of the Moorish peasants who, in the last instance, supported it. Reglá, the first historian to bring this important question into focus, transcribes an essential document proving that contemporaries of the expulsion were well aware of its consequences in the economic sphere. The Archbishop of Valencia wrote to a minister of Philip III in 1608, "All those who are necessary to the Republic, for its government and spiritual and temporal adornment, depend on the services of the Moriscos and live from the mortgages with which they or their ancestors have burdened the Morisco towns; and thus, when they see that they are unable to live, they will have to make an appeal to their rights and call upon His Majesty, lamenting their indigence and destruction."

To prevent this "indigence and destruction" the landholding aristocracy, not content with seizing the property of the expelled Moriscos, finally obtained a reduction of the interest on *censales* to 5%. Thus the cycle was complete: the measure which began by affecting agricultural economy made its immediate effects felt on the feudal economy, and finally affected the bourgeois economy which was its creditor. We may therefore conclude that, despite Hamilton's optimistic theory, the whole Spanish economic system suffered from the expulsion.

Along with the expulsion of the peasants who made a specialty of irrigation farming came the definitive victory of the old feudal concept that the basis of agrarian economy was cereals, olives, and vines. The only other crops that continued to be cultivated were sugar cane and cotton, in the southern part of Granada; silk in this same region, Valencia, and Murcia; linen and hemp in a number of regions in the North, and rice along the Mediterranean shore. No notable progress was made in a century which, to make matters worse, witnessed a constant drop in the price of agricultural products.

Decline of Herding and of the Mesta. One of the incontrovertible facts of Spanish economy in the 17th century is the loss in livestock. Although continuous statistical series do not exist, we know through Klein that during the second half of the century the number of head of sheep controlled by the Mesta was less than 2 million, a fact which confirms the diminution in numbers which had begun a century before. There were many causes for this phenomenon. Some authors attribute it to a period of drought undergone by the Mediterranean climate in the last decades of the 16th century and the early years of the 17th. Others add to this factor the disturbances which took place in the development of herding because of the wars in Catalonia and Portugal (1640–1641), interrupting use of the customary pastures and sheepwalks. And finally, we must not forget the attacks leveled against the Mesta, precursors of those which were to ruin it in the 18th century.

In the 17th century open warfare was declared on the Honorable Assembly of the Mesta. This powerful organization, so feared but at the same time so respected, became the target of every sort of criticism. Opposition to the privileged members of the Mesta arose from delegates to the Cortes, from the chanceries, the defenders of agriculture and enclosures, and from the great creditors of the Crown. The attacks converged particularly on the powers of the *Alcalde Entregador,* or President, who saw his powers limited on all sides and his jurisdiction questioned.

The Mesta gave way before these attacks inch by inch. Its chief support was its alliance with the monarchy, which, though in 1619, in exchange for the *millones* tax, it had granted the Pragmatic of Belén declaring entrance into the stockbreeders' brotherhood a voluntary act and limiting the functions of the organization's judges, had compensated the Mesta in 1633 by reestablishing all its privileges and granting full protection to its grazing grounds. The royal cedula of 1633 prohibited plowing up new ground and ordered all arable land granted since 1590—private as well as municipal, public, common and uncultivated lands—to be turned back into pasture with or without permission, if the term of the concession had expired. "The carrying out of this decree of famine," says Colmeiro, "for it condemned men to suffer want so that the flocks could prosper," necessitated a demarcation and survey of such lands, thus originating an infinite number of lawsuits and litigations which aroused many passions and plunged agriculture and nonmigratory herding into a calamitous condition.

In spite of this monopolistic legislation it was no longer possible to change the course of events, for the herding crisis pushed the Mesta into a dead-end street. Klein observes that after 1685 the threat of imminent bankruptcy can be seen in the Mesta's account books. In this last phase the great livestock trust could count less and less on royal support: "The impecunious later Hapsburgs were quite as ready to dicker with the opponents of the Mesta for subsidies as they were to bargain for 'loans' from a scarcely solvent organization. . . ." Thus, throughout the 17th century the defeat of this formerly all-powerful herding organization was slowly being prepared.

Collapse of Castilian Industry. "Even if we did not find convincing proof," wrote Colmeiro in 1863, "in the Parliamentary papers and the royal decrees, of the weakness and collapse of Spanish industry from the middle of the 16th century to the beginning of the 18th . . . we would be more than convinced of the sad truth by the inquiry of the Council of Castile in 1619, the very urgent *junta* of 1620 (though it bore no fruit because of Philip III's untimely death), and the efforts, pleas, and importunings of the impoverished and ruined cities, mainly Toledo, Cordova, Seville, Granada, and Valencia, which in 1655 were trying to bargain with the Court for a cure, or at least some relief from their troubles."

Though detailed studies are lacking, there are numerous memorials of the period (as for example Martínez de la Mata's, giving the list of seventeen guilds disbanded in 1655) which provide unequivocal evidence of this industrial decline. . . .

The population loss for Toledo and Segovia is particularly significant as an index of Castilian industrial evolution. The recovery of Burgos and Cuenca at the end of the 17th century has a possible connection with renewed export of raw wool.

One of the few encouraging events in this moribund 17th century was the establishment of ironworks for casting cannon and munitions in Liérgana and La Cavada (Santander). Assisted by the policies of the Count-duke of Olivares, the Belgian Jean Curtius and the Luxembourger Georges Labande set up an excellent metallurgical works in those towns in the year 1622.

This seems the appropriate place to sum up, with Larraz, the different factors contributing to the decline of Castilian manufactures: (1) industrial superiority of the Low Countries, England, and France over Castile, (2) the deviation of Spanish prices from European ones as a consequence of the influx of American silver, (3) the lesser capitalistic spirit of Castile in the 16th and 17th centuries, (4) the unhappy results of the Hapsburgs' European intervention.

A realization of this process of decline was so widespread that by the end of the century, during the reign of Charles II, there was a general desire for recuperation, and many projects to attain it were devised. In Castile, among the excellent proposals of the Count of Oropesa one at least survived: the *Junta de Comercio y Moneda,* or Board of Trade and Currency, created in 1679, which gave fruitful results in the following century. In 1674 thirty-two Aragonese deputies joined under the presidency of Don John of Austria to try to restore the kingdom's economic potential, but the committee was stalemated by a serious controversy over freedom versus limitation of trade. In Catalonia the efforts of a generation of men united around the doctrines of Narcis Feliu de la Penya obtained positive results with the aid of foreign technicians. Finally, in a general sense, the Royal Pragmatic of 1682 was—as Colmeiro says—the first step toward the rehabilitation of arts and trades, when it declared that possessing or having possessed factories for weaving silk, cloth, woolens, or other textiles was not unworthy of the nobility.

The Guilds and Industrial Decline. The guilds are usually blamed for the stagnation into which Spanish industrial production fell in the 17th century. Echoing the diatribes of the enlightened thinkers of the 18th, even apologists for the guilds attribute the stagnation of industry to them, because of the restrictions on entry into trades and the system of privileges enjoyed by the guilds.

The history of guilds under the Hapsburgs has not yet been written. The amount of material, both published and unpublished, is immense. But the published material is not very useful, for its authors based their studies on an idealistic view of the past and were unaware of even the rudiments of the economic life from which the guilds had sprung and out of which they developed. Just as they considered the institution to be very ancient—and we have already pointed out its relative modernity, even in Catalonia—they believed that its progress had been uniform, disregarding the tenacious opposition that had existed ever since the 16th century between the guilds of the old privileged cities and those which had arisen in the towns around them precisely to escape their monopolistic prerogatives. The relationship between the trade cycle and guild activity has also been forgotten, and, what is still more important, the State's tendency to submit guilds to uniform rules and strict control, not out of industrial policy but out of an obvious desire for tax revenue.

Now that we have cleared up these points, we can concentrate on guild history under the Hapsburgs and gauge its supposed responsibility for the country's industrial decline. After Ferdinand and Isabella's measures, which gave form to guild life in Catalonia and Valencia and encouraged creation of guilds in the Crown of Castile, the 16th century was characterized by the appearance of a considerable number of guild corporations. The motive was Spain's industrial expansion in the wake of the expanding economy of the period. A simple examination of the known foundations shows us that most modern guilds were founded in the second half of the 16th century, especially after 1530, starting point of the upward trend. In Burgos, for example, the market gardeners received their charter in 1509; the tanners in 1512; cobblers, 1528; and masons, 1529; after 1540, embroiderers (1544), dealers in skins (1545), shoemakers (1552), thong-makers (1570), charcoal-burners (1574), hatters (1589), and gamekeepers (1591). In Toledo, to the guild of the wax workers, recognized in 1446, were added the dyers (1530), butchers (1560), pastry cooks (1580), locksmiths (1582), sieve-makers (1588), and straw workers (1598). The same phenomenon is found in Saragossa (1540, blacksmiths; 1550, wool-combers; 1556, harness-makers, mattress-makers, locksmiths, and hatters; 1565, linen-weavers; 1567, wool-weavers; 1584, glass-blowers; 1590, carters), and even in Barcelona and Valencia, where numerous similar lists could be made.

Simultaneously, the guilds appeared in towns of secondary importance. Economic prosperity caused journeymen to move from the cities, where a mastership was difficult to obtain, and set themselves up as masters in nearby towns and even villages. Little attention has been paid to this phenomenon in Spain. However, its strength is undeniable. There is evidence of it in Catalonia (for example, foundation of the wool-weavers' guild in Sabadell in 1558, competing with the powerful wool-dressers' association of Barcelona). More examples could no doubt be found in other regions.

During the prosperous phase of the trade cycle there was no guild problem. It arose when Spanish foreign trade began to decline, and with the decline came a reduction in labor activity. Then the guilds became organizations of resistance to the contraction of economic life. Such is their history—a very unflattering one—in the 17th century. Caught between the devil of business stagnation and the deep sea of the State's tax demands, the guild corporations lived miserably and poorly, generally speaking, with the all-too-predictable sequel of obstructionism, oppression, fraud, oligarchic monopolies, and so on. Gradually people began to think of them as a dead weight, especially in places where they had been established relatively recently. In 1678 voices were raised in the Cortes of Calatayud asking for their suppression. However, in places where money was abundant the guilds continued to prosper; this was the case of those in Madrid. It was, in fact, during the 17th century that the Five Greater Guilds of Madrid were established, whose importance in Spanish economic life will be taken up in the next chapter.

The Crown's interest in keeping the guilds under strict control became accentuated in this same century, as its fiscal needs continued to grow. It was essential to the plans of the reformers of the Spanish treasury at the time to have an assured tax base. Hence, when the Board of Trade and Currency was created in 1679 the guilds came under its jurisdiction in administrative and economic matters. With the exception of the Catalonian and Valencian guilds, which maintained their traditional independence, the life cycle of the guilds was over: they returned fully to the control of the State which had created them, and in the end the State itself decreed their elimination.

Federico Chabod

10

In a culture that from Machiavelli to Venturi has produced great histori-ans, Federico Chabod stands with the greatest. As A. William Salomone writes, his was "one of the most brilliant and sensitive historical minds of the twentieth century." Chabod wrote extensively in a wide field. He is among a handful of masters in Machiavelli studies, he was expert on the European sixteenth century, he wrote a masterpiece on late nineteenth-century Italian diplomacy and politics, and he was an authority on contemporary Italian history. His works in any one of those fields would have gained him eminence as a historian.

Born on February 23, 1901, in the Franco-Italian Val d'Aosta of Northern Italy, Chabod enjoyed a happy and comfortable childhood, marred only by the exigencies of World War I. He entered the University of Turin in 1919, at which time he was already a passionate student of the life and works of Machiavelli. Like all young historians and philosophers of his time, he fell under the influence of Benedetto Croce, without ever accepting, however, all of Croce's dicta on history and historiography. He did learn from Croce to distinguish between the "facts" of history and man's consciousness of those facts. Consequently, all of Chabod's works are at least in part "intellec-tual history," analyses of the beliefs, opinions, and ruling ideas which move men to action. He further agreed with Croce that past reality—history—"can be grasped only through ourselves," that is, through the historian's thought and experiences, which are necessarily of the present. Acknowledging this inescapable condition, Chabod believed, was the first step toward mitigating if not overcoming its potentially distorting effects.

Chabod also studied at Florence under the liberal political historian Ga-etano Salvemini, whose work, in Croce's words, "re-established the bond between history and contemporary political experience." Chabod himself never wrote "present-minded" history; in fact, like many of his generation, he sought disengagement from the bitter realities of his contemporary Fascist

Italy. He did believe, however, that history deals with life and that the proper study of true history, while it demonstrates the limits of human freedom, illustrates also the potentialities open to men to make their own history. He further believed that any narrow monographic analysis must be, if not immediately applicable to a larger more general historical question, then at least preparatory to such an application. The "scientific" monograph, that is, had to serve the artistic or intuitive reconstruction of the historical reality.

To such influences and insights affecting the young scholar must be added those of Friedrich Meinecke, with whom Chabod studied at the University of Berlin from 1926 to 1928. Always respectful of Meinecke, Chabod nevertheless found him too much of an "idealist," too prone to accord to ideas an independent existence. He further faulted Meinecke for his "lack of a quality essential to historians of ideas, that of precision in demonstrating that one thing is a 'fact' and another thing is 'consciousness' of the fact." And yet he learned much from the great German historian.

Finally, although familiar with and impressed by the work of the *Annales* school of historiography, Chabod neither accepted its claims nor emulated its methods. He confessed that he did not see how "the secret of history" could be unlocked by the use of "statistical tables, percentages, medians, graphs, and diagrams." As befits a student of Machiavelli, he continued to stress political factors as being more decisive than others—economic, social, psychological—and to maintain that beyond technical precision and scientific rigor (in which Chabod had few peers) the historian had to rely upon his insights: "No logic and no appeal to concepts can ever be a substitute for intuition." These influences and principles pervade Chabod's works.

His essays on Machiavelli established Chabod's first claims to pre-eminence in history. Beyond such technical achievements as suggesting convincing dates for *The Prince* and thus clarifying the corollary problem of Machiavelli's "intentions," Chabod characteristically linked his apparently narrow subject to a much broader question, for, as he wrote, "Machiavelli is the true test of any view that is held of the Renaissance and of its historical significance." Chabod was instrumental in wrenching Machiavelli studies away from the "romantics," with their tendency toward idealizing and transfiguring the Florentine, and from the "realists," with their tendency to divorce political concerns from cultural history. Chabod's purpose, as he wrote, was "to present Machiavelli . . . as the expression, almost the synthesis of Italian life throughout the fourteenth and fifteenth centuries; to see reflected and clarified in his thought, as it were in its essential outline, the age-long process of development which leads from the downfall of the old Communal freedom to the triumph of the princely, the absolute State." Since Chabod's essays on Machiavelli, scholars have debated his interpretations but generally within the perimeters he himself established.

Chabod's stress on the primacy and even autonomy of politics appears quite clearly in his long essays on "The State of Milan in the Age of Charles V." There Chabod analyzes the "imperial idea" and the influence of economic and fiscal interests on Charles V's policies. He concluded that although Charles entertained seriously the imperial idea, in actual policy he followed political necessities; similarly, although Charles needed bankers' loans, financial considerations never played a role in his political decisions. Finally, the establishment of a centralized administration was neither an inevitable unfolding of a long process nor the triumph of the "idea" of the modern state over that of the feudal state. It was simply Charles' way of responding to the practical needs of his imperial policy.

Chabod brought all of his talents to bear in his last masterpiece, the *History of Italian Foreign Policy, 1870–1896* of which he completed only the first volume, entitled *The Premise* (1951). Based on exhaustive archival researches and rigorously bound by the most "scientific" methods of inquiry, *The Premise* is a brilliant analysis of politics and society, economics and culture, ideas and institutions, men and events. Chabod demonstrates, again, how after all the pertinent "facts" have been gathered in, it is the historian's "intuition" which must breathe life into them if history is to emerge. Italy's national existence began in the midst of a European crisis of values—political, social, and spiritual. Chabod's main theme is the travail of Italian statesmen seeking to found a liberal, progressive state within a European context of power politics dominated by Bismarck. *The Premise* is diplomatic history with a difference. Chabod demonstrates how complex and interrelated are foreign and domestic politics; he shows in a series of biographical sketches how Italian leaders responded as individuals to events and ongoing developments, even though they shared basic social characteristics; and he further shows how in that nationalistic age all statesmen worked, consciously and unconsciously, within a common European framework. Diplomatic history merges necessarily into intellectual history and European history emerges out of a consideration of Italian diplomatic history in *The Premise,* which one critic has called "one of the most important historical books published in the twentieth century."

Federico Chabod was clearly a master of the archives, a gifted writer, brilliantly imaginative, always in control both of his sources and his biases. He eschewed any philosophy of history, and he apparently regarded the search for general laws in history as wasted effort, "a vain neopositivistic aberration," in Salomone's words, "not worthy of serious attention." Chabod nevertheless insisted on the highest standards of historiographic methodology and on the validity of the "facts" unearthed in historical research. In his avoidance of any *Weltanschauungen* and in his defense of the validity of historical knowledge, as well as in his concern with values, Chabod reflects the prevailing mid-twentieth-century historiographic temper. His historical works, his labors as editor of the *Rivista storica italiana,* his presidency of the International Committee of Historical Sciences (1955), and his example as a teacher and colleague at the University of Rome combined to make of him, in Fernand Braudel's words, "one of those rare leaders whom historians may emulate but never match."

Selected Bibliography

The best introductions in English to Chabod and his works are the essays by A. William Salomone, "Federico Chabod: Portrait of a Master Historian," in *Historians of Modern Europe,* and by Sir Charles Webster, "Federico Chabod: An International Figure," *Rivista storica italiana,* LXXII (1960), 625–628. That issue of the *Rivista storica italiana* is devoted to the memory of Chabod and contains many informative essays by Chabod's colleagues and students. Felix Gilbert is perceptive on Chabod in his short essay "Three Twentieth-Century Historians: Meinecke, Bloch, Chabod," included in *History: The Development of Historical Studies in the United States,* edited by John Higham (1965). A. P. d'Entrèves offers a short but incisive introduction to Chabod's work in the English translation of the essays on *Machiavelli and the Renaissance* (translated by David Moore, 1958).

HISTORY OF ITALIAN FOREIGN
POLICY FROM 1870 TO 1896

ORDER AND LIBERTY

1. The Passion and the Idea

[After a discussion of the tenets of nineteenth-century Liberalism, Chabod proceeds:]

... But if such were the precepts of classical liberalism (that is, denying the division of society into rigidly opposed strata and positing a continuous intermingling between classes), completely new sociological concepts were beginning to emerge. These concepts insisted instead on the existence of opposed strata and on the reality of class or of *"stato"* (now emptied of its old-regime juridical content); and these classes were economic in essence. Such emergent sociological concepts were demanding the attention even of those who were hostile to socialism and Marxism. Italian liberal thought, which was beginning to follow Western and especially French liberal ideas, discovered that the notion of a society of political-economic groups was slowly but steadily encroaching upon the concept of a society composed of individuals. Nationalism, however, provided the greatest impulse toward the acceptance of new positions and different premises in political conflicts. Nationalists charged that the bourgeoisie, with their greed and cowardice, had short-changed, as it were, the fatherland. Years later, Crispi was to gain prominence as a voice of the right-wing bourgeoisie. A man of the old Left, he was yet persuaded of the sacred right of private property, and he praised the bourgeoisie for having given the Italian people political institutions, independence, and, even to the propertyless, civil rights. But he reproached these same bourgeoisie, not for their class egoism toward the populace, but rather for their materialism in the face of lofty national ideals; not for their social conservativism, but rather for their nationalistic deficien-

The following selection from *Storia della politica estera italiana dal 1870 al 1896* (1962), 2nd edition, Editori Laterza, Bari, 1962, pp. 350–365, was translated for this volume by Geremie Guercio Hoff of George Mason University with the collaboration of Gerald Cavanaugh.

248

cies. The bourgeoisie, Crispi charged, thought of their material interests, not of honor, and in that they were similar to the masses, who were affected with excessive concern for living conditions at the cost of any higher spiritual preoccupations.

However, whether the impulse was socialistic or nationalistic, in both cases society began to be seen as divided into blocs, bereft of the extreme fluidity with which classical liberalism of the early nineteenth century had endowed it. The two new forces of the contemporary world, both of which had emerged after 1870 and which together denied the individual while stressing a superior complex entity, be it class or country, began to assault liberalism from left and right. However, the affirmation that its own rule was not exclusive allowed the leading liberal bourgeois party to feel that it in fact constituted a regime that was not economic in nature but rather moral-political, one that reflected not social structure but rather civic functions. The word "bourgeoisie" [*borghesia*] was understood in the Italian not the French manner, as "received by all men in whose individual conscience there is joined a political conscience so strong as to enable them not only to judge public affairs but to enforce them, sustain them, and inspire them in a direct and conscientious way."

That such a regime could be unjust occurred even to some of the ruling party. They groped for words to express their dilemma and reflected on Piscane's bitter judgment: "The word 'democracy' which they used meant for them the reign of the bourgeoisie, which, if it was politically restricted, nevertheless preserved the social order as it was." Thus, Piscane noted, notwithstanding the "noble middle-class victims" who had suffered in redeeming the fatherland, there had been no substantial changes in the "sterile doctrines" that had triumphed in the French Revolution and which there had ushered in an extremely unequalitarian society, a new tyranny through which the middle classes "who, with their economic and intellectual power, had brought on the revolution, oppressed the masses who lacked everything." Similar arguments were uttered by those who held that the Italian people had brought about the political revolution for very precise economic ends, namely an improvement in their basic living conditions, lacking which made it ridiculous to talk of morality, education, and civic virtues. Others were publicly announcing that unification had benefited only the rich, who in the provinces were using their political powers to maintain and increase their domination over the ignorant and destitute masses. The great majority, they argued, sees the government only as an exactor of money and manpower; in many areas the wealthy had greatly increased their riches while the people gained little or nothing. In the House of Representatives, one delegate, Sonnino, observed, "Today the wealthy like to talk to the peasants' miserable conditions but only for their own purposes, to use

those conditions as a shield against the intrusion of civic interests, to
garner sympathy, by reflection, for their own problems, especially their
land taxes. But whenever they face the peasants directly, whether in
local administration or in private business, then, gentlemen, sentiments
of solidarity evaporate. Observe, in the south as in the north, the hordes
of hungry migrant peasants, the thousands of peasants evicted from the
most fertile and well-cultivated parts of Italy, and the hatred of the
sharecroppers toward the supposedly 'genteel' class. Look at the squalid
dwellings and the pitiful moral and physical living conditions of the
peasants in the lower Po Valley." In defense of the landowners
["borghesia"], Benedetto Cairoli reminded the legislators of "their un-
selfish, spontaneous, and endless philanthropy," and extolled as proof of
their self-abnegation the extension of voting rights, which he compared
to the sacrifices of the French nobility on the night of August 4, 1789. But
looming above the conflicts and controversies was the concrete fact that
society was indeed separating into different and opposed social strata.
Opening doors to individuals was no longer enough. The problem was
now seen to be one of political and social groups. The Italian bourgeoisie
had had their Revolution of 1830; there now began the Recrimination of
1830.

II

The Intellectual World

Now, inhibiting the formation of a reform movement which sought to
turn from notions of public beneficence and charity—a suitable remedy
for individual needs—to programs involving the organization of labor—
the remedy suitable for class needs—there stood first of all a deep-rooted
and widespread attachment to private property, inherited and acquired,
an attachment, however, especially strong among those who made up the
leading social group. This was, of course, an old tradition, and even the
French revolutionaries had secured property rights in Article 17 of the
Constitution of 1789; later, in the flood tide of Jacobinism in 1793, the
revolutionaries had reiterated the principle that property was a right of
the individual citizen, to dispose of as he wished. In a work well received
in Italy in 1848, Thiers had once again enunciated this inviolable principle, and even those most disposed toward alleviating the plight of the
people were angered by criticisms of private property and infringements
on property rights. Ricasoli, for example, was sincerely interested in his
peasants' well-being and often was moved by compassion and comprehension which prevailed over his personal interests. But if anyone even
hinted at timid innovations in the matter of customary property relation-

ships or suggested that perhaps the wishes of the peasants differed from the will of the landlords, Ricasoli would recoil with indignation and brusquely order his estate managers to inform the peasants that he was *il padrone,* that all of the land was his alone to dispose of as he saw fit, and that if any of his peasants spoke ill of him he would immediately be evicted. Once, when darker threats appeared, and during the gloomy and disquieting period of early 1849, when rumors circulated about investigations into Ricasoli's estates at Brolio, the iron-willed Baron reacted strongly: "If public authority appears with warrants," he announced to his tenants and stewards, "I will open my doors to it, but if it appears without legal authority, I shall resort to force against it. Arm yourselves, and if the brigands arrive, shoot them on sight. Brolio is private property, and no one can act against it; if the authorities charged with civic welfare cannot fulfill their duties, we must defend our persons and property ourselves."

To improve the living conditions of less fortunate people, both materially and morally, was held to be the principal duty of the wealthy; this principle had traditionally been expounded by Lambruschini, Ricasoli, and Minghetti. The rationale, of course, was largely one of self-interest. One must not allow the reins out of one's hands or give room for the exponents of socialism (that hard breed "come from hell to destroy everything they touched") to seduce the peasants with their devilish works and to precipitate a new age of barbarism by subverting society. Such a subversion would mean the prevalence of inferiors—peasants and workers. As human beings, workers are, of course, respectable people (Ricasoli and his peers believed), well deserving for the essential work they perform. But as a class operating in the political world, they heed only their passions and instincts; what was needed in politics was restraint, respect for traditions, and some knowledge of the world. Unfortunately, "education of the workers had not progressed sufficiently enough to bring about a fusion of classes," and their moral sense was correspondingly poorly developed.

The unprepared, uneducated masses were thus incapable of participating with their betters in politics. On that point there was general agreement, as when Cesare Balbo affirmed that only the educated were important in politics. As time went on, some among the educated moderated their disdain for the uneducated masses. "It seems to me necessary that there be ignorant wretches," Voltaire had written in 1766. A century later many people were openly wishing for the wretches to remain ignorant, but there were some leaders who hoped for the enlightenment through education of the masses; even they, however, thought it best to move circumspectly, there being insufficient moral and cultural material among the peasants and workers to speed up the process.

The workers clearly felt this disdain and fear, being granted no consideration even after the French Revolution, even though they were the basis of all society. "We work and our souls are in torment," went one labor manifesto. "It is the same today as it was in feudal times: we must acquire dignity and strength through the knowledge that we are needed." Education, free and compulsory education, became the primary social demand of organized labor. But, the answer came back, education alone was no longer sufficient; moral improvement was as necessary. This had been a favorite theme, expounded for decades, in different words and for different reasons, by Mazzini and d'Azeglio, Lambruschini and Ricasoli. But one group, with Mazzini, held the view that education was linked to conscience and revolutionary events, while others saw it as the last stage of a slow evolutionary process. The old conspirator Settembrini would say, Let the lower orders be content for now with the thoughtful supervision of the wise; let them place their trust in their prudent and experienced betters and slowly proceed, step by step, like children led by the teacher from the alphabet to novels, from numbers to complex mathematics. The people, he wrote, are like children who cry when their mother washes them but afterward smile at her with clear bright faces. To this question of education was applied Balbo's observation on the people in politics: the criteria for public good could be discerned only through private not public education. At a time when the notables of society believed it was God's decision when to perfect His people, the notion that education was as much a right as political freedom could hardly prosper.

Certainly, the theme of the immature people was constantly sounded. The common people are the future of the country, they are the nation's future resource; the people, therefore, must grow like seeds, naturally, and must not be harmed by being forced into social functions they cannot yet handle. Making the fateful transition from the social to the political field, this theme inspired aversion not only to universal suffrage but also to any broadening of popular electoral influence beyond certain limited, restricted boundaries. It was feared that the country's future might be abandoned to the care of an imperfectly educated populace who were either unprepared for public life or badly prepared by reading the most despicable newspapers; they would thus become easy prey to "Red" plots and transformed into "companies and battalions of voters who would be at the disposal of whoever would gain their leadership." The workers, it was believed, were daily becoming more riotous and vehement, displaying such foul language and aggressive attitudes that cities once known for their genteel customs were now degraded by the obscene and provocative language of the commoners. Lowering the voting age from twenty-five to twenty-one years, it was argued, would simply mean an increased membership for the socialistic subversive parties. Democracy was a beautiful word, the middle classes agreed, but it too often signified "a mere shift in society away from the insolence of the feudal barons" to the insolence of the mob. Beware, then, lest the reins of government slip into the hands of ignorant masses. Political passions among the lower classes precipitously injected into public affairs tended toward class egoism, and politics thus assumed the character of social struggle, allowing for the outbreak of class conflict based on economic issues, something as yet nonexistent in Italy. To institute universal suffrage would unleash conflict over "the social question," of which, thank heaven, there was no trace in Italy. As the loquacious Diomede Pantaleoni put it: "Property precedes the vote." Allow the masses to vote and sooner or later the have-nots will expropriate the haves. In the Senate (Lampertico) and in the Lower House (Codronchi) speakers affirmed that the cause of property and social order involved the cause of liberty itself and, further, that the needs of the "forgotten man," the property owner, had to be voiced and considered.

Among the other obstacles to the extension of the suffrage, this last fear was less immediate and less insistent. There remained alongside of it some room in which to consider matters such as the stability of political institutions and the actual threat posed to social unity by the potential dominance of the masses. Such fears were not merely a façade cloaking material interests, nor were concerns with ideals only a veneer covering mundane issues. If there were those who feared the working classes as meek agents of "Red" socialism and a potent threat to property, there were others who rather feared the peasant masses, controlled by "Black" reaction, who were no real threat to property but were certainly no supporters of individual freedoms and natural unity. Here again the liberal leaders found themselves confronting two extremes, the Red International and the Black International. Some feared one more than the other. Conservatives emphasized the "Red danger" and sought the support of the Catholic Party and of the moderate Rightists, which groups, "because of social conditions, material interests, and tradition, are the natural allies of the established government." More liberal groups, of course, rather emphasized the "Black" danger. The peasants were now invoked. They had in any case already been elevated by such apologists as Lambruschini to the position of being essential bulwarks against the arrogance and instability of the cities—those sources of false "progress" and subversive social and electoral schemes. Now a segment of the peasantry, the small propertied element, were exalted because "they hold the social order as dearly as their land and labor, which they do not wish to see suddenly swept away." This view was criticized as being divisive, setting town against country, and insuring the continued turbulence of the cities. It was also criticized on the grounds that the peasantry were ignorant and superstitious, willing tools of the clergy, who resisted liberalization and national unification and who sought a restoration of the old regime. If one side in the debate quoted Taine's harsh judgments of the French peasantry, the other side appealed to Vacherot's encomium of the peasants as the only stabilizing element amid France's chronic social turbulence.

More often, both "Reds" and "Blacks" were feared as a grave danger to the country, especially since they complemented each other, the Reds serving to fulfill the dire prophecies of the Blacks, while socialism of a sort became a Papal instrument. It was thus a bleak circumstance when don Margotti could unleash his paid orators on rural communities throughout Italy to harangue electoral assemblies, while petty speakers and corrupt journalists were working for the election of socialists. What a spectacle in "the opening of Parliament, with 300 deputies subscribing to the *United Catholic* and 200 editors of certain filthy papers which I neither read nor here mention."

Mingled with fears of the masses—who were viewed as a bloc not always distinguishable in its various elements—were other hopes, anxieties, and fears: love of freedom and of propriety; love of the nation and attachment to its liberal institutions; attachment especially to the monarchy now that the threat of universal suffrage, leading to a republic, appeared imminent; the instinct for preserving private property, prevailing at times but often replaced as a primary consideration by concern for political stability. Only an act of historical oversimplification could blend these two concerns as one—political and social—or make the social depend upon the political. The "Blacks," for example, did not threaten the material interests of the liberals—they were almost completely motivated by ideals, and fear of the Blacks dominated among liberals over fear of the Reds for many years after 1870. In 1872, Crispi announced the necessity of confronting the common enemy, which was . . . the Papacy; two years later Quintino Sella pressed the point that the "Black International," outwardly so benign, was in fact the greatest threat, since in order to achieve its patricidal goal—the ruin of the fatherland and of its freedom—it did not hesitate to join with foreign enemies while it prepared at home for its victory. Rather than deploring the Catholics' electoral absenteeism in 1871, Visconti-Venosta rejoiced in the Papacy's disdain for democracy which insured that the Quirinal [Capitol Hill] would not have to deal with the Vatican. It was logically-historically sound that the Blacks should appear the greater threat, given what seemed to be the strength of international reaction, which was powerfully evident in France and Austria and, between 1873–74, threatening to overtake Spain in a fearful Carlist reprisal. Devoid of any public national or international support, the Reds were then everywhere a heretical minority; the Blacks, however, were always and everywhere powerful and able to influence other countries' policies toward Italy. It must be added that in Italy the conviction was widespread that if great conglomerations of workers did not exist, as was the case in Italy, then the incendiary influence of the socialists would be nullified. This conviction was shared by Crispi, and for years he refused to acknowledge the "specter of socialism," until he finally had to admit that there was indeed combustible social material in Italy and that in fact it had been smoldering for some time. Before that admission, however, it was generally held that the Italian masses—who were not to be confused with the hooligans who demonstrated in public squares—were excellent and law-abiding citizens, as Jacini, an advocate of indirect elections, informed the Senate. Similarly, that resolute optimist Zanardelli advised his fellow senators that in Italy there were no deep social or class antagonisms such as other European nations knew, and he scorned the dark premonitions of his peers as baseless. Proof of the generally optimistic atmosphere prevailing was the emphasis on elementary education as a proper prerequisite for the expansion of the suffrage. Faith in science, widely taught in the schools, faith in peaceful and progressive development and social harmony blended together into one unity.

In the matter of Church lands, the question was viewed not as an attempt on property per se but as an effort for the fatherland. Popular attitudes toward rebellion did not mean a disruption of property rights, and among the rural masses neither sans-culottes nor urban incendiaries could ever be popular. Such French-style radicals were a threat, of course, not only to property but to the fatherland; the *Internationale* symbolized the negation of the ideals for which Italians had struggled. In this belief lay one of the most potent springs of Italian life. Once the country had been unified and made independent, the patriots, having done their duty, turned the nation over to the masses. But the populace had scarcely participated in the great adventure of unification, and often scorned the new regime as a façade behind which new masters ruled in ways similar to the old. Certainly, the alleged advantages of national unity seemed reserved for the propertied class, while the "donkey," the masses, bore the heaviest burdens as before, except now the burdens seemed weightier. If earlier the peasants had cried out for freedom and hoped for an era when the poor would live better and work less, they now lapsed into passivity and resignation: "Liberty and equality, but not material improvement." Fatherland and freedom were nice words, but for the hungry hardly enough. As one peasant of Lodi said to Carducci in 1881, "Enough of this talk of liberty! Let us talk about poverty!"

In this matter, too, there was a gulf between leaders and masses. Ear-

lier, Mazzini had warned against the possibility of a split occurring in
Italy as it had in France between the ideologists and doctrinaires on the
one hand and the people on the other. For this reason, he had made it a
fundamental part of his program to educate the people, and he even
glimpsed, if dimly, the social problem behind the political questions of
the day. After him, Andrea Luigi Mazzini, following Saint-Simon and
other French and Belgian socialists, had insisted more strongly on the
necessity of making the Italian Revolution more of a social process,
while Piscane wanted a revolution that would not merely change some
ministers or erect a Chamber but would obliterate the lazy rich and end
human want in a new society that would enable each citizen to enjoy the
fruits of his labor in an egalitarian atmosphere.

But the "Risorgimento" had been carried out by other means and with
different results. What might have been possible in the earlier days could
not be done at the dawn of the twentieth century, and once again the gulf
widened between the leaders and the masses. Turbulence and disorder,
resounding in the newspapers and journals, only increased the timidity
and fear of the upper classes, forcing them to perceive reform social
movements more and more as threats to freedom and stability. Thus,
Nation and Liberty began to be seen as antithetical to Social Reform. To
improve the lot of the masses appeared to require egalitarianism led by
despotism, a social leveling ending in a plebiscitarian dictatorship. Give
the masses the vote, the common view held, and anarchy would ensue,
followed by the surrender of political rights in return for material benefits, conferred no doubt by a military despotism. Such was the example
all too readily found by liberal historians in the French Revolution, with
its transition from Jacobinism to Napoleon. The "good" Revolution of
1789 was contrasted to the "bad" Revolution of 1793. Anti-socialism grew
naturally out of such nineteenth-century liberal thought. The theory
found confirmation not only in the French experiences of the two Napoleonic dictatorships but also in the so-called socialism of the Papacy,
which in recent years under Pius IX had denied the needs of sound
government by attempting to satisfy through public works and welfare
the needs of the poorer classes.

In other words, freedom was being threatened, the fatherland was
under attack by international socialism, and the leading groups in Italy
took at face value the polemical stance assumed by reformers. Socialism
was no longer the patriotic socialism and nationalism of a Piscane; it was
international, pitting class against nation, internationalism against nationalism. This is what led Mazzini to detach himself from the emerging
movement. It was destined for many years to fix a great gulf between the
socialist parties and the patriots, made unbridgeable because of the furious polemic between the two, one denigrating sentiments held dear by

the other. A great part of Italian history from 1900 to 1922 revolves around this painful split; it entailed great consequences.

Something else fed the ambivalence felt toward the masses. The question of education remained unsettled, but for many it held less promise of the elevation of others than of a certain detachment, separation, and even contempt of others. The disdain of the wise for the ignorant multitude was increasingly evident; the masses were regarded as creatures of instinct and devoid of reason. "We alone remain, we are the pure, the wise, the rational," Lambruschini exclaimed in 1849, and his boast reflected the social situation in which there was an invisible but formidable barrier between the cultured and the common, between the genteel and the merely literate. The situation could not be expressed in any simple formula and was more than that implied, for example, in the terms landowner and patriot. The wise man and the common man, or, more prudently, the wise man and the madman: such were the common dichotomies. The problem of the masses was clearly enunciated, from the leaders' point of view. These masses—whom the least critical described as having to be taken "not as one would wish but as one finds them," and whom the most fearful called "a crazy animal, filled with error and confusion, and devoid of taste, culture, or stability," "the beast with a thousand heads"—these masses here, as elsewhere among the upholders of the European cultural tradition, were regarded by Italian leaders with deep suspicion and even fear. Thus, from the fear of socialism and communism derived from universal suffrage there arose a fear of democracy—with unfortunate consequences for Italian political life.

Such were the fears which fed the antidemocratic bias of Flaubert, Renan, and the more moderate thinkers and writers of Italy. For such men the triumph of democracy meant a hopeless future, with society crushed under the weight of a military state, the precise beat of drums militaristically regulating every movement of the collectivity. Philistinism, ignorance, indifference to moral and spiritual values would prevail, allowing only preoccupation with material interests: a journey into the twilight of culture.

Desire for immediate material gratification: it was an accusation which for decades had been hurled at opponents on both sides of the Alps by political moderates. Those souls, the young Minghetti had written, who are mainly concerned with economic well-being, egotism, and greed demonstrate their love of pleasure and luxury which overcomes their desire for "dignity and honor." Minghetti had blamed the July Monarchy for France's materialism and condemned the actions of Pius IX, who, persuaded of the importance of satisfying people's material needs within the Papal states, prevented the most elevated spiritual ideas from emerging at the critical time. Minghetti was one of the many who feared that the satisfaction of physical needs was becoming the supreme end of humanity, and even Sella, so alien to Romanticism, at times evoked a nostalgia for the great days of 1848 when confronted by the cult of materialism of the new generation. Men like Luigi Blanch and Francesco De Sanctis had reason to protest that such judgments were too harsh, and they predicted that the new generation would employ in industry, commerce, and science the energies that the old generation had expended in conspiracies and speculation. The "materialistic" motto caught hold, however, and tended to become a stereotyped formula until enlivened by the heat of Flaubert's anti-materialist disdain. Benjamin Constant, too, had optimistically referred to his time as an age of commerce; he later realized that commerce implied not only the acquisition of wealth but also the oppression of human feelings, a discounting of affections and the spirit. He became skeptical of the benefits that flowed from the so-called magnificent and progressive sort of men and echoed the belief expressed in the poem "Palinodia" that "the virile age turned to economic studies and to public affairs." Men thus avoided any soul searching, seeking outside of themselves that which they no longer found within.

It was thus that ever since the July Monarchy the question was ceaselessly discussed whether technical progress was overshadowing moral progress and thus creating great perils for the future. There were many debates on how to make the two aspects progress together and especially on how the economy might be coordinated with or even made subordinate to moral principles. In this atmosphere of discussion and polemics, the candid soul of Luigi Luzzati attempted to confute Buckle's fashionable positivistic assertions (already forcefully debated by Droysen) and to demonstrate that virtue and morality were necessary for social progress, to the extent that without them advances in science and technology would have unfortunate consequences. Minghetti, too, sought to coordinate technical and moral progress, economics and morality, and emphasized that moral principles must control industrialism if it was to grow vigorously.

In the midst of such debates, the social question rapidly emerged. One aspect of the question was whether men were happier. If they were not, then how should the problems of the poor be alleviated, how should their rights be protected? Minghetti agreed on the necessity of social legislation which would take a moderate stand between complete laissez faire and direct and constant state intervention. A possible compromise existed consisting of a just socio-economic policy and including a leavening of pre-1848, pre-Marxist optimism which stressed the value of a good example: "When the people see a respectable man, honored by his family and society, paying attention to them, studying their needs, inspiring respect for their class, I believe that these keenly intuitive people will find the man benevolent and will turn to him and repel social agitators into the darkness from whence they shall never again emerge." The example of Lambruschini and Ricasoli was still fresh. The gentleman-seigneur could resume his old power in the state but in a different way. He could obtain leadership through knowledge and because of an irreproachable life instead of, as formerly, through wealth and power. The benevolent, public-spirited man could now guide the populace by good example; he could resolve the social problem by sheer moral strength. Minor writers pointed out for the workers the example of "the self-made man," while for the country squires there stood Lambruschini, Ricasoli, and Minghetti, classical examples of benevolent paternalism. The hero, banned from the political, reappeared in the social arena; the heroic enterprise was now social not political, its task, like that of enlightened despots, being to mediate between proprietors and dependents. Had not Bonghi discovered among the causes of the revolt of the Paris Commune the diminution of the intellectual and moral strength of the upper classes, which was in fact the diminution of the power of the good example, and which had led to the diminution of the influence of the upper over the lower classes?

Now, with all of this anxiety over the alleged decline of moral sense and the presumed triumph of egoism, the decline of the spirit and the rise of materialism, the demise of idealism and the birth of the profit motive, the wide-ranging political and social debate was an expression of the torments suffered by a substantial portion of the dominant Italian political party confronting not a definite problem but, rather, modern civilization in general. Stressing the increase of material wealth but fearing its effects and then appealing to the old anti-luxury, anti-materialistic slogans; extolling the new economic system but fearing its impact on culture and morality—these views express the ambivalence and fears generated by the rapid development of modern society. Politically, the moderates deplored the new spirit of conquest manifested in Bismarck's policies; economically, they feared the consequences of unrestrained competition, the dizzying fluctuations of the stock market. In both cases, power, strength, and numerical superiority were the only ideals or goals. In domestic politics, for example, the democrats aimed at imposing their wishes on the electors, stressing quantity over quality. The prevailing economic problem, disturbing and perplexing as it was, deeply affected politics. The decisive advance of modern industry throughout Europe was driving out the traditional and emotionally satisfying forms of production. These disturbing thoughts were rarely confessed explicitly. They were revealed in the hymns to a romanticized agriculture, a mothering, nourishing agriculture which people had always held to be primary and had endowed with a dignity and reputation never bestowed upon industry and trade, even during the most splendid commercial prosperity of the medieval Italian city-states.

Something new was undoubtedly being insinuated in these praises of rustic life, in this excited imparting of new meaning to agricultural employment. There was an effort to improve techniques, to modernize methods and systems, to approach English and French standards; there was a revival of agrarian studies, renewed discussions in journals, agricultural societies and congresses: these were among the major indications of an Italian renascence. It brought together men so socially and politically diverse as Cattaneo, Cavour, Ridolfi, Capponi, Lambruschini, and Ricasoli. Some were concerned with introducing Merino sheep at Villach, others with raising English hogs or setting up mechanical rice threshers, while still others, embarrassed by their tardiness, roamed the vineyards and wine cellars of Burgundy and Médoc, tasting wines, making comparisons, and developing techniques for improving their Chianti. Agreement on the desirability of technical improvement, however, cloaked a substantial divergence of general views.

For Cavour and Cattaneo, there was no antinomy but rather perfect symmetry between agriculture and modern commerce and finance. They viewed agriculture with the eyes of an economist, producer, and technician, as an essential economic factor. They ascribed to it no romantic pastoral meanings, nor did they cherish it as the sole great educator of the people or exalt it as the only basis of the country's economic and political structure. Cavour, initially a purely commercial agriculturalist *(par raison)*, fell under the fascination of the land and became immersed in the manifold and complex operations of farming; he ended by being an agriculturalist by preference, without, however, losing sight of the importance of industry and finance. Pushed by the necessity of making his way financially, Cavour, of the cadet branch of his family, had to express his "ardent and tormented will" as best he could in a country where industry was still viewed with suspicion and disdain; he planted his cabbages and tended his vineyards. Agriculture was, in a sense, Cavour's surrogate for politics, almost a refuge for political also-rans. Devoid of any of the fashionable idyllic sensitivity for the divine rural tranquillity, Cavour saw the fields only as fountains of production, as an industry, as an area for financial speculation and gambling on the price fluctuations of the various European markets. The old-regime country gentleman was assiduous in the cultivation of his lands, but his economic horizon was bounded by his estate; Cavour saw beyond his own fields to the farther markets of France and Russia. He followed the price trends from the Baltic to the Black Sea, buying and selling opportunely.

Thus we find no more prejudices, no more pretensions concerning the "primary role of agriculture" that marked the older, now rapidly disappearing political order whose hoary traditions had exalted the agricultural basis of civilization. Gone too was the presumed superiority of agriculture, a belief that had constituted an "ominous error fatal to many" and which in the past had led newly rich capitalists to invest in land "as if this would confer dignity on them and elevate them in society"; a belief which drew investment away from productive purposes such as improving industrial and commercial outputs. Nothing was left of all this except the recognition that "all of the industrial arts, daughters of labor, are of equal importance in the eyes of the state and people" because, all equally worthy, equally contribute to the public good. Cavour's philosophy was uprooting not only the political order in Italy but also the old noble-rural mentality. The first effect of the new politics and of the new freedom had to be a powerful industrial sector, because industry needed for its development "a certain amount of freedom and we affirm that its greatest progress will entail an impatient, restless environment endowed with freedom, a situation always preferable to the tranquillity of a constricting and repressive system."

Cavour, however, was a revolutionary, in deed if not in word. In contrast, for many others among the Italian leadership the quality of landowner was truly one which conferred more dignified social status; agriculture, in their view, was and had to remain primary. This was in accord with the ancient tradition which went back to old agricultural Rome and which had flourished even more during the fifteenth and sixteenth centuries. At that time, the pursuit of landownership and the titles of nobility that went with the land had drained capital and capitalists from industrial and commercial enterprises in Italy as in France and elsewhere, with the difference in Italy being that there were no heretical groups who might have carried out industrial and commercial activities (as the Huguenots did in France). In 1834, Salvagnoli rightly deplored the situation in Tuscany, where landed property was "so madly esteemed that the property owner *par excellence* was the possessor of land"; he mocked the "beautiful Castilian traditions" which nineteenth-century Tuscans yet maintained. In Lombardy in 1837, Cattaneo asserted that "most people in commerce have little esteem for merchants unless they have a non-commercial status," that is, unless they have landed estates; this was an extremely hurtful prejudice, in that capital would be lent only to those who owned real property, the least innovative and enterprising group. As late as 1855, Frattini, an advocate of economic innovation, was forced to agree that the prudent and cautious spirit of the landowner still predominated. Like Salvagnoli, he concluded that it was one of the effects of "that opprobrium in which for centuries Castilian ignorance kept those who dedicated themselves to commerce and industry." There was some proof of this in Piedmont, where Cavour suffered from social disdain because he was a businessman and speculator who did not live up to the traditional standards of his class.

In contrast to Cavour, Ricasoli found agriculture anything but a substitute for politics. When he went into politics, he found it a nuisance and always longed for his fields and vineyards and for those solitary and inhospitable regions "with which my soul comes to full accord of thought and feeling, thus giving my natural intelligence strength of purpose, where I dwell in open space unhindered by any restraints on memory or imagination; after four or five hours of a long spiritual journey in such an environment, my physical journey ends at the house toward which I was headed." Romantic sensibilities! When one compares other moderates, especially Tuscans, with Cavour, then the differences are glaring. For the Capponi and their friends—"the Capponi Church"—the passion for the land was exclusive. They opposed agriculture to industry, noting the gigantic and powerful factories thrown up by industry but stressing the social and moral problems they engendered. They judged the pace of industrialization as too swift and therefore disruptive and generative of misery and moral confusion. Preoccupied with the moral aspects of the question, Gino Capponi viewed the workers as reduced to machines, hands without minds, while the farmers retained their integrity of hand and mind. Industrial labor was mechanical; agricultural labor was intelligent. Continuing the contrast, he stressed "the sorrowful and desperate circumstances of workers in huge factories owned by a few capitalists"; he noted the plight of the workers, some of whom "raised their arms to heaven" in supplication, others of whom "raised their hands violently against their brothers"; he saw the new creation, the industrial world, frantically searching for equilibrium, striving to institute "a society resembling the agricultural system, which was coeval with civilization, and composed of proper relationships between proprietor and worker." The "slavery to the loom" was generating a slave revolt, it was evoking cries of passion, announcing by its rumbles an "approaching storm" destined to terrorize all Europe. The "golden mean" of agriculture [la mezzadria] was the way of ending the hatred that was ready to turn into fury.

The machine generated human misery. The "great and the terrible, the good and evil" character of the century was material progress, which brutalized man rather than elevated his soul, as rural life did, to God. Leopardi's sarcastic observations on railroads, on proliferating commerce, and on machines which emulated the works of heaven found sympathy even among those who rejected his cosmic pessimism and who sought refuge in a renewed moral and religious fervor. Was this new education, equal for all, bent on producing a generation of craftsmen? was the question asked by Gino Capponi. The mechanical populace was the supreme goal of the politicians and the subject of those philosophers who called themselves progressive: "Was this the freedom for which our fathers fought?" Industry was the subject, the glory, the weapon of the times; industrialists were "the priesthood of a century which worships money as its god." Such were the constant accusations against materialism and its consequent depression of the human spirit leveled by men who hated machinery and technological progress. "Mechanization" came to be disparaged as "soulless."

The powerful motor of industrial development was production, ever-increasing production that did not settle for the traditional demands of the market but rather excited new demands and created new markets. The romance or poetry of modern industry was already leading Cattaneo to speak of art as social existence and to find his industrial apotheosis in Henry Ford. Cattaneo himself feared that "the only thing which is desired today is production; this stress on production already suffices for England and France, but it is contrary to the nature of craft industry and the arts."

Let agriculture be innovative, then, but let us preserve agriculture as the primary occupation; let us preserve the peasant traditions and rural life, and maintain little industry. This was the only means of serving the cause of civilization, of morality, of national well-being, because the agricultural way of life [la mezzadria] was the repository of our ancient customs, the basis of our great and general prosperity, the sign of Christian charity and civil progress, and, finally, almost an innate condition of our national character. Agriculture was seen as an "ameliorating" force. The problem, then, was changing from a socio-economic to a moral-political one. Economic conservatism was becoming one with political conservatism; the fear of industry was becoming one with fear of the working classes.

How substantial the contrasts of complex views could be even among men who later agreed with each other as proponents of improved technology and increased production was shown by the discussions of the Tuscan agriculturalists (Georgofili), 1833–1834, and the contrasts between Gino Capponi (a great admirer of Pietro Leopoldo's proposed agrarian reforms and a man convinced of the supremacy of agriculture) and Salvagnoli. The latter, going beyond the specific problem of la mezzadria, insisted on the importance of studying agriculture in relation to commerce and industry and deplored the fact that Tuscany, once a manufacturing and trading center, was supposed to prostrate itself to the rural idol and to sacrifice to it all of its capital and industrial activity. "After shaking itself free of the rural mania [superstizione geofilia], Tuscany would find its capital, industry, and commerce gone, and thus reduced to carrying a few ears of corn and a handful of olives to the world market while its competitors sell all sorts of products."

From the conservative state of mind sprang the celebration of agriculture as the great moral educator, of agriculture as the mother of family and civil virtues, as the only certain source of peaceful, ordered progress. Here we are in a world alien to that of Cavour and Cattaneo. That the younger generation were in favor of mechanization did not mitigate the social fact that the majority of the older generation were still bound to traditional ways of life. Nature brought man back to God, the factory made him an atheist. The exponents of agriculture displayed renewed religious fervor in which God, nature, rural labor, and moral education were all blended into one concept. Even for Minghetti, although with less pathos than Ricasoli, the farmer and the true believer were fused together; and just as he wanted the economic system subordinated to morals and spirituality, so he wanted industry subordinated to "good laws, good institutions, education, and religion." Cavour admired Bentham's utilitarianism; Minghetti denounced it.

And if, according to Lambruschini, madmen lived in the cities and rural wisdom had to enter them to set them right, was this not proof enough that mechanization turned the soul to evil, while agriculture directed the soul to wholesome Christian precepts? The much debated problem of the relationship between economics and morality and between technical and spiritual progress found full realization in the discussions relative to agriculture and industry, stressing the educational power of the former and the debilitating moral effects of the latter. Both types of discussion were substantially the same, reflecting a similar attitude confronting the great problems which modern civilization was raising and which transcended mere politics.

This state of mind was supported as well by the humanistic cultural tradition still dominant in nineteenth-century Italy. That tradition contained no exaltation of mechanical inventions but rather stressed works of art and natural beauty. Since the Virgilian *Georgics,* praise for the rustic life had overwhelmed the urban merchant peddling his wares from town to town; trade had never attained a high level of dignity, not even in the great days of the Italian commercial city-states. In fourteenth-century Florence, Leon Battista Alberti had encouraged Gianozzo and Leonardo to exalt rural life: "The crystal-clear air, the happy country where the eye enjoys all its wholesomeness and purity." Only the countryside had "knowing, gracious, faithful, truthful" men and knew the work of "truly good and active men," where no envy, hatred, or malevolence existed. These words the proud Ricasoli repeated; for him the countryside signified tranquility, "the vigorous and elevated peace which is the effect of our souls' enlightenment, when our souls seem finally to have risen after long prostration. How many are the things which we take for granted, to which we give no thought, which in the city pain and distress us?"

Now, this cultural tradition in which Rome's walls, the high arches, and the mythological heroes alternated with vignettes of rural life was still predominant. Manzoni, who placed social economy at the basis of every other discipline, had freed himself from that tradition. Carducci had resumed it, however, at the same time. He found his most profound poetic inspiration in his abandonment to nature. For him, the green silence of the plain, the amber fields, the red clover meadows all infused peace and joy into his soul. Roaring furnaces did not stir his genius, those same blazing foundries which inspired Walt Whitman's Muses. Carducci's songs were most striking for their audacity of content; they seemed an attempt to mitigate extreme modernization with classical style. Carducci depicted the steam engine with its shrill whistle, its gloomy environs, as almost a monster, cruel and unholy, possessed of a metallic soul. As his classical style indicated, he saw industrialization as an extraordinary thing which pained him because it was taking from him his arcadian Lydia, tearing up the cypresses of Bòlgheri. He greeted the new, beautiful, and horrible monster as a Satanic force—the engine, a work of Enlightenment reason, creating artificial industries in verdant natural Umbria. The American poet—his chest swelling with pride at the sight of his powerful engines, the coal, the petroleum, the railroads—invited the Muses to abandon Greece, Italy, Europe and to look for a better, newer, and busier world, to forget the fairy tales of Troy, the castles of medieval times, and to sing the praises of industry, machinery, aqueducts, gasometers, and chemical fertilizer.

Two poets, two worlds. One poet sang the praises of the developing industrial civilization; the other looked back to the land, source of golden harvests and mother of all virtues.

But Carducci was already viewed as a scandalous semi-heretic. To be free and prepared to welcome the modern world meant to be like Cavour, far removed at times from the Italian humanist tradition, like Guicciardini, who also regretted not having gained more knowledge of literature but who was generally indifferent and even disdainful of literature and of *littérateurs,* heedless of stylistic refinement, and wholly taken up with economics and politics, persuaded of the necessity to analyze matters purely rationally. In terms of the Italian humanistic tradition, Cavour was a heretic. What else could be said of a man who having seen the tomb of Romeo and Juliet described it as "a watering place for buffalo, but pompously titled," who refused to give his opinions on Venice, since "the last tour guide will suffice to recall the things seen in that city," and who confessed to attaching little importance to the classics per se?

The eclectic Minghetti, although fully aware of his era's problems and capable of admiring the triumphs of science and industry, was still rooted in the old traditions of graceful humanists, artful writers, erudite orators. Unlike Cavour, he never freed himself from reverence for the classics—the classics meant the land not machines—and he never surrendered to an exaltation of feverish modern activity, as had Cavour and Sella, nor to the urge to elevate science to the level of divinity. Instead, he sharply defined its limits and, like Lambruschini and Capponi, he stressed the reality of man's inner life, religious sentiments.

Positivism was breaking into Italian cultural life, bringing with it a new spirit, upsetting old ideas, and, with all of its speculative deficiencies, opening up vistas in that cultural life. In a relatively short time, people noted that theretofore it had been impossible to speak without reference to Penelope's net, the sword of Damocles, and the rock of Sisyphus, but now one could not avoid evolution, natural selection, and the struggle for existence. Had a readers' referendum been held, Spencer and Darwin would have overpowered all of the ancient literary Olympians excepting only Dante, the Bible, and Shakespeare. Even while nearing its demise, however, the old culture struggled on.

The cult of "ideal beauty" and "moral beauty" thus contradicted industrialization and materialism. The past with its virtue and humanistic culture attempted to surmount the present vulgarity and crudeness, style opposed unrestrained appetite. From this confrontation came the theme of the relationship between technical progress and moral improvement. "Culture" was seen as a corrective to the materialistic tendencies of the age; literature was viewed as the savior of morality and aesthetics, threatened by modernization with extinction: "Beauty is the highest goal of nature and human intellect and I find in it the greatest argument against anything which tends to commercialize either nature or intellect." The polemics concerning education, then so lively, between those who demanded for teachers more practice, more modern procedures, and less classical training, and those who insisted instead on the absolute necessity of stressing above all else the classical tradition, with its superior "moral merits," such polemics were part of the more general debate in which proponents of the old and the new worlds were engaged. Love of classical culture, love of the beautiful, traditionally defined, the ambiguous position of the artist as one detached from mundane struggles and yet healing through his arts the wounds of those struggles, were joined together among Italian and European conservatives who shared a resistance to the new, modern, rational, industrial mass society being born.

Love of tradition, then; and, just as in the age of Burke and Cuocco, the basic idea of conservatism was that, in exalting tradition and the historical characteristics of individual countries, it repudiated revolutionary metaphysics and maintained the ideal of politics not as an abstraction but as a given order of institutions which had crystallized in good and proper time. This view was repeated by Minghetti, who declared that the loud affirmations of popular sovereignty, civic and political equality, the infallibility of the majority, and so forth were all being completely discredited.

Tradition: it was now time to protect it against the threatening roar of the "corrupt and violent" mob, which social entity was quite different from the real and peaceful people. Class struggle and the rights of the proletariat: these militant mottoes gave a solid and massive shape to general fears; they were aimed at a precise movement which was no longer social romanticism of a very uncertain and sentimental cast but rather the harsh, firm Marxist polemic or the perpetual revolutionary movement of Bakunin. The masses were stirring, and memories revived of public demonstrations which were so detested by the moderates now that 1848 had demonstrated how, once the fuse was lit, it was impossible to know where and with how much force the explosion would occur. Such demonstrations, even in other countries, made Ricasoli's blood boil with anger: "What have these demonstrations, at first spontaneous and then used by evil people, accomplished for us Italians?" The corrupt mob was a communist group who had already divided up all property even before occupying it; the street mob was "always an evil thing" and implied a Pellegrino Rossi assassinated or a Lambruschini chased from his home while "highwaymen" scaled the garden wall, or the cutting down of a Minghetti's forests. It implied Jacobinism, demagoguery, the triumph of shouters over thinkers, the end of the legality even though freedom existed only under the law; it meant accepting mob violence as the will of the people and dignifying as "the people" any mob who overwhelmed legitimate powers standing in its way; it was all of this, then, which to liberal thinkers was as repugnant as autocracy.

The fear of the fierce rabble armed with hatred and rancor enveloped freedom like a dark cloud. The moderates' rational principles could not win out amid tumult and violence; peaceful reform without revolution had always been and remained the moderates' hope. It was now shared by the Left, which, having achieved national unity and Rome, wanted to hear no more of revolution and preferred therefore an end to direct action.

It was only natural, then, that they should but reluctantly allow to the masses the right to vote. Men on the Right sincerely believed themselves alone to be pure and wise and were thus hostile to the notion of large numbers of new voters entering public life; they were not prompted so much by the fear of being voted out of office or of being forced to compete with popular parties, although that fear existed. There was something more involved. It was the fear of the unknown, of a great but obscure approaching menace whose outlines could not be perceived. "The painstaking prevision of future evils" thus confused souls who in their near despair of mankind sought refuge in the cry "may God protect Italy." Even to the more optimistic, however, the future looked bleak. Minghetti, like all European moderates, saw universal suffrage as an evil and defended the qualifications put on electoral rights, since they represented not only property "but also work, thrift, industriousness, and provenance." He himself was "very fearful" of the effects of electoral reform and anticipated sad days ahead for the country, now threatened with disorder, confusion, immorality, and degradation. As for Visconti-Venosta, he saw the electoral law of 1881 as "an enormous adventure": a most appropriate expression for defining the state of mind of these men and one which expressed their clearly evident fear of the triumph of "radicals" in future elections. Sella, who many years before had labeled universal suffrage the politics of adventure, deplored the futility of the nation's having thrown itself into a great unknown by so suddenly expanding the suffrage.

It was a frantic action only apparently liberal, and deplored even by Pasquale Villari, who contemptuously held that certain moderates had actually proposed universal suffrage out of fear of being openly defeated. It was also disapproved of by both Depretis and Zanardelli, the latter resigning himself "to handing the country over to the multitudes before purging them of their evils or calming their hatreds" and thus causing liberals to die "as retrogrades and . . . with an air of being too preoccupied to avoid dying."

Men of the Right, and thus conservatives. The fear, however, that things would end ruinously as a consequence of the extension of the suffrage was felt as well by the men of the Left who had themselves made the law. As Minghetti had predicted, Depretis himself would come to fear the dire consequences which followed the participation of the "new social class." Depretis henceforth took care to erect barriers against the threatening popular flood. The search was begun for a centrist parliamentary majority, obtained by eroding the parties as such, maneuvering over and through individuals, substituting for opposition in principle the principle of pragmatic cooperation. Since the threatening "flood" frightened Depretis as much as Minghetti, the Bolognese statesman and the man from Stradella joined together as a dike against "the invading demagoguery"; Minghetti went further than many of the old Right would have gone in his efforts to thwart the dangerous masses. The only means of avoiding a republican or socialist triumph was to unite all the supporters of existing institutions; as a result, political compromise [*trasformismo*], which Depretis succeeded in ably implementing. It was a practice that others of the Right had thought of and even attempted since Sella's efforts to form a ministry with Nicotera and the moderate Left in 1879, and again in 1881. These attempts anticipated *trasformismo,* an attempt in the style of Cavour to create a viable center capable of over-coming the rigidities of Left and Right.

Later, faced with socialism in full cry, other men of the Left who had remained tenacious advocates of the electoral law of 1881 and strong opponents of *trasformismo* ended up asking themselves whether they ought not regret "having expanded the suffrage before educating the plebes. We have placed a dangerous weapon in unskilled hands, and have paved the way for moral disorder and corruption."

Fear of the masses, resistance to bloc voting, reliance on individuals instead of parties in order to avoid rigid opposition—all these character-ized the politics of the center party. For strong reasons, these considera-tions were to make themselves socially acceptable, too. In order to face the problem as one of social structure, that is, by admitting class divi-sions, the politicians would have had to condone state intervention. If the state intervened in economic and social relationships and legislated, limited, and coerced people and economic interests, would not this be a flagrant, total contradiction in terms of individual interests, the basis of freedom? The state was guarantor of order, peace, and security for all but not the spokesman of the will and interests of any individual. At bottom, the nineteenth-century notion of freedom rested on individualism such as Benjamin Constant had stressed to the extent of refuting even the old myth, so dear to Montesquieu, of the Greek collective *polis.* There was already some concern expressed over the expansion of the state into society, the multiplying of its functions, its gradual penetration into vari-ous social activities. A new resistance to "state idolatry" was rising; the worship of the state was decried by leaders such as Spaventa and Sella.

State regulation and control of the railroads seemed a negation of liberal principles. It led in fact to parliamentary crises within the Right itself. The institution of postal savings banks was labeled as undue state interference in the economy, as further proof of the progress of the no-tion which allowed for greater governmental intervention in realms where freedom alone should reign. Compulsory elementary education evoked cries of protests against the invasion of the father's right of decid-ing whether to send his children to school. The opposition to an active state ran deep. The idea that "social interests" might limit the in-dividual's freedom was viewed as an innovator's monstrosity; no one wished to admit that society had a right to dictate to a landowner the use of his land: "You must cultivate these acres, fill in those ditches, channel that water, so that a part of the national wealth won't deteriorate; if not, you will be subject to fines and, if necessary, even to imprisonment."

Freedom meant always the right of the individual "to express his opinion, to choose his own work and to carry it out, to dispose of his property, and even to abuse it; to come and go without asking anyone's permission, and without having to give any account of his motives or actions."

We were then still following Cavour's example of deep hostility to any state interference in the economy. Cavour even opposed state experiments with model farms. We still witnessed the work of the Piedmont Agricultural Organization, which represented the highest stage reached in Italy of the free trade principle.

The state was, however, being asked to intervene in the socio-economic life of Italy with protective, assistance, and similar laws. Maximum damage was inflicted on the principle of individual freedom and property rights. Where did such a road lead? Straight to socialism and communism, toward which state supremacy was the first step.

The state, therefore, had to remain as defined in the Declaration of the Rights of Man and the Citizen, of August 1789. It was not to step beyond its limits of education and judicial functions; it would control the forces defending the country and the police maintaining public order. But beware of allowing everything to be so controlled. Spencer labeled such state substitution for private initiative "the coming slavery," and the Italian moderates, although not positivists, believed as he did: "Are we speaking of increasing the state's role? Doesn't the state limited to its legitimate duties as regulator of general and *valid* services have an immense, complex work to perform? Assignments to the state beyond its true tasks are deleterious first to the state itself and then to the individual citizen."

State intervention in social questions, even in forms which today would seem very mild, found fierce and tenacious opponents. The German Empire, baptized "socialist" because of its social legislation, appeared to the moderates not as the prototype of freedom, as the Left said, but rather as the prototype of authoritarianism in modern Europe. It was an authoritarianism which tried to compensate for the people's lack of freedom with Imperial charity and material well-being. Cavour's followers saw the enemy as "a type of idolatry of the state, which appears at times as state socialism, at other times as state tyranny over the Church." In this view, the distrust felt toward Bismarck's "spirit of conquest" and his anti-parliamentarianism revealed itself as concerned with an even more profound opposition which set off two different political worlds. Protesting against the "socialism of the lectern" of the German professors of economics and their Italian followers, Francesco Ferrara exclaimed that "the sense of freedom has died in us, it is buried with the corpse of Cavour, Cavour who had stimulated freedom, sustained it, and tried to pass on to his posterity the sacred pledge that each generation must uphold." In contrast, Minghetti was already by contemporary standards a semi-socialist. He proposed his "middle way": retain individual initiative but intervene on behalf of women and children workers because this was a valid exercise of power for a state responsible for education and assistance.

The natural and best remedy for social evils was thus always held to be through individual action, through private magnanimity, charity, the personal example of the wealthy and the noble who extend a benevolent hand to the destitute, helping them morally and materially. There remained always the emphasis on private philanthropic institutions, as in the establishments of Piemonte, the Marchioness of Barolo, and the canon Cottolengo Don Giovanni Bosco, along with renewed devotion to works of charity inaugurated and instituted by the leaders of the Counter Reformation: Saint Philip Neri, Saint Camillo de Lellis, the Houses of Charity, the hospitals, the orphanages, the nursing services, all with "maternal affection toward our neighbors so that we may care for them with charity of soul and of body." In fighting the terrible "Red threat," one armed oneself with charity and used it through the priest "so that people will recognize him not only as a spiritual but also as a material benefactor."

Cesare Balbo had written that charity was sacred, divine, incorruptible, and the unifier of all Christians; for him, the greatest book ever written was the *History of Charity,* and he believed that Christian charity was overcoming all other systems of philanthropy: socialism, social sentiment, humanitarianism.

A new note was sounded among the progressives. It was an appeal to go beyond charity, to the school: "the most beautiful and efficient source of civilization and education for the needy, a means by which to raise them, to gain for them bread and manners, to move their hearts to noble affections." The same faith in the proud ends of education which inspired disdain for the Vatican also inspired the conviction that social problems could be solved through books and that both Red and Black, Left and Right could in this way be repulsed. It availed nothing when some people urged improving the people's economic condition before talking of education, on the grounds that it was difficult to expect people who could hardly make a living to believe it a virtue to attend school.

Such in all their complexity were the attitudes of the leading Italian party. Against them stood the radical affirmation: class struggle, rights of the proletariat, war against the existing social structure. . . .

Lewis B. Namier

1888—1960

11

"Let us now consider the imposing and significant achievement of one whom most of us would regard as the greatest British historian to emerge on the academic scene since the First World War." Thus E. H. Carr describes Lewis B. Namier, with whom he profoundly disagreed philosophically. Namier's contribution to modern historiography may be gauged by the fact that he gave his name to a way of writing history. "To namierize" means to establish through close analysis of family identity, party status, and political loyalties the processes of political and social change and the workings of parliamentary systems. Namier was one of the first historians to apply to history the "prosopographical" approach—the collective study of the personal and social characteristics of an institutionally defined group of people who are historically important, e.g., senators, members of parliament, key civil servants. Namier applied this technique most effectively to the British "political nation" collected in "that marvelous microcosmos, the British House of Commons." The resulting book, *The Structure of Politics at the Accession of George III* (1929), established Namier's lasting reputation. Being "the most influential book (among professionals) ever produced by an English historian," it also transformed English historiography, an ironic consequence given the fact that Namier was and remained an "outsider" in Britain.

Lewis B. Namier was born Ludwik Bernstajn vel Niemirowski on June 27, 1888, in Galicia, Russian Poland. His father was a fairly well off "polonized" Jew who enjoyed the privilege, rarely extended to Jews, of landownership. The family did not practice Judaism. Like many Jews in like circumstances, the parents believed that assimilation was a way out of both the ghetto and the Jewish dilemma, and while they refrained from officially adopting any religion they allowed their children outwardly to observe the customs of the Polish Catholic Church. The father saw to it that his very intelligent and studious son received a good education at home through tutors, in the manner of the Polish gentry, until the boy was eighteen years old. Such enforced isolation from his peers distressed young Namier, who wished to attend a gymnasium. In quarrels with his father and in his daily experiences he discovered his ambiguous heritage and social situation. He was registered as a Jew in Warsaw but without any specific family religious affiliation. His father denied his Jewishness, while, the son discovered, neighbors, despite his landed estate, regarded him as "a Jew more Polish than the Poles."

History, the young Namier early learned, could not be overcome by denials, although, being human, he later engaged in denial himself. After attending law school at Lwow University, and experiencing there the bitter anti-Semitism and intense nationalism of his Polish peers, Namier was sent by his father to Lausanne to continue his education. At Lausanne, French friends convinced Namier that he ought to study at the Sorbonne, a move the father refused to allow. As a compromise, Namier transferred to the recently established London School of Economics.

Namier's career as a historian began in London when he met A. L. Smith, the Senior History Tutor at Oxford's Balliol College. Smith determined that Namier should go to Balliol; the unusually gifted young man acquiesced. His four years' experience there (1908–1912) was of central importance to Namier. "They taught me to think," he later remarked. Namier also then began, or perhaps accelerated, his search for an identity, shaking off his family and Central European ties. When his father announced that the family was adopting the Catholic faith, Namier defiantly announced his acceptance of Calvinism. He anglicized his name, became a British subject, and immersed himself ever more deeply in the history, society, and mores of the British. "His search for identity," Henry R. Winkler writes, "for a tradition of which he was part, explains, not only his Zionism but, even more revealingly, his unconcealed regard for the stable, self-confident society of upper-class England of the eighteenth century."

He had joined the typically English Fabian Society, but his "socialism" was much more oriented toward agrarian than urban affairs. His first sympathies had been for the Ruthenian peasants and their land problems. In his later historical works he would insist that "the relations of groups of men to plots of land, of organized communities to units of territory, form the basic content of political history." Such views militated against his sympathetic understanding of either proletarians or intellectuals, both urban and landless by definition, and nurtured his appreciation of the political and social traditions of the English landed aristocracy and of English society in general.

Being an "outsider" had some advantages. As Lady Namier recalls, "Belonging to no group, he was uniquely acceptable throughout Balliol." His Jewish background facilitated his acquaintance with Lord Balfour's niece, Mrs. Edgar Dugdale, a politically and socially influential personage who assisted Namier's entrée into the close corporation of aristocratic country

homes and London clubs whose archives, journals, and personal papers
Namier drew upon in his historical researches. Namier always spoke as if he
had penetrated the gates of "society." "In the phylogenetic history of the
Englishman the Oxford undergraduate of my own time corresponded to the
eighteenth-century man, and with him nearly foremost among social qualifications was that a man should be amusing. Anyone can enter English society
provided he can live, think, and feel like those who have built up its culture
in their freer, easier hours."

But there were sterner disadvantages. At Balliol, although first in the competition for an All Souls Fellowship (1911), he was passed over because of
his Polish-Jewish origin, and the pattern was set. Not until 1931 did he attain
an appointment as Professor of Modern History, at Manchester; and after
1945, by which time he had a pre-eminent reputation, he was passed over
by Oxford two or three times. Until his appointment at Manchester, Namier
experienced difficult times. In 1913, he came to America on business but
nonetheless continued his studies of "The Imperial Problem during the American Revolution" because in America "public libraries are open at night and
on Sundays." He served in the military in 1914–1915, before being transferred to the Foreign Office, which utilized his linguistic abilities and firsthand
knowledge of Central and Eastern European affairs. He taught for a while at
Oxford and then spent some years in Vienna and Prague as a journalist and
a businessman in order to earn money to finance his historical researches. In
those postwar years, too, Namier began his ambivalent, agonizing personal
connection with Zionism, working hard for the foundation of a free state for
"my own people, the Jews," but finally converting to Anglicanism. "His
Zionism," Lady Namier writes, "consisted of trying to join land and the
state." In 1925, he returned to England and over the next five years, living
on savings, loans from friends, and a few grants, he produced two "books"
(they are in fact compilations of long essays), *The Structure of Politics* and
England in the Age of the American Revolution (1930).

The two works, based on exhaustive research in hitherto untapped sources
and employing Namier's prosopographical technique, caused a profound
shift in the way historians perceived the unreformed House of Commons,
political labels such as Whig and Tory, the role of George III, in fact, the whole
structure of politics in the period from 1760 to 1783. Namier's purpose was
to expose complacent misconceptions and to offer historically valid explanations of eighteenth-century political life:

> Too much in eighteenth-century politics requires explaining. Between them and the
> politics of the present day there is more resemblance in outer forms and denomina-
> tions than in underlying realities; so that misconception is very easy. There were
> no proper party organizations about 1760, though party names and cant were
> current; the names and the cant have since supplied the materials for an imaginary

superstructure. A system of non-Euclidean geometry can be built up by taking a curve for basis instead of the straight line, but it is not easy for our minds to think consistently in unwonted terms; Parliamentary politics not based on parties are to us a non-Euclidean system, and similarly require a fundamental readjustment of ideas and, what is more, of mental habits.

His flat statement, "I deliberately refrain from discussing so-called parties and political groups, their meaning or lack of meaning; the political life of the period could be fully described without ever using a party denomination," and his equally flat defense of the unreformed House of Commons and the "deeper sense and usefulness" of the eighteenth-century electoral system shocked historians accustomed to party labels and to the notion of a "corrupt," unredeemed political structure. It forced upon them that "fundamental readjustment of ideas" Namier held essential if the true eighteenth-century were to be perceived. And one of the points to be perceived was the absence of ideology, of fanaticism, and of political theories and programs: "Englishmen learnt to leave things well alone—to refrain from drawing up elaborate, artificial, naïve schemes." Nor is "Parliamentary government based on the party system . . . an ingenious device, the product of creative thought." It is rather the organic unfolding of a process whose "bases are deep down in the political structure of the nation." These perceptions and conclusions were congenial to Namier. He was a true conservative who viewed society as an organism largely immune to the play of conscious efforts to change it. "The less, therefore, man clogs the free play of his mind with political doctrine and dogma, the better for his thinking." Namier's denigration of the positive role of political and social theories in human affairs led one commentator on "the Namier view of history" to write: "Darwin was accused of taking mind out of the universe; and Sir Lewis has been the Darwin of political history—in more senses than one."

Another of Namier's innovations was to eschew stereotypes such as "Whig" and "Tory." Instead, he analyzed groups of individuals to discover "Why Men Went into Parliament." He sought to grasp the meaning of the political mechanism by understanding the men who controlled and used it. The "History of Parliament," on which he labored to the end, was precisely such a prosopographical study. It was "based on the biographies of all the Members who sat in the House of Commons up to 1901: a demographic study of the most significant group-formation in the life of this country. . . . It is a new pattern of an aggregate character . . . that we are trying to delineate." Such an approach entailed psychological analyses to which Namier was by no means averse. Indeed, he was among the first historians to contemplate the application of psychoanalysis to history:

A neurotic, according to Freud, is a man dominated by unconscious memories, fixated on the past, and incapable of overcoming it: the regular condition of human communities. Yet the dead festering past cannot be eliminated by violent action any more than an obsession can be cured by beating the patient. History has therein a "psycho-analytic" function; and it further resembles psycho-analysis in being better able to diagnose than to cure: the beneficial therapeutic effects of history have so far been small; and it is in the nature of things that it should be so.

He believed psychoanalysis could help individuals toward understanding if not curing themselves (this appears to have been his own experience in such therapy). He further believed that history, a "sound historical education," might "wean men from expecting automatic repetition" and perhaps overcome "man's innate reluctance to think out the long-range consequences of his actions." But of the realization of this effect of history he was not sanguine.

After 1930, and for very personal as well as professional reasons, Namier by himself wrote but one other book, *1848: The Revolution of the Intellectuals* (1946). In it, he manifested 'his anti-German bias, his grasp of the peasant mentality, his scorn for intellectuals with their "programmes and ideals," and especially his conservative appreciation of the practical and realistic steps taken by the various monarchies in the face of concrete problems, in this case opposing armies to ideas and restless subjects. "States are not created or destroyed, and frontiers redrawn or obliterated, by argument and majority votes," he wrote. "Nations are freed, united, or broken by blood and iron, and not by a generous application of liberty and tomato-sauce." The book is a brilliant, incisive, and in some ways unfair assessment of 1848. After World War II, he churned out many essays on a wide variety of historical problems. In all of them, he displayed his mastery of language, his incisive analytical skills, his broad understanding of human nature, and a wide historical perspective not to be anticipated from the narrow concerns he devoted himself to in his monographs on the reign of George III. As an essayist, he maintained the greatness of his reputation.

Namier has been criticized for more than having taken the mind out of history. ("As though," G. R. Elton notes, "none of the people involved ever had an idea in their heads beyond some immediate and usually financial interest.") He has been accused of using, as it were, microscopes and telescopes but nothing in between in studying history; his narrow and one-sided concentration on political history has led to criticisms that he missed wide areas of vital importance to historical explanation, and to the corollary charge that the era he specialized in was uniquely suited to his methods and approach. Even, or especially, Namier's favorite enterprise, the "aggregate biography" of the House of Commons, has drawn criticism on the grounds that it neglects such things as the organization, the staff, and the proceedings of the House, and that, when the task is completed, its value may be less than such enormous labor warranted. "Bricks are important. But a pile of bricks is not a house. And should the master-builder spend his life in a brick-field?

Perhaps nemesis awaits the historian who seeks to expunge ideas from the historical process." All of this being noted, it remains true that Namier's work permanently swept away much of the conventional view of eighteenth-century English politics, and that prosopography as he practiced it has gained a permanent place among the disciplines historians must enlist in their labors.

Selected Bibliography

Perhaps the best approach to Namier the historian is by way of Namier the man, in Lady Julia Namier's superb study, *Lewis Namier* (1971). There are many excellent short studies of Namier and his career: Isaiah Berlin, "L. B. Namier: A Personal Impression," *Encounter,* XXVII (November, 1966), 32–42; John Brooke, "Namier and His Critics," *ibid.,* XXIV (February, 1965), 47–49; Herbert Butterfield, "Sir Lewis Namier as Historian," *The Listener,* LXV (May 18, 1961), 873–876, which should be complemented by Butterfield's *George III and the Historians* (1957); N. C. Phillips, "Namier and His Method," *Political Science,* XIV (March, 1962), 16–26; and Henry Winkler, "Sir Lewis Namier," *Journal of Modern History,* XXXV (March, 1963), 1–19. E. H. Carr makes some points on Namier's historiography in *What Is History?* (1961), and John R. Hale speaks of "The Age of Namier" in his collection *The Evolution of British Historiography from Bacon to Namier* (1964). George Steiner, "The Art of Memory," in *The New Yorker* (January 1, 1972), 61–64, and "Towering Outsider" by the anonymous reviewer in *The Times Literary Supplement* (May 21, 1971), 577–578, are informative in their responses to Lady Namier's biography.

Namier himself wrote little that was explicitly historiographic, but his essay "History," included in the collection *Avenues of History* (1952), offers an outline of his professional credo. Students who wish to pursue one aspect of Namier's work might consult Lawrence Stone's excellent article "Prosopography," in *Historical Studies Today,* edited by Felix Gilbert and Stephen R. Graubard (1972), 107–140.

PERSONALITIES AND POWERS

Monarchy and the Party System

I have chosen for my subject a story with a happy ending,with a striking dénouement, unforeseen and unpredictable while it was shaping. Constitutional monarchy—the union of a hereditary Crown with parliamentary government—is, to quote Mr. Churchill, "of all the institutions which have grown up among us over the centuries . . . the most deeply founded and dearly cherished." British monarchy detached from British politics has become the link of the Commonwealth of Nations, and the pivot of government in a number of co-ordinated countries; it is seen to secure basic continuity in government with a variability unequalled under any other system. But in the earlier stages the growth of constitutional monarchy was impeded rather than aided by conscious political thought—the "odious title" of Prime Minister was decried, and the extinction of party prayed for. Even now constitutional monarchy, though anchored both in the thought and affection of the nation, depends for its smooth working on the continuance of concrete factors by which it was moulded. Hence the importance of discerning them.

What are the basic elements of constitutional monarchy? A Sovereign placed above parties and politics; a Prime Minister and Government taking rise from Parliament, and received rather than designated by the Sovereign, yet as "H.M. confidential servants" deriving from the Royal Prerogative that essential executive character which an elected legislature could not impart to them; and an unpolitical Civil Service whose primary connexion is with the Crown, and which, while subordinated to party-governments, is unaffected by their changes: the two permanent elements, the Crown and the Civil Service, which not by chance together left the political arena, supply the framework for the free play of parliamentary politics and governments. Under royal government the sovereign was the undisputed, immediate head of the executive; under parliamentary government, it is the prime minister; but no clear-cut formula is possible for the intervening period of "mixed government," during

From *Personalities and Powers* (London: Hamish Hamilton, 1955), pp. 13–37. Copyright © 1955 by Sir Lewis Namier. Reprinted by permission of the publisher.

which the direction of government gradually passed from the sovereign to the prime minister by a process that can be logically defined but eludes precise dating. The prime minister replaced the sovereign as actual head of the executive when the choice of the prime minister no longer lay with the sovereign; the sovereign lost the choice when strongly organized, disciplined parliamentary parties came into existence; and party discipline depends primarily on the degree to which the member depends on the party for his seat. The sovereign can keep clear of party-politics only so long as it is not incumbent on him or her to choose the prime minister. Thus constitutional monarchy as now understood hinges to a high degree on the working of the modern party system.

In 1761 not one parliamentary election was determined by party, and in 1951 not one constituency returned a non-party member. To trace how that change has come about will require a most thorough knowledge of constituencies and elections, of members and parliaments, and of constitutional ideas and realities throughout the formative period: to acquire that knowledge is one of the tasks of the History of Parliament on which we are now engaged, and can only be accomplished by a great collective effort. In this lecture I propose to set before you tentative outlines: suggestions rather than conclusions. I shall deal mainly with the earlier period covered by my own research; still, in a broad survey I am bound to travel beyond its limits, and I have drawn on the help and advice most generously accorded by fellow workers in our field.

2

The king's business in parliament had at all times to be transacted through ministers; and as parliament grew in importance, so did the minister capable of managing it. Yet under "mixed government" even for the securing of parliamentary support royal favour and confidence were needed, and as late as 1786, Robert Beatson, in his *Political Index* dedicated to Adam Smith, placed the names of the leading ministers under the heading "A List of Prime Ministers and Favourites, from the accession of King Henry VIII to the present time." The personal element inevitably determined the exact relation between the sovereign and his advisers, and at all times there were kings who yielded easy assent to ministers or deferred to the guidance of favourites; and few more so than George III, especially in the first decade of his reign. Horace Walpole, accurately informed by his friend H. S. Conway, wrote in 1769 that George III "never interfered with his Ministers," but "seemed to resign himself entirely to their conduct for the time"—a statement borne out by the king's voluminous correspondence wherein, as a rule, he repeats with approval advice tendered by his ministers. He would become active only when, in Walpole's words, "he was to undo an administration." Still, "the King's independency," that is, his right to choose and dismiss ministers, was a constitutional axiom; and however hard politicians strove for office, they would, each and all, declare their extreme reluctance to enter or retain it unless assured of the king's favour willingly accorded. Newcastle in 1759 voiced "the most ardent wishes" for the Prince of Wales to succeed "in such a situation as shall leave his hands free . . . to form his plan of government with advantage"; George Grenville claimed to have "entered into the King's service . . . to hinder the law from being indecently and unconstitutionally given to him"—"to prevent any undue and unwarrantable force being put upon the Crown"; and Pitt repeatedly declared that he would not be forced upon the king by parliament, nor come into his service against his consent. When the Fox–North Coalition had succeeded in imposing themselves on the king driven to the brink of abdication, Fox, who treated Whig "anti-monarchism as the main principle of the British Constitution," addressed him, on 16 April 1783, in the following terms:

> Mr. Fox hopes that Your Majesty will not think him presumptuous or improperly intruding upon Your Majesty with professions, if he begs leave most humbly to implore Your Majesty to believe that both the Duke of Portland and he have nothing so much at heart as to conduct Your Majesty's affairs, both with respect to measures and to persons, in the manner that may give Your Majesty the most satisfaction, and that, whenever Your Majesty will be graciously pleased to condescend even to hint your inclinations upon any subject, that it will be the study of Your Majesty's Ministers to show how truly sensible they are of Your Majesty's goodness.

During the next forty years parties were gradually shaping in parliament, but they did not as yet dominate it, and in theory relations between king and ministers remained unchanged. "If you do not like us why do you not turn us out?" asked the Duke of Wellington of George IV in July 1821. And in March 1827 Stephen Lushington, M.P., Secretary of the Treasury, still attributed to the king the absolute and unqualified choice of his ministers; while Canning, in language curiously reminiscent of that held by Bute sixty-five years earlier, inveighed against aristocratic "confederacies," and discoursed on "the real vigour of the Crown when it chooses to put forth its own strength."

When in 1834 William IV had dismissed the Melbourne Government, Peel claimed a "fair trial" for the ministers of the king's choice; and its semblance was conceded by the Whigs, who, having won the ensuing general election, refrained from a direct vote of censure on the Address. As late as 1846, Wellington and Peel, at variance with a majority of their party, harped on their position and duties as Ministers of the Crown and declared that, were they to stand alone, they would still have "to enable

Her Majesty to meet her Parliament and to carry on the business of the country."

> I was of the opinion [declared Wellington] that the formation of a Government in which Her Majesty would have confidence, was of much greater importance than the opinions of any individual on the Corn Laws, or any other law. . . .

And Peel, whose ideas of an independent executive similarly seemed to hark back to the earlier period, thus attempted to define his position:

> I see it over and over again repeated, that I am under a personal obligation for holding the great office which I have the honour to occupy . . . that I was placed in that position by a party. . . . I am not under an obligation to any man, or to any body of men, for being compelled . . . to undergo the official duties and labour which I have undertaken. . . .

And next:

> I have served four Sovereigns. . . . I served each of those Sovereigns at critical times and in critical circumstances . . . and . . . there was but . . . one reward which I desired . . . namely, the simple acknowledgment, on their part, that I had been to them a loyal and faithful Minister. . . .

To this Disraeli retorted that the queen would never have called on Peel in 1841 had he not "placed himself, as he said, at the head of the Gentlemen of England."

> I say [continued Disraeli] it is utterly impossible to carry on your Parliamentary Constitution except by political parties. I say there must be distinct principles as lines of conduct adopted by public men. . . .
> Above all, maintain the line of demarcation between parties; for it is only by maintaining the independence of party that you can maintain the integrity of public men, and the power and influence of Parliament itself.

Here then were two conceptions of the ministers' relations to Crown and Party: one reflecting the past but still adducible without patent absurdity; the other, much more in harmony with the realities which then were shaping, and which, once shaped, were soon to be mistaken for primordial elements of the British Constitution. The past and the future, capable of neat definition, impinged on a period of mixed character, first, by a theoretical carry over, and next, by historical antedating. As a result, "by a double distortion," to quote Mr. Sedgwick's summing up, George III "has been represented as having endeavoured to imitate the Stuarts when he ought to have anticipated Queen Victoria."

3

According to contemporaries the complex system of the "mixed form of government" combined "by skilful division of power" the best of the monarchy, aristocracy, and democracy; and it was viewed by them with pride and satisfaction. Mechanically minded and with a bent towards the ingenious, they relished its "checks and controls," and the "mutual watchfulness and jealousy" which its delicate balance demanded from all concerned; and they cherished a constitution which safeguarded their rights and freedoms when "in almost every other nation of Europe" public liberty was "extremely upon the decline." George III, that much maligned monarch, was truly representative when, abhorring both "despotism" and "anarchy," he extolled "the beauty, excellence, and perfection of the British constitution as by law established." What was bound to escape contemporaries was the insoluble contradictions of a political system which, incongruously, associated a royal executive with parliamentary struggles for office. Yet the two had to coexist in an organic transition from royal to parliamentary government.

A parliamentary regime is based on the unhindered alternating of party-governments. But while contending party leaders can in turn fill the office of prime minister, how could the king freely pass from the one side to the other, and in turn captain opposite teams? It was far more consonant with his position to try to heal "the unhappy divisions that subsist between men" and form an administration from "the best of all parties" than to quit "one set of men for another." Could he give up with unconcern the ministers whom he had chosen and upheld, and in whose actions and policy he had participated? In 1779 it was but natural for him to stipulate that on a change of government past measures should "be treated with proper respect" and that "no blame be laid" on them. And here is a naïve but sincere statement of his position: "I have no wish but for the prosperity of my Dominions therefore must look on all who will not heartily assist me as bad men as well as ungrateful subjects." And on another occasion: "... whilst I have no wish but for the good and prosperity of my country, it is impossible that the nation shall not stand by me; if they will not, they shall have another King." He did not think in terms of parties; but their existence prevented the king, while he remained the actual head of the executive, from leading an undivided nation.

Yet it was impossible to eliminate party from parliament: an assembly whose leaders contend for office and power was bound to split into factions divided by personal animosities and trying to preserve their identity and coherence in and out of office. Consequently when in office they laid themselves open to the accusation of monopolizing power and of "keeping the King in fetters"; in opposition, of distressing the government with intention to "storm the Closet" and force themselves, unconstitutionally, on the king. No consistent defence of parties was possible under the "mixed form of government," and this undoubtedly retarded their development and consolidation. To Bolingbroke parties when based on a "difference of principles and designs" were "misfortune enough," but if continued without it an even greater misfortune, for then they were mere "instruments of private ambition." David Hume denounced them as subversive of government and begetting "the fiercest animosities" among fellow citizens; but he next conceded that to "abolish all distinctions of party may not be practicable, perhaps not desirable, in a free government." Burke squarely contended that party-divisions were, for good or evil, "things inseparable from free government"; and in his well-known eulogy of party as a union of men endeavouring to promote the national interest on a common principle, gave a forecast of parliamentary government. Men so connected, he wrote, must strive "to carry their common plan into execution with all the power and authority of the State"; in forming an administration give "their party preference in all things"; and not "accept any offers of power in which the whole body is not included." While professing adherence to the Revolution Settlement, by implication he eliminated the rights of the Crown, and obliquely argued that in fact the royal executive had ceased to exist, replaced by the monstrous contraption of a cabal set on separating "the Court from Administration." The "double Cabinet," a product of Burke's fertile, disordered, and malignant imagination, long bedevilled his own party and their spiritual descendants.

That the House of Commons might ultimately "engross the whole power of the constitution," wresting the executive from the Crown, was apprehended by Hume. How then could they be "confined within the proper limits"?

> I answer [wrote Hume] that the interest of the body is here restrained by that of the individuals. . . . The Crown has so many offices at its disposal, that, when assisted by the honest and disinterested part of the House, it will always command the resolutions of the whole so far, at least, as to preserve the ancient constitution from danger.

He thus discerned within the House itself the main obstacle to parliamentary government: a majority of its members were as yet by their ideas, interests, and pursuits, unfitted for a system of party politics.

4

Parliamentary struggles for office necessarily produce a dichotomy of "ins" and "outs"; and two party-names were current since the last quarter of the seventeenth century: hence in retrospect the appearances of a two-party system. In reality three broad divisions, based on type and not on party, can be distinguished in the eighteenth-century House of Commons: on the one side were the followers of Court and Administration, the "placemen," *par excellence* a group of permanent "ins"; on the opposite side, the independent country gentlemen, of their own choice permanent "outs"; and in between, occupying as it were the centre of the arena, and focusing upon themselves the attention of the public and of history, stood the political factions contending for power, the forerunners of parliamentary government based on a party-system. Though distinct, these groups were not sharply separated: wide borderlands intervened between them, in which heterogeneous types moved to and fro.

The Court and Administration party was a composite, differentiated body; but common to them all was a basic readiness to support any minister of the king's choice: even in their parliamentary capacity they professed direct political allegiance to the Crown, either on a traditional semi-feudal, or on a timeless civil-service basis, or merely as recipients, in one form or another, of the king's bounty; and adherence to the king's government, so long as compatible with conscience, was far more consonant with the avowed decencies of eighteenth-century politics than "formed opposition." A second, concomitant, characteristic of the group was that whether they were great noblemen, or minor ministers of an administrative type, or hard-working officials, or political parasites, they tried through a direct nexus with the Crown to secure permanency of employment: wherein they were, by and large, successful. A third common feature, induced by natural selection and inherent in the character of the group, was that its members did not play for the highest political prizes: peers of the first rank and great wealth and desirous of making a figure in the country, or great orators or statesmen in either House, would well-nigh automatically move into the centre of the arena and take their place among the leaders of political factions.

Here are examples of non-political groups in Court and Administration. The Brudenells were in the second half of the eighteenth century prominent at Court, and although they invariably had two, and mostly three, peerages, and at least four seats in the Commons—"I do not think," says their historian, Miss Joan Wake, "that they were ever much interested in politics." The Secretaries of the Admiralty were civil servants with expert technical knowledge, and though from Pepys to Croker they sat in parliament, in the eighteenth century not one went out on a change of government. Croker resigned with Wellington in 1830; "till our own day," he wrote in 1857, "the Secretary was not looked upon as a political officer, did not change with ministries, and took no part in political debate." The Secretaries of the Treasury, forerunners *inter alia* of the modern Parliamentary Whips, were civil servants concerned in the management of the House of Commons. In 1742, the Duke of Bedford took it for granted that Walpole's Secretary of the Treasury, John Scrope, would be dismissed, "through whose hands such sums of money have passed, and who refused to give any answer to the Secret Committee about those dark transactions. . . ."

> . . . what your Grace mentions is absolutely impracticable [replied Pulteney]. Mr Scrope is the only man I know, that thoroughly understands the business of the Treasury, and is versed in drawing money bills. On this foundation he stands secure, and is as immovable as a rock. . . .

When in May 1765 the king was obliged to take back the Grenvilles, they meant to exact explanations from some Members of Parliament who held quasi-civil service posts and of whose attachment they felt uncertain; but they dropped this design when told by one of them that

> he would faithfully support the administration of which he was a part but that he would on no consideration combine with any body of subjects against the undoubted right of the Crown to name its own officers. . . .

And in 1827 J. C. Herries, M.P., Secretary of the Treasury, thus defined his position:

> I am pursuing my own laborious vocation. . . . I am not in the following of any party. My business is with the public interests and my duty to promote the King's service wherever I am employed.

Horace Walpole admitted that among the "Treasury Jesuits," as he called them, were "some of the ablest men in the House of Commons, as Elliot, Dyson, Martin, and Jenkinson"; yet he ascribed to "secret influence" their continuance in office "through every Administration," and echoed Burke in calling them "the Cabinet that governed the Cabinet."

Whether a post was held by quasi-civil service tenure often depended on its holder. Lord Barrington, M.P., never out of employment between 1746 and 1778, was nineteen years at the War Office under Newcastle, Devonshire, Rockingham, Chatham, Grafton, and North; but Henry Fox as Secretary at War was a front-rank politician. Soame Jenyns, a littérateur of distinction and with good connexions, held the post of a Lord of Trade from 1755 till he left parliament in 1780; for Charles Townshend it was the first step in his political career. The character of Court offices was even more uncertain: Lord Hertford, the head of an eminently political family, who between 1751 and 1766 had been Lord of the Bedchamber, Ambassador to Paris, Lord Lieutenant of Ireland, Lord Steward, and then from 1766 onwards, Lord Chamberlain, wrote to the king on the fall of the North Administration: "Let me . . . as a personal servant to your Majesty, not be involved with Ministers to whom I have never belonged. . . ."

Not "to belong to Ministers" was sometimes raised to the level of a principle. Harry, sixth Duke of Bolton, early in the reign of George III

sided with the Opposition and rejoined them in 1770; but on succeeding
to the dukedom in July 1765, declared that in future

> his attachment shall be to the Crown only—that he sees how contemptible, and
> weak it is for a peer of England independent as he is, and with a great estate,
> to be dragged along in the suite of any private man or set of men whatever; and
> to become the mean instrument of their views, their faction, or ambition.

And Lord Egmont declared in the Cabinet on 1 May 1766: ". . . that I had
no predilection for this or that set of men—that my first duty was to Your
Majesty." Or again, in January 1783, Lord Hood, when put up in his
absence as candidate for Westminster, wrote that though he had no ambition for a seat in the House of Commons, he would accept, but would
then "studiously steer clear . . . of all suspicion of being a *party man
. . .* for or against the Minister," as he thought this "unbecoming a military servant of the King."

To sum up: so long as government was truly the king's own business,
and the king's permanent servants could sit in parliament, there was
nothing reprehensible or illogical in members refusing, from legitimate
interest or on grounds of conscience, to commit themselves to parties and
leaders.

5

The country gentlemen (and certain urban counterparts of theirs) were
the very antithesis of the Court party. Their watchword was independence: attachment to the Crown but no obligations to ministers. They
entered the House with a sense of duty to the public; their ambition was
primacy in their own "country" attested by being chosen parliamentary
representatives for their county or some respectable boroughs (or else
they sat for complete pocket boroughs of their own, preferably without
voters for whom favours might have to be obtained from Administration). Office, honours, or profits might have impaired rather than raised
their standing; the sovereign had therefore little occasion to disappoint
them, or the minister to reward them; and they were treated with the
respect due to the independent part they played. They were critical of
financial extravagance on Court, sinecures, or on costly (and unnecessary) wars; and they were suspicious, or even contemptuous, of the ways
of courtiers and politicians; they loathed government contractors and
pensioners in the House—the locusts that devoured the land-tax—and
were easily roused against them. But not playing for office, they were not
bound to factions: when on 12 February 1741, the Opposition Whigs
moved for Walpole's dismissal, 25 country gentlemen normally in opposition to him voted against the motion, while 44 left the House.

Governor Pitt wrote to his son on 16 January 1705:

If you are in Parliament, show yourself on all occasions a good Englishman, and a faithful servant to your country . . . Avoid faction, and never enter the House pre-possessed; but attend diligently to the debate, and vote according to your conscience and not for any sinister end whatever. I had rather see any child of mine want than have him get his bread by voting in the House of Commons.

About 1745 the story was told that a peerage had been offered to Sir Watkin Williams Wynn (M.P. for County Denbigh from 1722 till his death in 1749):

. . . his answer was that as long as His Majesty's Ministers acted for the good of their country, he was willing to consent to anything; he thanked His Majesty for the Earldom he had sent him, but that he was very well content with the honours he had and was resolved to live and die Sir Watkin.

And the boast of the typical country gentleman was that he was neither the minion of Administration nor the tool of faction.

Originally the country gentlemen tried to exclude all office-holders from the House; their failure left the door open for parliamentary government. But as a rule they practised what they had preached—it would have been a handicap for a knight of the shire, relying on the support of the country gentlemen, to hold office or to have received personal favours from government: in 1830 Sir Thomas Gooch, M.P. for Suffolk 1806–30, had to make excuses on the hustings for having solicited a Crown living for his son. Before about 1830 even "too marked a party line" was apt to be considered incompatible with true independence: in 1806, W. R. Cartwright (M.P. for Northamptonshire 1797–1830) was criticized for having consistently supported Pitt when "a Knight of the Shire should vote as an individual and not as a party man." In a speech in parliament, on 21 January 1819, Sir George Sinclair, M.P. for Caithness, thus defined the attitude of the country gentlemen:

. . . neither to withhold entirely their confidence from Government, nor implicitly to sanction their proceedings; sometimes to oppose their measures, but never to impeach their motives—to combine political candour with constitutional vigilance—rather predisposed to approve than predetermined to condemn; resolved to favour but not to flatter; to control, but not to embarrass.

And he rightly added:

I am well aware that no individual is more obnoxious to both parties than one who will not absolutely bind himself to either.

Thus the country gentlemen had this in common with the Court group that they too, though for widely different reasons, refused to be tied to parliamentary parties and leaders; further, that they also were neither orators nor leaders: for again, any one of them who rose to such pre-eminence, automatically joined the politicians in the central arena.

6

Little needs to be said about the outstanding, historical figures among the politicians: these were the men who played for the highest prizes, for Cabinet posts and the conduct of the king's business in administration and parliament. It was in their power to procure ease to the king's affairs in parliament, or to obstruct them; they could therefore claim the king's favour, and in a crisis compel it. But who were the rank and file of the political factions? In the first place the relatives, friends, and dependants of great peers usually returned for seats at their disposal; and next, the political following of Commoners who could aspire to the highest offices and hunt as equals with the oligarchical groups. But these followers, in search of places or profits, did not differ essentially from the minor ministers or political parasites of the Court party. In fact, the same men are found at various times on either side of the fence, and happiest when there was no fence: when their group was so firmly established in office that it could hardly be distinguished from the Court party.

Though there were three main groups in the eighteenth-century House of Commons, in action there could be but two: the ayes and the noes, the Government party and the Opposition—which fact has reinforced the delusion of a two-party system. The Government side was invariably a junction of the Court party with a group of politicians; to the attractive force of Crown patronage was added the political ability of parliamentary leaders. When the dissolution of the first Rockingham Administration seemed imminent in January 1766, members forming the core of the official group, in a survey of the political scene, thus described their own position:

> Those who have always hitherto acted upon the sole principle of attachment to the Crown. This is probably the most numerous body and would on trial be found sufficient to carry on the publick business themselves if there was any person to accept of a Ministerial office at the head of them, and this is all they want.

In other words, the Court could supply numbers and workers but not political leaders and a parliamentary façade—for this in 1766 it had to turn to the Rockinghams, or the Grenvilles and Bedfords, or to Chatham. Even when the leading minister was the king's choice—Bute in 1762, Chatham in 1766, North in 1770, or Pitt in December 1783—the king had often to accept some ministers displeasing to himself. But when his relations with the dominant political group were distant or uncertain, he would try to introduce into the Cabinet some ministers of his own: thus Northington and Egmont entered the Grenville and the first Rockingham

Administration, and Thurlow those of Rockingham and Shelburne in 1782–3; and it gave rise to comment in March 1783 when the king was not allowed a single member of his own choice in the Coalition Government. The theory of the Cabinet as a joint board of king's men and politicians was, unconsciously, formulated by Horace Walpole when the Duke of Richmond, in discussing Cabinet reconstruction in 1767, objected to Camden because he "would be the King's"—"I asked," writes Walpole, "if they expected that every man should depend on King Rockingham, and nobody on King George."

When a First Minister was known to enjoy the favour of the king, the Court party would naturally adhere to him; and every group of politicians in power tried to fill places at Court, administrative posts, and seats in government boroughs with their own men; these, if their group long continued in office, would permeate the Court party and coalesce with it. But if then a separation supervened, it remained to be seen how much government property the politicians would get away with—places for life, reversions, parliamentary seats, etc.—and how many friends, glued to the flesh pots, they would have to part with. Moreover, men who had long "upheld the rights of the Crown," condemning "formed opposition" as factious and disrespectful to the king, found it difficult to enter it themselves: as was seen in the case of Newcastle in 1762, and of Wellington in 1830.

In normal circumstances the king's authority and support were sufficient to keep the average group of politicians in office, but no government could survive for long if either the king or public opinion turned definitely against them. Between 1742 and 1832 the country gentlemen and their city counterparts increasingly became the spokesmen and indicator of public opinion; and that group, about a hundred strong, when solid would carry with it a good many men of its own type and class but of less pronounced independence and normally voting with the Court or with political groups. When in 1764, over General Warrants, a great many of the country gentlemen voted with the Opposition, the Government was in serious danger. When in February 1781, 59 out of 80 English knights of the shire, were listed by John Robinson, Secretary of the Treasury, as opposition, the end was near; and when on 18 March 1782, Thomas Grosvenor informed North "in his own name, and in those of some other country gentlemen" that they would withdraw their support from his Government, its fate was sealed. Even members of the Court party were now breaking away, or at least absenting themselves from the House: some from conviction, others from caution. When Wellington was defeated on 15 November 1830, only 15 out of 82 English county members voted for him and 49 against; and in 1831 "only six . . . English county-members in the new House were anti-Reformers."

Unengaged in struggles for office, the independent country gentlemen were a retarding element in the growth of parliamentary government, but the charge of favouring "prerogative," sometimes levelled against them, was as uncorrelated to political realities as were their own attempts at constructive action—for instance in the confusion after the fall of North, when the weight of the independent members was felt more than under stable conditions. Thus early in 1784, 78 members—the St. Albans Tavern group—endeavoured to contrive a reconciliation between Pitt and Fox and a coalition which was probably desired by neither, and least of all by the king: for these country gentlemen party wrangles were meaningless, and a nuisance if likely to bring on the dissolution of a parliament which had run only half its course. Another, even more naïve, move in 1788 is set forth in a circular endorsed by 30 Lords and Commoners. In this "such Members of the two Houses as hold themselves independent of, and unconnected with, the parties that now exist, and are desirous of contributing their best endeavours to promote the general interests of the Country," were invited, while not considering themselves "under any restraint, or tied down to follow the sentiments of the majority," to "act in unison with each other." And here is the "Analysis of the House of Commons" given in the circular:

I. Party of the Crown.. 185
> This party includes all those who would probably support his Majesty's Government under any Minister, not peculiarly unpopular.

2. The Party attached to Mr. Pitt.. 52
> Of this party were there a new Parliament, and Mr. P. no longer Minister, not above twenty would be returned.

3. Detached Parties supporting the present Administration viz:
> 1. Mr. Dundas.. 10
> 2. Marquis of Lansdowne 9
> 3. Earl of Lonsdale 9
> 4. East Indians 15

4. The independent or unconnected Members of the House .... [108]
> Of this body of men about forty have united together, in conjunction with some members of the House of Peers in order to form a third party for the purpose of preventing the Crown from being too much in the power of either of the two other parties who are contending for the government of the country, and who (were it really necessary) might with the assistance of the Crown, undertake to make up an administration to the exclusion both of Mr. Pitt and Mr. Fox, and of their adherents.

5. The Opposition to the present Administration
> 1. The Party attached to Mr. Fox... 138
> 2. Remnants of Lord North's Party... 17

6. Absentees and Neutrals 14

The names of Whig and Tory do not appear in this list, nor in any other compiled in those years; nor have I used them so far in this lecture, for they explain little, but require a good deal of explaining.

7

Whig and Tory were "denominations"—names and creeds—which covered enduring types moulded by deeply ingrained differences in temperament and outlook. But when was a clear party division covered by them? Even before 1714 some scholars now discern merely a number of groups and connexions of a Tory or a Whig hue, or of uncertain colouring; for hardly ever was there anything like straight party voting. About the middle of the century the names were deprecated, described as outworn and meaningless, and yet they were used; for names there must be in a political dichotomy, even if their meaning is uncertain and their use misleading. In parliament even under the first two Georges disaffected Whigs supplied the most inveterate leaders of the Opposition and most of its voting strength. But in a good many constituencies the names of Whig and Tory still corresponded to real divisions: partly perhaps because local factions could hardly have been denoted as "Government" and "Opposition," and partly because the most enduring distinction between Tory and Whig—High Church *versus* Low Church and Dissent— retained more vitality and significance in local struggles than at Westminster.

A ruling group will always try to place its opponents under a ban, and the natural consequence of the practice of Walpole and the Pelhams was that anyone who wished to play at politics and for office adopted the name of Whig: the Finches, Seymours, Legges, Leveson-Gowers, Wyndhams, Foxes, etc. In fact by 1750 everyone at Court, in office, and in the centre arena was a Whig, while the name of Tories, by a process of natural selection, was left to the residuum who did not enter politics in pursuit of office, honours, or profits, that is, to the country gentlemen and to the forerunners of urban radicals.

The nomenclature, as further developed in the first decade of George III's reign, is correctly stated by Horace Walpole in a passage of his *Memoirs,* penned late in 1768, or more probably in 1769: "The body of the Opposition," he says, "still called itself Whig, an appellation rather dropped than disclaimed by the Court"; "the real Tories still adhered to their old distinctions . . . and fluctuated according as they esteemed particular chiefs not of their connexion . . ."; but "their whole conduct was comprised in silent votes . . ." Thus Walpole knew the difference between "real Tories" and the Court Whigs who had become the "Tories" of Opposition Whig pamphleteers; but as he habitually flavours accurate perceptions with current cant, a footnote, added in the 1780's, emphatically asserts that Lord North "was a Tory." About the same time Burke, in a letter of 24 December 1782, describes the phalanx of 130–50 placemen and place-hunters ranged behind North to secure the survival of places, refers to them as "the body, which for want of another name, I call Lord North's"; and then adds: "I ought to have excepted out of the profligates of Lord North's corps five or six Tories who act on principle, such as it is." Less than two months later, the Rockinghams formed a coalition with the "profligates" by conceding to them that nothing more should be done "about the reduction of the influence of the Crown" by economical reform.

Who were now the "Tories"? The younger Pitt never used the name and after his death his successors went merely by that of "Mr. Pitt's friends" (apparently George Canning was the only one who occasionally called himself a "Tory"). On 5 October 1809, Perceval wrote to Lord Melville:

> Our Party's strength, dismembered as we are by Canning's and Castlereagh's separation from us . . . has lost its principle of cohesion. We are no longer the sole representatives of Mr. Pitt. The magic of that name is in a great degree dissolved, and the principle on which we must most rely to keep us together, and give us the assistance of floating strength, is the public sentiment of loyalty and attachment to the King. Among the independent part of the House, the country gentlemen, the representatives of popular boroughs, we shall find our saving strength or our destruction.

In short: here is once more the basic structure of eighteenth-century parliamentary politics, with increased regard for the country gentlemen but no trace of a two-party system, or at all of party in the modern sense; and the group which in 1760 went by the name of Tories, a generation later is referred to simply as "independent country gentlemen," the name of Tory being practically in abeyance. It is the history of those party-names, and how they were applied, which calls for careful study free of confusion between names and realities, or rather between the differing realities which the same names were made to cover; and next the history must be traced of party realities as shaped by interaction between the constituencies and the House of Commons. Nineteenth-century parliamentary historians now seem agreed in deferring the full emergence of the modern party till after the Second Reform Bill: what preceded it were intermediary forms which should not be treated anachronistically in terms of a later age.

With regard to the second half of the eighteenth century, the idea of party conducive to parliamentary government is usually linked up with the Whigs; which, for what it is worth, is a matter of nomenclature rather than of ideology: the politicians, and not the Court group or the independent country gentlemen, were the party-forming element, and the politicians called themselves Whigs. But among the politicians the attitude to sovereign and party did not depend on the degree of their Whiggery: those who enjoyed the favour of the Crown, and coalesced with the Court party, were naturally less of a party-forming element that those in disfavour, or uncertain of royal support, who had therefore to rely primarily on parliament and seek to form their following into a coherent party. This was specially true of political groups which had forced themselves on the king: the Grenvilles after September 1763, the Rockinghams in 1782, and the Coalition in 1783.

The fourth Duke of Devonshire, the "prince of the Whigs," was in every way an outstanding personality among them: disinterested and generous, he acted from a sense of duty but according to the canons of the time. As Lord Chamberlain he had to deal in August 1761 with a crisis in the King's Bedchamber.

> Lord Huntingdon Groom of the Stole [he writes] came to Lord Ashburnham who was in waiting and told him that he would put on the King's shirt. His Lordship reply'd to be sure if he pleased but then he must take the whole waiting. The other said no, I will only put on the shirt, Lord Ash [burnham] said I give you notice if you do it I shall quit the room. . . .

And so he did. Lord Rockingham and other Lords of the Bedchamber agreed with Ashburnham, "were much dissatisfy'd, thought it lowering their employments, and that they could not stay"; but when Bute became "very warm" over the matter Devonshire warned him that if five or six of the most considerable lords threw up their employment as beneath them, others too would quit, and Bute "would get nobody to take it that was worth having it." The late king, said Devonshire,

> had piqued himself on raising the Bedchamber by getting men of the first rank for them to take it, and that [if] it was lower'd they certainly would not remain in, that it was a very cheap way of keeping them steady to support Government.

Indeed, in 1761 the Lords of the Bedchamber included seventeen peers controlling at least double the number of seats in the House of Commons, and three courtesy lords, all in the House; and Devonshire was giving the right advice on how to put Court offices to the best use in managing parliament. But in that advice, given by a leading Whig at the end of the so-called Whig era, there is nothing which would even distantly foreshadow parliamentary government based on party.

For that, owing to circumstances, we have to turn much rather to the Grenvilles. Two months after the king had, in August 1763, unsuccessfully tried to get rid of them, a by-election occurred in Essex, and on 28 October, John Luther, one of the candidates called on Lord Sandwich, and expressed his concern at hearing that Sandwich was taking a part against him.

I told him [wrote Sandwich to Rigby] that I considered myself meerly with regard to Essex as a party man, that my interest and that of my best friends was at stake, as far as related to the support or downfall of the present Administration ... that I had seen Mr. Conyers, who had told me that he embarked himself in my system, and that he meant if he succeeded, to be a true and steady friend to *this* Administration. Mr. Luther answered me that he had given the same assurances to Mr. Grenville ... that he was a friend to *Government,* ... I said that *Government* was a loose word ... was he a friend to *this* Administration, and more so to *this* than he should be to any Administration of which Mr. Pitt was a member, at that he smiled and hesitated a little, but soon answered that he was a friend to this Administration and would shew himself as such while they acted *consistently....* I answered ... that his own words obliged me situated as I am to act against him; that this country must be governed by combinations of people, and that those who would act in the combination that I belonged to would have a right to my support. ...

But Luther, according to Sandwich, kept a back door open by constituting himself "the judge of what was *consistency* in the Administration."

Or again, in 1764 the Grenvilles intervened in East India Company elections (the first government to do so), with the purpose of helping Clive to get back his *jagir,* he having pledged himself to support them in or out of office—to which promise he adhered. And when they and the Bedfords were turned out by the king, they withdrew their men from Administration and the Court; whereas a year later, the Rockinghams showed so little understanding of party management that they left Chatham whomever he chose to retain. Ideas and a political practice are things of slow growth; parliamentary government, wise as it is as a system, was not born like Pallas Athene.

To sum up: Parliamentary government based on the party-system, is not an ingenious device, the product of creative thought, for which credit is due to one set of men, while another is to be blamed for lack of foresight or virtue in not anticipating it. Its bases are deep down in the political structure of the nation, which was being gradually transformed during the period of so-called mixed government. An electorate thinking in terms of nation-wide parties is its indispensable basis; and it is therefore at least as much in the constituencies as in parliament that the growth of these parties will have to be traced. In the eighteenth century parliament was without that background of enfranchised masses thinking in terms of party; it was to a high degree a closed arena, with its own life and divisions, still dominated by Court and Country on the periphery, but containing the forerunners of political parties in the centre. To clear up these antecedents must be the contribution of us, eighteenth-century historians, to the essential work on the least explored period of British constitutional history, the nineteenth century, now started by a group of keen, able, and what is important, mostly young, historians.

Erwin Panofsky

12

How history ever came to be defined within the narrow compass of "past politics" or of "state biography" is an interesting chapter in the evolution of historiography. After all, at least since the time of Voltaire, historians have recognized that their discipline encompasses the totality of human activity. "A canal which joins two oceans, a painting by Poussin, a fine play," as Voltaire put it, as well as the traditional political and economic factors in human activities deserved the historian's attention. Thus Voltaire, long before the *Annales,* outlined the scope of "total history." And he explicitly included the study of art. Certainly, the arts reveal man's feelings not only about art, but about God, nature, society, the state, and man himself. Properly approached as sources, they enable the historian to grasp more fully and knowingly man's history. In the twentieth century, "traditional" historians have increasingly accepted art works as documents of the past and have wisely co-opted art historians into the discipline. Erwin Panofsky was foremost among these new and highly regarded colleagues, and his definition of the scope of art history illustrates why other historians found his work so congenial and valuable:

> The art historian will have to check what he thinks is the intrinsic meaning of the work, or group of works, to which he devotes his attention, against what he thinks is the intrinsic meaning of as many other documents of civilization historically related to that work or group of works as he can muster: of documents bearing witness to the political, poetical, religious, philosophical, and social tendencies of the personality, period, or country under investigation.

In such a definition, art informs and does not transcend history.

Panofsky was born in 1892 in Germany, which was then the center of professional training in the history of art. That discipline, which Panofsky defined as "the historical analysis and interpretation of man-made objects to which we assign a more than utilitarian value, as opposed to aesthetics, criticism, connoisseurship, and 'appreciation' on the one hand, and to purely antiquarian studies on the other,'' had by then a long and respectable tradition in the German-speaking countries. The first book to employ the title "history of art,'' was Winckelmann's *Geschichte der Kunst des Altertums* (1764); as an American scholar has observed of the subject: "Its native tongue is German.'' By the 1930's, the only other country with a strong academic tradition of the history of art was America, and that tradition was given powerful reinforcement because so many art historians came to the United States as refugees from Hitler's tyranny. That is why Panofsky did so much great work in English, for example: *The Life and Work of Albrecht Dürer* (1943), *Studies in Iconology: Humanistic Themes in the Art of the Renaissance* (1939), *Meaning in the Visual Arts* (1955), and *Renaissance and Renascences in Western Art* (1960; the selection below is from this work).

After receiving a thorough classical education, the young Panofsky moved on to graduate studies in art history, studying at Berlin and Munich and earning his doctorate at the University of Freiburg. He rather quickly established himself as an authority on Renaissance art and in particular on the work of Albrecht Dürer. He attained a professorship at the University of Hamburg in 1926, and soon after became an associate of the Warburg Institute in Hamburg. Under the inspired direction of Aby Warburg, the Institute provided Panofsky and other scholars a combined specialized library, research institution, and lecture platform mainly devoted to the study and perpetuation of classical themes and ideas through the ages, especially the Renaissance. Panofsky accomplished some of his most important early works under the auspices of the Warburg Institute, for example, his study of Dürer's *Melancholia*. In 1931, he accepted an invitation to teach at New York University. From 1931 to 1933, he spent alternate terms teaching at Hamburg and New York. With the advent of the Nazi regime, he lost his post at Hamburg and in 1935 settled permanently in America, joining the Institute for Advanced Study at Princeton, where he remained until his death in 1968.

Perhaps Panofsky's greatest contributions to historical studies are to be found in his explications of the techniques and symbolism employed by medieval and Renaissance artists and in his clarifications of the transformations which occurred in art forms and motifs—"mutational changes" is his term—between 1300 and 1600. His demonstration that the invention of perspective meant presenting a picture to an individual consciousness which then controls the point of view around which pictorial space is organized helped substantiate the interpretation of the Renaissance as a period stressing individualistic and autonomous tendencies. Similarly, his analysis of the interactions of medieval thought and architecture, *Gothic Architecture and Scholasticism* (1951), cast much light on the philosophical and social norms, categories, and expectations of medieval man. In his superb studies of Albrecht Dürer, Panofsky discusses not only Dürer's works in their development but the social and professional contexts within which they were created. His analysis of Dürer's life and career is based on a sure knowledge of the historical, psychological, and philosophical conditions of late fifteenth-century and early sixteenth-century Germany. Panofsky shows Dürer's awareness of his German situation and the manner in which his art reflects that awareness; it thus tells us much of the historical reality of the period.

Panofsky was perhaps most influential in assisting traditional historians to deal with "the problem of the Renaissance." That problem centered around disputes over historical periodization and over concepts of continuity and change. The insights of the art historian, Panofsky maintained, could clarify these matters. As he wrote:

> The art historian, no matter how many details he may find it necessary to revise in the picture sketched out by Filippo Villani and completed by Vasari, will have to accept the basic facts that a first radical break with the medieval principles of representing the visible world by means of line and color was made in Italy at the turn of the thirteenth century; that a second fundamental change, starting in architecture and sculpture rather than painting and involving an intense preoccupation with classical antiquity, set in at the beginning of the fifteenth; and that a third, climactic phase of the entire development, finally synchronizing the three arts and temporarily eliminating the dichotomy between the naturalistic and the classicistic points of view, began at the threshold of the sixteenth.

Panofsky's vast erudition and mastery of critical inquiry have been enormously persuasive among historians involved in the debate over whether to retain the "Renaissance" as a valid period term.

Such qualities as erudition and methodological rigor are hallmarks of all great historians; they are supremely manifest throughout Panofsky's works. Panofsky himself regarded history as a humanistic enterprise. "An art historian," he wrote, "is a humanist whose 'primary material' consists of those records which have come down to us in the form of works of art" (which he defined as a "man-made object demanding to be experienced aesthetically"). But he insisted on the disciplined study of art. He noted the "very striking analogies between the methodological problems to be coped with by the scientist . . . and by the humanist" and concluded that "Science endeavors to transform the chaotic variety of natural phenomena into what may be called a cosmos of nature; the humanities endeavor to transform the chaotic variety of human records into what may be called a cosmos of culture." Because he deals with human actions and creations, however, the humanist-historian must "engage in a mental process of a synthetic and subjective character: he has mentally to re-enact the actions and to re-create the creations." The challenge of art history, and of all history, is, in Panofsky's words, "to build [it] up as a respectable scholarly discipline [when] its very objects come into being by an irrational and subjective process." It was a challenge Panofsky successfully responded to.

Within historiography itself, Panofsky observed that just as the art historian utilizes other historians' works, so conversely "the historian of political life, poetry, religion, philosophy, and social situations should make an analogous use of works of art. It is in this search for intrinsic meanings or content that the various humanistic disciplines meet on a common plane instead of serving as hand maidens to each other." It must be said that art historians like Panofsky, by drawing upon cultural and political history, have done more to broaden that common plane than have traditional historians whose interest in the visual arts as historical evidence has most often been slight. It nevertheless remains true that, while a canal between two oceans may command the studious attention of many historians, because of Erwin Panofsky and his colleagues a painting by Poussin now legitimately attracts the serious inquiries of more than a few historians, to the enrichment of all historiography.

Selected Bibliography

Panofsky's contributions to the historian's enterprise are perhaps most readily appreciated in two of his essays included in *Meaning in the Visual Arts:* "Art as a Humanistic Discipline" and "Three Decades of Art History in the United States: Impressions of a Transplanted European," and in the essay "Artist, Scientist, Genius: Notes on the 'Renaissance—Dämmerung,'" in *The Renaissance* (1953).

For an analysis of Panofsky's contribution to art history proper, with particular reference to iconography and iconology, students should consult Jan Bialostoki's essay on "Iconology" in *The Encyclopedia of World Art* (1967), 774–786. John Hale offers an insightful study of the potential contribution of art historians to historiography in his essay "What Help from Art?" in *The Times Literary Supplement,* April 7, 1966, 292–293; he is particularly perceptive on Panofsky's work. Peter Gay offers a brief discussion of the Warburg Institute, which incidentally moved from Hitler's Germany to London in 1936, in *Weimar Culture* (1968). Students who wish further information on the Institute, which both influenced and facilitated Panofsky's work, might begin with E. N. Gombrich's study of the founder, *Aby Warburg: An Intellectual Biography* (1970). Felix Gilbert's review essay "From Art History to the History of Civilization: Gombrich's Biography of Aby Warburg," *Journal of Modern History,* 44: 3 (September 1972), 381–391, is excellent on the intellectual background of Warburg.

RENAISSANCE AND RENASCENCES IN WESTERN ART

"Renaissance"—Self-Definition or Self-Deception?

Modern scholarship has become increasingly skeptical of periodization, that is to say, of the division of history in general, and individual historical processes in particular, into what the *Oxford Dictionary* defines as "distinguishable portions."

On the one hand, there are those who hold that "human nature tends to remain much the same in all times," so that a search for essential and definable differences between succeeding generations or groups of generations would be futile on principle. On the other, there are those who hold that human nature changes so unremittingly and, at the same time, so individually, that no attempt can and should be made to reduce such differences to a common denominator. According to this view, they are due "not so much to a general spirit of the age but rather to an individual's solution of . . . problems." "What we call 'periods' are simply the names of the influential innovations which have occurred constantly in . . . history," and it would therefore be more reasonable to name periods of history after individuals ("the Age of Beethoven") than to attempt their definition and characterization in general terms.

The first, or monistic, argument can be dismissed for the simple reason that, if it were true, everything would be possible everywhere at every moment, which would make the writing of history ("a written narrative constituting a continuous methodical record, *in order of time,* of important events") impossible by definition. The second, or atomistic, argument—reducing "periods" to the "names of influential innovations," and the "names of influential innovations" to the achievements of "individuals"—confronts us with the question how the historian may be able to determine whether and when an innovation, let alone an influential one, has taken place.

An innovation—the "alteration of what is established"—necessarily presupposes that which is established (whether we call it a tradition, a convention, a style, or a mode of thought) as a constant in relation to which the innovation is a variable. In order to decide whether or not an "individual's solution" represents an "innovation" we must accept the existence of this constant and attempt to define its direction. In order to decide whether or not the innovation is "influential" we must attempt to decide whether or not the direction of the constant has changed in response to the variable. And the trouble is that both the original direction of the constant and its subsequent deflection by an innovation—not difficult to detect as long as our interests do not reach farther than, as Aristotle would say, "the voice of a herald can be heard"—may take place within territorial and chronological boundaries limited only by the observability of cultural interaction (so that a history of Europe in the age of Louis XIV, though not a history of Europe in the age of the Crusades, would legitimately include what happened in America "at the same time").

If we are concerned with the history of book printing in Augsburg at the time of Emperor Maximilian, we shall find it easy to set down the invention of detachable flourishes as an "influential innovation" attributable to Jost de Negker—though even this very specific statement presupposes some investigation of the general state of affairs in Augsburg book printing before as well as after Jost de Negker's appearance on the local scene. And if we are concerned with the history of German music from *ca.* 1800 to *ca.* 1830, we may well decide to call this period the "Age of Beethoven"—though, in order to justify this decision, we must be able to show that the works not only of Haydn, Mozart and Gluck but also of many other German composers now nearly forgotten have so many significant features in common that they may be considered as manifestations of an "established style"; that Beethoven introduced significant features absent from this established style; and that precisely these innovations came to be emulated by a majority of such composers as had occasion to become familiar with his works.

If, on the other hand, we are concerned with the history of Italian painting in the first quarter of the sixteenth century, we shall find it very hard to designate this period by proper names. Even were we to limit ourselves to the three great centers of Florence, Rome and Venice, Leonardo da Vinci, Raphael, Michelangelo, Giorgione, and Titian would have legitimate claims to recognition as godfathers, and we should have to contrast them with so many predecessors and followers—and, again, to point out so many characteristics in which the innovators differ from the predecessors but agree with the followers—that we might find it more convenient (and, given the existence of such marginal yet indispensable figures as Andrea del Sarto, Rosso Fiorentino, Pontormo, Sebastiano del Piombo, Dosso Dossi, or Correggio, more appropriate) to resort to generic terms and to distinguish between an "Early Renaissance" and a "High Renaissance" phase of Italian painting. And if we are concerned with the history of Western European art (or literature, or music, or religion) in its entirety, we cannot help widening—or, rather, lengthening—these generic terms into such notions as "Mycenean," "Hellenistic," "Carolingian," "Gothic"—and, ultimately, "classical," "mediaeval," "Renaissance," and "modern."

Needless to say, such "megaperiods"—as they may be called in contradistinction to the shorter ones—must not be erected into "explanatory principles" or even hypostatized into quasi-metaphysical entities. Their characterization must be carefully qualified according to time and place and must be constantly redefined according to the progress of scholarship. We shall probably never agree—and, in fact, should not even try to agree in a number of cases—as to precisely when and where one period or "megaperiod" stopped and another started. In history as well as in physics time is a function of space, and the very definition of a period as a phase marked by a "change of direction" implies continuity as well as dissociation. We should, moreover, not forget that such a change of direction may come about, not only through the impact of one revolutionary achievement which may transform certain aspects of cultural activity as suddenly and thoroughly as did, for example, the Copernican system in astronomy or the theory of relativity in physics but also through the cumulative and, therefore, gradual effect of such numerous and comparatively minor, yet influential, modifications as determined, for example, the evolution of the Gothic cathedral from Saint-Denis and Sens to Amiens. A change of direction may even result from negative rather than positive innovations: just as more and more people may accept and develop an idea or device previously unknown, so may more and more people cease to develop and ultimately abandon an idea or device previously familiar; one may cite, for example, the gradual disappearance of the Greek language, the drama and the perspective representation of space from the Western scene after the downfall of the Roman Empire, the gradual disappearance of the devil from the art of the seventeenth and eighteenth centuries, or the gradual disappearance of burin engraving from that of the nineteenth.

In spite of all this, however, a period—and this applies to "megaperiods" as well as to the shorter ones—may be said to possess a "physiognomy" no less definite, though no less difficult to describe in satisfactory manner, than a human individual. There can be legitimate disagreement as to when a human individual comes into being (at the moment of conception? with the first heartbeat? with the severance of the umbilical cord?); when he comes to an end (with the last breath? with the last pulse? with the cessation of metabolism? with the complete decomposition of the body?); when he begins to be a boy rather than an infant, an adult rather than a boy, an old man rather than an adult; how many of his characteristics he may owe to his father, his mother, his grandparents, or any of his ancestors. Yet, when we meet him at a given moment within a given group, we shall not fail to distinguish him from his companions; to put him down as young or old or middle-aged, tall or short, intelligent or stupid, jovial or saturnine; and ultimately to form an impression of his total and unique personality. . . .

Renaissance and Renascences

The first of our preliminary questions may thus be answered in the affirmative: there was a Renaissance "which started in Italy in the first half of the fourteenth century, extended its classicizing tendencies to the visual arts in the fifteenth, and subsequently left its imprint upon all cultural activities in the rest of Europe." There remains the second: can qualitative or structural—as opposed to merely quantitative—differences be shown to distinguish not only this Renaissance from earlier, apparently analogous, revivals but also these earlier revivals from each other? And, if so, is it still justifiable to define the latter as "mediaeval" phenomena?

We all agree that the radical alienation from the Antique that characterizes the high and late phases of what we call the Gothic style—an alienation evident, *exceptis excipiendis,* in every work of art produced north of the Alps after about the middle of the thirteenth and before the end of the fifteenth century and, as will be seen, a prerequisite for the crystallization of the *buona maniera moderna* even in Italy—did not result from a steady decline of classical traditions. Rather it may be said to mark the lowest point on an undulating curve of alternate estrangements and *rapprochements;* and it is precisely because Byzantine art had never reached such a nadir that it would not have achieved a full-scale Renaissance even if Constantinople had not been conquered by the Turks in 1453.

The first of these *rapprochements* (already "intuited," as will be remembered, by Antonio Manetti) is known as the Carolingian revival or, to use the designation employed in Charlemagne's own circle, the Carolingian *renovatio.* During and after the disruption of the Western Roman Empire, the interrelated and overlapping processes of barbarization, Orientalization and Christianization had led to an almost total eclipse of classical culture in general and classical art in particular. Oases had been left in regions such as Italy, North Africa, Spain and South Gaul, where we can observe the survival of what has nicely been termed a "sub-antique" style; and in at least two centers we even find what amounts to revivals as opposed to survival. Determined efforts to assimilate Latin models were made in England, which produced, for example, the *Codex Amiatinus* and, in sculpture, the Crosses of Ruthwell or Bewcastle, and where the classical tradition was always to remain a force both more persistent and more self-conscious (either in the sense of purism or in the sense of romanticism) than was the case on the Continent. And a kind of Greek or Early Byzantine revival, apparently caused or at least promoted by the influx of artists fleeing from Arabic conquest or iconoclastic persecution, took place in seventh- and eighth-century Rome, whence it spread, to some extent, to other parts of the peninsula. But precisely those regions which were to form the nucleus of the Carolingian Empire—the northeast of France and the west of Germany—represented, from the classical point of view, a kind of cultural vacuum.

As happens so often in history (suffice it to remember the formation of the Gothic style in the thus far comparatively unproductive Ile-de-France or that of both the High Renaissance and the Early Baroque in Rome, where none of the great masters was either born or trained), it was in this very vacuum that there occurred a conflux and fusion of forces which resulted in a new synthesis: the first crystallization of a specifically Northwest European tradition. And chief among these forces was a deliberate attempt to reclaim the heritage of Rome, "Rome" meaning Julius Caesar and Augustus as well as Constantine the Great. When Charlemagne set out to reform political and ecclesiastical administration, communications and the calendar, art and literature, and—as a basis for all this—script and language (the documents emanating from his own chancellery during the early years of his regime still tend to be very illiterate), his guiding idea was the *renovatio imperii romani.* He had to invite a Briton, Alcuin, as his chief adviser in cultural matters (just as his grandson Charles the Bald had to enlist the help of an Irishman, John the Scot, to obtain a satisfactory translation of Dionysius the Pseudo-Areopagite's Greek); but all these efforts served, to use the contemporary phrase, to bring about an *aurea Roma iterum renovata.*

The reality and magnitude of this movement cannot be questioned. During the seventh and eighth centuries, when even in England a man as cultured as Aldhelm of Malmesbury (*ca.* 640–709) attacked pagan religion and mythology as furiously as any Tertullian or Arnobius, and when the content of Homer and Virgil, already trivialized by "Dictys" and "Dares" into what has been called "des procès-verbaux," was dragged down to an almost infantile level in the anonymous *Excidium Troiae,* few Roman poets and even fewer Roman prose writers were copied: a statistical survey of palimpsests in which the upper as well as the lower script antedates the year 800 has shown that in at least twenty-five of forty-four cases orthodox religious texts were superimposed upon secular Latin texts, whereas—in significant contrast to the practice of subsequent centuries—the opposite occurs only twice. Today we can read the Latin classics in the original largely because of the enthusiasm and industry of Carolingian scribes.

Nor can it be doubted that the employers and advisers of these scribes learned their lesson well. Their often excellent verses in classical meters fill four fat volumes of the *Monumenta Germaniae Historica,* and their ear became astonishingly sensitive to the refinements of Latin prose. Thanks to Charlemagne, writes the greatest representative of Carolingian scholarship, Lupus of Ferrières (a man who collated and corrected classical texts with an acumen akin to that of a modern philologist), to Eginhard, the biographer of the great emperor, studies had raised their heads; now (meaning under Louis the Pious, whose reign struck Lupus as an anticlimax after the fervent beginnings) they are disparaged again so that writers "begin to stray from that dignity of Cicero and the other classics which the best of the Christian authors sought to emulate." In Eginhard's work—epoch-making indeed in that it aimed at a revival of biography as a fine art, taking Suetonius' *Lives of the Emperors* as a model instead of indulging in simple-minded accumulation of alleged facts and no less simple-minded eulogy—Lupus still finds that "elegance of thought, that exquisiteness in the connection of ideas," which he admires in the classical writers (for him *auctores* pure and simple).

In art, the "back-to-Rome" movement had to compete with Orientalizing tendencies on the one hand and insular influence on the other; for the same British Isles which had been so important as a refuge of the classical tradition in pre-Carolingian times had simultaneously produced that antinaturalistic, "Celto-Germanic" linearism, either violently expressive or rigidly geometrical, which was to counteract and ultimately to triumph over this classical tradition. On the Carolingian continent, however, these opposing forces stimulated rather than weakened the energies of the *renovatio* movement.

Charlemagne's palace chapel in Aix-la-Chapelle is, in a general way, modeled upon the pattern of Justinian's San Vitale at Ravenna; but it received a west front suggested by Roman city gates, and its exterior was enlivened not by Oriental blind arcades as in San Vitale but by Corinthian pilasters of self-consciously classical cast. In the porch at Lorsch the polychromatic facing of the walls conforms to pre-Carolingian tradition; but its structural conception—not to mention the capitals of the pilasters, which evince the same classicizing spirit as do those of the palace chapel in Aix—harks back to the Arch of Constantine and, possibly, the Colosseum. The idea of incorporating towers with the basilica, so fundamentally important for the development of high-mediaeval church architecture, originated, it seems, in Asia Minor; but the plan of the basilica itself was revised *romano more,* that is to say, after the fashion of St. Peter's, St. Paul's and St. John in the Lateran. As Richard Krautheimer has shown, Constantinian edifices were, from the Carolingian architects' point of view, no less but perhaps even more "classical" than the Pantheon or the Theater of Marcellus—just as *Tulliana gravitas* was found and greeted in the Christian Fathers by Lupus of Ferrières.

In the decorative and representational arts the spirit of "aurea Roma iterum renovata" loomed even larger than in architecture. The Oriental component having been all but neutralized by the beginning of the ninth century, the *modus operandi* of painting, carving and goldsmithery was determined by two powerful influences: that of the British Isles and that of contemporary Italy where, as has been mentioned, the seventh and eighth century saw an artistic efflorescence doomed to be eclipsed by the very movement which it helped to produce in the North. Both these influences, however, were vigorously challenged by a third, that of classical antiquity. Drawing from all the sources that were accessible to them both physically and psychologically, the Carolingian masters resorted to Roman as well as Early Christian and "sub-antique" prototypes, book illuminations as well as reliefs in stone and stucco, ivory carvings as well as cameos and coins; for, as in architecture, no fundamental distinction was made between the pagan and the Christian Antique. But the very intensity and universality of their endeavor enabled them to develop, with surprising speed, a sense of discrimination as to the quality of their "material" and a certain ease and freedom in its exploitation.

In ornamental borders or initials classical motifs—the egg-and-dart pattern, the palmette, the vine *rinceau* and the acanthus—began to reassert themselves against the abstract interlaces and schematized animal patterns of insular and "Merovingian" art; and in the illustrative rendering of figures and things a first determined effort was made to recapture that affirmative attitude toward nature which had been characteristic of classical art. The more progressive masters attempted to do justice to the human body as an organism subject to the laws of anatomy and physiology, to space as a three-dimensional medium—in at least one case a Carolingian illuminator anticipated the Dugento and Trecento in appropriating from an Early Christian model a genuine interior with a reasonably well foreshortened ceiling—and to light as that which determines the surface appearance of solid bodies. In short, they sought a kind of verisimilitude which had long been absent from the West European scene.

The Anglo-Saxon schools had been at their best not when attempting to rival the lingering naturalism of Late Mediterranean art but when reducing the figure as well as its environment to a superbly disciplined pattern of planes and lines; only exceptionally did these opposites coincide in such insular manuscripts as a late eighth-century Gospel book in the Vatican Library or, above all, the famed *Codex aureus* at Stockholm. And when the continental illuminators, capable of rivaling the best of goldsmith's work in such marvels of abstract design and glowing color as the frontispiece of the mid-eighth-century *St. Augustine* in the Bibliothèque Nationale, ventured into the field of descriptive representation the results were as unsatisfactory, not to say ludicrous, as the Evangelists' figures in the exactly contemporary Gundohinus Gospels of 754.

Compared with these Evangelists, those in the Vienna "Schatzkammer-Evangeliar," the chief product of what is often called the "Palace School" of Charlemagne, give an impression so deceptively antique that they have been ascribed to artists from Byzantium; so vigorous is the modeling of the bodies beneath their white draperies, so gracefully are they posed in front of what has been called impressionistic landscapes. The mythological characters that represent the planets and constellations in such *Aratea* manuscripts as the *Codex Vossianus Latinus* 79 in the University Library at Leiden might have stepped out of a Pompeian mural. And the airy landscapes in the Utrecht Psalter of 820–830, organized in depth by undulating mountain ranges, dotted with buildings *all'antica* and feathery, light-dissolved trees, alive with bucolic or ferocious animals and teeming with classical personifications, are reminiscent of the wall paintings and stucco reliefs in Roman villas and palaces.

To mention mythological characters and classical personifications is to hint at what is, from our point of view, perhaps the most important aspect of the Carolingian *renovatio*. Personifications of localities, natural phenomena, human emotions, and abstract concepts as well as such familiar products of classical imagination as Victories, *putti,* Tritons, and Nereids had continued to play their role in Early Christian art up to the beginning of the seventh century. Then, however, they had disappeared from the scene, and it was left to the Carolingian artists not only to reinstate this interrupted tradition but also to make fresh excursions into the realm of Graeco-Roman iconography. Book illuminators reproduced, in addition to the illustrations of Prudentius' *Psychomachia* (where the warfare between the Virtues and the Vices is represented after the fashion of Roman battle scenes and Luxury appears in the guise of Venus accompanied by Jest and Cupid), innumerable pictures of an unadulteratedly secular character: the miniatures found in scientific treatises on botany, zoology, medicine, or the insignia of Roman public offices; in the *Comedies* of Terence and the *Fables* of Aesop; in calendars and encyclopaedias; and, above all, in those astronomical manuscripts, just mentioned, which more than any other single source served to transmit to posterity the genuine effigies of the pagan gods and heroes that had lent their names to the celestial bodies. Ivory carvers, gem cutters and goldsmiths assimilated classical models of all kinds, thus furnishing further material to the illuminators, while, on the other hand, freely appropriating the latter's designs.

Thus Carolingian art acquired a rich and authentic vocabulary of what I shall henceforth refer to as classical "images": figures (or groups of figures) classical not only in form—this, needless to say, applies to numberless motifs handed down by the Antique to Early Christian art and thus held in readiness for the Carolingian revival—but also in significance. And it is characteristic of the Carolingian *renovatio* that these classical "images," including the *dramatis personae* of the pastoral and the divinities of the pagan pantheon, were given liberty to escape from their original context without abandoning their original nature. In at least one case—and there may have been many more—a Carolingian *ivoirier* decorated the case and handle of a flabellum (a liturgical fan used to keep the flies away from the priest when saying Mass) with scenes from Virgil's *Eclogues* hardly susceptible to an *interpretatio christiana.* Some of the arches that enframe the Canon Tables and Evangelists' portraits in the Gospel Book of Ada, the putative sister of Charlemagne, are adorned with what may be called facsimiles of Roman cameos unchanged in iconography. And according to the most recent investigations it was in the Carolingian period that classical personifications—such as the Sun on his chariot drawn by four horses, the Moon on her chariot drawn by two oxen, the Ocean represented in the guise of the river-god Eridanus, the Earth nursing two infants or reptiles, Atlas or Seismos shaking "the foundations of the earth"—were permitted not only to proliferate in illustrations of the Octateuch and the Psalter (where they had played a rather modest role in Early Christian art) but also to invade the Passion of Christ, where, so far as we know, they had not been tolerated before at all.

This Carolingian revival, virtually ended with the death of Charles the Bald in 877, was followed by eight or nine decades that have been called "as barren as the seventh century." This judgment, chiefly reflecting the art historian's point of view, has lately been challenged. What may be described as the dark age within the "Dark Ages" has justly been credited not only with a number of important agricultural and technical improvements (mutually interrelated with an enormous and necessary increase in population) but also with noteworthy achievements in music and literature: in music, the acceptance of bowed instruments, a novel system of notation and a mistaken but fruitful theory of modes; in literature, apart from several beautiful hymns, Hrotsvitha of Gandersheim's touching attempts to place Terence in the service of monastic learning and morality, the very personal chronicles and memoirs of Liutprand of Cremona, and the even more personal outpourings of a man like Rather of Lobbes (or Verona).

These achievements, however, must be regarded as positive aspects of a negative or regressive development, as a kind of reaction against the Carolingian *renovatio* which, by ignoring or discarding the results of a somewhat self-conscious effort at living up to "classical" standards, liberated the inventive and expressive powers of outstanding individuals without, however, preventing a decline of culture in general.

As far as art is concerned, it remains true that the years from *ca.* 880 to *ca.* 970 amounted only to a "period of incubation"; it is not until the last third—in England about the middle—of the tenth century that we can observe a general resurgence of artistic competence and discipline —a resurgence so marked that it is often spoken of as the "Ottonian Renaissance" with reference to works produced in Germany, and as the "Anglo-Saxon Renaissance" with reference to works produced in England. In spite of such sobriquets, however, this new flowering does not primarily concern us here. It was a revival in all possible senses except in that of a concerted effort to revive the Antique. Imbued with the religious fervor of the Cluniac Reform, it proclaimed a Christocentric spirit profoundly opposed to the universalistic attitude which at the time of Charlemagne and Charles the Bald had tended to bridge the gulfs that separate the "era under Grace" from the "era under the Law," and the latter from the "era before the Law." The literary portrait of an Ottonian emperor could hardly have been patterned, like Charlemagne's in Eginhard's biography, after the model of a Roman Caesar; nor could he have been addressed as "David" by his intimates.

With only relatively few and well-motivated exceptions, the revival of *ca.* 970–1020 drew inspiration only from Early Christian, Carolingian and—very important—Byzantine sources. It thus widened and deepened that stream of tradition which carried classical motifs, placed in the service of the Judaeo-Christian faith, from Hellenistic and Roman sources into the sea of mediaeval art; but it did little to add to the volume of this stream by new and direct appropriations from the "pagan" antiquity. As far as classical "images" are concerned, the "Ottonian Renaissance" even tended to de-emphasize their importance and to de-classicize (if I may coin this word) their appearance. By and large the art of *L'An Mil* may be said to have been animated, in form as well as content, by a prophetic vision of the high-mediaeval future rather than by a retrospective enthusiasm for the classical past.

After another hundred years, however, when this high-mediaeval future was about to become a reality, when art approached the High Romanesque stage all over Europe and the Early Gothic stage in the Royal Domain of France, we do find a renascence movement in the sense here under discussion; or, to be more exact, two parallel and, in a sense, complementary renascence movements. Both began in the latter part of the eleventh century; both reached their climax in the twelfth and continued into the thirteenth; and both deliberately reverted to classical sources. They differed, however, from one another in place as well as in the direction of interests.

One of these movements is commonly—though somewhat loosely—referred to as the "proto-Renaissance of the twelfth century." In contrast to both the Carolingian *renovatio* and the Ottonian and Anglo-Saxon revivals of about 1000, it was a Mediterranean phenomenon, arising in Southern France, Italy and Spain. Though it drew strength, it seems, from an admixture of latent "Celto-Germanic" tendencies (so that the initial contribution of Burgundy was more vital than that of Provence, that of Lombardy, Apulia and Sicily more vital than that of Tuscany and even Rome), it originated outside the Carolingian territory: in regions where the classical element was, and in a measure still is, an inherent element of civilization; where the spoken language had remained fairly close to Latin; and where monuments of ancient art were not only plentiful but also, in certain regions at least, of real importance. In further contrast to the two earlier revivals, the "proto-Renaissance of the twelfth century" came into being at a time when—with the beginnings of urbanization on the one hand and the development of organized pilgrimages, not to mention the Crusades, on the other—the importance of local centers of production, mostly monastic, began to be superseded by that of more or less secularized regional schools (it is not until the eleventh century that we speek of the "schools of Auvergne, Normandy or Burgundy" rather than of the "schools of Reims, Tours or the Reichenau," and not until the middle of the twelfth that we encounter the professional lay architect), and when a determined attempt was made to extend the influence of art to the "common man." . . .

In contradistinction to the proto-Renaissance discussed in the preceding section, the second of the two renascence movements referred to at the beginning of this discussion may be called "proto-humanism"—provided that the term "humanism" is not considered as synonymous with such general notions as respect for human values, individualism, secularism or even liberalism but more narrowly defined as a specific cultural and educational ideal. This ideal, to quote its greatest mediaeval champion, John of Salisbury (d. 1180), is based on the conviction that "Mercury should not be torn from the embraces of Philology": or, in less poetic language, that it is necessary to preserve—or to restore—that union between clear thought and literate expression, reason and eloquence, *ratio* and *oratio,* which had been postulated by the classics from Isocrates to Cicero.

Thus understood, humanism conceives of a liberal education (*liberalia studia,* as John of Salisbury has it, *studia humanitatis,* to use the later academic term which survives in our expression "the humanities") as cultivating the classical tradition from the point of view of the man of letters and the man of taste rather than merely exploiting it for the purposes of the logician, the statesman, the jurist, the doctor, or the scientist. And thus understood, a "proto-humanistic" theme can indeed be isolated from the polyphony of twelfth-century culture, forming a kind of counterpoint to the revival of classical art which we have come to know as proto-Renaissance.

The revival of classical art originated, we recall, in Southern France, Spain and Italy, and the same is true of many other forms of cultural endeavor; but what was virtually absent from this Mediterranean scene was an analogous revival in what may be called (with due caution against the dangers attending the transference of modern terms to the distant past) *les belles-lettres.* "In Paris," says a disgruntled moralist, "the clerics care for the liberal arts; in Orléans, for [classical] literature; in Bologna for law books; in Salerno for pill boxes; and in Toledo for demons; but nowhere for morals." And with a certain number of adjustments—especially the addition of Montpellier and, later, Padua to "Salerno" and "Toledo," and the interpretation of "Orléans" as the symbol of a much wider area—this thumbnail sketch can still be accepted as reasonably true to life.

Within the orbit exemplified by "Bologna, Salerno and Toledo" intellectual interest was focused upon precisely those subjects which do not come under the heading of *studia humanitatis.* And it was only in these non-humanistic fields—most branches of philosophy, law, mathematics, medicine, and the natural sciences, which, especially in the South Italian and Spanish centers, included astrology and what we now would call the exploration of the occult—that genuine classical revivals took place.

That all the Greek texts translated (chiefly in Spain) from intermediary Arabic sources were purely scientific or "philosophical" in character goes without saying; but neither can an essayist, orator or poet be found among those authors who, first at the courts of William I and Roger I of Sicily, came to be directly translated from the original Greek. The numerous *Artes poeticae* and *Artes versificatoriae* produced in France and England during the twelfth and early thirteenth centuries do not have any parallel in Italy before Dante's *De vulgari eloquentia.* And Latin-writing poets in Italy almost exclusively limited themselves to historical, political and scientific matters. Their verses—and pretty poor verses they were, by and large, up to Petrarch—deal with the exploits of Robert Guiscard, the virtues of Mathilda of Tuscany, the triumph of the Pisans at Mallorca; or, on the other hand, with such medical subjects as the "four humors" or the Baths of Puteoli. The author of the last-named work, Peter of Eboli, even manages to introduce into his purely political *Liber in honorem Augusti* (a eulogy of Emperor Henry VI) a doctor from Salerno who, expatiating upon the unflattering characterization of Henry's rival, Tancred of Lecce, delivers a lengthy lecture on embryology and the causes of freakish malformation.

No Latin-writing Italian poet of the twelfth century thought of drawing from classical mythology or legend. This field of interest appears to have been pre-empted, as it were, by the practitioners of the *ars dictandi* or *ars dictaminis* (perhaps best rendered as the "art of letter writing"), where mythological and other classical motifs were used by way of erudite allusion, and by the vernacular poets, particularly in the south of Italy, whose works are at times distinguished by an Ovidian flavor largely imparted to them by Provençal influence. When at the end of the following century Guido delle Colonne wished to provide his educated contemporaries ("qui grammaticam legunt") with an up-to-date Latin version of that ever popular theme, the destruction of Troy, he could do so only by paraphrasing a romance composed by a Norman more than one hundred years before. And Petrarch's splendid hexameters describing the statues of classical gods in the third canto of his *Africa* are, to a large extent, still based upon the mythographical treatise of a twelfth-century Englishman.

It was, in fact, in an area remote from the Mediterranean—the northern sections of France, with Burgundy forming a kind of borderline district, West Germany, the Netherlands, and, most particularly, England—that proto-humanism as opposed to the proto-Renaissance came into being.

In this area—Romanized but not really Roman and roughly coextensive with the Carolingian Empire plus the British Isles—the revivalists of the eleventh and twelfth centuries may be said to have begun where men like Alcuin, Eginhard, Theodulf of Orléans or Lupus of Ferrières had left off. Looking upon the Antique as upon a sacred image rather than an ancestor's portrait, they were disinclined to neglect, let alone to abandon, the associative and emotional values of the classical heritage in favor of its practical and intellectual applicability. Only a "Northerner" could have written a letter like that addressed in 1196 by Bishop Conrad of Hildesheim to his old teacher, Herbord—a letter so full of pride because Italy was then in the hands of the Germans yet so full of reverent and credulous admiration for all that which the writer had heard about at school as "through a glass darkly" (Conrad does not mind mixing metaphors in his enthusiasm for both St. Paul and the world of the classics) and now "saw face to face": Cannae, where so many Roman nobles had been killed that their rings filled two bushels; but also a city called Thetis, founded by, and named after, the mother of Achilles; the little town Giovenazzo, the "birthplace of Jupiter"; Mount Parnassus and the Pegasian fountain, dwelling place of the Muses; and all the miraculous devices contrived by that greatest of magicians, Virgil.

Thus, while the Mediterranean revival of Roman law and Greek philosophy and science had a tremendous impact on intellectual life in the North (suffice it to mention, within the twelfth century alone, such men as Ivo of Chartres and Bernold of Constance, the canonists; Abelard and Gilbert de la Porrée, the dialecticians; Bernardus Sylvestris and William of Conches, the moral and natural philosophers; Alanus de Insulis, the metaphysician; Adelhard of Bath, the scientist), this impact promoted rather than impeded the spread of "humanistic" aspirations and activities (even Walter of Châtillon, it should be remembered, began his career as a law student at Bologna). In some individuals, for instance, Alanus de Insulis, the very distinction between philosophy and *belles-lettres* may be said to have ceased to exist; in others, such as John of Salisbury, an instinctive aversion to that dialectical method which, gaining momentum in his own time and environment, was to result in what we know as scholasticism, served only to deepen their devotion to the *liberalia studia.* And nearly everywhere in Northern territory we find a re-emphasis on good Latin both in prose and verse; a reintensification of the interest in classical fable and myth; and, as far as art is concerned, the emergence of what we should not hesitate to call an "aesthetic" attitude—an attitude now tinged with sentiment (let us not forget that English national literature began with a poem elicited by the awesome experience of Roman ruins), now almost antiquarian: instead of arousing the imitative instinct of the architect, the sculptor and the stone carver, the remnants of the classical past appealed to the taste of the collector, the curiosity of the scholar and the imagination of the poet.

Long before Frederick II acquired classical bronzes and marbles for his castles, Henry of Blois, Bishop of Winchester from 1129 to 1170, had imported from Rome, and set up in his palace, a number of "idols" produced by pagan artists "subtili et laborioso magis quam studioso errori." Long before Ristoro d'Arezzo, writing about 1280–1290, praised the specialty of his home town, those lustrous "Aretine" vases which—admirably decorated with "flying *putti,* battle scenes and fruit garlands"— "turned the heads of the *cognoscitori"* and seemed to have been "either produced by gods or descended from heaven," an English visitor to the Eternal City, Magister Gregorius of Oxford, had spent much of his time in describing and even measuring the classical edifices and had yielded so thoroughly to the "magic spell" *(magica quaedam persuasio)* of a beautiful Venus statue that he felt compelled to visit it time and again in spite of its considerable distance from his lodgings. And Hildebert of Lavardin, Bishop of Le Mans from 1097 to 1125, praised the majesty of Roman ruins and the divine beauty of the Roman gods in distichs so polished in form and so sensitive in feeling that they were long ascribed to a poet of the fifth century and are still quoted in the same breath with du Bellay's *Antiquitez de Rome,* although the good bishop was careful to stress, in a kind of palinode, that the destruction of so much pagan grandeur and loveliness was necessary to bring about the victory of the Cross.

There came into being an entirely new type of antiquarian literature, such as the *Graphia aurea Urbis Romae* and the *Mirabilia Urbis Romae* (composed *ca.* 1150), the content of which tended to merge with that of pseudohistorical expositions such as the *Gesta Romanorum.* And, most important, the world of classical religion, legend and mythology began to come to life as it had never come to life before—not only thanks to a growing familiarity with the sources (it is interesting to observe the gradual expansion and, if one may say so, liberalization of the "reading lists" drawn up for the benefit of students) but also, and even more so, thanks to an increasing emphasis on higher learning and literary skill as such. The rise of cathedral schools, universities and free associations not unlike the later academies facilitated the formation of a class of persons who thought of themselves primarily as *litterati* in contradistinction to *illitterati,* addressed each other in much the same vein as their spiritual descendants were to do in the fifteenth and sixteenth centuries and—even though most of them were still clerics and often rose high in the hierarchy—showed a characteristic inclination to withdraw into the bliss of pastoral seclusion. One has to go back to Cicero, Horace and Virgil—and, at the same time, forward to Petrarch, Boccaccio and Marsilio Ficino—to find the old theme "beata solitudo sola beatitudo" treated with so much introspective tenderness as in a poem by Marbod of Rennes, who died in 1123:

> Rus habet in silva patruus meus; huc mihi saepe
> Mos est abjectis curarum sordibus, et quae
> Excruciant hominem, secedere; ruris amoena
> Herba virens, et silva silens, et spiritus aurae
> Lenis et festivus, et fons in gramine vivus
> Defessam mentem recreant et me mihi reddunt,
> Et faciunt in me consistere . . .

(My uncle has a farm out in the woods, / Where I withdraw, having cast off the squalor / Of all the worries that torment mankind. / Its verdant grass, the silent woods, the gentle / And playful breezes, and the spring, vivacious / Amidst the herbs, refresh the weary mind—/ Restore my self to me and make me rest / Within me . . .)

The graceful *(levis)* Ovid, whose influence had been fairly limited in the early Middle Ages, became a "Great Power" in mediaeval culture after *ca.* 1100 and began to be commented upon with an assiduity previously reserved for such more "serious" or more erudite authors as Virgil or Martianus Capella. The knowledge of classical mythology, so necessary for the understanding of all Roman writers, was systematically cultivated and was conclusively summarized in the *"Mythographus III"* —the work of an English scholar traditionally referred to as "Albricus of London" and possibly identical with the renowned scholastic, Alexander Neckham (died 1217)—which was to remain the standard mythological handbook up to Petrus Berchorius' introduction to his *Metamorphosis Ovidiana moraliter explanata* (first version composed about 1340, second version about 1342) and Boccaccio's *Genealogia deorum*—and was to be read, exploited and criticized even later. And the intensity of the enthusiasm with which the Latin authors of the twelfth century immersed themselves in pagan legend, myth and history can be measured by the intensity of the opposition which this enthusiasm aroused among religious as well as philosophical rigorists—an opposition which, paradoxically and characteristically, tends to speak with the very voice which it endeavors to silence. . . .

From the eleventh and twelfth centuries, then, mediaeval art made classical antiquity assimilable by way of decomposition, as it were. It was for the Italian Renaissance to reintegrate the separated elements. Rendering unto Caesar the things which are Caesar's, Renaissance art not only put an end to the paradoxical mediaeval practice of restricting classical form to non-classical subject matter but also broke the monopoly of architecture and sculpture with regard to classicizing stylization (though painting did not catch up with their "maniera antica" until the second half of the fifteenth century). And we need only to look at Michelangelo's *Bacchus* and *Leda,* Raphael's Farnesina frescoes, Giorgione's *Venus,* Correggio's *Danae,* or Titian's mythological pictures to become aware of the fact that in the Italian High Renaissance the visual language of classical art had regained the status of an idiom in which new poems could be written—just as, conversely, the emotional content of classical mythology, legend and history could come to life in the dramas (non-existent as such throughout the Middle Ages), epics and, finally, operas devoted to such subjects as Orpheus and Eurydice, Cephalus and Procris, Venus and Adonis, Lucrece and Tarquin, Caesar and Brutus, Antony and Cleopatra.

When thirteenth-century Mantua resolved to honor its secular patron saint, Virgil, by public monuments, the poet was portrayed, like the representatives of the liberal arts on the Portail Royal at Chartres, as a mediaeval scholar or canonist seated before his desk and busily engaged in writing; and it was this image which took the place of the Christ in Majesty when Mantua decided in 1257 to pattern its coins after the Venetian *grosso*. But when in 1499, at the very threshold of the High Renaissance, Mantegna was asked to design a statue of Virgil—meant to replace another monument said to have been on the Piazza d'Erbe and to have been destroyed by Carlo Malatesta almost exactly one century before—he conceived of Virgil as a truly classical figure, proudly erect, clad in a toga and addressing the beholder with the timeless dignity of a Demosthenes or Sophocles.

This reintegration was, however, preceded—and, in my opinion, predicated upon—a general and radical reaction against the classicizing tendencies that had prevailed in proto-Renaissance art and proto-humanistic writing. In Italy the seals and coins postdating the *Augustales* of Frederick II and what I have called the "deceptively antique" cameos produced in the thirteenth century became progressively less rather than more classical in style. Nicolo Pisano's own son, Giovanni, while keenly responding to the expressive value of classical art and even daring to employ a *Venus pudica* type for the representation of Prudence in his Pisa pulpit, repudiated the formal classicism of his father and started what may be called a Gothic counterrevolution which, in spite of certain fluctuations, was to win out in the second half of the fourteenth century; and it was from this Trecento Gothic rather than from the lingering tradition of Nicolo's classicism that the *buona maniera moderna* of Jacopo della Quercia, Ghiberti and Donatello arose.

In France the classicizing style of Reims was—with such rare exceptions as the Auxerre reliefs just mentioned—submerged by an altogether different current exemplified by the *Mary Annunciate* right next to the famous *Visitation* and nearly contemporary with it; and next to this *Mary Annunciate* there can be seen the figure of the Angel Gabriel, produced only about ten or fifteen years later, in which classical equilibrium has been abandoned in favor of what is known as the "Gothic sway." How High Gothic ornament was purged of classical motifs, how the acanthus gave way to ivy, oak leaves and water cress and how the Ionic and Corinthian capitals, retained or even revived in Romanesque architecture, were banned is known to all. The series of *Constantines* patterned upon the *Marcus Aurelius* and, we recall, extremely popular throughout the twelfth century, abruptly breaks off in the thirteenth (it was not until the sixteenth century that, under the direct or indirect influence of the Italian Renaissance, equestrian monuments of a similar type were revived in the North). And about 1270–1275 an English workshop, commissioned to produce a retable that was supposed to resemble late-twelfth-century metal work but disinclined to change its pure High Gothic figure style and therefore concentrating its archaistic efforts upon the frame, attempted to stress the "Romanesque" character of this frame by the inclusion of simulated classical cameos: by this time classicizing tendencies were understood to be a thing of the past.

It would not be fair to speak of the classicism of Chartres and Reims as a "frustrated effort." On the contrary, the rise of that "intrinsic" classicism which culminated in the Reims *Visitation* is not only contemporary but, in a sense, coessential with the rise of those naturalistic tendencies which were to supplant it (again we may remember Goethe's dictum about the Antique as part of "natural nature"); and that sway or lilt which determines the High Gothic conception of human movement is nothing but a classical *contrapposto* in disguise. It is, however, precisely this disguise that matters. In a figure posed *all'antica,* the shoulder above the standing leg (the latter's function being comparable to that of a column supporting the load of the entablature) sags; in a figure dominated by the Gothic sway, the shoulder above the standing leg (the latter's function being comparable to that of a pier transmitting energy to the vault-ribs) rises. What had been the result of two natural forces in balance becomes the result of one preternatural force ruling supreme: the classical element is so completely absorbed as to become indiscernible. . . .

In short, before the Italian High Renaissance performed its task of reintegration, that undulating curve which, as I said, may serve to describe the fluctuations of classicizing tendencies in postclassical art had reached the zero mark in all genres as well as in all countries. The later phases of the Middle Ages had not only failed to unify what the Antique itself had left to its heirs as a duality—visible monuments on the one hand, texts on the other—but even dissolved those representational traditions which the Carolingian *renovatio* had managed to revive and to transmit as a unity.

The "principle of disjunction" thus cannot be accounted for by the accidents of transmission alone. It would seem to express a fundamental tendency or idiosyncrasy of the high-mediaeval mind which we shall re-encounter on several later occasions: an irresistible urge to "compartmentalize" such psychological experiences and cultural activities as were to coalesce or merge in the Renaissance; and, conversely, a basic inability to make what we would call "historical" distinctions. And this leads us back to the question which was posed at the beginning of this chapter: can the three phenomena which we have been considering—the Italian *rinascita,* the Carolingian *renovatio* and the twin movement known as proto-Renaissance and proto-humanism—be shown to differ from each other not only in scale but also in structure? And, if so, is it still possible to distinguish, within this triad of phenomena, between the Renaissance with a capital *"R"* and the two mediaeval revivals which I propose to call "renascences"? This question, too, deserves, I think, an affirmative answer; for, to put it briefly, the two mediaeval renascences were limited and transitory; the Renaissance was total and permanent.

The Carolingian *renovatio* pervaded the whole of the empire and left no sphere of civilization untouched; but it was limited in that it reclaimed lost territory rather than attempting to conquer new lands. It did not transcend a monastic and administrative *Herrenschicht* directly or indirectly connected with the crown; its artistic activities did not include major sculpture in stone; the models selected for imitation were as a rule productions of the minor arts and normally did not antedate the fourth and fifth centuries A.D.; and the classical values—artistic as well as literary—were salvaged but not "reactivated" (as we have seen, no effort was made either to reinterpret classical images or to illustrate classical texts *de novo*).

The classical revival of the eleventh and twelfth centuries, on the other hand, penetrated many strata of society. In art it sought and achieved monumentality, selecting models of greater antiquity than those normally chosen by the Carolingian masters, and emancipated classical images from what I have called the stage of quotation and paraphrase (it did precisely what the Carolingian *renovatio* had failed to do in that new meanings were infused into classical images and a new visual form was given to classical themes). But it was limited in several other respects: it represented only a special current within the larger stream of contemporary civilization (whereas Carolingian civilization as a whole was coextensive with the *renovatio* movement) and was restricted to particular regions; there was, according to these regions, a basic difference between a recreative and a literary or antiquarian response to the Antique; the proto-Renaissance in the arts was virtually restricted to architecture and sculpture as opposed to painting; and in art as well as literature classical form came to be divorced from classical content. Both these mediaeval renascences, finally, were transitory in that they were followed by a relative or—in the Northern countries—absolute estrangement from the aesthetic traditions, in art as well as literature, of the classical past.

How things were changed by the real, Italian Renaissance can be illustrated by a small but significant incident. The Carolingian *Aratea* manuscript which includes, among so many other classicizing pictures, the

Pompeian-looking Gemini had been left untouched for about four hundred years. Then a well-meaning scribe saw fit to repeat the entire text in the script of the thirteenth century because he evidently thought that the Carolingian "Rustic Capital" would stump his contemporaries, as well as future generations. But the twentieth-century reader finds Carolingian script easier to decipher than Gothic, and this ironic fact tells the whole story.

Our own script and letter press derive from the Italian Renaissance types patterned, in deliberate opposition to the Gothic, upon Carolingian and twelfth-century models which in turn had been evolved on a classical basis. Gothic script, one might say, symbolizes the transitoriness of the mediaeval renascences; our modern letter press, whether "Roman" or "italic," testifies to the enduring quality of the Italian Renaissance. Thereafter, the classical element in our civilization could be opposed (though it should not be forgotten that opposition is only another form of dependence); but it could not entirely disappear again. In the Middle Ages there was in relation to the Antique a cyclical succession of assimilative and non-assimilative stages. Since the Renaissance the Antique has been constantly with us, whether we like it or not. It lives in our mathematics and natural sciences. It has built our theatres and cinemas as opposed to the mediaeval mystery stage. It haunts the speech of our cab driver—not to mention the motor mechanic or radio expert—as opposed to that of the mediaeval peasant. And it is firmly entrenched behind the thin but thus far unbroken glass walls of history, philology and archaeology.

The formation and, ultimately, formalization of these three disciplines —foreign to the Middle Ages in spite of all the Carolingian and twelfth-century "humanists"—evince a fundamental difference between the mediaeval and the modern attitude towards classical antiquity, a difference which makes us understand the essential strength and the essential weakness of both. In the Italian Renaissance the classical past began to be looked upon from a fixed distance, quite comparable to the "distance between the eye and the object" in that most characteristic invention of this very Renaissance, focused perspective. As in focused perspective, this distance prohibited direct contact—owing to the interposition of an ideal "projection plane"—but permitted a total and rationalized view. Such a distance is absent from both mediaeval renascences. "The Middle Ages," as has recently been said, "never knew that they were mediaeval. The men of the twelfth century had none of that awareness of a Cimmerian night from which—as Rabelais wrote his friend Tiraqueau in 1532—humanity had emerged."

The Carolingian revival had been started because it was felt that a great many things needed overhauling: the administrative system, the liturgy, the language, and the arts. When this was realized, the leading spirits turned to antiquity, both pagan and Christian (and even with a strong initial emphasis on the latter), much as a man whose motor car has broken down might fall back on an automobile inherited from his grandfather which, when reconditioned (and let us not forget that the Carolingians themselves spoke only of *renovare* or *redintegrare* instead of using such words as *reflorescere, revivere* or *reviviscere,* let alone *renasci*), will still give excellent service and may even prove more comfortable than the newer model ever was. In other words, the Carolingians approached the Antique with a feeling of legitimate heirs who had neglected or even forgotten their property for a time and now claimed it for precisely those uses for which it had been intended.

In contrast to this untroubled sense of legitimacy, the high-mediaeval attitude toward the Antique is characterized by an ambivalence somewhat analogous to that which marks the high-mediaeval position toward Judaism. Throughout the Christian era the Old Testament has been recognized as the foundation of the New, and in Carolingian art the relation between the Church and the Synagogue still tended to be interpreted in a spirit of hopeful tolerance stressing that which perfect and imperfect revelation have in common instead of that which separates them: an initial in the Drogo Sacramentary produced at Metz between 826 and 855 depicts the Church and the Synagogue in a state of peaceful coexistence rather than as enemies. From the turn of the first millennium, however—witness the Uta Gospels, where the Synagogue, her brow and eyes disappearing behind the frame as the setting sun vanishes beneath the horizon, is opposed to the Church as a power of darkness that "tenet in occasum"—a feeling of hostility towards the living adherents of the Old Dispensation began to outweigh the respect for the dead patriarchs and prophets. And from the twelfth century, when this hostility resulted in discriminatory practices and physical persecution, the Synagogue came to be depicted blindfolded instead of merely turning away from the light and was occasionally shown in the act of killing an animal (although a man as tolerant as Abbot Suger of St.-Denis could still prefer to represent her, in one of his "anagogical" windows, in the role of precursor rather than foe, "unveiled" by God and thus belatedly endowed with sight, where her more fortunate sister receives a crown). In the high-mediaeval period, then, we can observe an unresolved tension between the enduring sense of obligation towards the prophetic message of the Old Law and the growing repugnance towards its bloody ritual and its contemporary manifestations. The Apostles could be shown seated or standing on the shoulders of the prophets much as Bernard of Chartres compared his generation's relation to the classics to that of dwarves "who have alighted on the shoulders of giants" and "see more numerous and distant things not by virtue of their own keen vision or their own stature but because they are raised aloft by the giants' magnitude"; but in the same iconographical context (in the "Fürstenportal" of Bamberg Cathedral) the Synagogue could be portrayed as a stubborn, benighted enemy of the Church, her statue surmounting the figure of a Jew whose eyes are being put out by a devil.

Similarly there was, on the one hand, a sense of unbroken continuity with classical antiquity that linked the "Holy Roman Empire of the Middle Ages" to Caesar and Augustus, mediaeval music to Pythagoras, mediaeval philosophy to Plato and Aristotle, mediaeval grammar to Donatus—and, on the other, a consciousness of the insurmountable gap that separated the Christian present from the pagan past (so that in the case of Aristotle's writings a sharp distinction was made, or at least attempted, between what was admissible and what should be condemned). The classical world was not approached historically but pragmatically, as something far-off yet, in a sense, still alive and, therefore, at once potentially useful and potentially dangerous. It is significant that the classical philosophers and poets were frequently represented in the same Oriental costumes as the Jewish prophets, and that the thirteenth century spoke of the Romans, their monuments and their gods as *sarrazin* or *sarazinais,* employing the same word for the pagans of old and the infidels of its own age.

For want of a "perspective distance" classical civilization could not be viewed as a coherent cultural system within which all things belonged together. Even the twelfth century, to quote a competent and unbiased observer, "never considered the whole of classical antiquity . . . it looked upon it as a storehouse of ideas and forms, appropriating therefrom such items as seemed to fit in with the thought and actions of the immediate present." Every phenomenon of the classical past, instead of being seen in context with other phenomena of the classical past, thus had to have one point of contact, and one of divergence, with the mediaeval present: it had to satisfy both the sense of continuity and the feeling of opposition: Hildebert of Lavardin's *Elegy of Rome* is followed, we remember, by a Christian palinode, and Marbod of Rennes' pastoral serves as an introduction for a *Sermo de vitiis et virtutibus.*

Now we can see why the union of classical form and classical content, even if retained in the images revived in Carolingian times, was bound to break apart, and why this process of "disjunction" was so much more radical in the arts—where the very fact that they provided a visual rather than intellectual experience entailed the danger of *curiositas* or even idolatry—than in literature. To the high-mediaeval mind Jason and Medea (even though she tended to perform her tricks of rejuvenation with the aid of the "water of Paradise") were acceptable as long as they were depicted as Gothic aristocrats playing chess in a Gothic chamber. Classical gods and goddesses were acceptable as long as they lent their beautiful presence to Christian saints, to Eve or to the Virgin Mary. But a Thisbe clad in classical costume and waiting for Pyramus by a classical mausoleum would have been an archaeological reconstruction incompatible with the sense of continuity; and an image of Mars or Venus classical in form as well as significance was either, as we have seen, an "idol" or talisman or, conversely, served to personify a vice. We can understand that the same Magister Gregorius who studied and measured the Roman buildings with the detachment of an antiquarian was filled with wonder and uneasiness by the "magical attraction" of that too beautiful *Venus;* that Fulcoius of Beauvais (died sometime after 1083) was able to describe a head of Mars discovered by a plowman only in terms of a violent conflict between admiration and terror ("Horrendum caput et tamen hoc horrore decorum, / Lumine terrifico, terror et ipse decet; / Rictibus ore fero, feritate sua speciosum"); that there sprang up, as a sinister accompaniment to proto-humanism, those truly terrifying tales (revived by the Romantics from Joseph von Eichendorff and Heinrich Heine to Prosper Mérimée and Gabriele d'Annunzio) about the young man who had put his ring on the finger of a Venus statue and thereby fell prey to the devil; and that, as late as in the second half of the fourteenth century, the Sienese believed the public erection of such a statue, recently excavated and much admired as a "work of Lysippus," to be responsible for their defeat at the hands of the Florentines (they took it down, dismembered it, and surreptitiously buried the fragments in enemy territory).

The "distance" created by the Renaissance deprived antiquity of its realness. The classical world ceased to be both a possession and a menace. It became instead the object of a passionate nostalgia which found its symbolic expression in the re-emergence—after fifteen centuries—of that enchanting vision, Arcady. Both mediaeval renascences, regardless of the differences between the Carolingian *renovatio* and the "revival of the twelfth century," were free from this nostalgia. Antiquity, like the old automobile in our homely simile, was still around, so to speak. The Renaissance came to realize that Pan was dead—that the world of ancient Greece and Rome (now, we recall, *sacrosancta vetustas,* "hallowed antiquity") was lost like Milton's Paradise and capable of being regained only in the spirit. The classical past was looked upon, for the first time, as a totality cut off from the present; and, therefore, as an ideal to be longed for instead of a reality to be both utilized and feared.

The Middle Ages had left antiquity unburied and alternately galvanized and exorcised its corpse. The Renaissance stood weeping at its grave and tried to resurrect its soul. And in one fatally auspicious moment it succeeded. This is why the mediaeval concept of the Antique was so concrete and at the same time so incomplete and distorted; whereas the modern one, gradually developed during the last three or four hundred years, is comprehensive and consistent but, if I may say so, abstract. And this is why the mediaeval renascences were transitory; whereas the Renaissance was permanent. Resurrected souls are intangible but have the advantage of immortality and omnipresence. Therefore the role of classical antiquity after the Renaissance is somewhat elusive but, on the other hand, pervasive—and changeable only with a change in our civilization as such.

Charles Beard

13

If Charles Beard was not the most influential, he was certainly the most controversial American historian in the first half of the twentieth century. He wrote, alone or in collaboration, forty-nine volumes of historical studies (and twenty-eight volumes of studies in political science), whose massive sales are an indication of his public reach; perhaps only Frederick Jackson Turner was more influential, and then because he established a "school," something Beard did not do. Clearly, however, some of Beard's works, especially *An Economic Interpretation of the Constitution* (1913) and his two studies of Franklin D. Roosevelt's foreign policy, *American Foreign Policy in the Making, 1932–1940* (1946) and *President Roosevelt and the Coming of the War, 1941* (1948), "excited more controversy and more denunciation," as H. K. Beale has said, "than any other history of the half century." Prolific and polemical, Charles A. Beard even today raises important historiographic and human questions.

Born in Indiana in 1874, Beard grew up in a family noted for its wealth, religious nonconformity, and respectable progressive politics. Intellectually active and politically involved as the family was, it also included a strong emphasis on pragmatic economic realism. "People ask me," Beard once recalled, "why I emphasize economic questions so much. They should have been present in the family parlor, where my father and his friends gathered to discuss public affairs." Beard received a good preparatory school education and, after serving some time as co-editor and publisher, with his older brother, of his father's newspaper, he went off to DePauw University. There he encountered Professor James R. Weaver, who introduced him to such political and social thinkers as Spencer, Buckle, Alfred Marshall, and Marx. "In Beard's intellectual life," Richard Hofstadter has noted, Weaver was "a decisive figure; his example probably suggested the possibility of teaching and scholarship as a career." During his college years, Beard visited Chicago and observed at first hand the effects of industrialization and urbanization. He worked for a time in Jane Addams' Hull House, coming in contact with working-class poverty and radical programs of amelioration.

In 1898, he volunteered for service in the Spanish-American War—a wholly idealistic act in defense of Cuban independence against Spanish imperialism. No doubt fortunately for Beard, enlistments surpassed need and he did not serve; he suffered, however, along with many of his peers when the noble passions of 1898 were succeeded by American imperialism in Cuba and the Philippines. Beard traveled to England that year and stayed for three years, active in public affairs while he studied at Oxford. He helped to found and then lectured at a workingmen's college—Ruskin Hall, named after the prescient critic of classical economic theory and of the industrial society it justified. Ruskin's ethical exhortations made a strong impression on the youthful Beard; his writings countered the pragmatic realism of Beard's upbringing and, as Richard Hofstadter has persuasively pointed out, their influence highlights "the profound ambiguity" in Beard's thought "between the moral passions that Ruskin addressed so directly and the desire for detached knowledge and scientific scholarship which Beard voiced on many occasions."

From 1899 to 1901, Beard published a number of short inspirational articles on reformers like Cobbett and Owen for *Young Oxford,* the Ruskin Hall periodical. "In taking up this work," he wrote, explaining their hortatory tone, "I do not pose as an historian; for it is his duty to leave ethics alone." He also published his first book, *The Industrial Revolution,* a respectable work in which, following a Ruskinian critique of laissez-faire economics, he emphasized the possibilities of progress still open to man rather than the horrors so far attendant upon the industrializing process. (Until rather late in his life, Beard maintained a robust faith in progress based on the application of modern science to society.) After considering a career as a labor organizer and political representative in England, he decided in 1902, "at length and with great reluctance," to return to America and to complete his graduate studies at Columbia University.

At Columbia, where Beard completed his dissertation ("The Office of the Justice of Peace in England in Its Origin and Development") and began to teach in 1904, he encountered a group of intellectuals and an intellectual movement that combined to complete his academic formation and would impel him through the rest of his academic life. The scholars included John Dewey, J. Allen Smith, and E. R. A. Seligman (whose *The Economic Interpretation of History* strongly influenced Beard's study of the Constitution), as well as such exponents of the "New History" as James Harvey Robinson and Harry Elmer Barnes. Morton White has aptly characterized this intellectual movement as the "Revolt Against Formalism." In Cushing Strout's words, "Antiformalism" means primarily "a concern for the vital matrix of social and economic forces and conditions which underlie institutional forms and theoretical constructions. As a temper of mind, 'antiformalism' tends to make an invidious contrast between the dynamic and the static, history and logic, experience and principle, practical adjustment and formal order, the utilitarian and the elegant. For the 'antiformalist' the first term of each antithesis is the honorific one."

The historiographical aspect of this revolt (which occurred in law, economics, and philosophy as well) entailed a rejection of the prevailing school of political history, of "scientific, objective history" in the style of Ranke. Historians were to seek for the living "reality" behind laws, institutions, philosophical systems, the "reality" of special interests, pressure groups, corporate greed, economic forces, and class conflict. (As Beard wrote in the preface to his most controversial book, "I print it in the hope that a few of this generation of historical scholars may be encouraged to turn away from barren 'political' history to the study of the real economic forces which condition great movements in politics." This "environmental determinism," as it has been called, was to evoke a response in the next generation from such historians of ideas as Arthur O. Lovejoy and Perry Miller.) Knowledge of these "realities" would allow for social control. History, therefore, was no longer to recount past wars or heroic exploits but, by uncovering historical and social relationships, would become an instrument for shaping the future. Beard and Robinson, for example, closed their collaborative effort, *The Development of Modern Europe* (1907–1908), with the prediction that "it well may be that men of science, not kings, or warriors, or even statesmen are to be the heroes of the future." It was in such an intellectual milieu, and within the larger ambience of the reforming, activist Progressive era, that Beard published his first book in American history, *The Supreme Court and the Constitution* (1912). The next year he published his irritating but now classic study, *An Economic Interpretation of the Constitution.* The book established Beard's reputation as a polemicist and initiated a debate not yet ended.

Without denying Beard's stature or his originality in *An Economic Interpretation,* one may agree with Richard Hofstadter's opinion that the work, "seen in historical context, seems more like a masterful summation of scattered insights and arguments than an altogether novel work." Sociologists and economists (e.g., E. R. A. Seligman) as well as historians of the Turner "school" had already begun to emphasize economic forces; the latter group were also mapping out geographic lines of political conflict. American socialist critics, along with novelists like Dreiser and journalists like Steffens, had for years been "unveiling" sinister economic interests entrenched behind legal and constitutional barricades. Legal philosophers and sociologists had been investigating the relationship of law to changing social conditions, and of the social position of judges to their interpretations of the law. Progressive reformers and critics of the Constitution had already pointed out the conservative, anti-democratic nature of the federal instrument of government. This scholarship perhaps explains why Beard's book engendered relatively calm debate and wide acceptance among historians, while it stirred up much controversy and no little invective outside of the professional arena. (William H. Taft and Warren G. Harding were among the public who were appalled by the book's thesis.)

It nevertheless remains true that Beard's assault on the traditional historiography of the Constitution was buttressed by new and powerful sources and insights. He found in James Madison's writings, especially "The Federalist," No. 10, the theoretical framework of economics, special interests, and political faction appropriate to his conception of political "realities." Beard drew upon the quantitative studies of voting patterns drawn by the Turner school; he surveyed the economic and social interests that were paramount in 1787; he attempted to ascertain through collective biography the economic interests and financial holdings of the delegates to the Convention; he sought to establish the Founding Fathers' "real" motives in so framing the Constitution. In short, he wished to demonstrate in "antiformalist" fashion the dynamic tension between ideas and interests. As he wrote of the book much later, "In political history, if not in all history, there are no ideas with which interests are not associated and there are no interests utterly devoid of ideas." He concluded that the Constitution as it emerged was "an economic document" best serving the interests of a discernible economic group—the holders of "personalty" (financial, mercantile, and personal property)—and that it was opposed by agrarian interests and backers of the use of paper money, that is, debtors. Further, the Constitution was ratified in a nondemocratic process; it was "the work of a consolidated group whose interests knew no state boundaries and were truly national in their scope."

Small wonder Warren Harding's newspaper railed against the book as filled with "filthy lies and rotten perversions . . . damnable in its influence." Beard himself maintained that the book was a work of scholarship done without reference to involvement in contemporary social and political reform movements, but it seems clear that his ambiguous position between passion and pure scholarship is manifest here as elsewhere in his writings. Beard's ironic observation that the book had been used by Progressives, socialists, and conservatives and praised as well as attacked by the historical establishment points up the ambiguities he himself felt.

The book engendered lasting discussion. Scholars have since advanced severe criticisms of its methodological and interpretative bases, and have thoroughly revised Beard's original revision. What is beyond dispute is that Beard initiated a new genre in American historiography. The opposite of a narrative, it is, in Richard Hofstadter's view, "probably the first truly exciting monograph in the history of American historiography; it achieved its excitement solely through the force and provocation of its argument."

In the years that followed, Beard produced other, similar works, such as *The Economic Origins of Jeffersonian Democracy* (1921) and *The Economic Basis of Politics* (1922)—all told he wrote twelve books between 1904 and 1922. He continued teaching at Columbia (and he was a superb and popular lecturer) until 1917, when he resigned over what in fact were infringements of academic freedom in the university. His resignation was not retirement; Beard remained active as a lecturer, writer, and engaged citizen. He was an adviser to the New York Bureau of Municipal Research; he helped found the New School for Social Research in 1919 and the Workers Education Bureau of America; he traveled with his family to Europe, to Japan (where he counseled the municipal government of Tokyo), and to China. If he later was an "isolationist," Beard was never parochial geographically or intellectually. Early in his career, he did much to introduce American scholars to the works of European thinkers like Marx and Marshall; late in his career, at the suggestion of his son-in-law, Alfred Vagts, he did much to popularize the work and interpretations of the young German revisionist Eckart Kehr. He was elected president of both the American Historical Association and the American Political Science Association, and he was throughout the interwar decades an outspoken civil libertarian.

The last three decades of his life were also devoted to unremitting scholarly productions. In the 1920's, Beard completed further studies of the economic interpretation of American history; he turned next to a consideration of the philosophical problems inherent in the concept of historical knowledge; and in the late 1930's, he undertook an almost obsessive analysis of American foreign policy. The shift of attention here manifested was symptomatic of Beard's intellectual conversion from a belief in economic determinism to historical relativism and eclecticism. The general disillusionment that followed World War I, the impact of the Great Depression, and the emergence of totalitarian regimes in Russia, Italy, and Germany (where, clearly, politics determined economics and "science" served whatever masters and purposes set to it) all tended to undermine Beard's optimistic belief in progress and to cast doubt upon his own historiographic tenets.

One could hardly have expected in 1913 that Beard would write in 1932 that "the world is largely ruled by ideas, true and false"; or in 1945 that "man hasn't sense enough to pursue economic interests consistently." Nor would one have expected the sober young "realist" later to confess (in 1933) that "written history is an act of faith," because "history is chaos and every attempt to interpret it otherwise is an illusion." But relativism and skepticism require suspension of judgment, a modest appreciation of the limits of human reason, a tentativeness in offering conclusions; and in his last writings, in his violent denunciation of Franklin Roosevelt's foreign policy, Beard lacked the modesty he had preached, or at least implied. His writings on foreign policy and his defense of his version of isolationism, which he called American continentalism, showed Beard's sturdy confidence in his ability to penetrate to the motives of men in power. He thought it was possible to demonstrate the economic basis of political and foreign policy decisions, and he argued his case as a prosecutor rather than candidly presenting the results of his historical inquiry. As Forrest McDonald concluded, the work of Charles Beard, "a man of . . . superior gift, massive intellect, and high moral purpose" was impaired by his political biases and by his confusion of the roles of historian and political activist.

If today "Beard's reputation stands like an imposing ruin in the landscape of American historiography," there remains much of consequence. The epistemological difficulties which inhere in any attempt to gain historical knowledge, the allure and peril of reductionism and determinism of any sort, the fruitfulness that may flow from new approaches and new questions, the impact on the historian of events in his own time, the effect of the historian's conscious and unconscious biases, are all exemplified in Beard's career. If most of his works have been superseded or at least thoroughly revised, it remains no small accomplishment to have inspired or impelled so many other historians to undertake so much fruitful work.

Selected Bibliography

The best introductory survey of Beard's career and the most probing analysis of his work is by Richard Hofstadter, in *The Progressive Historians, Turner, Beard, Parrington* (1968). Bernard C. Borning's *The Political and Social Thought of Charles A. Beard* (1962) is an excellent book, perhaps the best full-length study of Beard's thought. Howard K. Beale, editor, *Charles A. Beard: An Appraisal by Eric F. Goldman, Harold J. Laski, Howard K. Beale, Walton Hamilton, George Soule, Merle Curti, George R. Leighton, Richard Hofstadter, Max Lerner, Luther Gulick, George S. Counts, Arthur W. MacMahon* (1954), is, as its full title indicates, compendious on the man and his career. It includes an essay by Beale on "Beard's Historical Writings" and a "Bibliography of Beard's Writings" by Jack Frooman and Edmund David Cronon, the latter with a valuable section on "Major Articles and References about Beard." It may be supplemented by John C. Rule and Ralph D. Handen, "Bibliography of Works on Carl Lotus Becker and Charles Austin Beard, 1945–63," *History and Theory*, V (1956), 302–313.

Maurice Blinkoff's *The Influence of Charles A. Beard on American Historiography* (1936) is a helpful guide. Forrest McDonald analyzes and severely criticizes Beard's work in his essay "Charles A. Beard," in *Pastmasters: Some Essays on American Historians*, edited by Marcus Cunliffe and Robin W. Winks (1969). John Higham offers a valuable description of the traditions within which Beard worked and his reactions to them in *History: The Development of Historical Studies in the United States* (with Leonard Krieger and Felix Gilbert; 1965). Higham has a particularly good chapter on "The New History." Cushing Strout's *The Pragmatic Revolt in American History: Carl Becker and Charles Beard* (1955) is a sympathetic account of the two, in many ways similar, historians. "Like Becker," Strout writes, "Beard must be seen as a philosophical historian trying to pick his way through the tangled jungle of the modern world." Lee Benson, *Turner and Beard: American Historical Writing Reconsidered* (1960), offers a methodological "critique of Beard and his critics"; but before reading it, students ought to read, in sequence, Beard's *An Economic Interpretation,* Robert E. Brown's hostile *Beard and the Constitution* (1956), Forrest McDonald's *We the People* (1958), and *The Antifederalists* (1960) by Jackson T. Main, who is sympathetic to the Beard thesis.

AN ECONOMIC INTERPRETATION
OF THE CONSTITUTION OF THE
UNITED STATES

Introduction to the 1935 Edition

This volume was first issued in 1913 during the tumult of discussion that accompanied the advent of the Progressive party, the split in Republican ranks, and the conflict over the popular election of United States Senators, workmen's compensation, and other social legislation. At that time Theodore Roosevelt had raised fundamental questions under the head of "the New Nationalism" and proposed to make the Federal Government adequate to the exigencies created by railways, the consolidation of industries, the closure of free land on the frontier, and the new position of labor in American economy. In the course of developing his conceptions, Mr. Roosevelt drew into consideration the place of the judiciary in the American system. While expressing high regard for that branch of government, he proposed to place limitations on its authority. He contended that "by the abuse of the power to declare laws unconstitutional the courts have become a law-making instead of a law-enforcing agency." As a check upon judicial proclivities, he proposed a scheme for "the recall of judicial decisions." This project he justified by the assertion that "when a court decides a constitutional question, when it decides what the people as a whole can or cannot do, the people should have the right to recall that decision when they think it wrong." Owing to such declarations, and to the counter-declarations, the "climate of opinion" was profoundly disturbed when *An Economic Interpretation of the Constitution* originally appeared.

Yet in no sense was the volume a work of the occasion, written with reference to immediate controversies. Doubtless I was, in common with all other students, influenced more or less by "the spirit of the times," but

From *An Economic Interpretation of the Constitution of the United States* (New York: The Macmillan Company, 1913), pp. v–xvii, 292–295, 303–312. Copyright 1913, 1935 by The Macmillan Company, renewed 1941 by Charles A. Beard, and renewed 1963 by William Beard and Miriam Beard Vagts. Reprinted by permission of the publisher.

I had in mind no thought of forwarding the interests of the Progressive party or of its conservative critics and opponents. I had taken up the study of the Constitution many years before the publication of my work, while a profound calm rested on the sea of constitutional opinion. In that study I had occasion to read voluminous writings by the Fathers, and I was struck by the emphasis which so many of them placed upon economic interests as forces in politics and in the formulation of laws and constitutions. In particular I was impressed by the philosophy of politics set forth by James Madison in Number X of the *Federalist,* which seemed to furnish a clue to practical operations connected with the formation of the Constitution—operations in which Madison himself took a leading part.

Madison's view of the Constitution seemed in flat contradiction to most of the theorizing about the Constitution to which I had been accustomed in colleges, universities, and legal circles. It is true, older historians, such as Hildreth, had pointed out that there had been a sharp struggle over the formation and adoption of the Constitution, and that in the struggle an alignment of economic interests had taken place. It is true that Chief Justice Marshall, in his life of George Washington, had sketched the economic conflict out of which the Constitution sprang. But during the closing years of the nineteenth century this realistic view of the Constitution had been largely submerged in abstract discussions of states' rights and national sovereignty and in formal, logical, and discriminative analyses of judicial opinions. It was admitted, of course, that there had been a bitter conflict over the formation and adoption of the Constitution; but the struggle was usually explained, if explained at all, by reference to the fact that some men cherished states' rights and others favored a strong central government. At the time I began my inquiries the generally prevailing view was that expressed recently by Professor Theodore Clarke Smith: "Former historians had described the struggle over the formation and adoption of the document as a contest between sections ending in a victory of straight-thinking national-minded men over narrower and more local opponents." How some men got to be "national-minded" and "straight-thinking," and others became narrow and local in their ideas did not disturb the thought of scholars who presided over historical writing at the turn of the nineteenth century. Nor were those scholars at much pains to explain whether the term "section," which they freely used, meant a segment of physical geography or a set of social and economic arrangements within a geographic area, conditioned by physical circumstances.

One thing, however, my masters taught me, and that was to go behind the pages of history written by my contemporaries and read "the sources." In applying this method, I read the letters, papers, and documents pertaining to the Constitution written by the men who took part in framing and adopting it. And to my surprise I found that many Fathers of the Republic regarded the conflict over the Constitution as springing essentially out of conflicts of economic interests, which had a certain geographical or sectional distribution. This discovery, coming at a time when such conceptions of history were neglected by writers on history, gave me "the shock of my life." And since this aspect of the Constitution had been so long disregarded, I sought to redress the balance by emphasis, "naturally" perhaps. At all events I called my volume "an economic interpretation of the Constitution." I did not call it "the" economic interpretation, or "the only" interpretation possible to thought. Nor did I pretend that it was "the history" of the formation and adoption of the Constitution. The reader was warned in advance of the theory and the emphasis. No attempt was made to take him off his guard by some plausible formula of completeness and comprehensiveness. I simply sought to bring back into the mental picture of the Constitution those realistic features of economic conflict, stress, and strain, which my masters had, for some reason, left out of it, or thrust far into the background as incidental rather than fundamental.

When my book appeared, it was roundly condemned by conservative Republicans, including ex-President Taft, and praised, with about the same amount of discrimination, by Progressives and others on the left wing. Perhaps no other book on the Constitution has been more severely criticized, and so little read. Perhaps no other book on the subject has been used to justify opinions and projects so utterly beyond its necessary implications. It was employed by a socialist writer to support a plea for an entirely new constitution and by a conservative judge of the United States Supreme Court to justify an attack on a new piece of "social legislation." Some members of the New York Bar Association became so alarmed by the book that they formed a committee and summoned me to appear before it; and, when I declined on the ground that I was not engaged in legal politics or political politics, they treated my reply as a kind of contempt of court. Few took the position occupied by Justice Oliver Wendell Holmes, who once remarked to me that he had not got excited about the book, like some of his colleagues, but had supposed that it was intended to throw light on the nature of the Constitution, and, in his opinion, did so in fact.

Among my historical colleagues the reception accorded the volume varied. Professor William A. Dunning wrote me that he regarded it as "the pure milk of the word," although it would "make the heathen rage." Professor Albert Bushnell Hart declared that it was little short of indecent. Others sought to classify it by calling it "Marxian." Even as late as the year 1934, Professor Theodore Clarke Smith, in an address before the

American Historical Association, expressed this view of the volume, in making it illustrative of a type of historical writing, which is "doctrinaire" and "excludes anything like impartiality." He said: "This is the view that American history, like all history, can and must be explained in economic terms. . . . This idea has its origin, of course, in the Marxian theories." Having made this assertion, Professor Smith turned his scholarly battery upon *An Economic Interpretation of the Constitution.*

Now as a matter of fact there is no reason why an economic interpretation of the Constitution should be more partisan than any other interpretation. It may be employed, to be sure, to condemn one interest in the conflict or another interest, but no such use of it is imposed upon an author by the nature of the interpretation. Indeed an economic analysis may be coldly neutral, and in the pages of this volume no words of condemnation are pronounced upon the men enlisted upon either side of the great controversy which accompanied the formation and adoption of the Constitution. Are the security holders who sought to collect principal and interest through the formation of a stronger government to be treated as guilty of impropriety or praised? That is a question to which the following inquiry is not addressed. An answer to that question belongs to moralists and philosophers, not to students of history as such. If partiality is taken in the customary and accepted sense, it means "leaning to one party or another." Impartiality means the opposite. Then this volume is, strictly speaking, impartial. It supports the conclusion that in the main the men who favored the Constitution were affiliated with certain types of property and economic interest, and that the men who opposed it were affiliated with other types. It does not say that the former were "straight-thinking" and that the latter were "narrow." It applies no moralistic epithets to either party.

On the other hand Professor Smith's statement about the conflict over the Constitution is his *interpretation* of the nature of things, in that it makes the conflict over the Constitution purely psychological in character, unless some economic content is to be given to the term "section." In any event it assumes that straight-thinking and national-mindedness are entities, particularities, or forces, apparently independent of all earthly considerations coming under the head of "economic." It does not say how these entities, particularities, or forces got into American heads. It does not show whether they were imported into the colonies from Europe or sprang up after the colonial epoch closed. It arbitrarily excludes the possibilities that their existence may have been conditioned if not determined by economic interests and activities. It is firm in its exclusion of other interpretations and conceptions. Whoever does not believe that the struggle over the Constitution was a simple contest between the straight-thinking men and narrower and local men of the respective sections is to be cast into outer darkness as "Marxian" or lacking in "impartiality." Is that not a doctrinaire position?

Not only is Professor Smith's position exclusive. It is highly partial. The men who favored the Constitution were "straight-thinking" men. Those who opposed it were "narrower" men. These words certainly may be taken to mean that advocates of the Constitution were wiser men, men of a higher type of mind, than the "narrower" men who opposed it. In a strict sense, of course, straight-thinking may be interpreted as thinking logically. In that case no praise or partiality is necessarily involved. A trained burglar who applies his science to cracking a safe may be more logical than an impulsive night watchman who sacrifices his life in the performance of duty. But in common academic acceptance a logical man is supposed to be superior to the intuitional and emotional man.

Nor is there exactness in such an antithesis as "straight-thinking" and narrowness. Narrowness does not, of necessity, mean lack of straight-thinking. Straight-thinking may be done in a narrow field of thought as well as in a large domain. But there is a true opposition in national-mindedness and local-mindedness, and the student of economic history merely inquires whether the antithesis does not correspond in the main to an economic antagonism. He may accept Professor Smith's psychological antithesis and go beyond it to inquire into its origins. But in so doing he need not ascribe any superior quality of intellect to the one party or the other. To ascribe qualities of mind—high or low—to either party is partiality, dogmatic and doctrinaire partiality. It arbitrarily introduces virtues of intellectual superiority and inferiority into an examination of matters of fact.

In the minds of some, the term "Marxian," imported into the discussion by Professor Smith, means an epithet; and in the minds of others, praise. With neither of these views have I the least concern. For myself I can say that I have never believed that "all history" can or must be "explained" in economic terms, or any other terms. He who really "explains" history must have the attributes ascribed by the theologians to God. It can be "explained," no doubt, to the satisfaction of certain mentalities at certain times, but such explanations are not universally accepted and approved. I confess to have hoped in my youth to find "the causes of things," but I never thought that I had found them. Yet it has seemed to me, and does now, that in the great transformations in society, such as was brought about by the formation and adoption of the Constitution, economic "forces" are primordial or fundamental, and come nearer "explaining" events than any other "forces." Where the configurations and pressures of economic interests are brought into an immediate relation to the event or series of events under consideration, an economic interpretation is effected. Yet, as I said in 1913, on page 18, "It may be that some larger world process is working through each series of historical events; but ultimate causes lie beyond our horizon." If anywhere I have said or written that "all history" can be "explained" in economic terms, I was then suffering from an aberration of the mind.

Nor can I accept as a historical fact Professor Smith's assertion that the economic interpretation of history or my volume on the Constitution had its origin in "Marxian theories." As I point out in Chapter I of my *Economic Basis of Politics,* the germinal idea of class and group conflicts in history appeared in the writings of Aristotle, long before the Christian era, and was known to great writers on politics during the middle ages and modern times. It was expounded by James Madison, in Number X of the *Federalist,* written in defense of the Constitution of the United States, long before Karl Marx was born. Marx seized upon the idea, applied it with rigor, and based predictions upon it, but he did not originate it. Fathers of the American Constitution were well aware of the idea, operated on the hypothesis that it had at least a considerable validity, and expressed it in numerous writings. Whether conflicting economic interests bulk large in contemporary debates over protective tariffs, foreign trade, transportation, industry, commerce, labor, agriculture, and the nature of the Constitution itself, each of our contemporaries may decide on the basis of his experience and knowledge.

Yet at the time this volume was written, I was, in common with all students who professed even a modest competence in modern history, conversant with the theories and writings of Marx. Having read extensively among the writings of the Fathers of the Constitution of the United States and studied Aristotle, Machiavelli, Locke, and other political philosophers, I became all the more interested in Marx when I discovered in his works the ideas which had been cogently expressed by outstanding thinkers and statesmen in the preceding centuries. That interest was deepened when I learned from an inquiry into his student life that he himself had been acquainted with the works of Aristotle, Montesquieu, and other writers of the positive bent before he began to work out his own historical hypothesis. By those who use his name to rally political parties or to frighten Daughters of the American Revolution, students of history concerned with the origins of theories need not be disturbed.

For the reason that this volume was not written for any particular political occasion but designed to illuminate all occasions in which discussion of the Constitution appears, I venture to re-issue it in its original form. It does not "explain" the Constitution. It does not exclude other explanations deemed more satisfactory to the explainers. Whatever its short-comings, the volume does, however, present some indubitable facts pertaining to that great document which will be useful to students of the Constitution and to practitioners engaged in interpreting it. The Constitution was of human origin, immediately at least, and it is now discussed and applied by human beings who find themselves engaged in certain callings, occupations, professions, and interests.

The text of this edition remains unchanged, although I should make minor modifications here and there, were I writing it anew. Two facts, however, unknown to me in 1913, should be added to the record as it stands. Both were called to my attention by Professor James O. Wettereau, who has made important contributions to the history of the period. On page 93, I state that Benjamin Franklin "does not appear to have held any public paper." Evidence to the contrary is now available. In February, 1788, Franklin wrote concerning the public indebtedness: "Such Certificates are low in Value at present, but we hope and believe they will mend, when our new Constitution of Government is established. I lent the old Congress £3000 hard money in Value, and took Certificates promising interest at 6 per cent, but I have received no Interest for several years, and if I were now to sell the principal, I could not get more than 3s 4d for the Pound which is but a sixth part." This adds Franklin to the list on page 150.

The second fact pertains to the formulation of Hamilton's funding system, based on the authority of the Constitution. It was long believed that this system was largely, if not entirely, the child of Hamilton's brain. But two letters found by Professor Wettereau among the Oliver Wolcott Papers in the Connecticut Historical Society indicate an opposite view. Hamilton's First Report on the Public Credit was laid before the House of Representatives on January 9, 1790. In November of the preceding year, William Bingham, "Philadelphia merchant, capitalist, and banker," wrote a long letter to Hamilton, in which he recommended "virtually all of the essential measures subsequently proposed by the Secretary of the Treasury." During the same month of 1789, Stephen Higginson, "mariner, merchant, and broker," of Boston, also wrote a letter to Hamilton advocating measures similar to those laid before Congress by the Secretary of the Treasury, and warning him against the perils of the opposition certain to be raised. Bingham, who was actively engaged in speculating in public securities, asked Hamilton to inform him "how far any of my Sentiments coincide with yours." Whether Hamilton replied is unknown at present, but Thomas Willing, Bingham's father-in-law claimed to have seen Hamilton's "whole price" suggested for funding. These new historical discoveries by Professor Wettereau throw light on the spirit of Hamilton's financial system and his connection with the mercantile and banking interests.

To these notes of confirmation a memorandum of correction should be added. Page 29 may be taken to imply that the "landed aristocracy" of New York was *solidly* opposed to the Constitution, leaving no room for exceptions. Seldom, if ever, is there total class-solidarity in historical conflicts, and Doctor Thomas C. Cochran is entirely right in objecting to the implied generalization. He properly calls attention to the fact that "while the 'Manor Lords' feared land taxes they also held public securities to an extent which made many of them favorable to the establishment of adequate [federal] revenue. Thus while the strength of the Anti-Federalists rested on the landed classes, the most powerful of these landlords were often found in the opposition ranks." Hence, although his interpretation is economic, it corrects a generalization too sweeping in character, and should be properly noted.

Two other *caveats* should be entered. It has been lightly assumed by superficial critics, if not readers of the volume, that I have "accused the members of the Convention of working merely for their own pockets." The falsity of this charge can be seen by reference to page 73 of the original text still standing. There I say clearly: "The only point considered here is: Did they [the members] represent distinct groups whose economic interests they understood and felt in concrete, definite form through their own personal experience with identical property rights, or were they working merely under the guidance of abstract principles of political science?"

It has also been lightly assumed that this volume pretends to show that the form of government established and powers conferred were "determined" in every detail by the conflict of economic interests. Such pretension was never in my mind; nor do I think that it is explicit or implicit in the pages which follow. I have never been able to discover all-pervading determinism in history. In that field of study I find, what Machiavelli found, *virtù, fortuna,* and *necessitá,* although the boundaries between them cannot be sharply delimited. There is determinism, necessity, in the world of political affairs; and it bears a relation to economic interests; otherwise Congress might vote $25,000 a year in present values to every family in the United States, and the Soviet Government might make every Russian rich; but this is not saying that every event, every institution, every personal decision is "determined" by discoverable "causes."

Nevertheless, whoever leaves economic pressures out of history or out of the discussion of public questions is in mortal peril of substituting mythology for reality and confusing issues instead of clarifying them. It was largely by recognizing the power of economic interests in the field of politics and making skillful use of them that the Fathers of the American Constitution placed themselves among the great practicing statesmen of all ages and gave instructions to succeeding generations in the art of government. By the assiduous study of their works and by displaying their courage and their insight into the economic interests underlying all constitutional formalities, men and women of our generation may guarantee the perpetuity of government under law, as distinguished from the arbitrament of force. It is for us, recipients of their heritage, to inquire constantly and persistently, when theories of national power or states' rights are propounded: "What interests are behind them and to whose advantage will changes or the maintenance of old forms accrue?" By refusing to do this we become victims of history—clay in the hands of its makers.

The Economic Conflict over Ratification as Viewed by Contemporaries

Having discovered the nature of the social conflict connected with the formation and adoption of the Constitution, and having shown the probable proportion of the people who participated in the conflict and the several group-interests into which they fell, it is interesting, though not fundamentally important, to inquire whether the leading thinkers of the time observed the nature of the antagonisms present in the process. A full statement of the results of such an inquiry would require far more space than is at command in this volume; and consequently only a few illustrative and representative opinions can be given.

No one can pore for weeks over the letters, newspapers, and pamphlets of the years 1787–1789 without coming to the conclusion that there was a deep-seated conflict between a popular party based on paper money and agrarian interests, and a conservative party centred in the towns and resting on financial, mercantile, and personal property interests generally. It is true that much of the fulmination in pamphlets was concerned with controversies over various features of the Constitution; but those writers who went to the bottom of matters, such as the authors of *The Federalist,* and the more serious Anti-Federalists, gave careful attention to the basic elements in the struggle as well as to the incidental controversial details.

The superficiality of many of the ostensible reasons put forth by the opponents of the Constitution was penetrated by Madison. Writing to Jefferson, in October, 1788, he says: "The little pamphlet herewith inclosed will give you a collective view of the alterations which have been proposed by the State Conventions for the new Constitution. Various and numerous as they appear, they certainly omit many of the true grounds of opposition. The articles relating to Treaties, to paper money, and to contracts, created more enemies than all the errors in the system, positive and negative, put together."

Naturally the more circumspect of the pamphleteers who lent their support to the new system were careful about a too precise alignment of forces, for their strength often lay in the conciliation of opponents rather

than in exciting a more deep-seated antagonism. But even in such conciliatory publications the material advantages to be expected from the
adoption of the Constitution are constantly put forward.

Take, for example, this extract from a mollifying "Address to the Free-
men of America" issued while the Convention was in the midst of its
deliberations: "Let the public creditor, who lent his money to his country,
and the soldier and citizen who yielded their services, come forward next
and contribute their aid to establish an effective federal government. It
is from the united power and resources of America only that they can
expect permanent and substantial justice. . . . Let the citizens of America
who inhabit the western counties of our states fly to a federal power for
protection [against the Indians]. . . . Let the farmer who groans beneath
the weight of direct taxation seek relief from a government whose extensive jurisdiction will enable it to extract the resources of our country by
means of imposts and customs. Let the merchant, who complains of the
restrictions and exclusions imposed upon his vessels by foreign nations,
unite his influence in establishing a power that shall retaliate those
injuries and insure him success in his honest pursuits by a general system of commercial regulations. Let the manufacturer and mechanic,
who are everywhere languishing for want of employment, direct their
eyes to an assembly of the states. It will be in their power only to encourage such arts and manufactures as are essential to the prosperity of our
country."

It is in the literature of the contest in the states where the battle over
ratification was hottest that we find the most frank recognition of the fact
that one class of property interests was in conflict with another. This
recognition appears not so much in attacks on opponents as in appeals
to the groups which have the most at stake in the outcome of the struggle,
although virulent abuse of debtors and paper money advocates is quite
common. Merchants, money lenders, public creditors are constantly
urged to support the Constitution on the ground that their economic
security depends upon the establishment of the new national government.

Perhaps the spirit of the battle over ratification is best reflected in the
creed ironically attributed to each of the contending parties by its opponents. The recipe for an Anti-Federalist essay which indicates in a very
concise way the class-bias that actuated the opponents of the Constitution, ran in this manner: "Wellborn, nine times—Aristocracy, eighteen
times—Liberty of the Press, thirteen times repeated—Liberty of Conscience, once—Negro slavery, once mentioned—Trial by jury, seven
times—Great Men, six times repeated—Mr. Wilson, forty times. . . .—put
them altogether and dish them up at pleasure."

To this sarcastic statement of their doctrines, the Anti-Federalists replied by formulating the "Political Creed of Every Federalist" as follows: "I believe in the infallibility, all-sufficient wisdom, and infinite goodness of the late convention; or in other words, I believe that some men are of so perfect a nature that it is absolutely impossible for them to commit errors or design villainy. I believe that the great body of the people are incapable of judging in their nearest concerns, and that, therefore, they ought to be guided by the opinions of their superiors. . . . I believe that aristocracy is the best form of government. . . . I believe that trial by jury and the freedom of the press ought to be exploded from every wise government. . . . I believe that the new constitution will prove the bulwark of liberty—the balm of misery—the essence of justice—and the astonishment of all mankind. In short, I believe that it is the best form of government which has ever been offered to the world. I believe that to speak, write, read, think, or hear any thing against the proposed government is damnable heresy, execrable rebellion, and high treason against the sovereign majesty of the convention— And lastly I believe that every person who differs from me in belief is an infernal villain. AMEN."

Marshall's Analysis of the Conflict

. . . In fact, from the very beginning of the movement, the most eminent advocates of a new system were aware of the real nature of the struggle which lay before them. They knew that there was a deep-seated antagonism between the "natural aristocracy" and the "turbulent democracy" which was giving the government of Massachusetts trouble. Such an analysis of the difficulty is set forth by Stephen Higginson, a leading Federalist of Boston, in March, 1787: "The people of the interior parts of these states [New England] have by far too much political knowledge and too strong a relish for unrestrained freedom, to be governed by our feeble system, and too little acquaintance with real sound policy or rational freedom and too little virtue to govern themselves. They have become too well acquainted with their own weight in the political scale under such governments as ours and have too high a taste for luxury and dissipation to sit down contented in their proper line, when they see others possessed of much more property than themselves. With these feelings and sentiments they will not be quiet while such distinctions exist as to rank and property; and sensible of their own force, they will not rest easy till they possess the reins of Government and have divided property with their betters, or they shall be compelled by force to submit to their proper stations and mode of living."

Discerning opponents of the Constitution, as well as its advocates, were aware of the alignment of forces in the battle. Rufus King explained to Madison in January, 1788, that the opposition was grounded on antagonism to property rather than to the outward aspects of the new system. "Apprehension that the liberties of the people are in danger," he said, "and a distrust of men of property or education have a more powerful effect upon the minds of our opponents than any specific objections against the Constitution. . . . The opposition complains that the lawyers, judges, clergymen, merchants, and men of education are all in favor of the Constitution—and for that reason they appear to be able to make the worse appear the better cause."

The correctness of King's observation is sustained by a vigorous writer in the Boston Gazette and Country Journal of November 26, 1787, who charges the supporters of the Constitution with attempting to obscure the real nature of the instrument, and enumerates the interests advocating its adoption. "At length," says the writer, "the luminary of intelligence begins to beam its effulgent rays upon this important production; the deceptive mists cast before the eyes of the people by the delusive machinations of its INTERESTED advocates begin to dissipate, as darkness flies before the burning taper. . . . Those furious zealots who are for cramming it down the throats of the people without allowing them either time or opportunity to scan or weigh it in the balance of their intelligences, bear the same marks in their features as those who have been long wishing to erect an aristocracy in THIS COMMONWEALTH—their menacing cry is for a RIGID government, it matters little to them of what kind, provided it answers THAT description. . . . They incessantly declare that none can discover any defect in the system but bankrupts who wish no government and officers of the present government who fear to lose a part of their power. . . . It may not be improper to scan the characters of its most strenuous advocates: it will first be allowed that many undesigning citizens may wish its adoption from the best motives, but these are modest and silent, when compared to the greater number, who endeavor to suppress all attempts for investigations; these violent partizans are for having the people gulp down the gilded pill blindfolded, whole, and without any qualification whatever, these consist generally, of the NOBLE order of C—s, holders of public securities, men of great wealth and expectations of public office, B—k—s and L—y—s: these with their train of dependents from [form] the aristocratick combination."

Probably the most reasoned statement of the antagonism of realty and personalty in its relation to the adoption of the Constitution in Massachusetts was made in the letters of "Cornelius" on December 11 and 18, 1787: "I wish," he said, "there never might be any competition between the landed and the mercantile interests, nor between any different classes of men whatever. Such competition will, however, exist, so long as occasion and opportunity for it is given, and while human nature remains the same that it has ever been. The citizens in the seaport towns are numerous; they live compact; their interests are one; there is a constant connection and intercourse between them; they can, on any occasion, centre their votes where they please. This is not the case with those who are in the landed interest; they are scattered far and wide; they have but little intercourse and connection with each other. . . . I conceive a foundation is laid for throwing the whole power of the federal government into the hands of those who are in the mercantile interest; and for the landed, which is the great interest of this country, to lie unrepresented, forlorn, and without hope. It grieves me to suggest an idea of this kind: But I believe it to be important and not the mere phantom of imagination, or the result of an uneasy and restless disposition."

Connecticut.—There was no such spirited battle of wits over ratification in Connecticut as occurred in Massachusetts. Nevertheless, Ellsworth, in that state, produced a remarkable series of essays in support of the new Constitution which were widely circulated and read. In these papers there is revealed a positive antagonism between agrarianism and personalty, but an attempt is made at conciliation by subtly blending the two interests. Ellsworth opens: "The writer of the following passed the first part of his life in mercantile employments, and by industry and economy acquired a sufficient sum on retiring from trade to purchase and stock a decent plantation, on which he now lives in the state of a farmer. By his present employment he is interested in the prosperity of agriculture and those who derive a support from cultivating the earth. An acquaintance with business has freed him from many prejudices and jealousies which he sees in his neighbors who have not intermingled with mankind nor learned by experience the method of managing an extensive circulating property. Conscious of an honest intention he wishes to address his brethren on some political subjects which now engage the public attention and will in the sequel greatly influence the value of landed property."

The fact that the essential implications of this statement about his primary economic interests being those of a farmer are untrue does not affect the point here raised: Ellsworth recognised that the opposition was agrarian in character, and he simulated the guise of a farmer to conciliate it. Later on Ellsworth classifies the opposition. In the first rank he puts the Tories as leading in resisting the adoption of the Constitution because it would embarrass Great Britain. In the second class, Ellsworth puts those who owe money. "Debtors in desperate circumstances," he says, "who have not resolution to be either honest or industrious will be the next men to take alarm. They have long been upheld by the property of their creditors and the mercy of the public, and daily destroy a thousand honest men who are unsuspicious. Paper money and tender acts is the only atmosphere in which they can breathe and live. This is now so generally known that by being a friend to such measures, a man effectually advertises himself as a bankrupt. . . . There is another kind of people who will be found in the opposition: Men of much self-importance and supposed skill in politics who are not of sufficient consequence to obtain public employment, but can spread jealousies in the little districts of country where they are placed. These are always jealous of men in place and of public measures, and aim at making themselves consequential by distrusting everyone in the higher offices of society. . . . But in the present case men who have lucrative and influential state offices, if they act from principles of self interest will be tempted to oppose an alteration which would doubtless be beneficial to the people. To sink from a controlment of finance or any other great departments of the state, thro' want of ability or opportunity to act a part in the federal system must be a terrifying consideration."

Leaving aside the Tories and office-holders, it is apparent that the element which Ellsworth considers the most weighty in the opposition is the agrarian party. The correctness of his analysis is supported by collateral pieces of evidence. Sharon, one of the leading paper money towns which opposed the ratification of the Constitution in Connecticut had voted to assist Shays and had repeatedly attempted to secure paper emission legislation. In a few letters and speeches against the Constitution the plaintive note of the agrarian is discernible.

The opponents of the Constitution in Connecticut found no skilled champions such as led the fight in Pennsylvania and Massachusetts; and no such spirited discussion took place. The debates in the state ratifying convention were not recorded (save for a few fragments); but the contest in the legislature over the proposition to send delegates to the Philadelphia Convention showed that the resistance came from the smaller agrarian interests similar to those in Rhode Island and Massachusetts which had stood against the whole movement.

Mr. Granger from Suffield was opposed to the proposition to send delegates to Philadelphia because "he conceived it would be disagreeable to his constituents; he thought the liberties of the people would be endangered by it; . . . and concluded by saying that he imagined these things would have a tendency to produce a regal government in this country." Mr. Humphrey from the inland town of Norfolk sided with Mr. Granger and "concluded by saying that he approved the wisdom and policy of Rhode Island in refusing to send delegates to the convention and that the conduct of that state in this particular, was worthy of imitation." Mr. Perkins of Enfield "was opposed to the measure and said that the state would send men that had been delicately bred and who were in affluent circumstances, that could not feel for the people in this day of distress."

New York.—When it is remembered that the greatest piece of argumentation produced by the contest over ratification, *The Federalist,* was directed particularly to the electorate in New York, although widely circulated elsewhere, it will appear a work of supererogation to inquire whether the leaders in that commonwealth understood the precise nature of the social conflict which was being waged. Nevertheless, it may be worth while to present Hamilton's analysis of it. On the side of the Constitution, he placed the "very great weight of influence of the persons who framed it, particularly in the universal popularity of General Washington—the good will of the commercial interest throughout the states which will give all its efforts to the establishment of a government capable of regulating, protecting, and extending the commerce of the Union —the good will of most men of property in the several states who wish a government of the Union able to protect them against domestic violence and the depredations which the democratic spirit is apt to make on property . . . —a strong belief in the people at large of the insufficiency of the present confederation to preserve the existence of the Union."

Over against these forces in favor of the Constitution, Hamilton places the antagonism of some inconsiderable men in office under state governments, the influence of some considerable men playing the part of the demagogue for their own aggrandizement;—"and add to these causes the democratical jealousy of the people which may be alarmed at the appearance of institutions that may seem calculated to place the power of the community in a few hands and raise a few individuals to stations of great pre-eminence."

New Jersey and Delaware.—The speedy ratification of the Constitution in these states gave no time for the development of a sharp antagonism, even had there been an economic basis for it. In the absence of this actual conflict over the Constitution we can hardly expect to find any consideration of the subject by contemporary writers of note.

Pennsylvania.—The opposition between town and country, between personalty and realty in other words, was so marked in this commonwealth during the struggle over the ratification of the Constitution that it was patent to all observers and was the subject of frequent and extensive comment by leaders on both sides. On September 28, 1787, Tench Coxe wrote to Madison describing the disturbance over the resolution in the state legislature calling the ratifying convention, and after reciting the events of the day he added, "It appears from these facts that the Western people [*i.e.* the agrarians] have a good deal of jealousy about the new Constitution and it is very clear that the men who have been used to lead the Constitutional [or radical party] are against it decidedly." A month later Coxe again writes to Madison: "The opposition here has become more open. It is by those leaders of the constitutional [local radical] interest who have acted in concert with the Western interest. The people of the party in the city are chiefly federal, tho' not so I fear in the Counties."

Writing about the same time from Philadelphia to Washington, Gouverneur Morris said: "With respect to this state, I am far from being decided in my opinion that they will consent. It is true that the City and its Neighborhood was enthusiastic in the cause; but I dread the cold and sower temper of the back counties and still more the wicked industry of those who have long habituated themselves to live on the public, and cannot bear the idea of being removed from power and profit of state government which has been and still is the means of supporting themselves, their families, and their dependents." Such comments on the nature of the alignment of forces might be multiplied from the writings of other Federalist leaders in Pennsylvania, but it appears to be unnecessary to say more.

The leaders on the other side were constantly discanting upon the opposition between town and country. The recalcitrant members of the legislature in their protest to the people against the hasty calling of the state convention declared, "We lamented at the time [of the selection of delegates to the national Convention] that a majority of our legislature appointed men to represent this state who were all citizens of Philadelphia, none of them calculated to represent the landed interests of Pennsylvania, and almost all of them of one political party, men who have been uniformly opposed to that [state] constitution for which you have on every occasion manifested your attachment."

. . . It is evident that a considerable number of the voters in Pennsylvania clearly understood the significance of the division of powers created by the Constitution. In a petition circulated and extensively signed by Philadelphia citizens immediately after the completion of the labors of the Convention and directed to the state ratifying convention, the memorialists expressed their approval of the Constitution, and added: "The division of the power of the United States into three branches gives the sincerest satisfaction to a great majority of our citizens, who have long suffered many inconveniences from being governed by a single legislature. All single governments are tyrannies—whether they be lodged in one man—a few men—or a large body of the people."

Maryland.—The contest in Maryland over the ratification was keen and spirited and every side of the question was threshed out in newspaper articles and pamphlets. Through all the controversy ran the recognition of the fact that it was a struggle between debtors and creditors, between people of substance and the agrarians. Alexander Hanson in his considerable tract in favor of the ratification, dedicated to Washington, treats the charge that the Constitution was an instrument of property as worthy of a dignified answer. "You have been told," he says, "that the proposed plan was calculated peculiarly for the rich. In all governments, not merely despotic, the wealthy must, in most things, find an advantage from the possession of that which is too much the end and aim of mankind. In the proposed plan there is nothing like a discrimination in their favor. . . . Is it a just cause of reproach that the Constitution effectually secures property? Or would the objectors introduce a general scramble?"

Recognizing the importance of the interests at stake, another Federalist writer, "Civis," in the Maryland Journal of February 1, 1788, appeals to the voters for delegates to the coming state convention to be circumspect in order to procure the ratification of the Constitution. He laments that "men of property, character, and abilities have too much retired from public employment since the conclusion of the war," but expresses the hope "that, in this all-important crisis, they will again step forth, with a true patriotic ardour, and snatch their dear country from the dreadful and devouring jaws of anarchy and ruin." He cautions the citizens against voting for undesirable persons: "The characters whom I would especially point out as your particular aversion, in the present critical conjuncture, are all those in desperate or embarrassed circumstances, who may have been advocates for paper money, the truck-bill, or insolvent act; and who may expect to escape in the general ruin of the country."

On the other hand many opponents of the Constitution in Maryland definitely declared the contest to be one between property and the people of little substance. Such was practically the view of Luther Martin in basing his resistance on the ground that the new system prevented the states from interfering with property rights. The spirit of this opposition was also well reflected in a reply to the letter of "Civis," mentioned above, which took the form of an ironical appeal to the voters to support only men of property and standing for the coming state convention. "Choose no man in debt," it runs, "because being in debt proves that he wanted understanding to take care of his own affairs. . . . A man in debt can scarcely be honest. . . . Vote for no man who was in favor of paper money, for no *honest* man was for that measure. None but *debtors* and desperate wretches advocated the diabolical scheme. . . . Elect no man who supported the law allowing insolvent debtors to discharge their persons from perpetual imprisonment, by *honestly* delivering up *all* their property to the use of their creditors. The legislature *have* no right to interfere with *private* contracts, and debtors might safely trust to the humanity and clemency of their creditors who will not keep them in gaol all their lives, unless they deserve it. . . . Men of great property are deeply interested in the welfare of the state; and they are the most competent judges of the form of government, best calculated to preserve their property, and such liberties as it is proper for the common and inferior class of people to enjoy. Men of wealth possess natural and acquired understanding, as they manifest by amassing riches, or by keeping and increasing those they derive from their ancestors, and they are best acquainted with the wants, the wishes, and desires of the people, and they are always ready to relieve them in their private and public stations."

Virginia.—Madison remarked that he found in his state "men of intelligence, patriotism, property, and independent circumstances" divided over the ratification of the Constitution although in some other commonwealths men of this stamp were "zealously attached" to the new government. This general reflection is not borne out however by some of his contemporaries. Marshall, as we have noted above, regarded the conflict as being between two rather sharply divided parties, those who favored maintaining public and private rights in their full integrity and those who proposed to attack them through legislation. In fact, Madison himself at a later date declared that "the superiority of abilities" was on the side of the Constitution. Charles Lee claimed that "except a few characters, the members [of the Virginia convention] with the most knowledge and abilities and personal influence are also in favor of the Constitution."

In the opposition Patrick Henry put the whole mass of small farmers. "I believe it to be a fact," he declared in the Virginia convention, "that the great body of yeomanry are in decided opposition to it. I may say with confidence that, for nineteen counties adjacent to each other, nine-tenths of the people are conscientiously opposed to it. I may be mistaken but I give you it as my opinion; and my opinion is founded on personal knowledge in some measure, and other good authority. . . . You have not solid reality—the hearts and hands of the men who are to be governed."

North Carolina.—It would have been strange if the leaders for and against the Constitution in this commonwealth had not taken cognizance of the nature of the conflict they were waging. The popular paper money and debtor party had been powerful and active and had aroused the solicitude of all men of substance; and the representatives of the latter, as practical men, knew what they were doing in supporting an overthrow of the old system. "It is essential to the interests of agriculture and commerce," exclaimed Davie, in the state ratifying convention, "that the hands of the states should be bound from making paper money, instalment laws, and pine-barren acts. By such iniquitous laws the merchant or farmer may be defrauded of a considerable part of his just claims. But in the federal court, real money will be recovered with that speed which is necessary to accommodate the circumstances of individuals." Speaking on the same theme, paper money, Governor Johnston said: "Every man of property—every man of considerable transactions, whether a merchant, planter, mechanic, or of any other condition—must have felt the baneful influence of that currency."

The recognition of the nature of the clash of interests is manifest in scattered correspondence, as well as in speeches. For example, in a letter to Iredell, January 15, 1788, Maclaine says: "In New Hanover county the people if left to themselves are in favor of the change. Some demagogues, a few persons who are in debt, and every public officer, except the clerk of the county court, are decidedly against any change; at least against any that will answer the purpose. Our friend Huske is the loudest man in Wilmington against the new constitution. Whether ambition, or avarice, or a compound of both actuates him I leave you to judge. . . . I expect in a few weeks *The Federalist* in a volume. He is certainly a judicious and ingenious writer, though not well calculated for the common people. . . . Your old friend Huske and Col. Read have joined all the low scoundrels in the County [*i.e.* the country party] and by every underhand means are prejudicing the common people against the new constitution. The former is a candidate for the county."

This conflict between the town and country is explained by Iredell's biographer: "Soon after the [Revolutionary] War commenced a feud between the town of Wilmington and the county of New Hanover. The leading men 'upon 'Change' were either Tories or those whose lukewarmness had provoked suspicion: the agrestic population could but illy brook their prosperity. From that day to the present [1857] the politics of the burgess have been antagonistical to those of the former. The merchants have ever been the predominant class in the borough: daily intercourse has enabled them with facility to form combinations that have given them the control of the moneyed institutions while their patronage has added a potent influence with the press."

South Carolina.—The materials bearing on the ratification of the Constitution in South Carolina which are available to the northern student are relatively scanty. Nevertheless, in view of the marked conflict between the agrarian back-country and the commercial seaboard, it may easily be imagined that it was not unobserved by the leaders in the contest over ratification who championed the respective regions. This antagonism came out in a pamphlet war over the amendment of the state constitution which was being waged about the time of the adoption of the new federal system. In this war, "Appius," the spokesman for the reform party, is reported to have declared that "wealth ought not to be represented; that a rich citizen ought to have fewer votes than his poor neighbor; that wealth should be stripped of as many advantages as possible and it will then have more than enough; and finally, that in giving property the power of protecting itself, government becomes an aristocracy."

"Appius," after this general statement of his theory, then explains wherein the distribution of economic interests engendered antagonism in politics in that state. "The upper and lower countries, have opposite

habits and views in almost every particular. One is accustomed to ex-
pence, the other to frugality. One will be inclined to numerous offices,
large salaries, and an expensive government; the other, from the moderate fortunes of the inhabitants, and their simple way of life will prefer
low taxes, small salaries, and a very frugal civil establishment. One
imports almost every article of consumption and pays for it in produce;
the other is far removed from navigation, has very little to export, and
must therefore supply its own wants. Consequently one will favor commerce, the other manufactures; one wishes slaves, the other will be better
without them." In view of this opposition of interests, "Appius" holds that
there should be a redistribution of representatives which will give the
back-country its proper proportion and enable the majority to rule.

To this argument Ford replies in the language of Federalism. The
rights of property are anterior to constitutions; the state constitution
recognizes and guarantees these rights; the substantial interests of the
minority must be forever immune from attacks by majorities. Otherwise
"the weaker party in society," he declares, "would literally have no right
whatever: neither life, liberty, or property would be guaranteed to them
by the social compact, seeing the majority are not bound by it, but might
destroy the whole and by the same rule any part of it at pleasure. . . .
Virtue and vice would lose their distinction; the most vicious views would
be sanctified if pursued by the greater number, and the most virtuous
resistance punishable in the less. If the principles of justice are derived
from a higher source than human institutions (and who will deny it?) I
contend that the majority have no right to infringe them." Hence, any
change in the system which deprives the seaboard minority of their
preponderance in the state government cannot be too severely repro-
bated.

It can hardly be supposed that an economic antagonism in the state
that was so clearly recognized by publicists in 1794, and that manifested
itself in the vote on the ratification of the Federal Constitution six years
before, was overlooked in the earlier contest.

Indeed, evidence that it was not appears in a pamphlet written in
defence of the Constitution by Dr. David Ramsay, who was afterward a
member of the ratifying convention in South Carolina. He particularly
warns his fellow-citizens against the debtor element. "Be on your guard,"
he says, "against the misrepresentations of men who are involved in
debt; such may wish to see the Constitution rejected because of the following clause, 'no state shall emit bills of credit, make anything but gold
and silver coin a tender in payment of debts, pass any ex post facto law,
or law impairing the obligation of contracts.' This will doubtless bear
hard on debtors who wish to defraud their creditors, but it will be real
service to the honest part of the community. Examine well the characters

and circumstances of men who are averse to the new constitution. Perhaps you will find that the above clause is the real ground of the opposition of some of them, though they may artfully cover it with a splendid profession of zeal for state privileges and general liberty."

Georgia.—The speedy and unanimous ratification of the Constitution in Georgia seems to have prevented any very vigorous pamphleteering on the question. Indeed, the energies of the state were being strained to the limit in preparing for defence against the Indians, and there was little time for theorizing. Foreign invasion generally silences domestic discord.

Conclusions

At the close of this long and arid survey—partaking of the nature of catalogue—it seems worth while to bring together the important conclusions for political science which the data presented appear to warrant.

The movement for the Constitution of the United States was originated and carried through principally by four groups of personalty interests which had been adversely affected under the Articles of Confederation: money, public securities, manufactures, and trade and shipping.

The first firm steps toward the formation of the Constitution were taken by a small and active group of men immediately interested through their personal possessions in the outcome of their labors.

No popular vote was taken directly or indirectly on the proposition to call the Convention which drafted the Constitution.

A large propertyless mass was, under the prevailing suffrage qualifications, excluded at the outset from participation (through representatives) in the work of framing the Constitution.

The members of the Philadelphia Convention which drafted the Constitution were, with a few exceptions, immediately, directly, and personally interested in, and derived economic advantages from, the establishment of the new system.

The Constitution was essentially an economic document based upon the concept that the fundamental private rights of property are anterior to government and morally beyond the reach of popular majorities.

The major portion of the members of the Convention are on record as recognizing the claim of property to a special and defensive position in the Constitution.

In the ratification of the Constitution, about three-fourths of the adult males failed to vote on the question, having abstained from the elections at which delegates to the state conventions were chosen, either on account of their indifference or their disfranchisement by property qualifications.

The Constitution was ratified by a vote of probably not more than one-sixth of the adult males.

It is questionable whether a majority of the voters participating in the elections for the state conventions in New York, Massachusetts, New Hampshire, Virginia, and South Carolina, actually approved the ratification of the Constitution.

The leaders who supported the Constitution in the ratifying conventions represented the same economic groups as the members of the Philadelphia Convention; and in a large number of instances they were also directly and personally interested in the outcome of their efforts.

In the ratification, it became manifest that the line of cleavage for and against the Constitution was between substantial personalty interests on the one hand and the small farming and debtor interests on the other.

The Constitution was not created by "the whole people" as the jurists have said; neither was it created by "the states" as Southern nullifiers long contended; but it was the work of a consolidated group whose interests knew no state boundaries and were truly national in their scope.

Perry Miller

1905—1963

14

A distinction may be made between historiographic influence and achievement. This becomes apparent in any analysis of the work of Perry Miller, for, as Edmund Morgan has pointed out, Miller's "influence was incommensurate with his genius." And yet, since genius cannot be measured or contained, neither may its influence be easily gauged. What seems clear is that "it is possible today," as Michael McGiffert puts it, "to speak of American Puritan studies as a field of scholarship, and to appraise its estate and activity, because Perry Miller, above all others, made the American Puritans studiable." In works of enormous erudition and pervasive influence, Perry Miller rescued from myth and saved for true historical contemplation a vital element in America's past: the Puritan mind and heritage.

It is perhaps strange that Miller, an atheist, should have undertaken such a task; but as he said of the Puritans, one must penetrate surfaces to gain understanding. Miller was born in 1905, the son of a doctor in Chicago. The family was well off and mildly religious, and Miller attended private preparatory schools before entering the University of Chicago in 1922. He soon abandoned his studies, however, and from 1923 until 1926 roamed about the world in quest of adventure, trying his hand at various occupations, including professional acting in New York and service in the merchant marine. In the latter role, while in the Congo, Miller experienced, as he put it, "a sudden epiphany (if the word be not too strong) of the pressing necessity for expounding my America to the twentieth century. . . . To bring into conjunction a minute event in the history of historiography with a great one: it was given to Edward Gibbon to sit disconsolate amid the ruins of the Capitol at Rome, and to have thrust upon him the 'laborious work' of *The Decline and Fall* while listening to barefooted friars chanting responses in the former temple of Jupiter. It was given to me, equally disconsolate on the edge of a jungle of central Africa, to have thrust upon me the mission of expounding what I took to be the innermost propulsion of the United States, while supervising, in that barbaric tropic, the unloading of drums of case oil flowing out of the inexhaustible wilderness of America."

Miller returned to America to complete his formal education. Once "back in the security of a graduate school," he took up his self-appointed task. He thought it necessary to begin with the Puritan migration, despite the chronological priority of Virginia ("What I wanted was a coherence with which I could coherently begin"), and despite the advice of mentors who warned him that Puritan studies were a winnowed harvest. He attained the Ph.D. in 1931, at Harvard, and in 1933 published his first interpretative effort, *Orthodoxy in Massachusetts, 1630–1650.* After receiving his doctorate, Miller stayed on at Harvard as a professor of American literature. During World War II, he served with distinction in the Office of Strategic Services. He returned to Harvard after the war and resumed his scholarship, working until his death in 1963 on Puritanism and on "the life of the mind in America" (the title of his last, posthumously published work).

Miller's most substantial works, the basis of his reputation and influence, are *The New England Mind: The Seventeenth Century* (1939) and *The New England Mind: From Colony to Province* (1953). In those books and in many essays, anthologies, and biographical studies, Miller pressed his claim that America—that is, American historians—had failed to understand the Puritans and their thought and had consequently failed to perceive "the innermost propulsion of the United States." Miller was unabashedly, even arrogantly, a historian of ideas, of "mind," by which he meant "what was said and done publicly."

It is important to note the historiographic milieu in which Miller announced and implemented his program. The "Progressive" historians of the first decades of the twentieth century had stressed not ideas or thought but material factors as basic to historical explanations. Frederick Jackson Turner's frontier thesis, Charles A. Beard's economic and interest-group interpretations, and Merle Curti's emphasis on environmental conditions such as economic interests and the structure of capitalism are typical of the Progressivist tendency to relegate ideas to a secondary, derivative role in history. Such historians approached the Puritans with scant regard for their thought, emphasizing instead their economic and social conditions and their response to the impact of the American wilderness. At the same time, journalists like H. L. Mencken were defining as "Puritan" anything that smacked of social repression, political reaction, and anti-intellectualism. Prohibition thus represented the triumph of the Puritan message.

A reaction to this historical-journalistic denigration set in during the late 1920's and early 1930's. The Great Depression, the rise of totalitarianism, and the increasingly apparent power of political and social thought in impelling events and men all combined to cast doubt upon Progressivist historical views—Charles Beard himself revised his early deterministic interpretations. In the face of such developments, and following the isolated pioneering efforts of Moses Coit Tyler and Barrett Wendell, historians moved toward a reassessment of the conventional interpretation of Puritanism. Samuel Eliot Morison was the foremost of these early revisionists. He consciously attempted "to counteract the disparaging and, for the most part, inaccurate accounts of New England colonial culture that had been published during the previous forty years." In such works as *Builders of the Bay Colony* (1930) and *The Intellectual Life of Colonial New England* (published in 1936 as *The Puritan Pronaos*), he elaborated his opinion, "arrived at by considerable reading of what the puritans wrote, . . . that religion, not economics or politics, was the center and focus of the puritan dissatisfaction with England, and the puritan migration to New England." His sound scholarship and vigorous advocacy of a new, more truly historical conception of the Puritan world brought many young historians to the side of the revisionists. One of his students at Harvard was Perry Miller.

Responding, as he put it, "stubbornly" and "obstinately" to the "perverse tendencies" of the times and zealously to the example of his teacher, Miller plunged into Puritan studies as into combat. In his first published work, *Orthodoxy in Massachusetts* (1933), Miller defiantly announced that he had "attempted to tell of a great folk movement with an utter disregard of the economic and social factors," and proclaimed himself "so very naïve as to believe that the way men think has some influence upon their actions." As part of his manifesto against historians who neglected ideas, he later wrote, "I have difficulty imagining that anyone can be a historian without realizing that history itself is part of the life of the mind; hence I have been compelled to insist that the mind of man is the basic factor in human history."

In following through on this conviction, Miller undertook in *The New England Mind: The Seventeenth Century* an exhaustive "topical analysis of various leading ideas in colonial New England." He eschewed chronological, developmental, and morphological elements and instead concentrated on the "structure" and "anatomy" of the Puritan mind, a project, he wrote, "made . . . practicable by the fact that the first three generations in New England paid almost unbroken allegiance to a unified body of thought." He offered the work "as a chapter in the history of ideas" and "deliberately avoided giving more than passing notice to the social or economic influences." This was in keeping with his purpose, as he elsewhere expressed it: "I am not, let me insist, concerned with events, but with ideas, for history is often more instructive as it considers what men conceived they were doing rather than what, in brute fact, they did." Miller thus took the Puritans and especially their thought seriously, albeit not uncritically and certainly not out of pious devotion to them. As he wrote: "I wholeheartedly admire the integrity and profundity of the Puritan character, but . . . I am far from sharing in its code or from finding delight in its every aspect."

One of the side results of Miller's inquiry—and in this he was following the lead of Kenneth Murdock and Samuel Morison—was to humanize the Puritans: "In everyday life Puritanism did not mean that because Puritans were virtuous there should be no more cakes and ale." But Miller was most interested in analyzing the sources of Puritanism—Augustinianism, scholasticism, the works of English divines, Renaissance influences. He sought to show how the study of Puritan thought in its interrelations and significance "makes some contribution to our study of general intellectual history." To do this he had to immerse himself in the forbidding, alien, difficult, and prolific literature of Puritanism. He felt it necessary to quote from that literature at great length and to phrase Puritan ideas in the language of the times. His was an effort not only to understand Puritan concepts themselves but "to get underneath them," to "read for meanings far below the surface," to present them "as being comprehensible." One of his methods, as Donald Fleming observes, was "to take the men of the past at their word, but patiently to explicate this word, turn it about till every facet caught the light—perhaps for the first time in centuries—and then implicate it in a vanished or unsuspected context of ideas." It was such relentless probing that led Edmund Morgan to note that at Miller's level of analysis "thought will not bear leading." Perhaps only an atheist (or a Puritan) can thrive in the stern absolutes of Puritan theology. Certainly, few scholars have followed Miller's labyrinthine way.

The same intensity of purpose, the same exhaustive erudition, the same pursuit of the Puritans' meaning appeared in Miller's second volume on *The New England Mind: From Colony to Province*. In that volume, however, Miller dealt not with the unified structure of Puritan thought but rather its chronologically sequential "declension," "confusion," and "splintering." He maintained that these were not the results of economic development, of increased control by man of nature, of the new science, or of flourishing trade and commerce, although all of these impinged upon the New England mind. (He would say, for instance, that "it is evident that from the end of the seventeenth century down at least to the close of the nineteenth, the history of New England's 'mind' was written as much, if not more, by the actions of merchants and men of business as in the publications of theologians and politicians.") He rather argued, "unrepentantly, defiantly," that "the terms of Puritan thinking do not progressively become poorer tools than were the concepts of the founders for the recording of social change."

> On the contrary, they are increasingly the instruments through which the people strove to cope with a bewildering reality. Unless we also approach that buzzing factuality through a comprehension of these ideas, it becomes even more a tumultuous chaos for us than it was for those caught in the blizzard. Unless we can do this,

the writing of history ceases to be a work of the mind. But to proceed successfully from the intellectual to the social pattern requires of the historian—and the reader of histories—a sensitivity to the nuances of ideas at least as delicate as that of the best intellects in the period.

Such was the interpretative framework that Miller maintained throughout his work. Much as he may have noted environmental and social factors in his later works (so much so that Robert Middlekauff could write that Miller "ended as the historian of a culture"), he remained a historian of thought. As he wrote of the Puritan jeremiads:

> These ceremonial discourses do provide, taken in sequence, a chronology of social evolution; in them everything the historian pieces together out of records and documents is faithfully mirrored. They tell the story, and tell it coherently, of a society which was founded by men dedicated, in unity and simplicity, to realizing on earth eternal and immutable principles—and which progressively became involved with fishing, trade, and settlement. They constitute a chapter in the emergence of the capitalist mentality, showing how intelligence copes with—or more cogently, how it fails to cope with—a change it simultaneously desires and abhors.

He continued the history of Puritan thought in the eighteenth century with his stimulating, if perverse, intellectual biography of Jonathan Edwards, offering the view that Edwards "was so much ahead of his time that our own can hardly be said to have caught up with him. . . . Edwards was a puritan who would not permit mankind to evade the unending ordeal and the continuing agony of liberty."

Neither Vernon Parrington nor H. L. Mencken would have recognized this version of the Puritan Edwards, nor have all historians since Miller wrote accepted his interpretation either of Edwards or of Puritanism. For there is an element of perversity in Miller's act of resuscitating the Puritan mind and world. Some scholars question whether the Puritans in fact speak directly to modern man's predicament. Others doubt that every important experience finds expression in words and that verbalizations are always truly indicative of social realities. Miller was never clear on the point at which apostates become better witnesses than the orthodox, and he himself recognized the dangers attendant upon the search for "hidden meanings" even while he sought them.

Perhaps most important, it is arguable that Miller, in his search for coherence, in carrying out his "mission," made the Puritans and their thought more important than they in fact were. "Had he turned aside to examine the forces he slighted," Philip Haffender writes, "he must have puzzled less why in the end American thought 'betrayed itself' in moving from Puritanism to a wonder at Nature." Finally, if the Progressive historians looked forward, seeing progress, Miller looked backward, seeing "declension" interspersed with re-enactments and revivals. "His effort to pursue systematically 'the meaning of America' had nowhere to go," John Higham notes, "for he never established a terminus ad quem. Tragically, Miller's later work splintered into fragments, as the Puritan system had done in his brilliant account of it."

This being said, it remains undeniable that Miller was a great historian and, in the period after World War II, increasingly influential. American scholars have in general confirmed his stress on the importance of the Puritans. They have followed up his interpretations but perhaps with more regard to social and economic issues than Miller would have found congenial. Edmund Morgan, Miller's most renowned pupil, has suggested, for example, "another approach" to New England Puritanism, entailing a "town by town and church by church" inquiry into land ownership, patterns of habitation, taxation, church membership, and family structure, in order to establish firmer generalizations upon known specifics. Whatever new approaches are followed, it seems clear that Miller has imperishably established the necessity of dealing with the thought of Puritan America if historians, Americans, are to understand their own history.

Selected Bibliography

Perhaps the best introduction to Miller's historiography may be found in the several prefaces he wrote for the various editions of *The New England Mind: The Seventeenth Century* and *From Colony to Province*, and in the preface and headnotes he wrote for his collection of essays *Errand into the Wilderness* (1956). A number of Miller's colleagues and former students paid tribute to him and to his work in a series of essays collected as "Perry Miller and the American Mind" in *The Harvard Review*, II: 2 (1964). Edmund S. Morgan's "The Historians of Early New England," in *The Reinterpretation of American History*, edited by Ray Allen Billington (1968), contains a detailed discussion of Miller's contributions to Puritan historiography. Peter Gay, *A Loss of Mastery: Puritan Historians in Colonial America* (1966), includes a bibliographic essay on historiography in general and on the historians and historiography of the Puritans in particular. He criticizes Miller's work but concludes: "Every student of American Puritanism must begin with Miller, even if he does not end with him." Michael McGiffert, "American Puritan Studies in the 1960's," *William and Mary Quarterly*, XXXIX (January, 1970), 36–67, documents Miller's influence.

An interesting assessment of Miller's interpretations is George M. Marsden's article "Perry Miller's Rehabilitation of the Puritans: A Critique," *Church History*, 39:1 (March, 1970), 91–105. Although observing that "the vast majority of what Miller says about the Puritan mind still stands," Marsden criticizes Miller's comparative neglect of biblical sources, his omission of any discussion "of the person and work of Christ" in Puritan thought, and his attempt to dissociate the Puritans from Calvinism, all of which Marsden believes derived from Miller's desire to "rehabilitate" the Puritans in the eyes of the twentieth century. It is an interesting, provocative essay. John Higham, *Writing American History: Essays on Modern Scholarship* (1970), and Robert Allen Skotheim, *American Intellectual Histories and Historians* (1966), are both perceptive, with Skotheim more detailed, on Miller's work and milieu. David A. Hollinger, "Perry Miller and Philosophical History," *History and Theory,* VII (1968), 189–202; Robert Middlekauff, "Perry Miller," *Pastmasters: Some Essays on American Historians;* and Gene Wise, "Implicit Irony in Perry Miller's *New England Mind," The Journal of the History of Ideas,* 29 (1968), 579–600, are all helpful.

THE NEW ENGLAND MIND: THE SEVENTEENTH CENTURY

The Augustinian Strain of Piety

Four hundred years after Christ, Augustine of Hippo enacted an arduous pilgrimage, driven by his insatiable quest for satisfactions that nothing of this earth was ever able to supply him. Even while deluding himself with Manichean palliatives, he cried out,

> O Truth, Truth! how inwardly even then did the marrow of my soul pant after Thee, when they frequently, and in a multiplicity of ways, and in numerous and huge books, sounded out Thy name to me, though it was but a voice . . . I hungered and thirsted not even after those first works of Thine, but after Thee Thyself, the Truth . . . Yet they still served up to me in those dishes glowing phantasies, than which better were it to love this very sun . . . than those illusions which deceive the mind through the eye.

Twelve hundred years later, in a rude wooden structure by the Connecticut River, built in a newly cleared field that had just been named Hartford, Thomas Hooker preached to faithful Englishmen who had crossed an ocean that they might have the privilege of hearing him. He did not speak in the first person, for he was not uttering *Confessions,* but he spoke of what he and every one of his congregation could attest from their own experience. In his words sounded once more the accents of St. Augustine.

> *Sin is truly cross and opposite* . . . to the Nature of the soul in a right sense: Look at the soul in respect of the end for which it was created, and that impression which is enstamped and left upon it unto this day, whereby it's restlessly carried in the search, and for the procurement of that good for which it was made . . . The soul was made for an end, and good, and therefore for a better than it self, therefore for God, therefore to enjoy union with him, and communion with those blessed excellencies of his . . . this impression remains still upon the soul, though the work thereof is wholly prejudiced . . . Being possessed with sin,

the Judgment is blinded and deluded that it mistakes utterly, and perceives not this good, and so pursues other things in the room of it, yet restless and unsatisfied in what it hath, and attains, but it hath not that for which it was made.

Thus, when the wave of religious assertion which we call Puritanism is considered in the broad perspective of Christian history, it appears no longer as a unique phenomenon, peculiar to England of the seventeenth century, but as one more instance of a recurrent spiritual answer to interrogations eternally posed by human existence. The peculiar accidents of time and place did indeed entice Puritanism into entertaining a variety of ideas which were the features of its epoch, yet it was animated by a spirit that was not peculiar to the seventeenth century or to East Anglia and New England. The major part of this volume will necessarily be occupied with local and temporal characteristics, but these were not the substance or the soul of the movement. As Puritanism developed it became more and more encased in technical jargon and increasingly distracted by economic and social issues; as it wanted it partook more of the qualities of one age and became less of a gospel for all time. But as long as it remained alive, its real being was not in its doctrines but behind them; the impetus came from an urgent sense of man's predicament, from a mood so deep that it could never be completely articulated. Inside the shell of its theology and beneath the surface coloring of its political theory, Puritanism was yet another manifestation of a piety to which some men are probably always inclined and which in certain conjunctions appeals irresistibly to large numbers of exceptionally vigorous spirits.

I venture to call this piety Augustinian, not because it depended directly upon Augustine—though one might demonstrate that he exerted the greatest single influence upon Puritan thought next to that of the Bible itself, and in reality a greater one than did John Calvin—nor because Puritan thought and Augustine's harmonize in every particular. Some aspects of his work, his defense of the authority of the church and of the magical efficacy of the sacraments, were ignored by Puritans as by other Protestants. I call it Augustinian simply because Augustine is the arch-exemplar of a religious frame of mind of which Puritanism is only one instance out of many in fifteen hundred years of religious history. For a number of reasons many persons in late sixteenth-century England found themselves looking upon the problems of life very nearly as Augustine had viewed them, and, for reasons still difficult to expound, the number of such persons increased during the next six or seven decades. In the 1630's some twenty thousand of them, avowedly inspired by their religious views, settled New England and thus served to leave the impress of Augustine upon the American character. In England, as these spirits became more numerous, they came into conflict with other Englishmen, some of whom were certainly no less pious and no less Christian, but in very different fashions. When Puritans debated with Richard Hooker, the apologist of the Anglican church, they spoke at cross-purposes, for his intellectual affinities were entirely with Thomas Aquinas and scholastic tradition. The Puritans also were scholastics, but though they and Richard Hooker might use the same terms, their emphases were irreconcilable, and as between the two there can be no doubt that in the writings of Hooker's enemies we shall find the turn of mind and sense of values, even sometimes the very accent, of Augustine. There survive hundreds of Puritan diaries and thousands of Puritan sermons, but we can read the inward meaning of them all in the *Confessions.*

Puritan theology was an effort to externalize and systematize this subjective mood. Piety was the inspiration for Puritan heroism and the impetus in the charge of Puritan Ironsides; it also made sharp the edge of Puritan cruelty and justified the Puritan in his persecution of disagreement. It inspired Puritan idealism and encouraged Puritan snobbery. It was something that men either had or had not, it could not be taught or acquired. It was foolishness and fanaticism to their opponents, but to themselves it was life eternal. Surely most of the first settlers of New England had it; in later generations most of those who did not have it pretended to it. It blazed most clearly and most fiercely in the person of Jonathan Edwards, but Emerson was illuminated, though from afar, by its rays, and it smoldered in the recesses of Hawthorne's intuitions. It cannot be portrayed by description; to be presented adequately there is need for a Puritan who is also a dramatic artist, and Bunyan alone fulfills the two requirements. But in order that we may pursue the story of expression in New England, that we may find larger meanings in the formal intellectual developments, it has seemed advisable to attempt a description of this piety. The subsequent narrative will, I hope, take on added significance as an episode in the history of humanity if we can first of all conceive, even though we do not share, the living reality of the spirit that motivated this particular group of men. Thus I am here endeavoring to portray the piety rather than the abstract theology in which it was embodied, to present it not in the dry metaphysics of scholastic divines, but in such plain statements, thrown deliberately into the present tense, as the most scholastic of the clergy could utter, fortunately, in their less controversial moods. I shall undoubtedly do the material a certain violence by speaking of the sharply defined concepts of systematic divinity in the looser and vaguer language of human passion; yet the great structure of the Puritan creed, ostensibly erected upon the foundation of logic, will have meaning to most students today only when they perceive that it rested upon a deep-lying conviction that the universe conformed to a definite, ascertainable truth, and that human existence was to be had only upon the terms imposed by this truth.

Such a chapter as I am now attempting could never have been written by any true Puritan, for I am seeking to delineate the inner core of Puritan sensibility apart from the dialectic and the doctrine. In Puritan life the two were never so separated; they were indeed inseparable, for systematic theology, now become wearisome to the majority of men, provided Puritans with completely satisfying symbols; it dramatized the needs of the soul exactly as does some great poem or work of art. The religious emotion could not have existed, for them at least, except within the framework of dogma. Although we, starting from other assumptions and thinking as historians rather than as Puritans, may now ask what underlay the doctrine of predestination before we undertake to trace its evolution through the next two centuries, for Puritans themselves such a dissociation of the meaning from the formula was inconceivable. They saw no opposition between the spirit of religion and the letter of theology, between faith and its intellectualization, and they would have found no sense whatsoever in modern contentions that the words and parables of Christ may be understood without reference to an organized body of abstractions. It should also be confessed at once that many of the statements made in this chapter will be found at variance with the later sections. This is not to be wondered at when the nature of theology, and more particularly of theologians, is considered. Puritan sensibility was truly unified and coherent; but it was articulated only in dogmas and logical deductions. Dogmas can easily become severed from their emotional background, even by those who believe in them most passionately, whereupon they often become counters in an intricate intellectual chess game and lose all semblance of their original meaning. The effort to trace these permutations is triply difficult because transformation may come through a subtle shift in emotional connotation, or the same connotation may be preserved within a gradual reformulation of the doctrine, or else there may be a step-by-step progression in both signification and doctrine. It is not surprising, therefore, that among the basic assurances of early seventeenth-century Puritanism, after the Protestant cause had already been argued for a century, there should have been some that did not wholly correspond to the verbal symbols. Finally, we must remember that religion was not the sole, though it was indeed the predominant interest of the Puritans. They were skilled in many sciences besides theology, and they inevitably drew ideas from these sources, sometimes deliberately, more often unwittingly. We shall find that such ideas existed in their minds in more or less happy fusion with their religious convictions, and that when there was latent opposition among them, the Puritans themselves were at best only dimly aware of it. These considerations are almost too elementary to need restatement; still, they indicate cautions to be observed as we seek for a definition of Puritan piety, of the temperamental bias behind the thought, before we undertake to examine the thought itself.

It would, however, be a grave mistake to regard Puritan piety solely as an affair of temperament. We may declare that Puritans universalized their own neurasthenia; they themselves believed that their fears and anxieties came from clear-eyed perception of things as they are. We may say that they derived their ideas from the Bible, from Augustine and Calvin, Petrus Ramus and William Perkins, and that they were influenced by such and such factors in the environment. They believed that, the facts being what they are, one deduction alone was possible. The facts were in the Bible, which was of course the Word of God, but they were also in experience, and a man did not need the sermons of a godly minister to perceive the terms upon which all men struggle through existence; he needed merely to look about him. "Look," says the Puritan preacher, the doctrine is "as in nature, reason teacheth and experience evidenceth"; to deny it "is to go against the experience of all ages, the common sense of all men." It is obvious that man dwells in a splendid universe, a magnificent expanse of earth and sky and heavens, which manifestly is built upon a majestic plan, maintains some mighty design, though man himself cannot grasp it. Yet for him it is not a pleasant or satisfying world. In his few moments of respite from labor or from his enemies, he dreams that this very universe might indeed be perfect, its laws operating just as now they seem to do, and yet he and it somehow be in full accord. The very ease with which he can frame this image to himself makes reality all the more mocking; the world does give men food and drink, but it gives grudgingly, and when "the world says, peace, peace, then suddenly destruction comes upon them as a whirlwind." It is only too clear that man is not at home within this universe, and yet that he is not good enough to deserve a better; he is out of touch with the grand harmony, he is an incongruous being amid the creatures, a blemish and a blot upon the face of nature. There is the majestical roof, fretted with golden fire, and likewise there is man, a noble work that delights not himself. It is certain that the works of God "were all Good and Beautiful as they came out of his Hands," but equally certain that some deed of man "has put all out of Order, and has brought Confusion and Desolation on the works of God." There are moments of vision when the living spirit seems to circulate in his veins, when man is in accord with the totality of things, when his life ceases to be a burden to him and separateness is ecstatically overcome by mysterious participation in the whole. In such moments he has intimations of rightness, of a state of being in which he and his environment achieve perfect harmony, just as in his imagination he has fancied that once he did dwell in paradise. When these moments have passed he endeavors to live by their fading light, struggling against imperfection in the memory of their perfection, or else he falls back, wearied and rebellious, into cynicism and acrimony. All about him he sees men without this illumination, exemplifying the horrors of their detached and forlorn condition. They murder, malign, and betray each other, they are not to be relied upon, they wear themselves out in the chains of lust, their lives have no meaning, their virtues are pretenses and their vices unprofitable. What wonder that we see exorbitancies and confusions in human societies, "when fools and madmen have gotten the reins in their necks, and act all their own pleasure without any control"? Mortals pursue illusions, and success inspires only disgust or despair. They seek forgetfulness in idolatries and narcotics, or delude themselves in sophistical reasonings, and they die at last cursing the day they were born or clutching at the clay feet of their superstitions. Puritans did not believe that they saw things in these terms merely because they were victims of melancholia, but because such things were there to be seen. The so-called "Five Points" of Calvinism were simply a scholastical fashion of saying this much, and to living Calvinists they did not signify five abstract dicta, but a description of the plight of humanity.

The ultimate reason of all things they called God, the dream of a possible harmony between man and his environment they named Eden, the actual fact of disharmony they denominated sin, the moment of illumination was to them divine grace, the effort to live in the strength of that illumination was faith, and the failure to abide by it was reprobation. The heart of this piety was its sense of the overwhelming anguish to which man is always subject, and its appeal to anguish-torn humanity has always been its promise of comfort and of ultimate triumph. The Augustinian strain of piety flows from man's desire to transcend his imperfect self, to open channels for the influx of an energy which pervades the world, but with which he himself is inadequately supplied. It takes flight from the realization that the natural man, standing alone in the universe, is not only minute and insignificant, but completely out of touch with both justice and beauty. It cries out for forgiveness of the sins by which he has cut himself off from full and joyous participation. It proceeds upon the indomitable conviction that man, a part of created being, must once have been happy, though now he is everywhere miserable. It draws sustenance from the moments of exaltation in which glimpses of the original happiness are attained, a bliss which, though seen but faintly, extinguishes by contrast all other delights. It finds the infinite variety of the world's misery reducible to a concrete problem, the relation of the individual to the One. The substance of Augustine's message is this: "Deum et animam scire cupio. Nihilne plus? Nihil omnino."

If man once achieved knowledge of God and of his soul, the answer to all
other questions would soon follow. The irrepressible demand of the soul
for this knowledge is the driving force of the piety. On the one hand, the
facts are those ordained by a just God; on the other hand, there are the
desires of the soul. The soul must be satisfied, but the facts cannot be
denied. There can be no separating the attainment of happiness from the
attainment of truth. Solutions which pass lightly over the unpleasant or
ignore intractable realities are doomed to failure; so also are those in
which the aspirations of the spirit are given insubstantial answers.
Wherever the spokesmen for this strain of piety appear, whether in fifth-
century Rome or seventeenth-century New England, this is the burden
of their sermon, the substance of assertion and the problem for resolution. To the extent that the Puritan generations in New England were
able to think and to express their thought, this was the inevitable preoccupation of their discourse.

Long before the seventeenth century, theologians had discovered that
the endeavor to formulate this piety centered upon certain fundamental
conceptions: God, sin, and regeneration. Each of these ideas received
elaborate exposition in the creeds, confessions, and institutes that
streamed from the inexhaustible inkwells of Protestant writers; each of
them was divided into sub-doctrines, which in turn were sorted into still
further theological ramifications. Meanwhile, the basic ideas in their
essential meanings remained simple and inviolate. "God" was a word to
stand for the majesty and perfection which gleam through the fabric of
the world; He was Being, hardly apprehensible to man, yet whose existence man must posit, not so much as *a* being but as *The* Being, the
beginning of things and the sustainer, the principle of universal harmony and the guide. "Sin" was in effect a way of setting forth disharmony, of describing man's inability to live decently, his cruelties and his
crimes, and also a way of accounting for the accidents, the diseases, and
the sorrows which every day befall the good and the bad. On the definition of "regeneration" Protestants expended their greatest ingenuity and
differed among themselves most furiously, exemplifying in their controversies all the vindictiveness which they deplored in other men as an
evidence of innate depravity. Yet to all Protestants the general conception was the same; it meant substantially that there existed a way in
which supernal beauty could be carried across the gulf of separation. It
was an inward experience in which the disorder of the universe was
righted, when at least some men were brought into harmony with the
divine plan. It was the solution to the double problem of religion, reconciling the soul to fact and yet satisfying its desires. It joined God and man,
the whole and the particle. God reached out to man with His grace, man
reached out to God with his faith. Regeneration meant the repose and the

happiness toward which all men grope, because God "is the most pure, perfect, universall, primary, unchangeable, communicative, desirable, and delightfull good: the efficient, patterne, and utmost end *of all good;* without whom there is neither naturall, morall, nor spirituall good in any creature." All men seek the good, but only those who in unforgettable moments are ravished by it ever come to know it.

Since these three conceptions may be called the essentials of any Augustinian and Puritan point of view, our discussion of the piety can perhaps proceed most advantageously by considering them in turn. Once again, at the risk of needless repetition, I should remark that we are not here dealing with the verbal propositions through which the ideas were embodied in technical handbooks, but for the moment we are seeking to understand, as far as we can without resorting to sanctimonious and hackneyed phrases, with what emotional connotations the three beliefs were invested, what they meant, not so much as speculation, but as ever present realities to men of this particular piety, and especially to men in seventeenth-century New England.

God

Puritan thinking on the subject of the Deity always confronted the initial difficulty that in one sense thinking about Him was impossible. The Puritan God is entirely incomprehensible to man. The Puritan system rests, in the final analysis, upon something that cannot be systematized at all, upon an unchained force, an incalculable power. God can never be delineated even momentarily in any shape, contour, or feature recognizable to human discourse, nor may His activities be subjected to the laws of reason or of plausibility. He is a realm of mystery, in whom we may be sure that all dilemmas and contradictions are resolved, though just how we shall never in this world even remotely fathom. He is the reason of all things, and though men can "explain" the behavior of things, they cannot pretend to expound the reason of reasons. The seventeenth-century theologian, like the modern scientist, was perpetually explaining his world without being able to give the reason for its being precisely the kind of world which he explained.

The theologian was no more deterred than is his successor the scientist from the labors of exposition by this confession of fundamental ignorance. Time and time again a textbook or catechism begins with the incomprehensible God, and then proceeds to dogmatize confidently about His character and behavior. Some Puritans pay no more than lip service to the doctrine, and Cotton Mather in his heart of hearts never doubted that the divinity was a being remarkably like Cotton Mather. Yet, though individual Puritans might forget its implications, to Puritanism itself the idea was fundamental that God, the force, the power, the life of the universe, must remain to men hidden, unknowable, and unpredictable. He is the ultimate secret, the awful mystery. His essence "is capable properly of no definition"; all we can say is that He "is an incomprehensible, first, and absolute Being." He cannot be approached directly; man cannot stand face to face with Him any more than the stubble or the wax can draw near the fire: "He is a consuming fire to the sonnes of men, if they come to him immediately." His thoughts go beyond man's thoughts, "as much as the distance is betweene heaven and earth." We stand before Him, said John Preston, as a man upon the shore of an infinite sea:

> If he goes into the deepe, he is drowned: You may looke into *Gods* Essence, and see and admire it; but to think that thou couldest comprehend *God,* is, as if a man should think to hold the whole sea in the hollow of his hand.

The metaphors of the sea and of the sun were favorites with Puritan writers. Thomas Shepard used them both at Cambridge in Massachusetts Bay: the glory of God no man or angel shall know, "their cockle shell can never comprehend this sea"; we can only apprehend Him by knowing that we cannot comprehend Him at all, "as we admire the luster of the sun the more in that it is so great we can not behold it." At the end of the century Samuel Willard began his gigantic tome on the "compleat" body of divinity, in which over a thousand folio pages are required to tell what man may comprehend, by declaring that all reason is too finite to comprehend the infinite, "too shallow to contain the deep, the bottomless; too narrow to grasp the boundless; too little comprehensive to include this incomprehensible Object."

Men who could lose sight of this doctrine, who could say that God is such and such a being or that He conforms "of necessity" to these or those rules, could not be Puritans. "What God is, none can perfectly define, but that hath the Logicke of God himselfe"—this might well serve by itself for a definition of the Puritan spirit. However, it was also clear that no men, not even Puritans, could worship, much less obey, an illimitable mystery. Should human beings be required to contemplate forever an incomprehensible essence, their religious life might become an anarchic surrender to ineffable impulses, and no result was further from Puritan intentions. Therefore Puritan textbooks hastened to assert that while we cannot define God we may piece together "an imperfect description which commeth neerest to unfold Gods nature." This imperfect description was achieved by enumerating in logical sequence what were called God's "attributes." Strictly speaking the attributes have no existence outside the human intellect. God is one, indivisible, timeless act, but as such He is utterly meaningless to us: "we must needs have a diversified representation of it." The attributes are representations of the divine essence in terms with which the human reason can deal; they are "divine Predications, or Titles." They are not "divers things in God, but they are divers only in regard of our understanding, and in regard of their different effects on different objects." Diverse aspects of the divine essence cannot in fact be separated; yet from the human point of view they must be distinguished, and in thinking of them men are compelled to separate one from another "notionally." "They are not distinguished at all in God, but onely to us-ward, according to our manner of conceiving." Religion is what man believes about God, not necessarily what God in Himself is. . . .

That the Bible is the inspired word of God rested for the Puritans upon absolute conviction. They did not reject the help of historical confirmations, but when speaking most characteristically they did not stop to argue. The Mahometans, John Davenport declared, "have no Word for their beleeving in *Mahomet,* but the lying *Alchoran,* but we have the Scripture." The proof which a Christian has, said Cotton Mather, "is of that sort, that assures him, The *Fire* is indeed the *Fire;* even a *Self-evidencing, and scarce utterable Demonstration."* The Bible is fiat, it cannot be questioned, it alone is authority. "If the word speake for thee, it is no matter though all men and Angels speake against thee; and if the word condemne thee, it is no matter who speakes for thee." We must not shape our rule to suit men but must align men by the rules: "Crook not God's rules to the experience of men, (which is fallible, and many times corrupt,) but bring men unto the rule, and try men's estates herein by that." No sense or feeling nor any reasoning has the slightest validity "but that which is from and according to the Word of God." Any proposition asserted by Scripture is true: "When I am sure that God has said it, I believe it, for in things Divine there can be no sublimer proof then the testimony of God himself." Throughout the seventeenth century New England ministers reiterated this teaching, and there was hardly a man in the whole community who doubted it.

Consequently, as we endeavor to trace the history of Puritan thought in America we must remember that the Puritan looked upon discoverable truth as already discovered, set down in black and white, once and for all, by the supreme wisdom. There was nothing essential to be learned outside revelation. Puritan thought was incurably authoritarian and legalistic. Every proposition had to be bolstered by chapter and verse, and the margins of books, whether of divinity or politics, science or morals, the margins even of love-letters, had to be studded with citations. But one further consideration must at the same time be borne in mind, and it is of no less importance: the authority to which the Puritan thinker appealed as final and decisive was not itself the ultimate authority, and though the Puritan may have forgotten to distinguish between the two on occasion, he never did so for very long. The soul of Puritan theology is the hidden God, who is not fully revealed even in His own revelation. The Bible is His declared will; behind it always lies His secret will. His secret purpose "hee hath in himselfe, before al worlds, and hath not discovered it to the creature"; His revealed will is the purpose "which he hath made known to us by his word." His secret will is His decree of what shall be, His revealed will is His command of what ought to be. By the former, "God disposeth of all the affairs of his Creatures, according to his infinite wisdom, and good pleasure"; by the latter, He "prescribes to us our Duty, and how we ought to carry towards him in all things." Undoubtedly the two are not in fact opposed, but "in our manner of conception and expression," especially according to our experience, they come "under a diverse consideration," and can often seem thoroughly contradictory. We must obey the commanding will; we must pray for the things revealed, not for things according to His secret will, "for so we cannot guide our actions." We must not be wise "above what is written"; if we inquire further into the mystery of the Godhead than what is revealed, we will attain not knowledge but blindness. The visible church is not founded upon the secret intention, "but onely his revealed will signified in the Scriptures."

Thus the Puritan conception of God resulted in a Puritan habit of mind which must be called literalism. And yet, by the very terms of the conception, it was literalism up to a point; there was a reservation, however theoretical. The reservation may not seem very significant; to us it may appear quite superfluous, when there exists only one authoritative source for human knowledge, to give thought to a further realm of absolute knowledge beyond the explicit realm, since that region remains forever inaccessible to man. Yet the space between revelation and the inconceivable absolute, between the revealed will and the secret will, between the command and the decree, between knowledge and the searing flame, was from the point of view of orthodox apologetics the one fissure in the impregnable walls of systematic theology; from the point of view of history, it was the portal through which ran the highway of intellectual development.

Sin

Puritan divines counted that day lost in which they did not spend ten or twelve hours in their studies. They sacrificed their health to the production of massive tomes which demonstrated beyond the shadow of a doubt that man, created upright, fell of his own untrammeled choice into a corruption so horrible as to deserve the worst of punishments and so abject as to preclude all hope of recovery by his unaided efforts. Imposing though the sheer bulk of this literature may be as a monument to clerical industry, it probably never convinced anyone who was not already in profound agreement. The doctrines of original sin, of the depravity of man, and of irresistible grace were not embraced for their logic, but out of a hunger of the human spirit and an anxiety of the soul.

On this score the Puritans exhibit most clearly their descent from Augustine. The same subjective insight, the same turning of conscious-ness back upon itself, the same obsession with individuality, the same test of conclusions not so much by evidence or utility as by the soul's immediate approbation or revulsion—these qualities which appear in Augustine almost for the first time in Western thought and give him his amazing "modernity," reappear in force among the early Puritans. Like his, their meditations are intensely introspective, and in their own breasts they find the two fundamental issues: the natural emptiness of the heart and its consuming desire for fullness. From the depths of im-perfection the soul conceives of God as flawless perfection, whom it cannot hold responsible for its own desolation: "Because my soul dared not be displeased at my God, it would not suffer aught to be Thine which displeased it." The soul must therefore conclude that it is itself the cause for its plight; becoming further aware that the will nevertheless deliber-ately persists in evil, the soul cries out in anguish, "O rottenness! O monstrosity of life and profundity of death! Could I like that which was unlawful only because it was unlawful?" From such an insight flows the piety of Augustine, from the double conviction that in a world emanating from all-good, all-perfect Being, man lives at odds with it, and that never-theless the maimed soul, even while persisting in evil, longs for deliver-ance from the body of this death, for reinstatement in the created har-mony.

The similarity of mood between Augustine and the Puritans could be illustrated merely by the frequency with which he is quoted in Puritan writing. Thomas Hooker begins a discussion of regeneration thus:

> There is an old phrase, which Saint *Augustine* propounded in his time, and Divines take it up with one consent in this case, and that is this, *that God of an unwilling will, doth make a willing will.*

The high estimation in which Puritans held the name of Augustine is revealed when Hooker continues to call him "Saint," though this use of the word was generally proscribed as a Popish corruption. But even when they were not directly borrowing Augustine's phrases, the Puritans were speaking out of the same spirit. New England diarists had not the literary genius of the author of the *Confessions* and the *Soliloquies,* nor could the divines put autobiographies into their sermons; still at their more pedes-trian pace they followed his example in relying for the demonstration of original sin and innate depravity upon an analysis of the soul. If the soul, which is a spiritual substance, is ever to find peace, it must return to its creator: "Its rest must bee in God; as the Rivers runne into the Sea, and as every body rests in its center." Even souls that have never been touched by compunction still betray the soul's desire; even those too blind to know that they lack sight exhibit an unconscious craving for vision:

> For, looke what the Soule is to the body, the same is the grace of Gods Spirit to the Soule. When the Soule is deprived of Gods Spirit, there followes a senselesse stupidnesse upon the heart of a man. . . .

Goaded by his appetite for happiness, man ranges over the world, glutting his senses with enjoyments which give no relief beyond the delusive moment; in his inability to find enduring comfort in a surfeit of pleasures man exhibits at once the desperateness of his present condition and the loftiness of his origin:

> The eyes and the eares are the inlets or doores of the soule, through which innumerable objects enter, yet is not that spacious roome filled, neither doth it euer say it is enough, but like the daughters of the horsleach, crys giue, giue! and which is most strang, the more it receius, the more empty it finds it self, and sees an impossibility, euer to be filled, but by him in whom all fullnes dwells.

A "Leprous person" can have little use for a gold chain, and rich apparel is wasted upon "a dead carkasse." Unless he find forgiveness, unless he be reinstated, man cannot overcome separateness; his appetites will grow only the more exorbitant by feeding upon substitutes.

> The want of this takes off the sweetness of al the comforts, contentments, the sap and rellish of al priviledges, and the confluence of all Earthly Excellencies that can be enjoyed in this Pilgrimage, when the soul is under the pressures of Gods displeasure, and the tyranny of his own distempers, which carries him from God, and keeps him under the dreadful indignation of the Almighty, present him then with the beauty of al the choycest blessings that ever any man had on Earth, yea, what ever others hoped for, but in vain. Put them into his hand, conceive him possessed of the fulness of al worldly perfections, Crowns, Kingdoms, Honors, and preferments, the broken heart tramples al under foot with neglect, what is that to me, saies the soul? had I al the Wealth to enrich me, al Honors to advance me, Pleasures and Delights to content me, and my sins stil to damn me? miserable man that ever I was born in the midst of al these falsly conceived comforts. This sowr Sawce spoils al the Sweetmeat, this dram of poyson makes deadly al the delights and pleasures that possibly can be attained or expected.

Terrifying though such a prospect is, the ultimate horror is not merely the vanity of the worldly quest, but the willfulness with which man persists in it. "We not only have these lusts, but we love them." We are swaggerers who reply to correction by exaggerating our faults; because we are unable of our own power to escape the tools of desire, we refuse the offered help.

> There is an incapability in our minds to receive this spiritual light by which we might be enabled to come to the right discovery of our Corruptions . . . The sinner at first would not see his sinnes were it in his power and might he have his own mind, he would have the ghastly visage of them gone out of his sight.

Yet even such defiance is a sham, a piece of bravado, springing from a secret knowledge that though mercy and salvation "were laid downe upon the naile for believing and receiving of it," a man cannot do it of himself. As long as the heart continues cross to the Almighty, as long as it is separate from Him, the burden will remain insufferable and insupportable. Again and again analysis of the heart reveals that "as long as this remains unsubdued, there is no end of his sorrows, nor end of his prayers in suing to the Almighty for succor and relief." The lesson does not have to be learned by reading the history of Adam or by memorizing the logic of predestination; it is familiar to all men in their terrors, their inferiorities, and their insecurities; no sentence of reprobation can visit them with more condemnation than they themselves know they deserve, at least in the awful moments of honest self-recognition which no man can escape.

At the same time, while the conception of original sin is made vivid by inward knowledge of a man's self, it is reinforced by what a man observes of humanity in general. Even if he be undisturbed by an innate grief of spirit, a man may behold in the spectacle of the race enough to convince him that no created being could have been intentionally assigned the rôle which he sees men enacting every day of their miserable existences. Reason alone, said Willard, "will say that he could not be made such as he is now become, consistent with the wisdom and goodness of his maker." Since there can be no suspicion of the maker's wisdom or goodness, the present plight of mankind cannot have been a part of His original design. When we look over the world, when we see therein the children of men born to affliction as surely as sparks fly upwards,

> when we see Sicknesse, Diseases, Deaths, Perplexities, Disappointments, Discontents, and all manner of Miseries, let us stand still and enquire, How a Creature so excellent in his Creation, is become so Sorrowful and Miserable in his present condition; and to satisfy our Minds about it, let us look back to Man's Apostacy.

Puritan theologians cited testimony of this sort ostensibly to corroborate revelation; they did not expect that in itself the force of such reflections would be sufficient to humble sinners. Even in the face of indisputable facts men persist in their blindness and refuse to make the inescapable inferences. The degradation of man will be realized to the full extent only when viewed with the light of grace, and without that light no amount of factual perception will lead to spiritual understanding. Yet, for all that, the theologians themselves continued to press upon men not yet regenerated the arguments from common knowledge, and their persistent appeal to experience may be taken by us as a sign that the piety was derived as much from it as from Biblical instruction, that the doctrine came not only from the book of Genesis but also from the lesson of mortality. To any objective scrutiny man as he exists seems "like an old House gone to decay"; yet the observer must infer that the ruinous heap indicates "what a famous Structure it once was, but is now nothing but Rubbish." From the miserable fragments can be imaginatively reconstructed the nature with which man was created, "like a fair House, new built, fit to entertain the King of Glory, fit for a Temple for the Holy Ghost to dwell in." Certainly He who created man could not have marred His own handiwork; the fault must lie entirely with man himself. The edge of the doctrine of innate depravity was made sharp on the whetstone of human responsibility. It was obvious that men had contrived to bring upon themselves all the anguish they suffered; it was still more obvious that neither this awareness nor the anguish itself liberated them from the trammels of perversity. A being who brought such a destiny upon himself could hardly expect to find within himself the power to master it. The force of this conclusion gave the Puritan cry for deliverance through the grace of God its urgency and its poignance.

Regeneration

In a handbook that was widely used in New England John Ball defined faith as "the gift of God, and the act of man: a wonderfull and supernaturall gift of God, and a liuely motion of the heart renewed by grace, and powerfully moued by the Spirit." The moment of regeneration, in which God, out of His compassion, bestows grace upon man and in which man is enabled to reply with belief, was the single goal of the Augustinian piety. Without it individual life was a burden, with it living became richness and joy. Other people have found other names for the experience: to lovers it is love, to mystics it is ecstasy, to poets inspiration. Even ordinary men have their ups and downs, know seasons when they are filled with something more than their usual vitality. That there is some such phenomenon hundreds have testified, though their explanations have varied from calling it a merging of the self with an all-pervading substance to taking it for a physiological crisis caused by the excess secretions of a ductless gland. To the Puritans there was of course only one interpretation. It was the act of communion in which the infinite impinged upon the finite, when the misery of the fragmentary was replaced by the delight of wholeness. Regeneration was the receiving by man of "the fulnesse of the infinitenesse of all perfections which are in the Lord," who alone is "able to fill up all the emptie chinks, void places, the unsatisfied gaspings & yawnings of the spirit of a man." It was the resolution of the problem of sin, and of all other problems that torture humanity.

No other subject in the repertoire of theological debate was more bewritten and no other riddle so exercised the ingenuity of the clergy and the patience of the laity. We shall have occasion to sympathize with the Sysiphean labors of the divines as we behold them again and again almost finishing exhaustive systematizations of the doctrine, only to have their structure collapse because some obstinate fact simply will not fit in. As Thomas Hooker rightly said, "The point is difficult, and the mysterie great." Yet we must not be deceived by the mass of black-letter type devoted to the elucidation of regeneration into thinking that it was not a real conception to Puritan sensibility, that it did not correspond to a vivid experience. Throughout all the laborious analyses the fundamental idea remained clear, and if Puritans could never satisfactorily define faith they were not therefore hindered from living by it.

Theological formulation was difficult because regeneration is a mystery. Those who have it, or think they have it, cannot tell exactly how it was wrought or precisely what happened, and those who do not have it cannot conceive what it might be; furthermore, there are some who are never quite sure whether they have it or not, and they make the problem exceedingly difficult. We have little right to patronize the Puritans for their ignorance. With all the laboratory facilities now at hand and all their clinical study, modern psychologists differ among themselves no less than did the theologians in their diagnosis of what occurs to human beings during the seizure; the layman of the seventeenth century becomes the patient of the twentieth and overhears his case as hotly disputed among doctors of the mind as formerly he beheld his symptoms argued among doctors of divinity. The result once more is a tribute to the bewildering variety of the religious experience. No one can deny that some such psychological event does take place; dispute arises over the nature of the theoretical frame in which the explanation is set. For Puritans the frame was inevitably theological; its outlines were predetermined by the system of belief inherited from the past, from Augustine in particular, to which a renewed precision had been given by the Reformation.

The Puritan theory of regeneration began with the premise of an omnipotent God and an impotent man. It seemed obvious that a man, bound in the slavery of sin, could not liberate himself; before he could stand once more erect the effects of his sin had to be canceled and the transgression pardoned. Regeneration therefore must begin with an act of absolution, performed before the divine tribunal, an act in which man himself could take no part. A change must be wrought in his status before any could be made in his nature. In theological parlance this first act of regeneration was known as "justification," and it meant that God, having decided to acquit a particular individual, says to him, in effect, "that his Justice and Law is fully satisfied, that hee will lay nothing upon your score, require no satisfaction at your hands, but he will fully and freely discharge you of all your sins which you have committed." Thereupon divine grace reaches forth to the prostrate man in two ways: first it comes as a call to new life, a summons from above—which was called "vocation"—and then it penetrates his being and there it generates—or, in view of Adam's original nature, "re-generates"—a power to respond. John Milton's tutor at Cambridge, William Chappell, compiled a bibliography of theological works for the guidance of divinity students, and under the heading "Treatises on True Conversion" he listed only New England writers; the divines of the Puritan colonies excelled as analysts, and of them all Thomas Hooker was esteemed the most profound. He illustrated justification and regeneration by the simile of a sick apprentice: to make a free man of him there must be a double change; his master must tear up the indenture, thus working a "moral change," and then the physician must cure him, working a "real change."

> Just so it is in this change of the soule: there is a morall change in justification, a man is bound to the Law, and liable to the penaltie of it, and guiltie of the breach of it: now God the Father in Jesus Christ, acquits a man of this guilt, and delivers him from this revenging power of the Law, and thats not all, but withall hee puts holinesse into the heart, and wisedome into the minde . . . & this is called a naturall change, because there are new spiritual abilities put into the heart.

Therefore grace is to be understood as something inward and spiritual, and when it has wrought upon a man in regeneration "it leaves an impression upon the most inward motions of the soul, as they meet with God in the most retired and refined actions thereof." It is a renewal of man out of sin, a resurrection from death. It regenerates not merely his mind and his will, but the whole man, giving him a new inclination, a new heart, a completely new life.

The one bedrock certainty about the matter is that grace is a supernatural power and that no man can enact regeneration by his own exertions. The natural disposition is not only bound by sin, it cleaves to sin; though the soul may cry out for deliverance it fights against the deliverer. Grace must pursue the soul, forcibly seize upon it, violently reverse the will. It is "a marvellous strong work, when the Spirit of God comes to act things contrary to nature." Man instinctively wishes to do for himself and to rely upon his own prowess; faith "is the going out of the soule to another, and to see all-sufficiencie in another, and to fetch all from another." So we cannot properly say that in regeneration a man comes to possess Christ but rather we must say that he is possessed by Christ, "because the worke lies on Christs part." The peace that passes understanding must come from above the understanding. Only a supernatural power can withdraw the natural heart "from all those secret bosome distempers . . . which breed . . . discontentment within a man," and compel the soul to "resigne up it selfe to the good will of God." Regeneration must be done "by an irresistible power" or else it will never succeed in overturning the dominion of sin.

Consequently, the initial requirement for a description of regeneration is a rigorous distinction between the effects of divine grace and all behavior elicited by natural causes. This distinction was not always an easy one for the Puritan to establish, because in fallen men there are faculties which can sometimes produce actions remarkably similar to those that result from faith, even at times seeming to excel them. The presence of these faculties argues no saving worth in man, it only proves the fiendish subtlety of his corruption. Sin does not always manifest itself as violence and rapine, but masquerades as virtue itself, thus setting a trap by which the unwary may be betrayed into resting content with a performance that has nothing of God in it. For example, certain natural influences or physical causes will work a life of seeming virtue; fear of punishment, "the good Temperament of the Body," a decent education will often lead to well-regulated conduct and everyday probity. But all such effects come from mechanical and comprehensible causes, the results are temporary and relative. Grace is absolute and supernatural. It is, Hooker said, "a holy kind of violence." It is not wrought by "morall perswasion" but by "his powerfull operation, and omnipotent hand put forth for such a purpose." Faith is not a thing "which our nature can attaine to with outward helpes," there are no seeds of belief within us. "Neither education, nor examples of others, nor our own resolutions, can settle our hearts upon God, till we find an inward power and authority causing divine truths to shine into our hearts." A child may have the "most towardly natural disposition" and "be advantaged by the most likely way of education"; he may have instilled into him arguments to convince the most obdurate mind, and "yet till the heart be changed and over-poured by a work of supernatural grace, the life will alwayes be found barren of any good fruit, void of holiness, and sincere obedience."

It is also true that in natural man there exists an internal conflict which to the uninitiated seems to be the struggle of grace and sin. There is in man something of a conscience; he was created with it, exactly as he was created with eyes or limbs, and no more could it have been obliterated at the fall. It is now extremely unreliable, but still strong enough to restrain most men from the more extravagant vices. It accuses men of their sin, and it can make them so uncomfortable that some will fly to religion for refuge. A few may even fight and die for the truth, but if their motive is no more than self-preservation, if they are driven by nothing more than a haunting conscience, they commit in effect an act of suicide; "this is but a principle of nature, not an inward principle of life, whose property is to seek the subversion of corrupt nature, as natural conscience seeks the garnishing of it and the actions thereof." In wicked men the conscience is at odds with the will, and because all men are compounded of spirit and matter they are torn by a never ending contention between the soul and the body. But in them the conflict is natural, mechanical, all on the same plane; it is a crossing of one faculty by another, each wanting its own advantage. When grace is poured into the reluctant soul, the inward struggle takes on vastly more complex dimensions. Grace injects into every faculty a new element, by which each learns to judge its own sinfulness and thereupon commences a civil war with itself:

> In the Saints the Controversie is between every faculty and it selfe, between the understanding and it selfe, betweene the whole Soule, as it is compared with it selfe, there is something good in every part of it, and something ill, and these two contend.

Natural men alternate between joy at one moment and sorrow at another; gracious persons are filled simultaneously with exultation and grief. They are elevated by the glory of grace and cast down by the knowledge of sin, and therefore only they can at one time be both diligent in worldly business and yet untainted by the world.

> Where ever the heart of a man is sanctified by the Spirit of grace; where you have the life of sanctification in a Christian, you shall finde variety of graces in them, some of them of such diversity and opposition one to another, that in nature the like temper is not to be found in one person at the same time, and in the same businesse.

Grace comes from God, who is, as we have seen, possessed of attributes which in nature are not compatible with each other, and it makes man in some measure capable of the same supernatural balance of qualities.

It was difficult enough in practice to keep from taking some of the natural perturbations of the unregenerate for the stirrings of authentic grace; it was still more difficult to distinguish accurately between the powers of natural reason and those of divine grace. If there are remnants of conscience in the progeny of Adam there are also fragments of the intellect, for without a mind man would cease to be. When the Puritan spoke of "the light of reason" or of "the light of nature" he meant these ruins of the image of God; the phrases signified the amount of innate rationality that descendants of the first man still retain, though in a sadly dilapidated condition.

> The light of nature, remaining in *Adams* posterity, since the lapse: is so little as that it is not to be mentioned the same day, with what was in *Adam*, before the fall. The light of nature, consists in common principles imprinted upon the reasonable soul, by nature: inclining man, to assent unto some naturall, and manifest trueths upon the representation of them; without waiting for any proofe; that is, as it were by instinct, without argument. Viz. *that it is impossible for the same thing, at once, for to be, & not to be.*

By the same tokens, even before the mind begins to think, it already knows that there is a God, that parents are to be honored, that there is a difference between good and bad. Consequently some men, for example Seneca or Plutarch, guided solely by the light of reason, building upon merely natural principles, are able to acquire the "morall virtues" inculcated by supernatural light. Puritans did not deny that such virtues had their uses—in fact, they allowed them rather too much utility—but they were positive that such were not the stuff of divine grace and contributed nothing toward salvation. Men can learn some things from "the book of creation," from the arts and sciences, by the light of nature, but not what the elect learn by the light of glory. Rational conviction at best makes things appear but as they seem, whereas spiritual conviction presents them as they really are. The holy spirit may use argumentation, but it goes much farther and enables the soul to see intuitively as well as through the point-by-point demonstrations of logical discourse.

> Reason can see and discourse about words and propositions, and behold things by report, and . . . deduct one thing from another; but the Spirit makes a man see the things themselves, really wrapped up in those words. The Spirit brings spiritual things as well as notions before a man's eye; the light of the Spirit is like the light of the sun—it makes all things appear as they are.

The life of reason, though lived never so well, "is but a dead life." Faith "exceeds the most lively and heroicall performances of the best of the Heathens that ever was," because what they did was from their own strength; their finest actions "are but so many dead works, because the heart is dead." Knowledge will not cure a wounded spirit, and though a man "bee acquainted with all the motions of heaven, they cannot bring him to heaven: With all the secrets of nature, they cannot bring him out of the dreggs of nature." There was for the Puritan a hierarchy of comprehension, what Preston called a "three-fold kinde of Truth": on the first plane there was natural truth within the heart of men; on the second there was the common knowledge that natural men could acquire from theologians and books; on the third was spiritual knowledge. All men had the first, all might gain the second, only grace could give the third; yet on that level alone was redemption to be secured. The life of the Christian was not sustained by wisdom, or brilliant abilities, or by philosophical fortitude, but by faith.

The danger that the natural convictions of reason might be mistaken for the supernatural impress of the spirit was real enough. To the Puritans the danger was made the more threatening as they recognized the existence of a species of belief which accepts not merely natural religion but revelation as well, which nevertheless is merely a belief of the mind, not of the soul. It is what the seventeenth century called "historicall faith"—"a beleeving, not of the stories of the Bible only to be true, but a beleeuing of the whole Word of God, the articles of the faith; but beleeved onely in a historicall manner generally, not applyed particularly to himselfe." It is not saving faith for all its confession of Christianity. Like heathen morality, it is a thoroughly natural product; under favorable circumstances it can be cultivated in any by good teachers. Men can be instructed in the meaning of Scriptural words and be made proficient in its logic, but in order that they may "see the spiritualnesse of the work that is manifested and communicated in that reason there," they must be instructed by the spirit. It is as though, Hooker explained, an ignorant man should be shown a clock and be told how it was put together; he might understand the words and the reasons, but he could not on the spot acquire the art of clockmaking.

> There is a curious frame in the soule of a Christian, of grace, of faith, of repentance, of holinesse, of love, patience, and the like . . . but I that read what he hath written of these things, being a naturall man, though happily I understand the sence, and apprehend the meaning of the words, yet the true knowledge of the nature of repentance, or faith, or hope, I cannot possibly attain to, so long as I remain a meer naturall man . . . When I finde my own heart wrought upon, then I can best discover it to another, then doe I know that which before I never understood; though happily I could discourse something concerning such things, and understand the outside as it were, yet that was all, I never knew the bottom, as I doe now.

Most of the divines were ready to admit that in extent of knowledge a wicked man might go as far as any saint under heaven, and all agreed that religion learned by rote was not the religion of the heart, that an understanding of theology was not an experience of grace.

Natural reason could not be expected to reach so high as grace because

by definition it had been corrupted. It had shared in the general conta-
gion of sin; Adam no doubt was created as upright in his reason as in his
will, but what now remains as the light of reason is almost certain to
prove a will-o'-the-wisp. No matter how successfully reason may upon
occasion contrive actions that resemble those of grace, so long as it remains unregenerate it is not only incapable of true excellence but vigorously hostile to it. Reason will bend the arguments of Scripture and wrest
the words to devious meaning; when a man is first accused of sin he gets
reason, like a hireling lawyer, to defend him before the court of God, "to
plead against the word of God lest it should prevaile, or his sins should
lie so heavy upon him as to tire and weary him out of them." In many
men of great ability "for depth of brain and strength of understanding"
the sway of reason becomes so firm that they can never be brought to the
truth; where there is "wiliness, depth and subtilty of wit, large reaches
of carnal reason," there is apt to be but little faith. For the Puritan further
and conclusive proof of the enmity of reason to faith was the Papacy and
its teachings; the principles of the Roman church were in their eyes
eminently satisfactory to human reason, and the institution deserved
damnation if for that sin alone. Faith demands the acceptance of things
above reason, grace fills men with the power to believe the impossible.
Up to a certain point rational arguments may be used to prepare and
confirm, but they cannot serve for persuasion. Even when reason is legitimately employed, its conclusions must always be tested by the proposition of faith, and whatever reason turns up to the contrary must be at
once discarded. "Almost all the sin and misery that hath filled the World,
hath broke in at this door, hearkening to reason against Institution." We
should note in passing that it was not reason itself, conceived in the
abstract, that the Puritans condemned, but reason as men employed it.
The light of pure reason, said John Norton, is "an effect proceeding from
the Word," but man, endowed with no more of it than remains in him
after the fall, is in virtual darkness. Pure reason is therefore inaccessible
to man, like the essence of God; man has only "carnal reason," a mere
caricature of that which he once possessed as the badge of his lordship
over all other creatures.

> Star-light, cannot make it, otherwise then night. The light of nature since the
> fall, compared with the light of the image of God, before the fall, hath not the
> proportion of Star-light, to the bright Sun-light at noon-day. This indeed is but
> darkness. But, if compared with the light of the Gospell, it is worse then gross
> darkness.

As we pursue the story of New England thought we must bear in mind
the complete separation which the founders made between supernatural
grace and all its natural simulacra. Puritanism could exist only on condi-

tion that it maintain the distinction, and when we shall find the division closing up, we shall perceive the dwindling of piety.

The effort to set off supernatural grace from natural morality and reasonable conduct involved also a metaphysical difficulty which was to become of great importance, down even to the time of Emerson. Grace was to be distinguished from natural powers; but was it not true, according to the doctrine of concursus, that God created and sustained all natural processes, and that by the doctrine of providence He directed and controlled all the operations of mind and body? To say that grace was supernatural seemed to say therefore that it was above God Himself, or that there was a division of the Deity into an ordinary self and an extraordinary self. Most of the issues that were so hotly contested among seventeenth-century theologians were connected with attempts to resolve this discrepancy between the God of everyday providence and the God who dispensed His grace according to no rule but His own pleasure, who then condemned to damnation those who, never receiving the grace, lived as well as they could in the strength of natural conscience, unregenerate reason, and historical faith. For the orthodox Puritan there was no way out except to keep the two activities of God, providence and regeneration, on separate planes. God diffuses Himself through space to create and sustain the world, but there is a second emanation, over and above the original one, which is grace. When He puts grace into the heart of a man it is as though He made a new and gratuitous concretion of his substance in addition to that already precipitated in creation. The omnipotent Being fills all space, controls all actions, directs all destinies; out of Him comes all life, and without the constant play of His sustaining power physical being would disintegrate into nothing. He fills heaven and earth with His presence, says Hooker, "His infinite Being is every where, and one and the same every where in regard of himself; because his being is most simple, and not subject to any shadow of change, being all one with himself." There is, says Shepard, an essential presence of the spirit "that is in every man, as the Godhead is every where, in whom we live and move." The spirit lives in the most wicked men, in "the vilest creature in the world." Therefore the presence of God in the regenerate soul must follow upon a second act of creation, a new radiation reaching directly across to man, overleaping the regular channels of influence. "Yet he is said to take up his abode in a special manner, when he doth put forth the peculiar expression of his Work." Our union with the spirit in faith, while we live in a world sustained and governed in every detail by that spirit, is not with that aspect of it which regulates the course of events or our everyday life, but that which comes to us of itself. Natural life is common to all, "but this special Presence of God, he affords only to his Redeemed, Chosen and Called." It is not enough that God has spoken once; the fall of man has made it necessary that He speak again. He must re-create those He would redeem, He must bring them under more than the government of His providence, even under the dominion of grace.

The distinction between God's energy put forth in governing the universe and in regenerating the saints furnished metaphysical grounds for a theological distinction between God's decreeing will, as seen in the events, and His commanding will, as seen in the Bible. As we study this distinction we come close to the Puritan's innermost sense of the living process. It is as though a pulsating energy were continuously pumped through creation's veins by the beat of a mighty heart, which yet at irregular intervals, by an exceptional contraction of the ventricles, sends forth a stream of still more tremendous force. Out of the same being have proceeded the stars, animals, men; but in some incarnations the being has taken forms superior to others. "The least spear of grass has the same power to make it that made heaven and angels," says the Puritan, but he does not then chant with the author of *Leaves of Grass* that the least thing in creation is equal to any other. A fly is above the cedar because it has another life which the cedar has not, "so the meanest believer is better than the most glorious hypocrite." In the regenerate, the author of all life ordains yet another life superior to the other forms, giving them something which the others have not. In the course of providence God often provides men with powers and gifts, bridles their violence, overcomes their pride, teaches them the truth of Scripture. But these things He does by managing secondary causes, sending men to the right teachers, instructing them through their experience or through science. What is achieved in this fashion is a work of "common grace." Supernatural grace is a work peculiar to the elect, which comes upon them with irresistible force and depends upon no antecedent conditions or preparations. This conception, that for the relation of God and man a new line of communication must be opened over and above the relation of creature to creator and of life to the source of life, a special contact, a designation by name and a specific bond, is the very heart of Puritanism. To the Puritan, cosmic optimism was not enough. The scheme of perfection became monotonous if restricted to flawless regularity; the human quest, the deep longings of the soul, went unsatisfied if the wheels of the world ground slowly, justly, and implacably. There must be room in the universe for a free and unpredictable power, for a lawless force that flashes through the night in unexpected brilliance and unaccountable majesty. It was better in Puritan eyes that most men be passed over by this illumination and left to hopeless despair rather than that all men should be born without the hope of beholding it, or that a few should forgo the ecstasy of the vision.

Richard Hofstadter 1916—1970

15

Richard Hofstadter has been called the finest historian of his generation. His death in 1970, at the height of his powers, represents an incalculable loss to American historiography. As an interpreter of the American past, in such original studies as *The American Political Tradition* (1948), *The Age of Reform: From Bryan to F.D.R.* (1955), and *Anti-Intellectualism in American Life* (1963) Hofstadter made powerful contributions to the unending debate that American historians carry on with one another and themselves. His active contemplation of such influential historians as Turner, Beard, and Parrington—the entire Progressive tradition, in fact—and his assessments of the role of the social sciences in history have been instrumental in providing a fund of new ideas to American historiography in an age of what Robert A. Skotheim has called "convergence and new directions" within the discipline.

Hofstadter was born in Buffalo, New York, in 1916. He earned his B.A. at the University of Buffalo, majoring in philosophy and history, and then began graduate work in 1937 at Columbia University, where, after four years of teaching at the University of Maryland (1942–1946), he taught until his untimely death. That he was an Easterner by birth and a New Yorker by desire should be stressed. His social perspective armed him, as it were, against the beguiling frontier interpretation of American history and enabled him to perceive and to analyze "the agrarian myth" of America: "a notion of the [urban] educated classes" that became "a mass creed, a part of the country's political folklore and its nationalist ideology." Further, the cultural life of the city in the 1930's and 1940's had much to do with the formation of Hofstadter's historiographic concerns. Those were decades of intellectual ferment, of a radicalism sharpened by the exigencies of the Great Depression and the "war against Fascism." As Hofstadter himself later described it:

> I belong to the generation that came of age during the middle thirties. This was a period, of course, of tremendous conflict on a world scale and of intense and lively controversy in American domestic politics. A battle of ideologies roughly similar to

that which took place in a world-wide theatre of action could be seen at home as well. For many of us an interest in studying the formation and development of ideologies was a natural intellectual response to the conflict raging around us. But to a detached observer these ideologies were far more interesting for their extraordinary appeal to various types of individuals than they were for their rational or philosophic content. I found myself, therefore, becoming interested in individual and social character types, in social mythologies and styles of thought as they reveal and affect character, and in politics as a sphere of behavior into which personal and private motives are projected.

Hofstadter found congenial the role of "detached observer," which is perhaps why Alfred Kazin, knowing him to be a political liberal, could describe him in the 1930's as "a natural conservative in a radical period, with a melancholy knowledge of the shoals and traps of human nature." His ability to attain such detachment (even in regard to his own works) and his awareness of the ambiguities of human nature informed all of Hofstadter's professional interests, which lay at what he called the "intersection" of political and intellectual history:

> When I was first attracted to history as a vocation, it was by a two-fold interest: I was attracted both by what might be called orthodox political history and also by the history of ideas. At first these two seemed parallel rather than converging. Not only did I not have a very clear idea of how the two might be put together, but I had little interest in doing so. As time went on I realized that what I most wanted to write about were things marginal to both political historians and to practitioners of the history of ideas who stem, say, from the severe tradition in which Arthur O. Lovejoy has done such impressive work. My interests lay between the two fields, at the intersection of their perimeters.

His first book, *Social Darwinism in American Thought* (1944), illustrates the influence on the young scholar of Charles Beard and Vernon Parrington, with their emphasis on the primacy of social and economic "realities" over ideas. This "Progressive" influence remained vital in Hofstadter's second major work, *The American Political Tradition,* in which he pursued the other of his major interests, political history, in this case the "ideology of American statesmanship." The book is a series of portraits "analyzing men of action in their capacity as leaders of popular thought," from "The Founding Fathers: An Age of Realism" to "Franklin D. Roosevelt: The Patrician as Opportunist." Hofstadter's thesis was that

> However much at odds on specific issues, the major political traditions have shared a belief in the rights of property, the philosophy of economic individualism, the value of competition; they have accepted the economic virtues of capitalist culture as necessary qualities of man. Even when some property right has been challenged—as it was by followers of Jefferson and Jackson—in the name of the rights of man or the rights of the community, the challenge, when translated into practical policy, has actually been urged on behalf of some other kind of property.

The sanctity of private property, the right of the individual to dispose of and invest it, the value of opportunity, and the natural evolution of self-interest and self-assertion, within broad legal limits, into a beneficent social order have been staple tenets of the central faith in American political ideologies; these conceptions have been shared in large part by men as diverse as Jefferson, Jackson, Lincoln, Cleveland, Bryan, Wilson, and Hoover. The business of politics—so the creed runs—is to protect this competitive world, to foster it on occasion, to patch up its incidental abuses, but not to cripple it with a plan for common collective action. American traditions also show a strong bias in favor of equalitarian democracy, but it has been a democracy in cupidity rather than a democracy of fraternity.

Only Franklin Roosevelt, Hofstadter argued, sensed the failure of the American political tradition and recognized the need for innovation. But Roosevelt, daring in practice, offered no new systematic or consistent social and political conceptions as the basis of a new tradition, and this lacuna explains the post-Roosevelt "rudderless and demoralized state of American liberalism."

In its emphasis on "shared beliefs" and "staple tenets," the book seemed to contribute to what came to be known as the "consensus history" of the 1950's, the view, that is, that American politics "has been built socially upon a middle-class basis and ideologically upon a liberal consensus." In John Higham's robust metaphor, the new consensus history "amounted to a massive grading operation that smoothed and flattened the convulsive dialectic of progressive history." But Hofstadter never accepted the label of consensus historian. He did accept, however, the contribution of consensus history to, as he put it, "the rediscovery of complexity," which had been obscured by the clear, conflicting polarities posited and celebrated by Progressive historians.

Progressive history [Hofstadter later wrote] had been written to meet several needs that are no longer felt in the same way, and it began to seem, to members of my generation, somewhat too insular and too nostalgic. Those of us who grew up during the Great Depression and the Second World War could no longer share the simple faith of the Progressive writers in the sufficiency of American liberalism. We found ourselves living in a more complex and terrifying world, and when we set about criticizing the Progressive historians I believe it was with a keener sense of the difficulties of life and of the problem of rendering it in intelligible historical terms. Even those of their guiding ideas that still seemed to be valid now seemed marginal rather than central; and many of their interpretative ideas rested on some kind of identification of the past and present that we could easily see through, not because we were cleverer but because their present was no longer ours. Gradually they ceased to be the leading interpreters of our past and became simply a part of it.

Progressive history thus no longer sufficed for Hofstadter's generation; but consensus history (Hofstadter was to write in 1956), while an "indispensable corrective," was "an essentially negative proposition" which could not explain such salient features of the American past as the Civil War and chronic racial and ethnic conflict. The task before American historians if they were to encompass the varieties and ambiguities of both conflict and consensus was therefore "to return to the assessment of conflict in American life and thought without going straight back into the arms of the Progressives."

In all of Hofstadter's works, one finds a dual concern with historians' previous interpretations ("He reacted more keenly to historians than to history," Arthur M. Schlesinger, Jr., writes) and with his own time and milieu. "The political and moral controversy of the New Deal naturally influenced" his first book, *Social Darwinism*. The necessity "in a time of cultural crisis to gain fresh perspectives on the past" impelled at least partially the writing of *The American Political Tradition*. "The need for an analysis from the perspective of our own time" inspired *The Age of Reform. Anti-Intellectualism in American Life* was "conceived in response to the political and intellectual conditions of the 1950's." Hofstadter's belief in the positive values of parties and recognized partisan opposition, at a time "when discontent with the workings of the American party system is at a high pitch," informed his last complete book, *The Idea of a Party System* (1970). "I still write history," he said in 1960, "out of my engagement with the present." Hofstadter's achievement testifies to the truth that while natural science progresses by forgetting its past, history advances by remembering its intellectual forebears, and, by utilizing present perspectives and new insights, moving beyond them. "One always has to reckon with the generation that has gone before," Hofstadter wrote. "I think where one gets one's real intellectual impetus is reacting against ideas one had felt strongly."

In the process of liberating himself from his intellectual fathers while recognizing his debt to them, Hofstadter drew upon materials and insights that had not been available to his predecessors. He took the lead in introducing into American historiography a professional (as opposed to a lay) appreciation of nonrational social and psychological elements in human affairs. He also helped to induce historians to accept and to apply the insights of the social sciences. Already in *The American Political Tradition,* he drew upon the notion of "psychic crisis" in describing America in the 1890's and employed psychiatric concepts in his explanations of such leaders as Theodore Roosevelt and William Jennings Bryan. In an essay written soon after, Hofstadter ventured "onto the high and dangerous ground of social psychology" in an effort to explain "Manifest Destiny" and the American takeover of the Philippines. He justified such steps on the grounds that "we have little other choice than to move into this terrain wherever simple rationalistic explanations of national behavior leave us dissatisfied."

In other studies, Hofstadter made use of such social psychological concepts as status and interest politics, regressive classes, and status tensions. He himself avowed his debt to Karl Mannheim, who "provided the link I had been seeking between ideas and social situations." He found in Mannheim a justification for his view that historical knowledge is in many ways an extension of present consciousness backward into the past: "That our social thinking is determined by our social position is not necessarily a source of error. On the contrary, it is often the path to political insight." The influence of psychoanalysis upon historians, Hofstadter noted in 1956, was growing: "The intellectual revolution that we associate with Freud is beginning to have some effect, however subtle and unformalized, upon the way they see their materials." Hofstadter saw in the use of social science techniques and concepts an opportunity to unite in a fruitful way the technical monographic work of historians with their essential narrative tasks, making, as it were, a happier marriage of analysis and literary exposition.

His coupling of the scientific with the literary is typical, for he always emphasized the artistic function of the historian. Like the literary critics who most influenced his manner—Mencken, Wilson, Trilling—Hofstadter was a stylist. And, as Schlesinger writes, even "in his forays into the domain of the social sciences, Hofstadter always took care to civilize his captives and teach them English." In commending the social sciences to historians, he believed that they would necessarily "be persuaded to accept the imaginative as well as the cognitive side" of historiography and to realize "more fully than before how much history is indeed akin to literature."

Prolific, widely read, vastly curious, undogmatic, and supremely intelligent, Hofstadter was a master of language and of modern cultural analysis; this enabled him to encompass "the complexity of social interests, the variety of roles and motives of political leaders, the unintended consequences of political actions, the valid interests that have so often been sacrificed in the pursuit of other equally valid interests," in short, the stuff of history.

Selected Bibliography

Arthur M. Schlesinger, Jr., offers a helpful and judicious essay, "Richard Hofstadter," in *Pastmasters: Some Essays on American Historians.* Christopher Lasch's "On Richard Hofstadter," *The New York Review,* March 8, 1973, 7–13, is a perceptive tribute to "the finest historian of his generation." John Higham, *History,* and Robert A. Skotheim, *American Intellectual Histories and Historians,* are particularly useful for establishing Hofstadter's milieu. The best introduction to Hofstadter is by way of his own works, but most revealing are "Interview: Richard Hofstadter," *History,* 140 (1960); his essay "History and the Social Sciences," in *The Varieties of History,* edited by Fritz Stern (1972); and his *The*

Progressive Historians (1968). Students may find worth reading Morton White's curious review of this last work in *American Historical Review* (1969), 601–603— curious because the philosopher takes the historian to task for his vagueness concerning conceptions that only philosophers appear able to clarify, and so far have not, at least in any way usable by historians.

A bibliography of Hofstadter's works and an informal analysis of the "progress of his mind" is included in the excellent collection of essays edited by Stanley Elkins and Eric McKitrick, *The Hofstadter Aegis. A Memorial* (New York, 1974).

THE AGE OF REFORM

THE AGRARIAN MYTH AND
COMMERCIAL REALITIES

I. *The Yeoman and the Myth*

The United States was born in the country and has moved to the city.
From the beginning its political values and ideas were of necessity
shaped by country life. The early American politician, the country editor,
who wished to address himself to the common man, had to draw upon
a rhetoric that would touch the tillers of the soil; and even the spokesman
of city people knew that his audience had been in very large part reared
upon the farm. But what the articulate people who talked and wrote
about farmers and farming—the preachers, poets, philosophers, writers,
and statesmen—liked about American farming was not, in every respect,
what the typical working farmer liked. For the articulate people were
drawn irresistibly to the noncommercial, nonpecuniary, self-sufficient
aspect of American farm life. To them it was an ideal. Writers like
Thomas Jefferson and Hector St. Jean de Crèvecœur admired the yeoman
farmer not for his capacity to exploit opportunities and make money but
for his honest industry, his independence, his frank spirit of equality, his
ability to produce and enjoy a simple abundance. The farmer himself, in
most cases, was in fact inspired to make money, and such self-sufficiency
as he actually had was usually forced upon him by a lack of transportation or markets, or by the necessity to save cash to expand his operations.
For while early American society was an agrarian society, it was fast
becoming more commercial, and commercial goals made their way
among its agricultural classes almost as rapidly as elsewhere. The more
commercial this society became, however, the more reason it found to
cling in imagination to the noncommercial agrarian values. The more
farming as a self-sufficient way of life was abandoned for farming as a
business, the more merit men found in what was being left behind. And

the more rapidly the farmers' sons moved into the towns, the more nostalgic the whole culture became about its rural past. The American mind was raised upon a sentimental attachment to rural living and upon a series of notions about rural people and rural life that I have chosen to designate as the agrarian myth.[1] The agrarian myth represents a kind of homage that Americans have paid to the fancied innocence of their origins.

Like any complex of ideas, the agrarian myth cannot be defined in a phrase, but its component themes form a clear pattern. Its hero was the yeoman farmer, its central conception the notion that he is the ideal man and the ideal citizen. Unstinted praise of the special virtues of the farmer and the special values of rural life was coupled with the assertion that agriculture, as a calling uniquely productive and uniquely important to society, had a special right to the concern and protection of government. The yeoman, who owned a small farm and worked it with the aid of his family, was the incarnation of the simple, honest, independent, healthy, happy human being. Because he lived in close communion with the beneficent nature, his life was believed to have a wholesomeness and integrity impossible for the depraved populations of cities. His well-being was not merely physical, it was moral; it was not merely personal, it was the central source of civic virtue; it was not merely secular but religious, for God had made the land and called man to cultivate it. Since the yeoman was believed to be both happy and honest, and since he had a secure propertied stake in society in the form of his own land, he was held to be the best and most reliable sort of citizen. To this conviction Jefferson appealed when he wrote: "The small land holders are the most precious part of a state."

In origin the agrarian myth was not a popular but a literary idea, a preoccupation of the upper classes, of those who enjoyed a classical education, read pastoral poetry, experimented with breeding stock, and owned plantations or country estates. It was clearly formulated and almost universally accepted in America during the last half of the eighteenth century. As it took shape both in Europe and America, its promulgators drew heavily upon the authority and the rhetoric of classical writers—Hesiod, Xenophon, Cato, Cicero, Virgil, Horace, and others—whose works were the staples of a good education. A learned agricultural gentry, coming into conflict with the industrial classes, welcomed the moral strength that a rich classical ancestry brought to the praise of

---

1. By "myth," as I use the word here, I do not mean an idea that is simply false, but rather one that so effectively embodies men's values that it profoundly influences their way of perceiving reality and hence their behavior. In this sense myths may have varying degrees of fiction or reality. The agrarian myth became increasingly fictional as time went on.

husbandry. In France the Physiocrats preached that agriculture is the only true source of wealth. In England the rural entrepreneurs, already interested in breeding and agricultural improvement, found the praise of husbandry congenial. They enjoyed it in James Thomson's *Seasons,* or in Dryden's translation of Horace:

> How happy in his low degree,
> How rich in humble poverty, is he,
> Who leads a quiet country life,
> Discharged of business, void of strife,
> And from the griping scrivener free?
> Thus, ere the seeds of vice were sown,
> Lived men in better ages born,
> Who plough'd with oxen of their own,
> Their small paternal field of corn.

"There is, indeed, scarcely any writer," declared Samuel Johnson in 1751, "who had not celebrated the happiness of rural privacy."

Wherever the peasantry was being displaced by industry or commercial farming, and particularly in England, where rustic life was devastated by the enclosures, such literature took on special poignancy. Oliver Goldsmith's classic statement, "The Deserted Village," became well over a hundred years later the unchallenged favorite of American Populist writers and orators. Chiefly through English experience, and from English and classical writers, the agrarian myth came to America, where, like so many other cultural importations, it eventually took on altogether new dimensions in its new setting. In America such men as Jefferson and Crèvecœur, Thomas Paine, Philip Freneau, Hugh Henry Brackenridge, and George Logan propagated the myth, and after them a multitude of writers whose lives reach well into the nineteenth century. So appealing were its symbols that even an arch-opponent of the agrarian interest like Alexander Hamilton found it politic to concede in his *Report on Manufactures* that "the cultivation of the earth, as the primary and most certain source of national supply, . . . has intrinsically a strong claim to pre-eminence over every other kind of industry." And Benjamin Franklin, urban cosmopolite though he was, once said that agriculture was "the only *honest way*" for a nation to acquire wealth, "wherein man receives a real increase of the seed thrown into the ground, a kind of continuous miracle, wrought by the hand of God in his favour, as a reward for his innocent life and virtuous industry."

Among the intellectual classes in the eighteenth century the agrarian myth had virtually universal appeal. It was everywhere: in tracts on agricultural improvement and books on economics, in pastoral poetry and political philosophy. At once primitivist and rationalist, it could be made congenial to almost every temperament. Some writers used it to give simple, direct, and emotional expression to their feelings about life and nature; others linked agrarianism with a formal philosophy of natural rights. The application of the natural-rights philosophy to land tenure became especially popular in America. Since the time of Locke it had been a standard argument that the land is the common stock of society to which every man has a right—what Jefferson called "the fundamental right to labour the earth"; that since the occupancy and use of land are the true criteria of valid ownership, labor expended in cultivating the earth confers title to it; that since government was created to protect property, the property of working landholders has a special claim to be fostered and protected by the state.

At first, as I have said, the agrarian myth was a notion of the educated classes, but by the early nineteenth century it had become a mass creed, a part of the country's political folklore and its nationalist ideology. The roots of this change may be found as far back as the American Revolution, which, appearing to many Americans as the victory of a band of embattled farmers over an empire, seemed to confirm the moral and civic superiority of the yeoman, made the farmer a symbol of the new nation, and wove the agrarian myth into its patriotic sentiments and republican idealism. Still more important, the myth played a role in the first party battles under the Constitution. The Jeffersonians appealed again and again to the moral primacy of the yeoman farmer in their attacks on the Federalists. The family farm and American democracy became indissolubly connected in Jeffersonian thought, and was inherited from the Jeffersonians by exponents of popular causes in the Jackson era. By 1840 even the more conservative party, the Whigs, took over the rhetorical appeal to the common man, and elected a President in good part on the strength of the fiction that he lived in a log cabin.

The Jeffersonians, moreover, made the agrarian myth the basis of a strategy of continental development. Many of them expected that the great empty inland regions would guarantee the preponderance of the yeoman—and therefore the dominance of Jeffersonianism and the health of the state—for an unlimited future. In his first inaugural address Jefferson spoke of the United States as "a chosen country, with room enough for our descendants to the thousandth and thousandth generation." The opening of the trans-Allegheny region, its protection from slavery, and the purchase of the Louisiana Territory were the first great steps in a continental strategy designed to establish an internal empire of small farms. Much later the Homestead Act, though temporarily blocked by the South (the only section of the country where the freehold concept was seriously contested as an ideal), was meant to carry to its completion the process of continental settlement by small homeowners.

The failure of the Homestead Act "to enact by statute the fee-simple empire" was, as we shall see, one of the original sources of Populist grievances, and one of the central points at which the agrarian myth was overrun by the commercial realities.

Above all, however, the myth was powerful because the United States in the first half of the nineteenth century consisted predominantly of literate and politically enfranchised farmers. Offering what seemed harmless flattery to this numerically dominant class, the myth suggested a standard vocabulary to rural editors and politicians. Although farmers may not have been much impressed by what was said about the merits of a noncommercial way of life, they could only enjoy learning about their special virtues and their unique services to the nation, could hardly mind hearing that their life was intrinsically more virtuous and closer to God than the lives of many people who seemed to be better off. Moreover, the editors and politicians who so flattered them need not in most cases have been insincere. More often than not they too were likely to have begun life in little villages or on farms, and what they had to say stirred in their own breasts, as it did in the breasts of a great many townspeople, nostalgia for their early years, and perhaps relieved some residual feelings of guilt at having deserted parental homes and childhood attachments. They also had the satisfaction in the early days of knowing that in so far as it was based upon the life of the largely self-sufficient yeoman the agrarian myth was a depiction of reality as well as the assertion of an ideal.

Oddly enough, the agrarian myth came to be believed more widely and tenaciously as it became more fictional. At first it was propagated with a kind of genial candor, and only later did it acquire overtones of insincerity. There survives from the Jackson era a lithograph that shows Joseph Ritner, Governor of Pennsylvania, standing by a primitive plow at the end of a furrow. There is no pretense that the Governor has actually been plowing—he wears broadcloth pants and a silk vest, and his tall black beaver hat has been carefully laid in the grass beside him—but the picture is meant as a reminder of both his rustic origin and his present high station in life. By contrast, Calvin Coolidge posed almost a century later for a series of photographs that represented him as haying in Vermont. In one of them the President sits on the edge of a hay rig in a white shirt, collar detached, wearing highly polished black shoes under a fresh pair of overalls; in the background stands his Pierce Arrow, a secret-service man on the running board, plainly waiting to hurry the President away from his bogus rural labors. That the second picture is so much more pretentious and disingenuous than the first is a measure of the increasing hollowness of the myth as it became more and more remote

from the realities of agriculture. Well on into the twentieth century eminent Americans continued to pay this ritualistic obeisance to what one
writer has called "agricultural fundamentalism." Coolidge himself, who
showed monumental indifference to the real problems of farmers in the
1920's, none the less declared: "It has been attested by all experience that
agriculture tends to discouragement and decadence whenever the
predominant interests of the country turn to manufacture and trade."
Likewise Bernard Baruch, a metropolitan financier whose chief contact
with agriculture consisted in the absentee ownership of a country estate,
asserted: "Agriculture is the greatest and fundamentally the most important of our American industries. The cities are but the branches of the
tree of national life, the roots of which go deeply into the land. We all
flourish or decline with the farmer."

Throughout the nineteenth century hundreds upon hundreds of thousands of farm-born youths had set the example that Coolidge and Baruch
only followed: they sang the praises of agriculture but eschewed farming
as a vocation and sought their careers in the towns and cities. For all the
rhetoric of the pastoral tradition, nothing could keep the boys on the
farm, and nothing could conceal from the farm population itself the
continuous restless movement not merely to farms farther west but to
urban areas, East and West. Particularly after 1840, which marked the
beginning of a long cycle of heavy country-to-city migration, farm children repudiated their parents' way of life and took off for the cities,
where in agrarian theory, if not in fact, they were sure to succumb to vice
and poverty. Farm journals were full of editorials, stories, and poems
voicing the plaintive theme: "Boys, Stick to the Farm!" and of advice to
farmers on how to rear their sons so that farming as a way of life would
be attractive to them. A typical bit of this folklore runs:

> The great busy West has inducements,
>   And so has the busiest mart,
> But wealth is not made in a day, boys,
>   Don't be in a hurry to start!
>
> The bankers and brokers are wealthy,
>   They take in their thousands or so;
> Ah! think of the frauds and deceptions—
>   Don't be in a hurry to go.
>
> The farm is the safest and surest;
>   The orchards are loaded today,
> You're free as the air of the mountains,
>   And monarch of all you survey.
>
> Better stay on the farm a while longer,
>   Though profits come in rather slow;

> Remember you've nothing to risk, boys—
> Don't be in a hurry to go.

In the imagery of these appeals the earth was characteristically a mother, trade a harlot, and desertion of ancestral ways a betrayal that invited Providential punishment. When a correspondent of the *Prairie Farmer* in 1849 made the mistake of praising the luxuries, the "polished society," and the economic opportunities of the city, he was rebuked for overlooking the fact that city life *"crushes, enslaves,* and *ruins so many thousands of our young men* who are insensibly made the victims of *dissipation,* of *reckless speculation,* and of *ultimate crime."* Such warnings, of course, were futile. "Thousands of young men," wrote the New York agriculturist Jesse Buel, "do annually forsake the plough, and the honest profession of their fathers, if not to win the fair, at least from an opinion, too often confirmed by mistaken parents, that agriculture is not the road to wealth, to honor, nor to happiness. And such will continue to be the case, until our agriculturists become qualified to assume that rank in society to which the importance of their calling, and their numbers, entitle them, and which intelligence and self-respect can alone give them."

Rank in society! That was close to the heart of the matter, for the farmer was beginning to realize acutely not merely that the best of the world's goods were to be had in the cities and that the urban middle and upper classes had much more of them than he did but also that he was losing in status and respect as compared with them. He became aware that the official respect paid to the farmer masked a certain disdain felt by many city people. In time the eulogies of country life that appeared in farm journals lost their pleasantly complacent tone and took on some of the sharpness of a "defensive gesture against real or imagined slurs." "There has . . . a certain class of individuals grown up in our land," complained a farm writer in 1835, "who treat the cultivators of the soil as an inferior caste . . . whose utmost abilities are confined to the merit of being able to discuss a boiled potato and a rasher of bacon." The city was symbolized as the home of loan sharks, dandies, fops, and aristocrats with European ideas who despised farmers as hayseeds. One writer spoke in a magnificent stream of mixed metaphor of "the butterflies who flutter over them in British broadcloth, consuming the fruits of the sweat of their brows."

The growth of the urban market intensified this antagonism. In areas like colonial New England, where an intimate connection had existed between the small town and the adjacent countryside, where a community of interests and even of occupations cut across the town line, the rural-urban hostility had not developed so sharply as in the newer areas where the township plan was never instituted and where isolated farmsteads were more common. As settlement moved west, as urban markets grew, as self-sufficient farmers became rarer, as farmers pushed into commercial production for the cities they feared and distrusted, they quite correctly thought of themselves as a vocational and economic group rather than as members of a neighborhood. In the Populist era the city was totally alien territory to many farmers, and the primacy of agriculture as a source of wealth was reasserted with much bitterness. "The great cities rest upon our broad and fertile prairies," declared Bryan in his Cross of Gold speech. "Burn down your cities and leave our farms, and your cities will spring up again as if by magic; but destroy our farms, and the grass will grow in the streets of every city in the country." Out of the beliefs nourished by the agrarian myth there had arisen the notion that the city was a parasitical growth on the country. Bryan spoke for a people raised for generations on the idea that the farmer was a very special creature, blessed by God, and that in a country consisting largely of farmers the voice of the farmer was the voice of democracy and of virtue itself. The agrarian myth encouraged farmers to believe that they were not themselves an organic part of the whole order of business enterprise and speculation that flourished in the city, partaking of its character and sharing in its risks, but rather the innocent pastoral victims of a conspiracy hatched in the distance. The notion of an innocent and victimized populace colors the whole history of agrarian controversy, and indeed the whole history of the populistic mind.

For the farmer it was bewildering, and irritating too, to think of the great contrast between the verbal deference paid him by almost everyone and the real status, the real economic position, in which he found himself. Improving his economic position was always possible, though this was often done too little and too late; but it was not within anyone's power to stem the decline in the rural values and pieties, the gradual rejection of the moral commitments that had been expressed in the early exaltations of agrarianism. It was the fate of the farmer himself, as we shall see, to contribute to this decline. Like almost all good Americans he had innocently sought progress from the very beginning, and thus hastened the decline of many of his own values. Elsewhere the rural classes had usually looked to the past, had been bearers of tradition and upholders of stability. The American farmer looked to the future alone, and the story of the American land became a study in futures. In the very hours of its birth as a nation Crèvecœur had congratulated America for having, in effect, no feudal past and no industrial present, for having no royal, aristocratic, ecclesiastical, or monarchical power, and no manufacturing class, and had rapturously concluded: "We are the most perfect society now existing in the world." Here was the irony from which the farmer suffered above all others: the United States was the only country in the world that began with perfection and aspired to progress.

II. *The Farmer and the Realities*

To what extent was the agrarian myth actually false? When it took form in America during the eighteenth century, its stereotypes did indeed correspond to many of the realities of American agricultural life. There were commercial elements in colonial agriculture almost from the earliest days, but there were also large numbers of the kind of independent yeomen idealized in the myth, men who had remarkable self-sufficiency and bequeathed to their children a strong penchant for craftsmanlike improvisation and a tradition of household industry. For a long time the commercial potentialities of agriculture were held in check by severe obstacles. Only the farmers very near to the rivers and the towns had adequate transportation. The small industrial population provided a very limited domestic market, and the villagers raised a large part of their own food. Outside the South operations above the size of the family farm were cramped by the absence of a force of wage laborers. At the beginning of the nineteenth century, when the American population was still living largely in the forests, poised at the edge of the Appalachians, and standing on the verge of the great drive across the prairies that occupied settlers for half a century, the yeoman was by no means a fiction.

The early panegyrists of the agrarian myth were, of course, aware of the commercial farmers, but it was this independent yeoman who caught their fancy. Admiring the natural abundance produced and consumed by the family on its own farm, they assumed that the family farm would always be, as it so frequently was in the early days, a diversified and largely self-sufficient unit. Even Jefferson, who was far from a humble yeoman, and whose wants were anything but simple, succeeded to a remarkable degree in living up to the ideal of self-sufficiency. Like many planters, he numbered among his slaves a balanced group of craftsmen; and even if the luxuries of Jefferson the planter had to be imported, the necessities at least of Jefferson the farmer, and of all his "people," were yielded by his own land. This was also the goal set by the theorists for the yeoman. Making at home almost everything he needed, buying little, using each year but a pocketful of cash, he would be as independent of the marketplace as he was of the favors of others. The yeoman, too, valued this self-sufficiency and the savings it made possible, but he seems to have valued it more often than not as a means through which he could eventually enter the marketplace rather than as a means of avoiding it. "My farm," said the farmer of Jefferson's time, "gave me and my family a good living on the produce of it; and left me, one year with another, one hundred and fifty silver dollars, for I have never spent more than ten dollars a year, which was for salt, nails, and the like. Nothing to wear, eat, or drink was purchased, as my farm provided all. With this saving, I put money to interest, bought cattle, fatted and sold them, and made great profit." Here, then, was the significance of self-sufficiency for the characteristic family farmer: "great profit." Commercialism had already begun to enter the American Arcadia.

From colonial days there had always been before the eyes of the yeoman farmer in the settled areas alluring models of commercial success in agriculture: the tobacco, rice, and indigo planters of the South, the grain, meat, and cattle exporters of the middle colonies. In America the spirit of emulation was exceptionally strong, the opportunities were considerable. The farmer knew that without cash he could never rise above the hardships and squalor of pioneering and log-cabin life. Self-sufficiency produced savings, and savings went into the purchase of more land, of herds and flocks, of better tools; they erected barns and silos and better dwellings, and made other improvements. When there was spare time, the farmer often worked off the farm to add to his cash resources, at first in trapping, hunting, fishing, or lumbering, later in the maintenance and repair of railroads. Domestic politics were persistently affected by his desire for the means of getting a cash crop to market, for turnpikes and canals. The foreign policy of the early Republic was determined again and again by the clamor of farmers to keep open the river outlets for American produce.

Between 1815 and 1860 the character of American agriculture was transformed. The independent yeoman, outside of exceptional or isolated areas, almost disappeared before the relentless advance of commercial agriculture. The rise of native industry created a home market for agriculture, while at the same time demands arose abroad, at first for American cotton and then for American foodstuffs. A network of turnpikes, canals, and railroads linked the planter and the advancing Western farmer to these new markets, while the Eastern farmer, spurred by Western competition, began to cultivate more thoroughly the nearby urban outlets for his products. As the farmer moved out onto the flat, rich prairies, he found possibilities for the use of machinery that did not exist in the forest. Before long he was cultivating the prairies with horse-drawn mechanical reapers, steel plows, wheat and corn drills, and threshers. The cash crop converted the yeoman into a small entrepreneur, and the development of horse-drawn machinery made obsolete the simple old agrarian symbol of the plow. Farmers ceased to be free of what the early agrarian writers had called the "corruptions" of trade. They were, to be sure, still "independent," in the sense that they owned their own land. They were a hardworking lot in the old tradition. But no longer did they grow or manufacture what they needed: they concentrated on the cash crop and began to buy more and more of their supplies from the country store. To take full advantage of mechanization, they engrossed as much land as they could. To mechanize fully, they borrowed cash. Where they could not buy or borrow they might rent: by the 1850's Illinois farmers who could not afford machines and large barns were hiring itinerant jobbers with machines to do their threshing. The shift from self-sufficient to commercial farming varied in time throughout the West and cannot be dated with precision, but it was complete in Ohio by about 1830 and twenty years later in Indiana, Illinois, and Michigan. All through the great Northwest, farmers whose ancestors might have lived in isolation and self-sufficiency were surrounded by jobbers, banks, stores, middlemen, horses, and machinery; and in so far as this process was unfinished in 1860, the demands of the Civil War brought it to completion. As the *Prairie Farmer* said in 1868: "The old rule that a farmer should produce all that he required, and that the surplus represented his gains, is part of the past. Agriculture, like all other business, is better for its subdivisions, each one growing that which is best suited to his soil, skill, climate and market, and with its proceeds purchas[ing] his other needs."

The triumph of commercial agriculture not only rendered obsolete the objective conditions that had given to the agrarian myth so much of its original force, but also showed that the ideal implicit in the myth was contesting the ground with another, even stronger ideal—the notion of opportunity, of career, of the self-made man. The same forces in American life that had made Jacksonian equalitarianism possible and had given to the equalitarian theme in the agrarian romance its most compelling appeal had also unleashed in the nation an entrepreneurial zeal probably without precedent in history, a rage for business, for profits, for opportunity, for advancement. If the yeoman family was to maintain itself in the simple terms eulogized in the myth, it had to produce consistently a type of character that was satisfied with a traditional way of life. But the Yankee farmer, continually exposed to the cult of success that was everywhere around him, became inspired by a kind of personal dynamism which called upon the individual to surpass traditions. He was, in terms that David Riesman has made familiar, not a tradition-directed but an inner-directed man. Agrarian sentiment sanctified labor in the soil and the simple life, but the prevailing Calvinist atmosphere of rural life implied that virtue was rewarded, after all, with success and material goods.

From the standpoint of the familiar agrarian panegyrics, the supreme irony was that the immense interior that had been supposed to underwrite the dominion of the yeoman for centuries did as much as anything else to destroy the yeomanlike spirit and replace it with the spirit of the businessman, even of the gambler. Cheap land invited extensive and careless cultivation. Rising land values in areas of new settlement tempted early liquidation and frequent moves, and made of the small entrepreneur a land speculator. Already in the late eighteenth century writers on American agriculture noticed that American farmers were tempted to buy more land than they could properly cultivate. George Washington wrote apologetically to Arthur Young about the state of American farming, admitting that "the aim of farmers in this country, if they can be called farmers, is not to make the most they can from the land, which is, or has been cheap, but the most of the labour, which is dear; the consequence of which has been, much ground has been scratched over and none cultivated or improved as it ought to have been. . . ." This tendency was strengthened by the rapid march of settlement across the prairies. In 1818 the English immigrant Morris Birkbeck wrote from Illinois that merchants, professional men, and farmers alike were investing their profits and savings in uncultivated land. "The farmer, instead of completing the improvement of his present possessions, lays out all he can save in entering more land. In a district which is settling, this speculation is said to pay on the average, when managed with judgment, fifteen per cent. Who then will submit to the toils of agriculture, further than bare necessity requires, for fifteen per cent? Or who would loan his money, even at fifteen per cent, where he can obtain that interest by investing it in land? Thus every description of men, almost every man, is poor in convertible property."

Frequent and sensational rises in land values bred a boom psychology in the American farmer and caused him to rely for his margin of profit more on the process of appreciation than on the sale of crops. It took a strong man to resist the temptation to ride skyward on lands that might easily triple or quadruple their value in one decade and then double again in the next. It seemed ultraconservative to improve existing possessions if one could put savings or borrowings into new land. What developed in America was an agricultural society whose real attachment was not to the land but to land values. In the 1830's Tocqueville found this the prevailing characteristic of American agriculture: "Almost all the farmers of the United States combine some trade with agriculture; most of them make agriculture itself a trade. It seldom happens that an American farmer settles for good upon the land which he occupies: especially in the districts of the far West he brings land into tillage in order to sell it again, and not to farm it: he builds a farmhouse on the speculation that, as the state of the country will soon be changed by the increase of population, a good price will be gotten for it. . . . Thus the Americans carry their business-like qualities into agriculture; and their trading passions are displayed in that as in their other pursuits."

The penchant for speculation and the lure of new and different lands bred in the American farmer a tremendous passion for moving—and not merely, as one common view would have it, on the part of those who had failed, but also on the part of those who had succeeded. For farmers who had made out badly, the fresh lands may have served on occasion as a safety valve, but for others who had made out well enough on a speculative basis, or who were beginning a farming "career," it was equally a risk valve—an opportunity to exploit the full possibilities of the great American land bubble. Mobility among farmers had serious effects upon an agricultural tradition never noted for careful cultivation: in a nation whose soil is notoriously heterogeneous, farmers too often had little chance to get to know the quality of their land; they failed to plan and manure and replenish; they neglected diversification for the one-crop system and ready cash. There was among them little attachment to land or locality; instead there developed the false euphoria of local "boosting," encouraged by railroads, land companies, and farmers themselves; in place of village contacts and communal spirit based upon ancestral attachments, there was professional optimism based upon hopes for a quick rise in values.

In a very real and profound sense, then, the United States failed to develop (except in some localities, chiefly in the East) a distinctively *rural* culture. If a rural culture means an emotional and craftsmanlike dedication to the soil, a traditional and pre-capitalist outlook, a tradition-directed rather than career-directed type of character, and a village community devoted to ancestral ways and habitually given to communal action, then the prairies and plains never had one. What differentiated the agricultural life of these regions from the practices widespread in European agriculture—or, for that matter, from the stereotype of the agrarian myth—was not simply that it produced for a market but that it was so speculative, so mobile, so mechanized, so "progressive," so thoroughly imbued with the commercial spirit.

Immigrant farmers, who really were yeomen with a background of genuine agrarian values, were frequently bewildered at the ethos of American agriculture. Marcus Hansen points out: "The ambition of the German-American father, for instance, was to see his sons on reaching manhood established with their families on farms clustered about his own. To take complete possession of a township with sons, sons-in-law and nephews was not an unrealizable ideal. To this end the would-be patriarch dedicated all his plodding industry. One by one, he bought adjacent farms, the erstwhile owners joining the current to the farther West. Heavily timbered acres and swamp lands which had been lying unused were prepared for cultivation by patient and unceasing toil. 'When the German comes in, the Yankee goes out,' was a local proverb that varied as Swedes, Bohemians or other immigrant groups formed the invading element. But the American father made no such efforts on behalf of his offspring. To be a self-made man was his ideal. He had come in as a 'first settler' and had created a farm with his ax; let the boys do the same. One of them perhaps was kept at home as a helper to his aging parents; the rest set out to achieve beyond the mountains or beyond the river what the father had accomplished in the West of his day. Thus mobility was fostered by family policy." The continuing influx of immigrants, ready to settle on cleared and slightly improved land, greatly facilitated the Yankee race across the continent.

American agriculture was also distinguishable from European agriculture in the kind of rural life and political culture it sustained. In Europe the managers of agriculture and the owners of land were characteristically either small peasant proprietors, or substantial landholders of traditional and conservative outlook with powerful political and military connections. The American farmer, whose holdings were not so extensive as those of the grandee nor so tiny as those of the peasant, whose psychology was Protestant and bourgeois, and whose politics were petty-capitalist rather than traditionalist, had no reason to share the social outlook of the rural classes of Europe. In Europe land was limited and dear, while labor was abundant and relatively cheap; in America this ratio between land and labor was inverted. In Europe small farmers lived in villages, where generations of the same family were reared upon the same soil, and where careful cultivation and the minute elimination of waste were necessary to support a growing population on a limited amount of land. Endless and patient labor, including the labor of peasant women and children exploited to a degree to which the Yankee would not go except under the stress of pioneering conditions, was available to conserve and tailor the land and keep it fertile. On limited plots cultivated by an ample labor force, the need for machinery was not urgent, and hence the demand for liquid capital in large amounts was rare. Diversification, self-sufficiency, and the acceptance of a low standard of living also contributed to hold down this demand. Much managerial skill was required for such an agricultural regime, but it was the skill of the craftsman and the traditional tiller of the soil. Village life provided a community and a cooperative milieu, a pooling of knowledge and lore, a basis of common action to minimize risks.

In America the greater availability of land and the scarcity of labor made for extensive agriculture, which was wasteful of the soil, and placed a premium on machines to bring large tracts under cultivation. His demand for expensive machinery, his expectation of higher standards of living, and his tendency to go into debt to acquire extensive acreage created an urgent need for cash and tempted the farmer into capitalizing more and more on his greatest single asset: the unearned appreciation in the value of his land. The managerial skill required for success under these conditions was as much businesslike as craftsmanlike. The predominance in American agriculture of the isolated farmstead standing in the midst of great acreage, the frequent movements, the absence of village life, deprived the farmer and his family of the advantages of community, lowered the chances of association and co-operation, and encouraged that rampant, suspicious, and almost suicidal individualism for which the American farmer was long noted and which organizations like the Grange tried to combat. The characteristic product of American rural society was not a yeoman or a villager, but a harassed little country businessman who worked very hard, moved all too often, gambled with his land, and made his way alone.

III. THE FRONTIER OR THE MARKET?

The American farmer was unusual in the agricultural world in the sense that he was running a mechanized and commercialized agricultural unit of a size far greater than the small proprietary holdings common elsewhere, and yet he was running it as a family enterprise on the assumption that the family could supply not only the necessary capital and managerial talent but also most of the labor. This system, however applicable to the subsistence farm or the small yeoman's farm, was hardly adequate to the conditions of commercial agriculture. As a businessman, the farmer was appropriately hardheaded; he tried to act upon a cold and realistic strategy of self-interest. As the head of a family, however, the farmer felt that he was investing not only his capital but his hard work and that of his wife and children, that when he risked his farm he risked his home—that he was, in short, a single man running a personal enterprise in a world of impersonal forces. It was from this aspect of his situation—seen in the hazy glow of the agrarian myth—that his political leaders in the 1890's developed their rhetoric and some of their concepts of political action. The farmer's commercial position pointed to the usual strategies of the business world: combination, co-operation, pressure politics, lobbying, piecemeal activity directed toward specific goals. But the bathos of the agrarian rhetoric pointed in a different direction: broad political goals, ideological mass politics, third parties, the conquest of the "money power," the united action of all labor, rural and urban. When times were persistently bad, the farmer tended to reject his business role and its failures to withdraw into the role of the injured little yeoman. This made the differences between his situation and that of any other victim of exploitation seem unimportant to him. As a Southern journalist wrote of the situation in the cotton country: "The landowner was so poor and distressed that he forgot that he was a capitalist . . . so weary of hand and sick of spirit that he imagined himself in precisely the same plight as the hired man. . . ."

The American farmer thus had a dual character, and one way of understanding our agrarian movements is to observe which aspect of the farmer's double personality is uppermost at a given time. It is my contention that both the Populist rhetoric and the modern liberal's indulgent view of the farmers' revolt have been derived from the "soft" side of the farmer's existence—that is, from agrarian "radicalism" and agrarian ideology—while most farm organizations since the decline of the Populists have been based primarily upon the "hard" side, upon agricultural improvement, business methods, and pressure politics. Populism itself had a hard side, especially in the early days of the Farmers' Alliance and the Populist Party, but this became less and less important as the depression of the nineties deepened and other issues were dropped in favor of the silver panacea.

Most of our views of the historical significance of Populism have been formed by the study of the frontier process and the settlement of the internal empire. This approach turned attention to some significant aspects of American agrarian development, but also diverted attention from others. To a writer like Frederick Jackson Turner the farmer on the plains was significant above all as the carrier of the traditions of the frontier. To Turner the frontier, or the West, was the primary source of most of "what has been distinctive and valuable in America's contributions to the history of the human spirit. . . ." Hence the primary interest of the Populist lay in the fact that he was "a survival of the pioneer, striving to adjust present conditions to his old ideals." While Turner did on occasion comment on the capitalistic and speculative character of the farmer, he saw this as something of no special importance, when compared with the farmer's role as the bearer of the yeoman tradition and "the old pioneer ideals of the native American. . . ." The chief difference between Populist thinking and the pioneer tradition, Turner felt, was that the Populists showed an increasing sense of the need for governmental help in realizing the old ideals. His explanation of this change in philosophy—indeed, of the entire agrarian revolt of the 1890's—was formulated in the light of the frontier theory and the alleged exhaustion of "free" land. "Failures in one area can no longer be made good by taking up land on a new frontier," he wrote in 1896. "The conditions of settled society are being reached with suddenness and with confusion. . . . The frontier opportunities are gone. Discontent is demanding an extension of governmental activity in its behalf. . . . A people composed of heterogeneous materials, with diverse and conflicting ideals and social interests, having passed from the task of filling up the vacant spaces of the continent, is now thrown back upon itself and is seeking an equilibrium." The idea that the agrarian uprising was precipitated by the disappearance of the frontier and the exhaustion of the public domain has also been given the scholarly support of John D. Hicks's standard history of *The Populist Revolt.* Earlier discontents, Hicks concluded, had been lightened by the departure of the restless and disgruntled for the West, a process that created new opportunities for them and eased the pressure on those they left behind. But by the nineties, "with the lands all taken and the frontier gone, this safety valve was closed. The frontier was turned back on itself. The restless and discontented voiced their sentiments more and fled from them less."

The conclusion that it was the West, the frontier spirit, that produced American democracy, and that Populism was the logical product of this spirit, is a deceptive inheritance from the Turnerian school. The decisive role played by the South in Populism suggests instantly the limitations of this view. Terms that are superficially appealing when applied to Kansas become meaningless when applied to Georgia. Southern Populism, which could hardly have been close to the frontier spirit, was at least as strong as the Western brand and contained the more radical wing of the agrarian revolt of the nineties. Moreover, the extent to which "the West" as a whole supported the agrarian revolt has commonly been exaggerated, as the distribution of Populist votes in 1892 and of Bryan votes in 1896 clearly shows. Populism had only three compact centers. Each was overwhelmingly rural. Each was dominated by a product whose price had catastrophically declined: the South, based chiefly upon cotton; a narrow tier of four Northwestern states, Kansas, Nebraska, and the two Dakotas, based upon wheat; and the mountain states, based chiefly upon silver. Silver is a special case, though strategically an important one, and we can for the moment postpone consideration of it, except to remark that the free-silver Populism of the mountain-states variety was not agrarian Populism at all, but simply silverism. Elsewhere agrarian discontent, where it reached a peak of local intensity sufficient to yield an independent Populist Party of notable strength or to win a state for Bryan in 1896, was roughly coterminous with the cash-staple export crops and the burden of heavy mortgage indebtedness.

The common tendency to focus upon the internal frontier as the matrix of Populism has obscured the great importance of the agrarian situation in the external world, which is profoundly relevant to both Southern and Western Populism. The frontier obsession has been identified in America with a kind of intellectual isolationism. The larger and more important answer to the causes of the agrarian crisis of the 1890's must be found not in the American West, but in the international market. While American Populism has been seen almost solely in terms of domestic events and the internal frontier, the entire European and American world was shaken by an agrarian crisis that knew no national boundaries and that struck at several nations without internal frontiers on the verge of real or imagined exhaustion. "Almost everywhere," declared an English observer in 1893, "certainly in England, France, Germany, Italy, Scandinavia, and the United States, the agriculturists, formerly so instinctively conservative, are becoming fiercely discontented, declare they gain less by civilization than the rest of the community, and are looking about for remedies of a drastic nature."

During the last three decades of the nineteenth century a revolution took place in international communications. For the first time the full effects of steam locomotion and steam navigation were felt in international trade. In 1869 the Suez Canal was opened and the first transcontinental railroad in the United States was completed. Europe was connected by submarine cable with the United States in 1866, and with South America in 1874. A great network of telegraph and telephone communication was spun throughout the world. Huge tracts of new land being settled in Argentina, Australia, Canada, and the American West were now pulled together in one international market, while improvements in agricultural technology made possible the full exploitation of areas susceptible to extensive and mechanized cultivation. Agrarian depressions, formerly of a local or national character, now became international, and with them came international agrarian discontent, heightened by the almost uninterrupted international price decline that occurred from the early 1870's to the 1890's. It is hardly accidental that the products of the American staple-growing regions showing the highest discontent were the products most dependent upon exports.

The notion that the unavailability of free land for further expansion of the American farming system was chiefly responsible for the remarkable surge of agrarian discontent no longer seems credible. It is true that many Americans, including some Populist spokesmen, were concerned during the 1890's about what they thought to be the imminent disappearance of the public domain. There was also a school of thought among those interested in the agrarian problem that took pleasure in the prospect that the approaching exhaustion of new lands would lower the expansion of the agricultural economy to the point at which the values of already settled land would begin to rise sharply, and thus put an end to the problem of settled farmers. However, the entire conception of exhausted resources has been re-examined and found to be delusive; actually an abundance of new land was available long after the so-called disappearance of the frontier in 1890. During the decade 1890–1900, in which the discontent was most acute, 1,100,000 new farms were settled, 500,000 more than the number in the previous decade. In the twenty years after the farmers' organizations met in 1890 at Ocala, Florida, to formulate their demands, 1,760,000 new farms and 225,600,000 new acres were added to the nation's agricultural domain. More land, indeed, was taken up after 1890 under the terms of the Homestead Act and its successors than had been taken up before. True, a high proportion of this was suitable only for grazing and dry farming, but the profitability of land is a result not merely of soil chemistry or soil humidity but also of the economic circumstances under which the land is cultivated; the condition of the market in the early years of the twentieth century admitted of more profitable cultivation of these relatively barren lands than of much richer lands in the depressed period. Finally, there were after 1890 still more supplies of rich land in Canada, which farmers from the United States did not hesitate to occupy. In 1914, Canadian officials estimated that 925,000 Americans had moved, chiefly during the sixteen years past, across the border to the lands of Alberta and Saskatchewan. Lavish opportunities to settle on new lands or open new acres were still available after 1890, and in fact much use was made of these opportunities during the nineties. In so far as farmers were deterred from further settlement, it was not by the absence of land but because the international agrarian depression made the nineties a hazardous time to begin a farm.

The conception that the end of free or cheap land was primarily responsible for precipitating discontent implies that the existence of such land had been effective in alleviating it, and suggests that the effects of the Homestead Act up to about 1890 were what had been hoped for at the time of its passage. But the Homestead Act had never been successful in creating the inland freehold empire that agrarian reformers had dreamed of. Its maladministration and its circumvention by speculators and railroads is by now well known. From 1860 to 1900, for every free farm entered and kept by a bona fide farmer under the act there were about nine bought from railroads or speculators or from the government itself. Speculators, engrossing immense tracts of land under the privilege of unrestricted "entry," which was not abolished until 1888, did far more damage to rural society in the West than merely transmitting "free" land to farmers at substantial prices. They drove immigrants to remote parts of the frontier; they created "speculators' deserts"—large tracts of uncultivated absentee-owned land—and thus added to the dispersal of the population, making the operation of roads and railroads far more costly than necessary; they refused to pay taxes, thus damaging local government finances and limiting local improvements; they added to all the characteristic evils of our rural culture while they built up land prices and kept a large portion of the farm population in a state of tenancy.

The promise of free Homestead land or cheap land was self-defeating. The Homestead Act itself, which required five years of residence before title to a free farm was granted, was based upon the assumption that settlement would take place in a gradual and stable way, after the manner of the mythical yeoman. It made no allowance for the mobile habits of the American farmer. The number of forfeited entries under the Homestead Act was extraordinary. What effect the Homestead Act *might* have had if the West had been gradually settled by yeoman farmers protected from speculators and living after the fashion of the myth seems no more than a utopian conjecture. As it worked out, the Homestead Act was a triumph for speculative and capitalistic forces, and it translated cheap or free land into a stimulus for more discontent than it could quiet. The promise of the Homestead Act was a lure for over-rapid settlement in regions where most settlers found, instead of the agrarian utopia, a wilderness of high costs, low returns, and mortgages.

The self-defeating tendency of relatively cheap land in a speculative society is perfectly illustrated in an intensive contemporary study of a Nebraska township by Arthur F. Bentley. This township was first settled in 1871–2. In the early days when land prices were low, there was a prosperous period of rapid settlement, and the farmer's rate of profit was high whenever he had good crops; this encouraged him to buy and work more land than he could properly manage. The rapid appreciation of the price of land led him to try to realize his gains in advance by mortgaging. As fast as he could increase his loan he would do so, using the funds either to pay temporary losses or for further investment or speculation. "It is true," Bentley observed, "the farmer may often have suffered from excessive interest and grasping creditors; but it was less frequently the avarice of the lender that got him into trouble than the fact that he was too sanguine and too prone to believe that he could safely go into debt, on the assumption that crops and prices in the future would equal those in the present." At any rate, the typical farmer soon found himself in such a vulnerable position that one bad crop year or a brief temporary cessation of increase in land values, such as that of 1890–1, would put him on the verge of failure. Those farmers who came in early and took government land, who managed with some skill and got clear of heavy debt, made out well; those who came later, took railroad land, and made the usual errors of management were in straits. By 1892, when Bentley made his study, he concluded that a would-be purchaser who did not have enough capital to buy his farm outright and to hold it over subsequent periods of hard times "had almost better throw his money away than invest it in farming operations in Nebraska at the current prices of land and under the present agricultural conditions; unless, he be possessed of unusual energy and ability."

It is evident that Western Populism was, among other things, the out-
growth of a period of incredible expansion, one of the greatest in the
world history of agriculture. From 1870 to 1900 more new farm land was
taken up than in all previous American history. By the mid-eighties a
feverish land boom was under way, and it is the collapse of this boom that
provides the immediate background of Western Populism. We may take
the experience of Kansas as illustrative. The boom, originally based on
the high prices of farm produce, had reached the point of artificial infla-
tion by 1885. It had swept not only the country, where the rapid advance
in prices had caused latecomers to buy and mortgage at hopelessly in-
flated values, but also the rising towns, which were all "bonded to the
limit for public improvements [and] public utilities." As a state official
later remarked, "Most of us crossed the Mississippi or Missouri with no
money but with a vast wealth of hope and courage. . . . Haste to get rich
has made us borrowers, and the borrower has made booms, and booms
made men wild, and Kansas became a vast insane asylum covering 80,-
000 square miles." In the winter of 1887–8 this boom, which had been
encouraged by railroads, newspapers, and public officials, abruptly collapsed—in part because of drought in the western third of the state, in
part because farm prices had stopped going up, and in part because the
self-created confidence upon which the fever fed had broken.

The fathers of the Homestead Act and the fee-simple empire had acted
upon a number of assumptions stemming from the agrarian myth which
were out of date even before the act was passed. They trusted to the
beneficence of nature, to permanent and yeomanlike nonspeculative settlement; they expected that the land really would pass without cost into
the hands of the great majority of settlers; and they took it for granted
that the native strength of the farmer would continue to rest upon the
abundance produced on and for the farm. These assumptions were incongruous with the Industrial Revolution that was already well under
way by 1862 and with the Communications Revolution that was soon to
come; they were incongruous even with the natural character of the
plains, with their winds, sandstorms, droughts, and grasshoppers. And
the farmer, caught in the toils of cash-crop commercial farming, did not,
and could not, reckon his prosperity by the abundance produced on the
farm but rather by the exchange value of his products as measured by
the supplies and services they could buy. His standard of living, as well
as the security of his home, became dependent upon his commercial
position, which in turn was dependent upon the vicissitudes of the world
market.

In pointing to the farmer's commercial role I am not trying to deny the
difficulties of his position or the reality and seriousness of his grievances:

the appreciation of debts through deflation, the high cost of credit, ine-
quitable tax burdens, discriminatory railroad rates, unreasonable eleva-
tor and storage charges. Populism can best be understood, however, not
as a product of the frontier inheritance, but as another episode in the
well-established tradition of American entrepreneurial radicalism,
which goes back at least to the Jacksonian era. It was an effort on the part
of a few important segments of a highly heterogeneous capitalistic
agriculture to restore profits in the face of much exploitation and under
unfavorable market and price conditions. It arose as a part of a transitional stage in the history of American agriculture, in which the commercial farmer was beginning to cast off habits of thought and action
created almost as much by the persistence of the agrarian myth as by the
realities of his position. He had long since taken from business society its
acquisitive goals and its speculative temper, but he was still practicing
the competitive individualism that the most advanced sectors of industry
and finance had outgrown. He had not yet learned much from business
about its marketing devices, strategies of combination, or skills of self-
defense and self-advancement through pressure politics. His dual identity itself was not yet resolved. He entered the twentieth century still
affected by his yeoman inheritance but with a growing awareness of the
businesslike character of his future.